Eminent Europeans

Eminent Europeans

Personalities who shaped contemporary Europe

EDITED BY MARTYN BOND,
JULIE SMITH & WILLIAM WALLACE

The Greycoat Press

The publishers wish to record their thanks to the following organisations for their permission to reproduce the photographs of Eminent Europeans on the front cover:

The Imperial War Museum

The European Parliament

The Council of Europe

The Office of the President of the Czech Republic

First published in 1996 by The Greycoat Press, London

ISBN 1 899908 00 5

© 1996 The Greycoat Press

The Greycoat Press, PO Box 10586, London SW1P 2ZE.
Email: *greycoat@jbltd.demon.co.uk*

Set in 11/13 point Bodoni.
Graphic reproduction by Chappell Graphics Ltd, Bromley.
Printed in the United Kingdom by the Ipswich Book Company, Ipswich.

Contents

Preface

The Rt Hon Lord Jenkins of Hillhead OM

This collection of essays takes us over what might be thought by seasoned European warriors to be familiar terrain. Yet the essays do so with such a freshness of view and acute eye for unusual corners of knowledge that I found them as usefully informative as they were entertaining to read. From an early perusal of the book I gleaned two strikingly original quotations – one from the 3rd Marquess of Salisbury, the other from Dean Acheson – which greatly embellished a speech which I had to make the following week.

All the four great themes in the European symphony of the past fifty years are well developed. First there is the story of the founding fathers and of the success of the Six. Alongside this is the crucial off-stage and mostly supportive rôle of the Americans. Also a little apart – but for different reasons – there is the endemic semi-detachment of the British, except when the Single Market was being created, for that was an affair of packages and not of ideology, and therefore acceptable. Fourthly, perhaps the most important issue facing Europe today, the consequences of the lifting of the Iron Curtain and the extension of the idea of Europe to the whole continent rather than just its Western part are treated in several well-informed essays.

Inevitably in such a collection the essays vary considerably in style: some (those by Julian Critchley and Alan Watson, for instance) are very funny; others light up little-known clefts of ground. They all help to give a sense of background and perspective to a European debate which in Britain tends to be obsessive without being illuminating.

19.iii.96

Vision and Reality

An introduction to Eminent Europeans

'The past is a foreign country; they do things differently there.' Fifty years after the end of the Second World War it requires an imaginative leap of historical empathy to grasp the hopes and fears, the passions and the interests, which moved people of that generation to try to rebuild our shattered continent on a new basis. For those for whom the Cold War itself is a matter of history rather than of personal memory the apparent stability of the socialist regimes of central and eastern Europe ten years ago must itself be hard to understand, let alone the scepticism and suspicion in the West which Mikhail Gorbachev had to overcome as he set out to 'westernise' the USSR by claiming a place for Russia within 'our common European home'. With the collapse of the Soviet Union, the ideological battleline between the Western values of liberal democracy and social markets and the Communist values of state social-ism, so bitterly contested in the postwar years, has disappeared beyond recall. The passionate idealism of European federalists who witnessed the collapse of their own states in the Second World War has faded. The urgency with which de Gaulle de-fended the sovereignty of France has given way to a more qualified determination among his contemporary successors to maintain the essence of national sovereignty amidst the unavoidable pressures of interdependence.

The aim of this volume is to provide an insight, for readers who have come of age in a peaceful and integrated Western Europe and who take its hard-won achievements for granted, into the motivations of some of the leading personalities who shaped Western Europe and its institutions. The men – they were almost without exception men – who grappled with the problems of postwar reconstruction after 1945 were born mostly towards the end of the nineteenth century. They had survived two Euro-pean wars, in one or both of which most fought; and they feared that the aftermath of the second might be as unstable as that of the first. They witnessed Communist revolution in Russia, and revolutionary disorder across central Europe; fascism in Italy, and later national socialism in Germany; economic depression leading to na-tional protection, rearmament leading to renewed war. Occupation and resistance revealed the weakness of the nation state and the divisions within national societies. They faced the recurrent problem of Germany, Europe's central power and largest nation: a state without clear or agreed boundaries, an economy on which most of its neighbours depended historically for their prosperity.

With active American political and economic support and under Communist threat, external and internal, they set out to rebuild state structures and national legitimacy within a broader framework. But they did not start their regional experiment with a blank piece of paper. Monnet and Adenauer recalled failed schemes of Franco-German reconciliation from the 1920s, attempts to harness Saar and Ruhr coal to Lorraine steel; Schuman had grown up as a Lotharingian citizen in this contested region. Churchill had flirted with Franco-British union (under Monnet's wartime persuasion) before he turned to Anglo-American integration. Catholic thinkers had struggled to develop theological and philosophical responses to totalitarian regimes and racist ideologies, devising doctrines of subsidiarity, Christian democracy, and personalism which continued to influence European politics half a century later. Socialists in exile, in the resistance or in concentration camps, had also recast their political approaches under the bitter experience of war. Prisoners on both sides had time to reflect and to dream; Walter Hallstein, for instance, transported to prison camp in the USA, devoted himself to the study of American federalism. Governments in exile in London, in intermittent contact with resistance movements within their occupied states, were forced to consider the lessons of the interwar years and prepare the compromises they needed to strike between sovereignty and international cooperation when the guns fell silent.

Socialist, Liberal and Christian Democratic Internationals were created in the immediate postwar years by these exiled and resistance politicians, competing with the international Communist movement in appealing to the hearts and minds of the peoples of Europe. In France and Italy the Communists emerged from the Resistance with considerable prestige, effective overt and covert organisations, and mass support; the French and Italian Communist Parties in 1946-7 were the largest outside the USSR itself. It seemed quite possible that many disillusioned Germans, after 1945 as after 1918, might also turn to the Communist alternative which was being established in government in the Soviet zone. Millions of refugees (or 'displaced persons', commonly known in postwar Britain as 'DPs') from the lost German territories, the Baltic states, Poland and the Ukraine were encamped across Western Europe. Returning deportees and prisoners of war had to be absorbed, ruined industries to be reconstructed, shortages of food and fuel to be overcome. This desperate effort at national reconstruction took place within an international context in which US forces withdrew from Central Europe while the Red Army stayed: first imposing Communist rule on Poland, then on Hungary, Romania and Bulgaria, then supporting a coup in Czechoslovakia which triggered the fear of Communist takeovers further west. The onset of the Cold War and the beginnings of West European integration went together in the heated and anxious postwar years.

For the next generation of political leaders, following the men who gave Western Europe its postwar shape and taking office in the 1960s, 1970s and 1980s, the Second World War alone was their reference point. Edward Heath, Denis Healey and Helmut Schmidt fought for their countries, the first two in Normandy and the last on the Eastern front; Willy Brandt fought for his beliefs against his country. Hugh Gaitskell and Harold Wilson experienced the European war from the home front in England. Helmut Kohl came of age in the immediate postwar years, with the trauma of defeat and the question of Germany's responsibility as motivating ideas. Margaret Thatcher was just twenty years old in 1945, and, although without wartime service, with a lasting image of Britain standing firm and emerging victorious while continental states collapsed into occupation and collaboration. François Mitterrand, that deeply ambiguous figure, bridged the images and the generations: an officer in the defeated French army, an official of the Vichy regime, a member of the Resistance, a minister in the postwar French government, a participant in the 1948 Congress of the Hague – becoming President of France two years after Mrs.Thatcher became Prime Minister, and remaining President for five years after she lost office. Only with Jacques Delors do we reach the clearly postwar generation: a leader whose personal experience was not directly marked by the Second World War.

Europe between the wars stretched as far east as Brest-Litovsk, with the revolutionary (and largely unknown) Soviet Union beyond. During the war the Soviet Union became America's and Britain's most crucial ally, bearing the main brunt of the conflict against Germany for three years from the summer of 1941 until the Western allies invaded Normandy. The victorious Red Army established a new frontier across the centre of Europe, with socialist regimes imposed on the states it 'liberated'. Postwar 'Europe' in the minds of most 'Europeans' was for most purposes only western Europe, summed up by Adenauer's remark that, in the trauma of 1945, 'Asia had reached the Elbe'. Disillusionment with authoritarian socialism led many in Central Europe – like Vaclav Havel, Gyorgy Konrad, or Milan Kundera – to dream of a future 'return to the West'; others, like József Antall, took the path of inner migration from the outset, waiting for more propitious times. It was the re-emergence of Westernisers in Russia, among the postwar generation of Mikhail Gorbachev and others too young to have been overwhelmed by the experience of the great purges of the 1930s and the Great Patriotic War from 1941-45, which brought this wider Europe back into the international society from which it had been cordoned off for fifty years.

History is shaped by the interaction between events and human responses, mediated by the continuing processes of technological and environmental change. There was a tendency in the first histories of European integration, written in the 1960s and 1970s, to ascribe its success to the heroic qualities of a small number of great men – Robert Schuman, Konrad Adenauer, Alcide De Gasperi, Jean Monnet, Paul-Henri Spaak – presented as saintly and visionary figures who placed the secular interests of European civilisation before the short-term interests of its separate nation states. In this hagiographic version of history there were also dark figures who struggled against the march of progress and civilisation: de Gaulle chief amongst them, defending a nineteenth-century concept of the nation state in the face of political and economic logic, with Mrs.Thatcher inheriting the Gaullist mantle a generation later.

Eminent Europeans does not subscribe to such an approach. As John Harper makes clear in his essay, the American intellectual and political contribution to the construction of Western Europe in the postwar years was substantial, reinforced by West European dependence on American economic assistance and military support. West European leaders reacted to circumstances as they saw them, struggling to respond to crises as they arose. Monnet's plan for Franco-German integration in 1950 was in some ways as opportunistic as his 1940 plan for Franco-British union. The earlier scheme failed in the chaos of a disintegrating French Government; the later scheme caught the imagination of key players within another divided French government, and prospered through strong American support.

Many of the men who built postwar Europe borrowed their ideas from others, and reshaped them to fit immediate and pressing needs. One of the oddities of the history of West European integration is that so many of the early prophets of an integrated Europe came, as John Pinder notes, from outside the six states which constituted its core: from the successor states to the Austro-Hungarian empire, from Switzerland and from England. English rhetoric, and British prestige, were at the peak of their influence in the immediate aftermath of the Second World War, as Julian Critchley recalls, with the European Movement itself under British leadership. But through their experience of the war the British had become more conscious of the differences rather than the similarities between them and the European continent. Travelling across the Channel to visit war-compromised politicians in shaky coalition governments presiding over still unstable societies, it seemed to most British leaders only practical commonsense to hold back: to encourage others to commit themselves to a path of integration which they considered inappropriate for their own country. The idealistic rhetoric of the Congress of the Hague and of the early Council of Europe did not, however, play a determining role in shaping the real structures of European institutions. That came from careful bargaining among governments, often under American pressure, led by politicians who were prepared to take risks to achieve long-term security and economic objectives.

The rebuilding of postwar Western Europe required both a structure for regional political integration *and* a reconstruction of the nation state. The first was essential to security and to economic recovery; American security guarantees and Marshall Plan aid were both conditional on West Europeans accepting moves in this direction. The second was essential to re-establish legitimacy and democratic stability after the social conflicts of the 1930s and the traumas of state collapse, occupation, collaboration and resistance.

Perceptions differed about the balance to be struck between these two imperatives. Paul-Henri Spaak concluded in his London wartime exile that a postwar Belgian government would 'have to combine... a certain reawakening of nationalism and an indispensable internationalism'. Altiero Spinelli, exiled on a Mediterranean island, imagined a new Europe in which the people would throw off old loyalties to failed states in favour of a larger entity as enthusiastically as Neapolitans and Tuscans had done in favour of a united Italy a century before. Charles de Gaulle, carrying the honour of France in wartime London by permission of the Anglo-Saxons, was clear that the state and the nation were the fundamentals to be rebuilt, with international cooperation a necessary but clearly secondary priority. Spinelli maintained his faith in popular support for a united Europe, against all setbacks, through to the 1980s, persuading the newly-elected European Parliament to agree to a radically federalist draft treaty on European Union. But it was Monnet's strategy of limited integration, its political implications camouflaged in technical language and administrative style, which carried reluctant national governments and publics, not Spinelli's more direct and explicit assault.

Circumstances always constrain available choices. But personalities count in what is chosen, in which opportunities are seized or missed. It was crucial to the successful launch and acceptance of Monnet's proposals of June 1950 that the French foreign minister was Robert Schuman, rather than (for example) Guy Mollet or Antoine Pinay. If the francophile Adenauer had given way to the atlanticist Erhard in 1956, if Blankenhorn had conducted the negotiations rather than Hallstein, the Treaties of Rome might have given birth to the wider but weaker free trade area which the British, and some within the German government, preferred. If de Gaulle had returned to office a year earlier, the treaties once negotiated might not have been ratified. If, a generation later, Helmut Kohl and Margaret Thatcher, the two leading European conservatives of their time, had understood each other better and struck up a constructive relationship, the pattern of West European politics in the 1980s would have been significantly different. Jacques Delors's distinctive style of leadership marked the European Commission and the wider politics of European integration over ten years of office, but it was constrained or supported at different moments by the shifting political and personal alliances of nation states and national leaders.

Each new generation of leaders was marked, too, by individual admiration – or dislike – for those who had gone before. Helmut Kohl explicitly saw himself as Adenauer's political heir; Mrs.Thatcher was fond of quoting Churchill; Mitterrand's entire career was dialectically linked to that of de Gaulle. Differences of style in political leadership made for distinctive images, some more politically appealing, others more open to admiration than affection. Schuman and Delors were both ascetics, contrasting with the evident enjoyment of life of Spaak or Kohl. Delors, like

Hallstein before him and Mrs.Thatcher in the opposite camp, worked and read seven days a week, both serious thinkers who relaxed by informing themselves further on other and wider issues. Monnet cultivated his country weekends, thinking politics as he walked alone or with friends and advisers.

The Europe which they shaped, and which in turn constrained the choices which they made, has been transformed since the late 1980s by the unification of Germany, the transition of East and Central Europe from state socialism to market democracy, the disintegration of the Soviet Union and the partial withdrawal of the United States. The structures which these eminent Europeans built and worked through remain, though strained now under the pressures of enlarging membership and expanding tasks for the European Union. The political leaders who grapple with the contemporary European agenda are children of the postwar years, with Chancellor Kohl defining himself as 'the last European' among a successor generation who took for granted what his political heroes struggled to achieve. It remains to be seen what imaginative leaps they may make in adapting European institutions to new tasks, what lessons they recall to inform the decisions they take. Our objective here is to show the reader something of what motivated the leaders who built our prosperous, stable and peaceful Europe, with all its underlying political ambiguities and contradictions. We hope it will encourage the intelligent reader to look with a constructively critical eye both at the tasks which now face European political leaders and at the quality of contemporary leadership shown in tackling them.

Martyn Bond, Julie Smith and William Wallace

Prewar Ideas of European Union – The British Prophets

John Pinder

The vision of a united Europe has recurred through the centuries. Among the more notable visionaries were Sully and Penn in the seventeenth century, the Abbé de Saint-Pierre and Kant in the eighteenth, Saint-Simon, Mazzini and Proudhon in the nineteenth. But it was not until the dreadful period of European history which began with World War One that the political project for a Union of the kind that Europeans have been building since World War Two began to take shape.

Signs of this were already evident in the months following the outbreak of war in 1914. In Berlin, an association called *Neues Vaterland* was founded, with Albert Einstein as one of its supporters, to promote the idea of supranational European unification. In London, Norman Angell and Ramsay MacDonald were among the sponsors of the Union for Democratic Control, which aimed to replace the balance of power by a European federation of states. Disappointment with the postwar settlement and the League of Nations was to lead to more influential proposals in the 1920s. In 1923 Count Richard Coudenhove-Kalergi launched his book, *Paneuropa*, and founded the Pan-European Union. His energetic propagation of the message that Europe faced the choice between a voluntary federation and a union forced by absolutist Russia had a powerful impact on opinion. But his proposals for a compulsory arbitration court followed by a customs union and eventually a United States of Europe were too far-reaching to have practical effect in Europe between the wars.

In 1929 came Ortega y Gasset's famous book, *The Revolt of the Masses*, in which he advocated that a great nation be constructed from the peoples of Europe. But he gave no convincing idea of the structure of a Union that would serve the purpose he had in mind. Nor did Aristide Briand, then French Foreign Minister, who, also in 1929, launched at the League of Nations General Assembly his proposal for 'some kind of federal bond' among the European states. But he went on to assert that they would be associated 'on the basis of absolute sovereignty', as were the member states of the League itself; and since most of these were European, it is not clear what added value the proposal would have brought. Winston Churchill was, as we shall see, attracted by Briand's initiative. But the

1

British government was not and, with insufficient support elsewhere, the Briand plan came to naught. In the 1930s, Hitler and Mussolini blocked any further political initiatives towards European Union.

This did not deter those prophets who continued to promote the idea of European Union against the day when it should become politically feasible. One group whose thinking was to contribute to the development of the European idea was the Parisian *Ordre Nouveau*. Their starting point was the personalist philosophy, opposed to both individualism and collectivism, which focused on the relationship between the person and the community. The leader of the personalist movement was Emmanuel Mounier, whose writings were to influence Jacques Delors, as Charles Grant notes elsewhere in this book. The moving spirit of the more specifically federalist personalists, who believe that the smallest communities, political, economic and social, should federate with each other in larger communities, up to the level of the region, the nation and eventually Europe and the world, was Alexandre Marc, who has remained active in European federalist circles up to and beyond his ninetieth birthday in 1994. Born in Odessa, he left Russia after the Bolsheviks seized power, then studied in Paris and, for a year, at Freiburg under Husserl. Immensely active and intelligent, he was attracted to personalism and, with Mounier, founded in 1930 the review *Esprit*. He went on to found the *Ordre Nouveau* and the review of that name together with like-minded friends, including the profoundly cultured Swiss Denis de Rougement who, like Marc, was to be influential in the formation of the European Union of Federalists after the Second World War. De Rougement and the Swiss organisation *Europa-Union*, launched in 1933 and led for many years by the economist and editor Hans Bauer, were particularly insistent on the need for decentralisation, following the Swiss example, in a European federal system.

The personalists had, however, unfortunately associated the atomistic individualism they abhorred with liberal democracy and its political institutions. Thus although Marc and his friends worked vigorously to help found the European Union of Federalists (EUF) and the European Movement (EM), they sought to mobilise the *forces vives*, or civil society, rather than the political parties, parliaments and governments. But without a commitment to the institutions of liberal democracy, nothing effective would have been done to set in train the process of European Union along Community or federal lines. So the leadership of those who were working to realise their vision of such a Union through political action in the EM and the EUF passed to a man whose idea of European Union had been shaped by the thinking of writers imbued with the principles of liberal and constitutional democracy: Altiero Spinelli.

Spinelli's federalism was based on his reading, while incarcerated by Mussolini on the island of Ventotene, of the works of British federalists. He was to recall decades later how his introduction to the federal idea, through reading these works around the time of the Second World War began, had:

> remained to this day impressed on my memory like a revelation. Since I was looking for mental clarity and precision, I was not attracted by the foggy and contorted ideological federalism of a Proudhon or a Mazzini, but by the clean, precise thinking of these English federalists, in whose writings I found a very good key to understanding the chaos into which Europe was plunging and for devising alternatives.

In the 1930s a number of Britain's foremost intellectuals had indeed been writing about a project for a federal union in Europe and some leading British statesmen, present and future, spoke in favour of it. The intellectuals included Sir William Beveridge, Lionel Curtis, Ivor Jennings, Harold Laski, Lord Lothian, Kim Mackay, Lionel Robbins, Arnold Toynbee, Barbara Wootton and, recently naturalised as British, Friedrich von Hayek; the statesmen included Clement Attlee, Ernest Bevin, Winston Churchill and Harold Wilson. Some of these people were among the most influential prophets of the postwar movement towards European Union. Because of their influence on Spinelli and the postwar federalist movement and hence on the international European Movement, and because their works, though of exceptionally high quality, have been almost entirely forgotten in Britain, the rest of this chapter will be devoted to these British federalists.

Given the mediocrity of Britain's postwar contribution to the development of European Union, and the myth, sedulously spread by some politicians, that the federal idea is an unwelcome alien invention, all this may seem surprising, even unbelievable. But it was so. The aim of this essay is to provide evidence and explanation of a forgotten episode in which the British should take some pride. The fresh memory of the carnage in the First World War was one reason for it. A sense of responsibility for the state of the world, strong when Britain was still a great power, was another. A third was the imminence of renewed disaster in the Second World War. A fourth was the strength of the British tradition of federalist thought and action. But since this too has been forgotten, we should start with evidence that the federal idea is a product of British political culture and had an important place in British political thought.

British political culture and the federal idea

The federal idea was the result of an accommodation between those Americans who saw the need for a strong central government for the defence and development of the former colonies and those who set more store by local autonomy. The agreement to meet both needs by dividing powers between two levels of government, democratic at both levels, was the invention of people who were imbued with British political philosophy, from which the idea of the separation of powers had stemmed. If powers could be divided among different institutions, they could also be divided between different levels of government. So the federal idea can be seen as a product of the British political tradition, alien not to the British but to the absolutist systems then prevalent on the Continent.

It was not until the second half of the nineteenth century that the British became aware of the significance of what the Americans had done. But in 1863 Edward Freeman, later to become Regius Professor of Modern History at Oxford, published a weighty book on the history of federal government which analysed the American division of power and sovereignty between 'coordinate authorities'. This established federalism as a subject of academic study at the highest level. Two decades later it became a subject of political significance too, with the rise of two major political projects: Imperial Federation and a federal version of Home Rule to answer the Irish question.

Imperial federation

In the early 1880s Sir John Seeley, Regius Professor of Modern History at Cambridge, wrote *The Expansion of England*, which achieved great fame because it responded to mounting concern about the future of the Empire on which British power was based. His argument was that all the historic European powers would be eclipsed by America and Russia, but that Britain could escape this fate if it federated with the self-governing colonies, later called Dominions. This, he insisted, would not be an empire, but a large federal state. His book was to provide a basis for an influential political movement. But first it is interesting to see how he had applied the federal idea in another direction.

In 1871 the London Peace Society, shocked by the Franco-Prussian war, asked Seeley to give them a lecture with his thoughts on how war could be abolished. His answer, which was published in an article entitled *United States of Europe*, was a European federation that would have exclusive control of the armed forces, hitherto controlled by the member states. The forces would have to be controlled by democratic federal institutions, including an impartial federal judiciary and a federal legislature and executive, all to have direct links with the citizens rather than relying, as alliances had done, only on intergovernmental relations. Seeley realised that this would be harder for Europeans than it had been for Americans, but he believed it possible, provided that a vast popular movement could be generated to achieve it. He concluded by evoking the vision of a new federation arising 'like a majestic temple from the tomb of war'.

While Seeley saw the potential of the federal idea for Europe, that was not the lesson which British politicians were to draw from the Franco-Prussian war, with its striking evidence of the rise of German power. They were more responsive to the idea of consolidating the power of the British Empire: hence the success of Seeley's book a decade later.

The Imperial Federation League was founded in 1884, with strong political support, Liberal as well as Conservative, the Liberals laying particular emphasis on Britain's role as the principal bastion of political freedom in the world, and both being concerned that Britain's position was threatened by the rise of German power. Seeley himself was a Liberal, as was James Bryce, the Regius Professor of Civil Law at Oxford, who was to serve in three of Gladstone's Cabinets. Bryce was the author of the definitive treatise on American federal government, at the conclusion of which he considered how far the American experience could be relevant for Europeans. He, like Seeley, supported the Imperial Federation League and contributed to its thinking. But the political leader of the imperial federalists was Joseph Chamberlain, who did much to ensure that federalism in this form occupied a prominent place in the British politics of that period. Thus neither politicians nor academics could ignore the significance of the federal idea; and the point was driven home by another burning issue of that time: the Irish question.

A federal UK to answer the Irish question

Lord Acton replaced Seeley as Regius Professor of Modern History at Cambridge in 1895. He was a man who wrote brilliant essays rather than books; and he had, in the preceding three decades, written four essays on federalism that were later published in his famous *History of Freedom and other Essays*. Acton was concerned with the decentralisation rather than the concentration of power, so he saw federalism as a protection for minorities and a defence against the over-mighty state. Federalism was, he believed, 'the most efficacious and most congenial' of all the checks on centralised oppression of minorities; and 'the coexistence of several nations under the same State' was 'the best security of its freedom'. The same decentralist aspect of federalism was taken up by Ernest Barker, also to become an eminent Cambridge professor, who advocated decentralisation into smaller national groups 'on which large powers are to be conferred by way of devolution' and who, in the early years of this century, envisaged the rise of a new Socialism and a new Liberalism based on this federal principle.

For Acton, the immediate practical application of the federal idea should be to resolve the Irish problem. He had been a Liberal MP for six years and was a close adviser to Gladstone, particularly on Home Rule for Ireland; and his advice was to establish Irish Home Rule in the context of a federal United Kingdom. This idea, like that of imperial federation, was to gain powerful political support from the 1880s on. Here again, Chamberlain was to play a prominent part, promoting the proposal for a federal United Kingdom in 1885-6 and causing the defeat of Gladstone's first Home Rule Bill on the grounds that it was not federal enough. Home Rule was still a critical issue for British politics in 1911, when Winston Churchill and Lloyd George put a federal proposal to the Cabinet Committee on the subject, and for a time the Cabinet was preoccupied by federalism. Federalism was supported by *The Times*, *The Observer* and the *Daily Mail*; and in 1912 Churchill made speeches in favour of a federal United Kingdom. On 19 June 1918, *The Times* affirmed that 'the future is clearly with the federal solution'. As far as Ireland was concerned, it was too late. But here again, it was hardly possible for politicians to be unaware of the federal idea as a solution to political problems.

The idea of European federation

Acton had understood that the federal idea could have general application. He wrote that it completed the principles of the liberal constitution 'in a way that was capable of unlimited extension', and that it offered 'the only way of avoiding war', allowing different nations to 'live in harmony side by side'. As Seeley had foreseen as early as 1871, it offered a way of avoiding war in Europe in particular; and in *The Development of European Polity*, published in 1903, Professor Sidgwick, who did a great deal to establish the subject of political science at Cambridge, drew on the work of Freeman and Bryce to expound the federal idea and concluded that a European federation was 'the most probable prophecy'.

As editor of the influential *Pall Mall Gazette* and *Review of Reviews*, W. T. Stead was a passionate advocate of the federal idea, whether applied internally to the UK, or to the Empire or to Europe. About the last of these he wrote a book on *The United States of Europe on the Eve of the Parliament of Peace*, referring to the Peace Conference at The Hague in 1899. The first issue of the *Review of Reviews* after the outbreak of the First World War led with an article on ' The United States of Europe: The Only Way Out'.

We have dug into the history of the half century before the First World War in order to demonstrate that the notion that federalism is an alien concept, which the British have always ignored, is a myth. To the contrary, there was a great deal of distinguished academic work on the subject; both Ireland and the Empire had brought it to the fore in British politics from the 1880s onwards; and proposals for European federation had been discussed, though without reaching the political agenda. Barker was not exaggerating when he wrote in 1915 that 'there is much talk of federalism these days'. That the talk did not lead to concrete achievement was, of course, due to entrenched opposition to constitutional change. Albert Dicey's reaction to what he called the current notion 'that federalism contains the solution of every constitutional problem that perplexes British statesmanship' was to insist that 'the absolute sovereignty or despotism of the King in Parliament' was 'the one fundamental dogma of English constitutional law'. That dogma has to this day prevented the British from playing a constructive part in the development of European Union. But it did not inhibit the extensive discussion of the federal idea that took place in Britain, more than anywhere else in Europe, before the First World War, bequeathing a stock of knowledge of the subject that enabled the British of the interwar period to produce a remarkable generation of prophets of European federation.

The prophets and their ideas, 1938-40

Knowledge of the federal idea was passed to the interwar generation not only through the written word but also by people who had understood its value before the First World War: in particular Philip Kerr (later Lord Lothian), Lionel Curtis, Winston Churchill and Harold Laski.

Lothian and Curtis

Lord Milner, who was a prominent imperial federalist, assembled his 'Kindergarten' of bright young men in South Africa in the early years of the nineteenth century, among them Lionel Curtis and Philip Kerr. Confronted with the problem of designing a constitution to make a new state out of four existing colonies, they became inspired by the federal example of the United States. Although their proposals for a federal constitution were not adopted, after returning to England in 1909 they founded the Round Table, dedicated initially to the causes of imperial and UK federation. After a visit to Canada in 1911, however, Kerr realised that imperial federation was not wanted, and transferred his commitment to the idea of international federation more generally.

From 1916 to 1921 Kerr was Lloyd George's private secretary and as such played a significant part in the Peace Conference after the War. Realising that the League of Nations offered no secure basis for peace, he developed his ideas about international federation in two books in the early 1920s. As a leader of the Liberal Party, in 1931 Lord Lothian, as he by then was, became a Cabinet Minister in the coalition government, but resigned in 1932 in protest against the protectionism of the Ottawa Agreements. He continued to be preoccupied by the threat of another war and by the federal idea as the antidote; and in 1935 he published his federalist classic, *Pacifism is not Enough – Nor Patriotism Either*, in which he identified national sovereignty as the root cause of war, which the League of Nations had allowed to remain intact. Affirming that 'peace is a positive thing', requiring a system based on justice rather than merely the absence of violent conflict, he advocated a federation to establish the rule of law through judicial power, together with a federal legislature and executive.

Recognising that opinion was not yet ripe for so radical a change, he urged the peace movement to work for such a genuine peace system. Events, he predicted, would bring the need for federation to the fore. Such events were not long in coming; and in the spring of 1939, Lothian was to give strong support to the founders of the Federal Union movement, which was soon to become extraordinarily popular. He wrote the movement's first substantial pamphlet, *The Ending of Armageddon*. This, in line with the recently published *Union Now* by the American Clarence Streit, envisaged Atlantic rather than European federation. But like many of the British who were soon to become committed to the federal idea, he then turned to advocacy of a European federation, to be based at first on union between Britain and France. During the first months of the war, as Ambassador to Washington, he departed from the conventional ambassadorial role by promoting that idea in a number of his American speeches.

Meanwhile his old friend Lionel Curtis, who had played a leading part in the Kindergarten and the Round Table, among other things persuading Churchill in 1911 to favour the federal option for the UK, and whose federalist commitment was such that his friends used to call him 'The Prophet', had been in Oxford writing a vast book called *Civitas Dei* which, with religious principles as its starting point, traced through history the development of individual rights and thus of liberal democracy. This, he argued, pointed towards federation, eventually to world federation; and Britain and the United States, as the major powers with the greatest experience of liberal democracy, should lead the way.

With American isolationism precluding such a role for the United States, Curtis, like Lothian, spurred by the outbreak of war, came to accept the idea of moving towards European federation through union with France. By 1939 Arnold Toynbee was directing a research unit set up by the Foreign Office to provide background thinking for British policy, and Curtis was his Chairman. Toynbee wrote a paper advocating such a union and Curtis responded by insisting that it must have unequivocally federal institutions, although as regards its powers he was a minimalist, wanting to confine them to defence, foreign affairs and directly associated matters. Curtis, like Lothian, had been drawn from the Atlantic to the European project by the close alliance with France, the hard fact of American isolationism, and the onset of the war.

Churchill

Even before the First World War, Churchill had been an advocate of a federal solution to a pressing political problem. So it is not perhaps surprising that a man with his imaginative reach should have responded sympathetically to Aristide Briand's proposal for European Union, with an article in the *Saturday Evening Post* of 15 February 1930 entitled 'The United States of Europe'. He wrote that European citizens could realise themselves simultaneously as, for example, French, German, Spanish, Dutch; as European; and finally, as citizens of the world. He envisaged European unification or 'federal links'; but Britain with its Empire would remain alongside this European Union, associated but 'not comprised'. In the later 1930s, Churchill was President of the British section of New Commonwealth, which called for an international court for compulsory arbitration, with international troops to enforce its decisions. In June 1940, as Prime Minister, he made the offer of union to France, but too late to prevent French capitulation. Finally, in Zurich in September 1946, he said that 'We must build a kind of United States of Europe' and that 'the first step must be a partnership between France and Germany'. This was a truly historic speech, which made the idea of a federal Europe seem politically feasible to many on the Continent and thus helped launch the movement towards the European Union of today. Moreover it pointed towards the Franco-German partnership as the idea's prime mover, a relationship regarded by most people as inconceivable, coming so soon after the end of the war. He was understandably not so far-sighted as regards Britain's role, because the old imperialist could still look out on an Empire comprising a quarter of the world's population, which made Britain a world power. He would not, it may be surmised, have been so exclusive had the British Empire been reduced to the few small islands that remain today. But here we are concerned with the prophets of European Union, whether or not Britain is included; and among these, Churchill surely has an honourable place.

Laski

Harold Laski had been a most brilliant student of Ernest Barker and was imbued with his ideas of decentralist federalism. In his early twenties Laski wrote two books analysing the concept of sovereignty from this standpoint. He started to teach at the London School of Economics in 1920 and became Professor of Politics there in 1926, having great influence over students for the next thirty years. In 1926 his *Grammar of Politics*, which was for many years the standard work on political science, was published. In it he wrote that 'society is essentially federal in nature ... authority must be federal also'. This form of federalism had much in common with those of Continental thinkers such as von Gierke, who had influenced Barker, and Proudhon, whom Laski much admired. Laski also stressed the need for a federal union of states. 'Peace cannot be built on a system of separate sovereign states', he wrote, in the preface to the third edition of his *Grammar*, affirming 'the incompatibility of the sovereign state with that economic world order so painfully struggling to be born'.

Laski's own struggle to come to terms with the world of the 1930s, however, led him to espouse marxism, though without abandoning his libertarian principles. He still regarded federal union as necessary, but thought that the working class would first have to secure political control, which should in liberal democracies be achieved peacefully.

Active in the Labour Party, Laski moderated his views and became its Chairman by the time of its victory at the general election of 1945. Addressing the Congress of the French Socialist Party in that year, he proposed that the two nations unite to form a single state, 'open to immediate or ultimate accession by all European democracies'. Thus he too became a prophet of European Union, without, however, abandoning his vision of an eventual world federation. Speaking soon after the shock of Hiroshima, he saw such a European federation as 'an essential step to that World Government' which the atomic bomb had now made urgently necessary.

Laski's teaching introduced many generations of students to the federal idea. His federalism may also have made an impression on the Director who appointed him to his post at the LSE, Sir William Beveridge, who was to become powerfully committed during the first year of the Second World War to the project of a European federation.

Beveridge

Beveridge, as a great social reformer, was essentially a problem-solver. This trait led him from what had looked like the start of a promising academic career into social work and then into a campaign for a national system of labour exchanges, to help deal with the problem of unemployment. Churchill, as President of the Board of Trade in the Liberal government, appointed Beveridge as personal assistant in 1911, and he rose by 1919 to be, at the age of 39, one of the youngest ever Permanent Secretaries. He was appointed Director of the LSE in that year; and by 1937, when he left to become Master of University College, Oxford, he had transformed it from a small school with mainly part-time students to a world leader in the social sciences. The appointment to the teaching staff of a number of stars in the social sciences, among whom were four of the federalist prophets included in this chapter, Laski, Hayek, Jennings and Robbins, was part of this process. The interactions among them contributed to the efflorescence of British federalism in the late 1930s and certainly influenced other members of the staff at the LSE, including R.H.Tawney, who concluded his renowned book on *Equality* by presaging the collapse of 'the system of independent sovereign states, each claiming full sovereignty as against every other'.

After the start of the Second World War in September 1939 Beveridge, now at Oxford, gave a great deal of his time to the newly established Federal Union movement and in particular to its Federal Union Research Institute. Here, as he had done at the LSE, he assembled the best available talent, this time to study the constitutional and economic aspects of a federation embracing, as a minimum, Britain, France, Germany, the four Scandinavian countries, Belgium and Holland, to be established after the war, when Germany had returned to democracy. As well as being Chairman of the Institute, Beveridge chaired both its economic and constitutional committees and conferences. Both Lionel Robbins and Barbara Wootton wrote reports for the economic conferences and memoranda were supplied by James Meade, later a Nobel Prizewinner, and Harold Wilson, subsequently Prime Minister. Wilson, in addition to making some interesting proposals, engaged in a polemic with von Hayek reminiscent of the debate in the 1980s and 1990s over the Social Charter. Hayek, too, was an active participant in the economic meetings, including an Anglo-French conference that the Institute held in Paris in the spring of 1940. The constitutional conferences had two draft federal constitutions put before them, by Ivor Jennings and Kenneth Wheare, two of the foremost constitutional lawyers of their generation, who were later to become Vice-Chancellors of Cambridge and Oxford respectively.

Fortified by this remarkable input of economic and constitutional expertise, Beveridge himself wrote the first of the Institute's series of Federal Tracts, entitled *Peace by Federation?*, published in May 1940. In it he proposed that the federal powers be limited to defence, foreign policy, trade, currency and migration, all other powers to remain with the member states; and he defined the federal institutions as a two-chamber legislature, an executive responsible to it and a judiciary that would interpret the federal constitution. This was a far from original, but clear and cogent outline of a European federal polity and of the case for it. Beveridge knew that the social reforms he wanted to see would come to naught if Europe continued to be disrupted by wars; and the relationship with France seemed then to make federation a feasible project. This prospect was altered by the fall of France in the following month; and Beveridge was soon to be called to the government service to design his historic proposals for the welfare state. But during a crucial period he, too, was to be numbered among the prophets of European Union.

Jennings, Robbins, Hayek

Both Ivor Jennings and Lionel Robbins joined the LSE in 1929 and both became deeply committed to the Federal Union movement ten years later. Friedrich von Hayek joined the LSE in 1930 and was likewise to play his part in the Federal Union Research Institute.

Jennings, as Reader in English Law at the LSE, wrote his three great books on the British constitution. In the 1930s he enjoyed intense discussions with Laski and others, in the course of which the subject of a federal Europe must have arisen. In 1938, he wrote a paper on 'The Idea of a United State of Europe'. By 1939, he became committed to the newly founded Federal Union, serving on its Council; and he became very active in its Research Institute, attending almost all the meetings. The constitution he wrote for it, short and beautifully drafted, was published in 1940 as an annex to his book, *A Federation for Western Europe*. Such was the state of opinion at the time that he observed in its first sentence that 'The desirability of replacing international anarchy by international government is so generally recognised in Great Britain that it needs no demonstration'.

Robbins, who had been just old enough to be an officer in the Royal Artillery in the First World War, was such an outstanding economist that he was appointed to his Chair at the LSE when only thirty years old. He retained it for over thirty years, punctuated by four years as Director of the economic section of the War Cabinet's secretariat; and on leaving the LSE in 1961, he became chairman both of the *Financial Times* and of the government committee on higher education which led to the great expansion in the 1960s and also proposed replacing the binary by a unitary structure, a reform that was not implemented until the 1990s. In 1934 he had written to Lothian, expressing 'the greatest of interest and the most complete agreement' with Lothian's speech on 'Liberalism in the Modern World' which presaged his *Pacifism is not Enough.* This was one key to Robbins's unique contribution to economic thought: his exposition of the need for law and government at the international level as a framework for the international economy. Another key came from Edwin Cannan, who had been professor of economics at the LSE until 1926 and had, during the First World War, envisaged that the allies would become the nucleus of a federation that would include the defeated powers. At the same time he had pointed out that free trade economists 'did not understand that the actual harmonious cooperation of the world was dependent on institutions the development of which requires law and government'.

Robbins built on his understanding of both the political and the economic case for federal union in two books, published in 1937 and 1939. Referring in the first one, *Economic Planning and International Order*, to Cannan's observation about a serious deficiency of nineteenth century liberalism, he reasoned that an international liberal economy needs both security and a legal frame for effective markets, which should include laws of property and contract, assured freedom of trade as well as of capital and labour movements, anti-monopoly policy, and if possible an international money. These requirements of a liberal economy were inconceivable without government, which would have to be neither an alliance nor a unitary state, but federal.

The second book, called *The Economic Causes of War*, was concluded just after the Second World War began. Robbins argued that it was not capitalism, but national sovereignty, aggravated by protectionism, that was the root cause of war; that the American Founding Fathers were right, and 'unless we destroy the sovereign state, the sovereign state will destroy us'; and that, while world federation was not yet feasible, European federation would be possible once the Germans, 'this great people', had been 'coerced into free and equal citizenship of the United States of Europe'. Robbins, like many others at that time, had been led by hard political facts from an idea of the general merits of federal government to advocacy of a European federation. Unlike others, he managed to develop an economic theory that explained the need for institutions of international government if an open liberal economy is to be secured. This major contribution to economic thought could have helped greatly towards an understanding in Britain of the political implications of the interdependent modern economy. But it has unfortunately largely been ignored.

Robbins had remarked, in May 1939, how 'so many people, working quite independently, are finding themselves led more and more to the adoption of the federal idea'. He was to work enthusiastically with a number of them in the Federal Union Research Institute, and wrote one of the Federal Tracts, *The Economic Aspects of Federation*. This was his last contribution to the development of federal thought before being drawn into the government service for the duration of the war.

Friedrich von Hayek, or plain Hayek as he called himself after becoming naturalised British in 1938, was appointed Took Professor of Economic Science at the LSE in 1930. He was close to Robbins, who benefited greatly from the intellectual stimulus of Hayek's seminars, which Robbins usually chaired; and Robbins made particular acknowledgement to him in the preface to *The Economic Causes of War*. Hayek went on to be awarded the Nobel Prize in 1974 and to become the economic guru of neo-liberals, especially in Britain, some of whom may be surprised to learn that he, too, contributed to the literature in favour of federal union in the late 1930s. His article on 'The Economic Conditions of Inter-State Federalism' appeared in the *New Commonwealth Quarterly* in September 1939, in which, referring to Robbins, he affirmed that the international liberal economy needs international federation, and that nineteenth century liberalism did not succeed more fully largely because of its failure to develop in this direction. 'The abrogation of national sovereignties and the creation of an effective international order of law', he wrote, 'is a necessary complement and the logical consummation of the liberal programme'. While the economic benefits could 'hardly be overestimated', security would be enhanced by becoming a common federal responsibility as well as through the removal of protection as a cause of conflict. This dimension of liberalism was not a party matter, but a *'point d'appui* for all liberals'. While Hayek and Robbins were economic liberals, Jennings was a Fabian, and in the 1930s Laski was, although a member of the Fabian Society's Executive Committee, farther to the left. While Hayek's economic arguments did not appeal to socialists, or to social democrat economists such as Harold Wilson, the federal idea appealed to people across the spectrum of democratic politics.

Wootton, Mackay

Barbara Wootton was still a young student at Cambridge when her first husband, John Wootton, died of wounds in 1917. 'The implications of international anarchy in a shrinking world', she was to write in her contribution to the Federal Tracts, could be seen 'in the graves of France and Flanders', poignantly expressing what was a powerful motive for many British federalists. On leaving Cambridge she became a research officer for the Labour Party and the Trades Union Congress, then Director of Studies for extra-mural classes at the University of London from 1926 to 1942. After that she was Professor of Social Studies; and finally she became the Leader of the Labour Party in the House of Lords. From 1939 to 1943 she was extremely active in Federal Union. An inspiring speaker, she carried her share of the political and administrative leadership, chairing the Executive Committee in the winter of 1939-40 and then the National Council until 1943. Her Federal Tract, *Socialism and Federation*, contested the view, prevalent among left-wingers at the time, that socialism had to come before federation. Social progress was 'contingent upon international order' and was undermined by war. So a European federation should be established after the Second World War; and socialists should help to shape it, in the interests of civil and political freedom and of social and economic security.

Kim Mackay also argued that federal union was a necessary condition of socialism. His origins were very different from those of Barbara Wootton. He was an Australian who had been a lecturer in economics at Sydney University and who came to London in 1934 to practise as a solicitor, then pursued a career in Labour Party politics and in business. He rescued Federal Union from near bankruptcy in 1940, when its membership had plunged after the fall of France and the onset of total war, and he chaired its Executive Committee from then until he entered wartime service in the Ministry of Aircraft Production in 1941. In the winter of 1939-40 he wrote a book, *Federal Europe*, in which, like Jennings, he included a constitution that he himself had drafted. He argued like Robbins about the economic causes of war and like Wootton about socialism and federation, adding that the notion of socialism in one country was completely impractical. After analysing the failure of the League of Nations and criticising Briand's proposals for reforming the League as being likewise based on national sovereignty and therefore ineffective, he developed a powerful argument for a federal Europe, with Britain, France and Germany at its core.

Mackay pursued his European federalist commitment with undiminished energy after the war. Following his election as a Labour MP in 1945, he sent a copy of his *Federal Europe* to each Member of Parliament and campaigned with such success that nearly two hundred MPs, drawn almost equally from the two main parties, signed a resolution in March 1948 in favour of a democratic federation of Europe, with a constitution based on common citizenship, political freedom and representative government, and with powers including currency, trade, external affairs and defence, to be drafted by a constituent assembly of representatives chosen by their parliaments. Prime Minister Attlee, replying to the debate, expressed his sympathy with the idea, saying that 'ultimately I believe we must come to federation of Europe'; but evidently not yet. Attlee, while rejecting any immediate action in that direction, spoke more positively of it than subsequent Prime Ministers. But it was not so long since he had been distinctly more positive than that.

Attlee, Bevin, Wilson

Churchill was not the only postwar leader who had favoured the federal project. Labour leaders had done so too. Foremost among them was Clement Attlee, who in

November 1939 said in a speech at Caxton Hall, echoing a slogan coined by W. T. Stead, that 'Europe must federate or perish'. Attlee was carried on the wave of enthusiasm for European federation at that time. But he was not particularly oriented towards Europe. After the war, when Europe seemed a less promising theme to so many British politicians, he turned his attention to the wider world. But he did not abandon the federal idea. He later became President of the British Association for World Government, which advocated reform of the United Nations in a federal direction.

Ernest Bevin, Labour's first postwar Foreign Secretary, also spoke in favour of European Union before the war but preferred the idea of world federation after it. As a highly pragmatic trade union leader, Secretary General of the Transport and General Workers Union since 1922, he spoke at the Trades Union Congress in 1927 in favour of British association with a United States of Europe, in order to create on this side of the Atlantic the conditions that had made America so rich. In 1939 he visited the newly established office of Federal Union and offered his help in spreading the idea in the TGWU; and he followed this up by signing the declaration with which Federal Union launched itself in May 1939, to the effect that national sovereignty must be replaced by federation. After serving as Minister of Labour and National Service during the war, he became Foreign Secretary in 1945; and he then again made clear his federalist commitment, but at the world, not the European, level. His advocacy of world federal government in the House of Commons in November 1945 could hardly have been more precise, when he called for a world federation with world law, a world judiciary to interpret it, a world police force to enforce it, and a world assembly as 'the world sovereign elected authority'. While this was not European, it was certainly federal, demonstrating once more the fallacy of the notion that the British cannot grasp the federal idea.

Harold Wilson, from a younger generation of Labour leaders, was Prime Minister from 1964 to 1970 and again from 1974 to 1976. When the Labour government sought to join the Community in 1967, Wilson was remarkably quick to embrace this cause and to demonstrate his understanding of what it was all about. This is not so surprising, since he had been actively engaged in the Federal Union Research Institute in 1939-40 when he was a Fellow of University College, Oxford, assisting Beveridge with his research projects. He attended all the meetings on economic and on constitutional questions and wrote a paper on 'Economic Aspects of Federation' which was published in the Institute's first Annual Report. He took issue with Hayek, not about the need for federation, which both accepted, but about the economic policies required, Wilson insisting on freedom for the member states to adopt labour standards as the French had done and wanting significant federal powers in this field far beyond what could result from the EU's Social Charter in the 1990s. He proposed that economic union be an objective of the European federation, in order both to contribute to political unity and to offer the potential for 'a greatly increased standard of life'. He also presciently proposed that tariffs within the federal union should be reduced by a stepwise process, anticipating what has in fact been done in the Community. While he did not give much evidence of commitment to the federal idea, he certainly had good knowledge of it and made a constructive contribution to thinking about the process of moving towards it by a series of steps.

Toynbee

Arnold Toynbee's fame rests on the twelve volumes of *A Study of History*, published between 1934 and 1961; and it was his studies of history that led him to the federal idea. As a brilliant classical scholar he pursued his classical and archaeological studies on foot through Greece and Italy before the First World War. Having picked up dysentery on the way, he was unfit for active service, so he worked in the Political Intelligence Department of the Foreign Office throughout the war; and in 1919 he was, like Lothian, in the British delegation to the Peace Conference. He was then appointed, like Robbins at the age of only thirty, to a Chair at London University, in Byzantine and Modern Greek language, literature and history. In 1924, while retaining a research professorship at London University, he became the Director of Studies at Chatham House. So he was in close touch with the contemporary scene while at the same time unfolding his historical grand design.

In 1914 Toynbee had been struck by similarities between the war then beginning and the Peloponnesian War; and that was the origin of his plan for a study of history comparing all known civilisations. Unable to forget the loss of so many of his contemporaries in the terrible battles of the First World War, he was particularly anxious to understand the conditions that led to war. In the introduction to his *History*, he explained that during a lengthy period up to 1875, the two dominant institutions of industrialism and nationalism had, in Europe, been 'working together to build great powers'. But after 1875 they began to work in opposite directions: industrialism towards a global reach; nationalism focusing on smaller communities. The First World War had brought this contradiction to the surface, with enormous damage to the great powers in particular. There were two divergent reactions to this: militant nationalism, favouring protectionism and military power; or international cooperation, whereby states 'accommodate their sovereign independence' to international controls. 'The spirit of Nationality,' Toynbee wrote, 'is a sour ferment of the new wine of Democracy in the old bottles of Tribalism'; but 'in the new age, the dominant note ... is the sense of being parts of some larger universe' rather than for nations to aspire to be 'universes in themselves'. We were, Toynbee thought, entering a new phase, in which 'the consciousness of Western Society' is dominated by wider institutions, while the existing states are seen as 'parochial and subordinate'. The widespread welcome for the federal idea in the late 1930s showed that there were some grounds in Britain at that time for Toynbee's sanguine view. But as the 1930s wore on it became increasingly clear that in some other countries militant nationalism prevailed.

Faced by the prospect of another terrible war, Toynbee signed the Federal Union declaration of May 1939, promoting the federal idea. Unlike many of the signatories, Toynbee had no doubt that Europe was the context in which Britain should federate. In his *History* he had emphasised at the outset that British history was a part of European history. In July, two months before the war began, he wrote a memorandum for Chatham House entitled 'First Thoughts on a Peace Settlement', in which he asserted that 'we must aim at a political union (a full and permanent federation, not just a limited temporary alliance) between Great Britain and France'. By October, in his 'Second Thoughts on a Peace Settlement', he outlined two alternatives: either dismember Germany or induce the Germans to enter a European federation voluntarily. Although Toynbee's aim was federation, it was clear from the memorandum that he envisaged a period of defence association before political union. Such pragmatism was unacceptable to Curtis, who insisted that there must be a common government responsible to a common parliament, with direct authority over the citizens, who must have loyalty to the Union as a whole. This was certainly not news to Toynbee, who knew the meaning of the word federation. But he must have been concerned with the process whereby a federal union could be brought about. He doubtless wanted his ideas to be assimilable for policy-makers in the Foreign Office, for whom Chatham House had set up a research unit, located in Balliol College, Oxford, and directed by Toynbee himself.

Toynbee's ideas did indeed before long find an echo in the Foreign Office. By February 1940, Orme Sargent, a senior official with European responsibilities, recommended that Britain offer France a 'close and permanent cooperation – political, military and economic – as will for all intents and purposes make of the two countries a single unit in postwar Europe', following which Toynbee was asked to produce a draft for a Treaty of Union. With the help of his old friend Sir Alfred Zimmern, then a professor at Oxford, he produced within ten days an Act of Perpetual Association between the United Kingdom and France. While this had some federal elements, it was certainly not a blueprint for a federal state. But it was put before a committee chaired by Lord Hankey, a bureaucrat of the old school who had been Secretary to the Cabinet from 1916 to 1938 and who was now a member of Neville Chamberlain's Cabinet. The committee's reception of the draft Act gave a preview of British civil servants' reactions to the postwar proposals for establishing and developing the Community: objections from the Board of Trade to the idea of a customs union, from the Treasury to monetary integration, from the Colonial Office on Commonwealth grounds and from Hankey himself on any sharing of sovereignty whatsoever. It was clear from Hankey's attitude that the original idea would not have survived the committee. But the committee itself did not survive the fall of France.

June 1940 and after: the British forget

The Federal Union movement was at a high point when France fell in June 1940. It had the support of illustrious intellectuals and eminent politicians. Aside from those already mentioned, they included the scientist Julian Huxley; Captain Liddell Hart, the military historian; Kingsley Martin, the editor of the *New Statesman*; the author J.B.Priestley; Benjamin Seebohm Rowntree, businessman and philanthropist; Henry Wickham Steed, former editor of *The Times*; the composer Ralph Vaughan Williams; and William Temple, Archbishop of York, who said that 'the whole scheme of Federal Union has made a staggeringly effective appeal to the British mind'. There was also William Curry, whose Penguin Special, *The Case for Federal Union*, sold a hundred thousand copies within six months; and behind him was the Federal Union movement, which by the spring of 1940 had ten thousand members in 253 branches spread throughout the country, and which enjoyed the editorial support of *The Manchester Guardian*, the *New Statesman* and *The Times*. Public opinion was ready to welcome Churchill's offer of Union with France, transmitted to Prime Minister Reynaud on 16 June 1940.

Churchill offered 'indissoluble union'. There were no longer to be two nations, but one Franco-British Union with a shared citizenship. There would be joint organs for defence and for foreign, financial and economic policies. A single war cabinet would direct all armed forces. 'And', the offer ended with a Churchillian flourish, 'thus we shall conquer'. Churchill was to recall his surprise, when he put this proposal to the Cabinet, to see 'the staid, solid, experienced politicians engage themselves so passionately in an immense design'. Perhaps he was not aware how deep the federal idea had penetrated in Britain by then. His Assistant Private Secretary, Sir John Colville, who was sitting in the office outside the Cabinet room that day, was evidently aware of this, not only recalling later that 'it was a marvellous idea and I have never seen such enthusiasm', but writing at the time that 'we had before us the bridge to a new world, the first elements of European or even World Federation'.

The offer came too late. Reynaud wanted to accept it but the French Cabinet decided instead to replace him by Marshal Pétain and to capitulate. The project of an Anglo-French Union as the foundation for a federal Europe was laid to rest. Hankey's reaction was predictable: 'I shall resist to the uttermost of my power any sacrifice of our nationality or any permanent fusion with France'; and if, for France, you read Europe, that attitude has influenced British policy to this day.

What remained, then, from this remarkable episode of British enthusiasm for the federal idea, and for its European form in particular? Most important was, of course, Churchill's role in launching the European Union project in 1946. Mackay's brave efforts in the federal cause should not be forgotten. As we saw from Spinelli's tribute to the British federalists, moreover, their writings had a decisive influence on his thinking and hence on that of the postwar European federalist movement. But as far as British policy and the British public are concerned, this element of the national heritage seems to have sunk almost without trace.

The reason cannot be that the British are unable to understand the federal idea which has inspired much of the movement towards the European Union we have today. Federalism was prominent in British politics in the 1880s, in the second decade of this century and in the period around the outbreak of the Second World War; and in that period attention was focused on the project for a European federation. It was the experience of the War following the fall of France that caused the British to resist close ties with Europe afterwards; and the federal idea suffered in the eyes of Westminster and Whitehall from its association with the project of building up the European Community and, later, the Union. But the heritage of federalist thought bequeathed by these prophets of the period up to June 1940 remains available for the British when they finally decide to adopt the European project wholeheartedly.

Selected Bibliography

Acton, Lord (1907) *The History of Freedom and other Essays*, London: Macmillan.

Attlee, C.R. (1940) *Labour's Peace Aims*, London: Peace Book Co.

Barker, Ernest (1915) *Political Thought in England from Herbert Spencer to the Present Day*, London: Williams and Norgate.

Beveridge, Sir William (1940) *Peace by Federation?*, London: Federal Union.

Bosco, Andrea (1992) *Federal Union and the Origins of the Churchill Proposal*, London: Lothian Press.

Bosco, Andrea and Cornelia Navari, eds (1994) *Chatham House and British Foreign Policy 1919-1945*, London: Lothian Foundation Press.

Burgess, Michael (1995) *The British Tradition of Federalism*, London: Pinter Publishers.

Cannan, Edwin (1927) *An Economist's Protest*, London: P.S. King and Sons.

Charlton, Michael (1983) *The Price of Victory*, London: BBC.

Churchill, Winston S. (1948) *The Second World War*, Vol.2, London: Cassell.

Colville, Sir John (1985) *The Fringes of Power: Downing Street Diaries 1939-55*, London: Hodder and Stoughton.

Coudenhove-Kalergi, Count Richard (1923) *Paneuropa*, Vienna: Paneuropa-Verlag, in English as (1926) *Pan-Europe*, New York: A. Knopf.

Curry, W. B. (1939) *The Case for Federal Union*, Harmondsworth: Penguin Special.

Curtis, Lionel (1934-7) *Civitas Dei*, 3 vols, London: Allen and Unwin.

(1939) 'World Order', *International Affairs*, May-June.

Dicey, A.V. (1915) *Introduction to the Study of the Law of the Constitution*, London: Macmillan, 8th edn.

Fasnacht, G.E. (1952) *Acton's Political Philosophy*, London: Hollis and Carter.

Freeman, Edward A. (1863) *History of Federal Government from the foundation of the Achaian League to the disruption of the United States*, Vol.1, London: Macmillan.

Jalland, P. (1980) *The Liberals and Ireland: The Ulster Question in British Politics to 1914*, Brighton: Harvester Press.

Jennings, W. Ivor (1940) *A Federation for Western Europe*, Cambridge: Cambridge University Press.

Kinsky, Ferdinand and Knipping, Franz, eds (1996) *Le Fédéralisme Personnaliste aux sources de l'Europe de demain: Hommage à Alexandre Marc*, Baden-Baden: Nomos Verlag.

Laski, Harold J. (1938) *A Grammar of Politics*, London: Allen and Unwin, 1st edn 1925.

Lothian, Lord (1934) 'Liberalism in the Modern World' reprinted in Pinder and Bosco, eds (1990).

(1935) *Pacifism is not Enough – Nor Patriotism Either*, Oxford: Clarendon Press.

(1939) *The Ending of Armageddon*, London: Federal Union.

(1941) *The American Speeches of Lord Lothian*, London: Oxford University Press.

Loughlin, John (1989) 'French Personalist and Federalist Movements in the Interwar Period' in Peter M. R. Stirk, *European Unity in Context: The Interwar Period*, London: Pinter Publishers

Ludlow, Peter (1978) 'The Unwinding of Appeasement' in Lothar Kettenacker, *Das Andere Deutschland im Zweiten Weltkrieg*, Stuttgart: Klett Verlag.

Mackay, R.W.G. (1940) *Federal Europe*, London: Michael Joseph.

Mayne, Richard and John Pinder with John Roberts (1990) *Federal Union: The Pioneers*, Basingstoke: Macmillan.

Ortega y Gasset, J. (1929) *La Rebelión de las Masas*, Madrid; in English as (1961) *The Rebellion of the Masses*, London: Allen & Unwin.

Pinder, John and Andrea Bosco, eds (1990) *Pacifism is not Enough*, London: Lothian Foundation Press.

Robbins, Lionel (1937) *Economic Planning and International Order*, London: Macmillan.

(1939) *The Economic Causes of War*, London: Jonathan Cape.

(1941) *Economic Aspects of Federation*, Federal Tracts No. 2, London: Macmillan.

Seeley, John (1871) 'United States of Europe', *Macmillans Magazine*, Vol.23, March, pp.436-48.

(1883) *The Expansion of England*, London: Macmillan.

Sidgwick, Henry (1903) *The Development of European Polity*, London: Macmillan.

Stead, W.T. (1899) *The United States of Europe on the Eve of the Parliament of Peace*, London: The Review of Reviews Office.

Streit, Clarence K. (1939) *Union Now*, London: Jonathan Cape.

Tawney, R.H. (1938) *Equality*, London: Allen and Unwin, 3rd edn.

Toynbee, Arnold (1934) *A Study of History*, Vol.1, London: Oxford University Press.

von Hayek, F.A. (1939) 'The Economic Conditions of Inter-State Federalism' in *New Commonwealth Quarterly*, September.

Wootton, Barbara (1941) *Socialism and Federation*, Federal Tracts No.6, London: Macmillan.

Schuman, De Gasperi, Spaak – The European Frontiersmen

Richard Mayne

The integration of Europe is a process involving countless people and much collective effort; but it has also crucially depended on the mould-breaking efforts of a few. Most historians rightly believe that its essential initiator was Jean Monnet: without him it might not have begun – or would have taken a different and no doubt less radical form. Monnet himself, however, always insisted on the role of others. 'It's easy to have ideas,' he used to say: 'what's hard is to get them applied in practice'. In his *Memoirs* he defined his own task: 'To influence those who held power, and try to ensure that they used it when the opportunity arose... These men, after all, take the risks; they need the kudos'. Monnet's ideas, in fact, might well have foundered without the support of several key figures. Robert Schuman, Alcide de Gasperi and Paul-Henri Spaak were three of them.

All played a decisive part at early stages in the building of Europe. Robert Schuman formally proposed the first step – the European Coal and Steel Community (ECSC). Alcide De Gasperi steered Italy into a Community founded on the reconciliation of France and Germany. Paul-Henri Spaak helped bring to birth the Benelux Memorandum which relaunched the whole enterprise in 1955. All three were in some respects alike; and yet all three were very different. Robert Schuman was bookish, monkish, almost saintly. Alcide De Gasperi was a skilful Italian statesman who held together a centre-right coalition. Paul-Henri Spaak was a Belgian Socialist. Yet they all shared one important characteristic. All three came from frontier regions.

Schuman was born in Luxembourg, the tiny Grand Duchy squeezed between France, Belgium and Germany, and was educated partly in Germany but spent his political life in the service of France. De Gasperi was born in the Tyrol when it was part of Austria-Hungary, and entered politics as an Italian representative in the Austrian parliament before Trentino was annexed to Italy. Paul-Henri Spaak, born in Schaerbeek, Brussels, came from a country divided linguistically between Flanders and Wallonia; although himself a Francophone, he bore a Flemish name.

Accidents of birth and geography are not, of course, reductionist explanations of conscious political options; but in these cases they surely helped make evident the possibility of choice. Frontiers, like fences, are both vital and potentially dangerous: vital, because they help define communities and make them viable; potentially dangerous, because they too often alienate those they divide. Living on, near, or across frontiers can turn some people into xenophobic chauvinists. In others, it can stir impatience with artificial barriers and encourage common humanity – a sense that all men and women are equal even if they are seldom alike.

Robert Schuman

Robert Schuman was born on 29 June 1886, in Clausen, to the north-east of Luxembourg city centre, looking across the valley of the Pétrusse and the Alzette to the great cliff of the Bock, with the spires of the upper city in the distance. The Grand Duchy of Luxembourg, with its mixture of French and German landscapes and languages, neutral since 1867 but in a customs union with Germany since 1842, was an apt birthplace for a pioneer European: but Schuman's own ancestry was also mixed. His father had been born in Lorraine, at Evrange near the Luxembourg border, when it was still part of France, before the 1871 Treaty of Frankfurt gave it to Germany until the end of the First World War. Schuman *père* had not, however, opted for French nationality in time to avoid becoming a German citizen after 1871, and he had not settled in Luxembourg until 1881. Robert Schuman's mother was a Luxemburger, although she had spent some time with her parents in the Vosges; but she had become German by her marriage – a fact that she had failed to record in her first census form as a married woman: an official had corrected her 'Luxemburger' to 'German'. On later census forms, both parents called themselves 'Lotharingians'.

At home, Robert Schuman spoke Letzeburgesch. 'It was in Luxembourg,' he said later, 'that I acquired the first notions of patriotism. The year was 1890, and we were under the Grand-Ducal balcony. The crowd was cheering Grand Duke Adolphe, who had just made his formal entry into the capital. I was a little boy of four, lost in the throng. I was thrilled by its enthusiasm and I shared its pride. Like everyone else, I did my best to sing the *Feierwôn*: "*Mir wölle keng Preise sin!*" ' The desire for independence expressed in that song was partly a reaction against the growing influence of Germany, which led to a wave of Francophilia, culminating in the establishment of the *Alliance Française* in 1905. By that time, however, Robert Schuman had already left Luxembourg to study for a final year at the lycée in Metz, where he took the Abitur, before going on to study law at the universities of Berlin, Munich, Bonn and Strasbourg. As he wrote later, 'I went to continue my studies in Germany, to which I was linked by the annexation of Alsace-Lorraine'. He then, in fact, joined the Alsace-Lorraine Bar, setting up his office in Metz.

In 1914 he received call-up papers for the German army, but failed his medical and never wore a German uniform: a photograph of him in a German helmet published by the French Communist press in the 1950s was a fake. Instead, and for the rest of the First World War, he was seconded to the civil administration. In 1918, when the war was over, he was appointed to the Municipal Commission in Metz, and in the following year he was elected to the French Chamber of Deputies as representative of the Moselle. Looking back in 1949, he explained to the *Luxemburger Wort* newspaper what he acknowledged as 'this kind of desertion, which made me keep my French nationality whereas I could legally have opted for Luxembourg citizenship. I remained what I was' – an allusion to the Luxembourg national motto 'Mir wölle bleiwe wat mir sin' – 'French and Lotharingian, especially since at that time Lorraine as a whole had been in exile'. Schuman was regularly re-elected deputy for the Moselle until the outbreak of the Second World War.

On 14 September 1940, after the fall of France, Robert Schuman was arrested by the Gestapo. In the following April he was assigned to house arrest in Neustadt, but in August 1942 he escaped and went into hiding until 1944, when he returned to his father's birthplace at Evrange.

Speaking in Letzeburgesch, Robert Schuman told a Radio Luxembourg audience in September 1952: 'Et ass ken Zo'fall, dass d'Ide vun enger Gemengschaft vu Stohl, Eisen a Kuelen grad engem Letzbuerger Jong komm ass, dem seng Elteren erlieft hun, waat et hescht Krich ze hun'. But if it was, as he said, no coincidence that the idea of a European Coal and Steel Community should come from a son of Luxembourg, the Community's true originator, Jean Monnet, played down such apparent determinism:

> It has been said that Monsieur Robert Schuman was better prepared than others, because of his origins, to make that choice. He had known all the dramas of frontier regions. I am not sure that this is a conclusive explanation. If he was able to act on 9 May 1950, it was because he had never been afraid of responsibility and had accepted so important a post only in order to build a better world. His action seems to me to have been determined less by his memories of the past, which could on the contrary have blinded him, than by his lucid vision of Europe's future.

A lucid vision had always guided Robert Schuman's career. A cradle Catholic, at the age of 17 he had helped to organise the 1913 German Catholic Congress in Metz; and he always saw his subsequent political work as a corollary to his commitment as a Christian. Photographed as a boy, he looked both earnest and eager. When he was 14, his father died. He remained very attached to his mother; but in 1911, when he was 25, horses bolted with a coach at a wedding reception, throwing her to her death. This bereavement was the great sorrow of Robert Schuman's life. His faith sustained him: a photograph taken shortly afterwards shows the young barrister in a state of resigned tranquillity more common in middle age. In old age, when I knew him, he was courteous and benevolent, a formal, bald, straight-backed figure with wise eyes and a firm, wide mouth under his short grey moustache. He never married, and lived simply, like a priest: but he was a shrewd and experienced statesman.

His first official appointment had been in 1920 on the Alsace-Lorraine Consultative Committee, of which he was successively Secretary, Vice-President, and President. His first government post was in 1940 as Under-Secretary of State to the French Prime Minister, dealing with refugees in Paul Reynaud's administration and then in that of Marshal Philippe Pétain. He resigned in July 1940 when Pétain was voted plenary powers. In 1945, after his wartime captivity and clandestinity, he was again elected deputy for the Moselle, this time as a member of the Christian-Democratic Mouvement Républicain Populaire (MRP). In the following year he became Minister of Finance in Georges Bidault's government, then in 1947 in that of Paul Ramadier, whom he succeeded as Premier. In 1948 he was Minister of Foreign Affairs, briefly doubling this post with that of Prime Minister; and he remained Foreign Minister when Bidault returned as Prime Minister in October 1949.

Thus it came about that Robert Schuman was in the right place at the right time to launch the proposal for a European Coal and Steel Community – the Schuman Plan – that Jean Monnet had designed. But his espousal of it was no accident. In May 1948 he had been one of the 750 statesmen from all over Western Europe who attended the Congress of Europe in The Hague, which proposed among other things the Council of Europe inaugurated in Strasbourg in August 1949. Five months later, in mid-January 1950, Schuman paid his first official visit to Germany as French Foreign Minister. His aim was to iron out some of the problems that were now arising between the two countries. In October 1949 the West and the Soviet Union had once again failed to agree on a German peace treaty. The Germans were growing restive under continued foreign tutelage by the International Ruhr Authority – all the more so since France was seeking to annex the Saar. When Schuman reached Germany, he was shocked and hurt by the atmosphere he encountered. His official hosts in Mainz, Bonn and Berlin were polite, if distant: but the press and the opposition were outspokenly hostile. No less disconcerting was the attitude of the United States, eager to revive the German economy so that the Ruhr's heavy industry could contribute to the recovery of Western Europe. To many in France at the time, Germany still seemed menacing – at best an economic rival, at worst a political threat.

In March 1950 the German Chancellor Konrad Adenauer made public an idea that he had already discussed in January with John J. McCloy, the US High Commissioner in Germany. In an interview with Kingsbury Smith of the International News Service, he proposed a political union between France and Germany, open also to Britain, Italy, and the Benelux countries. To Adenauer, this was no novelty: he had toyed with similar thoughts in the 1920s. But in the political climate of early 1950 it seemed both premature and misplaced. The French, in particular, were none too happy at the way it had been revealed to an American journalist rather than through official channels: France would wait, a spokesman said, to receive 'concrete proposals'. They finally came, of course, not from Germany but from Jean Monnet.

Monnet had been in touch with Schuman since May 1947 when, as *Commissaire au Plan*, he proposed to Robert Schuman, then Finance Minister, a fund to finance basic industry. This first letter was addressed to 'Monsieur le Ministre'. Most of its successors were addressed to 'Mon cher Président', while Schuman responded to 'Cher Monsieur Monnet', 'Mon cher Président' or, later, 'Mon cher Président et Ami'. Friendship grew out of formality through work together on common concerns: it was some time before, one hot day, Monnet suggested that they take their jackets off. Schuman hesitated. 'I wear braces,' he explained – but finally disrobed.

In his *Memoirs*, Monnet recalled their discussion of Franco-German reconciliation:

'Peace can be founded only on equality,' I told him. 'We failed in 1919 because we introduced discrimination and a sense of superiority. Now we are beginning to make the same mistakes again'.

Schuman very much agreed with me, and we easily understood each other. I liked his simplicity and common sense, and I respected his transparent honesty and strength of spirit. The French people clearly sensed it too, and they trusted him. It was important for him to realise this and to overcome his modesty in order to make his mark with the public as he did with his colleagues, gently but firmly. He was to play a crucial role in the great changes that our foreign policy was going to have to undergo, and I took care to keep in touch with him, both in person and through his *directeur de cabinet*, Bernard Clappier, for whom like Schuman I had both admiration and friendship.

When Monnet and his colleagues drafted what became the Schuman Declaration of 9 May 1950, he had to find someone, he recalled,

who had the power, and the courage to use it to trigger off so great a change. Robert Schuman seemed to me the ideal man to do so; but owing to a misunderstanding I did not approach him first. What happened was this. I had had a long conversation with Bernard Clappier... I had spoken in general terms about my ideas, which had interested him greatly.

'M. Schuman,' he said, 'is looking for an initiative that he can propose in London on May 10 [when Britain, France and the United States were to discuss the future of Germany and the raising of her production quotas]. I have the feeling that this has been his one great preoccupation since the Big Three met in New York last September..'.

'Well,' I said, 'I have some ideas'.

I thought that Clappier was going to call me back after having spoken to his Minister. But a combination of circumstances gave him no time to do so; and on Friday 28 April, thinking that Schuman was not interested, I decided to send the plan to Georges Bidault, the Prime Minister, under whose aegis the Planning Commission worked.

That very same day, only a few moments after I had had the dossier taken round to Pierre-Louis Falaize, Bidault's *directeur de cabinet*, Clappier got in touch with me again, apologising for his long silence.

'Here's the proposal,' I said. 'I've just sent it to Bidault'.

Clappier read the text, and quickly made up for lost time.

'It's excellent,' he said. 'May I show it to M. Schuman?'

I gave him a copy and he took it straight to the Gare de l'Est, where Schuman was about to take the train for Metz, to spend the weekend as usual in the solitude of his country house at Scy-Chazelles. Clappier found him already sitting in his compartment.

'Could you read this paper of Monnet's?' he asked. 'It's important'.

On Monday morning, Clappier was back at the Gare de l'Est to meet the incoming train. No sooner had Schuman got off than he said:

'I've read the proposal. I'll use it'.

Those few words were enough.

Of course, more was needed. Schuman showed the paper to Bidault, who 'in a furious rage' complained to Monnet: 'I should have appreciated your telling me first'.

'I did,' I said. 'I wrote to you on Friday'.

He looked for the letter; it was on his desk. Had he read it? In his memoirs he affirms that he had, and I believe him. Probably the plan clashed with his own concern at the time, which was to set up an Atlantic High Council. What might have happened to the project if Bidault had taken it over, and what might have happened to Europe, are questions that others have tried to answer. Myself, I have never wondered what consequences might have followed something which has not occurred; that seems to me an utterly barren speculation. The fact is that there was no Bidault Plan, but a Schuman Plan.

And Schuman earned the right to its title. Very discreetly, he and Monnet brought others into the secret: Alexandre Parodi, Secretary-General at the Foreign Ministry, and René Mayer and René Pleven, respectively Ministers of Justice and of Overseas Affairs. The two Ministers arranged for the French Cabinet to meet a day early that week, on Tuesday 9 May instead of the usual Wednesday. Meanwhile, on Monday morning, Schuman summoned Robert Mischlich, an official of the Ministry of Justice who also worked in his private office at the Ministry of Foreign Affairs. Mischlich was to undertake 'a delicate and secret mission' – to go to Bonn with two letters for Konrad Adenauer, outlining the Schuman Plan which the French Cabinet was to tackle on the following day.

Interrupting a Federal Cabinet meeting, Adenauer at once agreed. 'All my life,' he told Mischlich, 'I have fought to reconcile France and Germany. Today Robert Schuman's generous initiative fulfils all my hopes. This French proposal is in every way historic: it restores my country's dignity and is the cornerstone for uniting Europe'. Mischlich telephoned to Clappier in Paris – just as the French Cabinet was reaching the end of its agenda. Until then, Schuman had not dared raise the subject. Now – some say none too clearly – he sought permission to announce the proposal; and at 6.00 p.m. that day he did so, at a press conference summoned hastily to the Salon de l'Horloge at the Quai d'Orsay, seat of the Foreign Ministry.

Schuman's role was by no means over. Next day he was in London for the Three-Power negotiations. He had to appease Ernest Bevin, the British Foreign Secretary, surprised by the French announcement and later annoyed to find that Dean Acheson, the US Secretary of State, had been let into the secret when passing through Paris. The Schuman Declaration, moreover, was a statement of intent, not a fully-fledged plan; and Schuman, as Foreign Minister, had to explain it not only to Belgium, Italy, Luxembourg and the Netherlands, which accepted its open invitation, but also to Britain, which at that time declined. Both Schuman and Monnet spent much time trying to quell British fears of the unknown, but not at the expense of their project's basic principles: the merger of sovereignty and the establishment of joint independent institutions. Schuman, who knew Britain less well than Monnet, was thought by some to be less eager to recruit her: but in reality both were adamant that any negotiation must be based on these principles, to save the future Community from the weak inter-governmentalism of the Organisation for European Economic Cooperation (*OEEC*) and the Council of Europe, both severely limited by nationalist constraints. At the Quai d'Orsay, Schuman was formally responsible for the long series of French telegrams politely but firmly explaining this to the British Government; but it was Monnet who drafted them and stuck to his guns.

At 4.00 p.m. on 20 June 1950, again in the Salon de l'Horloge, Schuman opened the conference to negotiate the Coal and Steel Community Treaty:

> We believe that we cannot afford to fail, to give up without reaching a conclusion. But never before have States undertaken or even envisaged the joint delegation of part of their national sovereignty to an independent supranational body...

> We shall have to think about the technical details that will be the subject of conventions to be concluded later, but without writing them into the Treaty now. We shall work as a team, and not as a negotiating conference with rigid, pedantic rules.

It was Monnet who in practice led the negotiations; but Schuman returned in mid-July when the institutions were being settled. As Monnet wrote in his *Memoirs*:

> He slipped almost unnoticed into the room, to join the conference whose chairman he had been since the very first day, after which he had not reappeared. Sitting down at the head of the table, he apologised for being 'an intruder'. Then he quietly expressed his firm conviction that the High Authority must be independent.

> 'But independence has never meant irresponsibility,' he said; 'and in your work you have achieved a balance between national and Community power which to my mind is a remarkable system of democratic safeguards'.

Modesty, firmness, balance – these were qualities that Schuman embodied throughout his life. During the long process of negotiating and ratifying the Coal and Steel Community Treaty, he lent the project his full authority, tirelessly insisting, like Monnet, on its essentials: equality among the member States, merging their national sovereignty under common rules and institutions subject to democratic and judicial control. Schuman similarly backed Monnet's Pleven Plan for a European Defence Community (EDC), defending it to the very last moment, when it was defeated on a procedural vote in the French National Assembly on 30 August 1954. Most of that time he had remained Foreign Minister, leaving the post only in January 1953, when Bidault succeeded him in René Mayer's new government. He returned to office as Minister of Justice in Edgar Faure's administration in 1955; but when Guy Mollet became Premier in 1956 he withdrew from government, and served as a deputy until he retired from politics in 1962. But he remained active, first as President of the European Movement and then, from 1958 to 1960, as President of the European Parliament.

When he died, on 4 October 1963, it was at the end of a brilliantly constructive life. Only five years after the most murderous war in history, he had taken revolutionary action to reconcile France and Germany. He had succeeded: the Schuman Plan had laid the foundations of European union: it had survived the defeat of EDC and had led on to the European Economic Community and Euratom. The way ahead was clear. True, there were problems. Charles de Gaulle had blocked the Community's first attempt at enlargement, and would soon try to curb its use of majority voting. There were troubles to come. But, as Jean Monnet had said ten years earlier at a ceremony in Schuman's honour on 9 May 1953, in Luxembourg, his birthplace:

> 'Monsieur Robert Schuman, since 9 May 1950, you and we have held to the same course. And if today we face storms, we know that by pressing forward we shall come through them and at length achieve the United States of Europe conceived on 9 May 1950, for which you will always enjoy the gratitude of all people of goodwill'.

Alcide De Gasperi

Alcide De Gasperi was born on 3 April 1881, at Pieve Tesino, not far from Trento in the Tyrol, then part of Austro-Hungary. His family's origins were modest; all his life he stressed the need for greater social justice. Like Schuman, he was bookish: in later life, austere and bespectacled, he looked like a strict and incisive music teacher. Like Schuman, he was deeply Christian. He used to classify politicians as men of prey, men of power, or men of faith; according to his daughter Maria Romana he hoped to be remembered as a man of faith. He read sacred texts, including Thomas à Kempis's *De Imitatione Christi*, he prayed regularly and took Communion every Sunday. His brother, who died young, was a priest, and his daughter entered a religious order after the Second World War.

And, again like Schuman, De Gasperi came from a disputed frontier region: in 1919, when Schuman became a French citizen at the age of 33, De Gasperi became an Italian citizen at the age of 38. But he had always considered himself Italian. From the age of 24 he had edited *La Voce Cattolica*, which in the following year became *Il Trentino* and later *Il Nuovo Trentino*, defending Italian culture and his region's economic interests. In 1911 he was elected to the Austrian Parliament, joining other Italian deputies who sought to have the Trentino made part of Italy. In the 1919 peace settlement, their wish was granted: the Trentino was ceded to Italy by the Treaty of Saint-Germain. In the same year, a number of Catholic associations founded the Partito Popolare Italiano, led by Don Luigi Sturzo. It was not an official Catholic party, because the Holy See refused to be involved in Italian politics; but it was sanctioned by the Vatican as a vehicle for the mass of Italian Catholics to take part in political life. Its programme included individual and family liberty, social and political reform, and a degree of decentralisation. In its first election, its representatives won 100 seats.

Alcide De Gasperi was one of its founder members. Even at that time, the Partito Popolare contained three contrasting elements – one strongly clerical and conservative, the second small and left-wing, the third more moderate but very actively radical, eager for social and especially agrarian reform. De Gasperi was always a reformer.

This soon led him to clash with Benito Mussolini's Fascists, who came to power in 1922. In April 1923, just before the Partito Popolare's fourth Congress, some of its right-wing members, who supported the Fascists, formed a breakaway National Union. At the Congress, Sturzo reaffirmed that the Partito Popolare was 'the antithesis of lay Liberalism [in Italian politics, right-wing], of Socialist materialism, of the pantheist State and of the Nation deified'. These, he said, 'together make up the great heresy that we have inherited from the 19th century, and which dominate the convulsions of today'. The Congress finally endorsed only 'conditional collaboration' with Mussolini's Government.

Don Sturzo's speech and the Congress's conclusions unleashed a violent anti-Catholic campaign in the Fascist press. In July, on orders from the hierarchy, Sturzo resigned as the Partito Popolare's Political Secretary. De Gasperi took his place and led the party into the April 1924 election. Despite intimidation and violence, it won nine per cent of the vote and 40 parliamentary seats.

By this time, however, the Partito Popolare had virtually split into supporters and opponents of the Fascist regime, and the opponents were no longer safe from Mussolini's rubber truncheons and castor oil. Already in the previous August the Fascists had murdered Don Giovanni Minzoni, a Romagna priest. Now, in June 1924, they assassinated the Socialist deputy Giacomo Matteotti. In October, the Vatican ordered Don Luigi Sturzo to leave Italy, and he took refuge in Paris with several colleagues. On 9 November 1926, the Partito Popolare's deputies were expelled from parliament and the party itself was dissolved. In 1927 Alcide De Gasperi was arrested and sentenced to four years' imprisonment.

He served his sentence for sixteen months. At the end of that time, through the intervention of Pope Pius XI, he was released and appointed as a librarian in the Vatican. Under the 1929 Lateran Treaties, this had become Vatican City, an independent Papal territory in the heart of Rome, with its own coinage, police, radio station and postal system. Here, by day, De Gasperi was employed to catalogue the Vatican Library; at night, he translated books from German to earn extra money for his family. From 1933 onwards, he also wrote political commentaries for the Vatican bi-monthly *Illustrazione Vaticana*, not only reacting to current events but also stating political principles. Over the years, too, he made stealthy contact with other anti-Fascist groups in Milan, Florence and elsewhere. One such organisation in Lombardy was the Guelph Action Party, led by Piero Malvestiti (long afterwards a member of the EEC Commission and then President of the ECSC High Authority). It had as its motto 'Christ, King and People'. In July 1942 another group of democrats, including Count Carlo Sforza, Ugo La Malfa and Ferruccio Parri (the partisan leader 'General Maurizio'), founded the Action Party, with a name harking back to Mazzini and a programme of radical but not Marxist change. In August and September of that year, Alcide De Gasperi brought representatives of Malvestiti's and Sturzo's groups together in the house of a friend in Milan. Other important allies were to be found in movements like the Federazione Universitaria Cattolica Italiana (FUCI) led by Igino Righetti and Mgr Giovanni Battista Montini. This was in part responsible for the 1943 Camaldolì Code, a programme for the post-war reconstruction of Italy on Christian but pluralist, not clerical lines. Its ideas were very close to those set forth by De Gasperi in July 1943 in *Christian Democracy's Ideas for Reconstruction* and in *The Programme of Christian Democracy* in January 1944. By this time, the new Christian Democrat party was establishing itself as successor to the Partito Popolare, and profiting greatly from the links between priests and parishes that spread across the country like an ecclesiastical web.

When Mussolini fell on 25 July 1943, Italy was thrown into dangerous confusion. With the war not yet over, Nazi forces still fighting in the peninsula, and the interim Government of King Victor Emmanuel III and Marshal Pietro Badoglio soon discredited and in flight, the real new centres of civil power were the Committees of National Liberation (CLN), composed of all Italy's anti-Fascist movements. Their central committee in Rome was headed by Ivanoe Bonomi, who had been Prime Minister in 1921-2. When the Nazis occupied Rome, the CLN there and its Northern counterparts went underground; but the Naples and Bari CLNs continued to work openly for political reconstruction rather than Allied occupation. On 9 June 1944, five days after Rome's liberation, the CLN central committee set up a Provisional Government with Bonomi as Premier and a number of Christian Democrat members, including De Gasperi as Minister without Portfolio. On 29-30 July, Christian Democracy held its first Congress, in Naples; it elected De Gasperi as its Political Secretary.

In 1945, with the support of the Northern Italian CLNs, and with general consent in the country, the Action Party's Ferrucio Parri was made Prime Minister in the Provisional Government. But by this time the Action Party had been weakened by a Left-Right split; and in November 1945 it lost the support of the Liberals and the Christian Democrats. On 10 December De Gasperi, who has been Foreign Minister, replaced Parri as Prime Minister. He was 64, and remained in office for more than seven years.

In the following April, 1946, the Christian Democrat party Congress in Rome voted to end the Monarchy, compromised by the years of Fascism. The decision was endorsed, more narrowly, by the Italian people in the referendum of 2 June 1946 – the day of the national elections for Italy's Constituent Assembly. In these, Christian Democracy came top of the poll, though without an absolute majority, and De Gasperi was confirmed as Prime Minister. Once the new constitution had been set in place, in January 1948, fresh elections were held that April. With 48 percent of the vote, De Gasperi and his party won an absolute majority in the Chamber of Deputies. A pattern of Christian Democrat dominance had been set that was to last for a generation and more.

In 1945 De Gasperi told his party that its mission was 'to protect the integrity of our people's Christian spiritual heritage'. But he was in no sense a fundamentalist. Some of the Catholic hierarchy, as well as some purist members of Christian Democracy (including Giorgio La Pira and Amintore Fanfani, a later Prime Minister), would have liked to use their electoral victory to build what they called 'a Christian State', forming a Christian Democrat Government without the 'lay', non-clerical parties they had worked with in the CLNs. De Gasperi refused. Resolutely hostile to any clericalisation of the regime, he invited the moderate lay parties into a coalition. His clericalist critics were furious: there were angry scenes at the next party Congress, at Venice in June 1949. But De Gasperi's view prevailed. He was similarly obdurate in 1952 when the Church proposed an alliance with the neo-Fascist MSI to beat the Communists in the Rome municipal elections. Coalition with the lay democratic parties was another matter. It gave him a Ministry of all the Talents – including that of Count Carlo Sforza, the former diplomat and Action Party member, who remained his Foreign Minister until ill-health forced him to retire in 1951 at the age of 77.

Italian foreign policy under De Gasperi and Sforza was firmly anchored to the West and to Europe. In Italy the hope of European unity was nothing new. As early as July 1941 Altiero Spinelli, Ernesto Rossi and Eugenio Colorni, all exiled by Mussolini to the island of Ventotene, had produced a Manifesto calling for a 'European Federation'. In the autumn of 1941, Spinelli wrote a second Memorandum on 'The United States of Europe'. In December, the founders of the later Action Party (which Spinelli and Rossi joined) proposed 'a European federation of free democratic states within a framework of world-wide co-operation'; and when the Action Party formally came into being in 1943 it urged:

> the bringing about of a European federation of free democratic countries... which decisively rejects the principle of absolute state sovereignty, advocates the renunciation of all purely territorial claims, and favours the creation of a legal community of states with the necessary institutions and the means to establish a regime of collectively organised security.

In the spring of 1943 De Gasperi himself had drafted a paper calling on nations to accept 'restrictions on their sovereignty in favour of overall solidarity'. The foundation programme of Christian Democracy, made public on 25 July 1943, proposed:

> a federation of freedom-loving Europeans – an expression of the solidarity of all peoples – within a revived League of Nations. Direct representation of peoples as well as of governments... Armed forces and voluntary recruitment under the sole control of the international community. Nations to be allowed to choose their own legal systems and to have European as well as national citizenship.

The party adopted this programme at its first Congress in April 1946.

Article II of the 1947 Italian Constitution declared that:

> Italy consents, on condition of parity with other states, to limitations of sovereignty necessary to an order for assuring peace and justice among nations; it promotes and favours international organisations directed towards that end.

In the same year, during the parliamentary debate on the Marshall Plan, Sforza insisted that only its ratification could create 'a climate of trust and co-operation with those European powers which, like ourselves, wish to create Europe'. Italy likewise enthusiastically backed the Council of Europe – only to share, later, many people's disappointment at its limited powers and scope.

However, when the Schuman Plan was launched upon the world, the first reaction of Pietro Quaroni, the Italian Ambassador in Paris, as he reported to Sforza, was to tell Robert Schuman that 'it would have been as well, in this case, and to avoid unpleasant comments in Italy and elsewhere, if his declaration had specifically mentioned Italy'. Schuman duly promised to do so in his remarks to the press. That said, Quaroni recommended a rapid and positive response. He gave three reasons: the reconciliation of France and Germany and the building of Europe were in line with Italian policy; to be in the negotiations from the start would give Italy full rights; and it was only thus that she could defend her interests, notably that of Italian steel. Sforza and De Gasperi agreed. Appointing Paolo Taviani, a young Christian Democrat deputy, to head the Italian delegation at the Schuman Plan conference, Sforza wrote to him:

> All your colleagues must understand that we recognise in the Schuman Plan the first serious attempt to establish in today's Europe a supranational authority. This, with the possibility of eliminating once and for all the Franco-German divide that caused so many wars, is one of the greatest hopes of the present time. Italy, which has everything to gain from peace and everything to risk in war, must support to her utmost the Schuman Plan. Naturally, you and your colleagues will have to defend Italy's specific interests. This will be all the more effectively achieved if it is clear that we are not espousing protectionism.

He added a point that very much echoed Jean Monnet's sentiments:

> You and your colleagues must maintain the best possible relationship with the other delegations, and always encourage contact with the British, leaving the door open to them. It is in our political and economic interest that Britain should finally join the agreement. When it becomes clear that agreement is on its way, she will join; facts, actual facts, are what the British prize above all.

When Sforza retired in July 1951, De Gasperi himself took over the Ministry of Foreign Affairs and recalled Taviani to Rome as his Secretary of State. Taviani's replacement in Paris was Ivan Matteo Lombardo, a long-standing member of the European Federalist Movement.

By this time, the Schuman Plan conference had produced the ECSC Treaty, signed on 18 April 1951. Meanwhile, however, on 24 October 1950, the French Prime Minister, René Pleven, had proposed what was essentially Jean Monnet's plan for a European Defence Community (EDC), and the representatives of the six ECSC countries were busy in Paris negotiating the EDC Treaty. De Gasperi, in particular, was convinced that any European Army would necessitate what he called 'a central political authority'; and at a meeting in Santa Margherita Ligure near Genoa, on 12-13 February 1951, he put the case very convincingly to Robert Schuman. In June of that year he received Adenauer in Rome. The two men got on well. On 23 August Adenauer wrote to Robert Schuman:

I regard it as a particularly favourable and even providential sign that all the weight of the tasks to be undertaken rests on the shoulders of men who, like you, our mutual friend President De Gasperi and myself, are filled with the desire to build the new edifice of Europe on Christian foundations. I believe that few occasions in the history of Europe have offered better opportunities for achieving such a goal.

It was with Adenauer's and Schuman's support that De Gasperi was able to have included in the EDC Treaty its unique Article 38, which explicitly provided for further steps towards political federation to be prepared by the EDC Assembly. On 10 September 1952, without waiting for this to be formally established, the Council of Ministers of the ECSC asked its nascent Common Assembly to co-opt further members into a so-called 'Ad Hoc Assembly' in order to draft the Treaty for a European Political Community (EPC).

Five days later Alcide De Gasperi made a resounding speech to the Consultative Assembly of the Council of Europe. Recalling that the EDC Treaty had been signed on May 27, that the ECSC Treaty had come into force on August 10, and that the British Government had decided to seek association with the new Community, he said:

> These events have encouraged us to go forward. I am convinced that without a central political authority the kind of solidarity envisaged by the EDC Treaty, which is a matter of life and death, would not be able to resist the separatist and individualistic tendencies that at times might emerge in some national Parliament.

De Gasperi was not proposing a monolithic super-state or a revival of the Carolingian Empire. 'Forget any fantasies about Charlemagne and the Middle Ages!' he had told the Italian Senate in March, during the debate to ratify the ECSC. 'We are talking about a coalition of democracies, based on the principle of freedom'. Now, at the Council of Europe, he went further:

> The first and most important problem we have to tackle, I think, is to decide which aspects of our countries' life should be subject to the central political authority... I am convinced that we cannot guarantee solidarity in our military efforts, in peace or war, without achieving a minimum of solidarity in work and the economy. For this economic solidarity there is a whole range of possibilities, from a customs union to lower or preferential tariffs, from a single confederal bank based on a monetary agreement among the various international banks to a single currency, from a single market to the abolition of quotas...

> We need to pool only what is strictly necessary to reach our immediate goals using flexible methods that can be applied gradually and progressively so as to reconcile the Latin legal approach with the pragmatism of the British...

> But above all in our work it is the political will to achieve European Union that must be the determining factor, the motive force. Economic co-operation is necessarily a compromise between every participant's naturally autonomous demands and those of the over-riding political interest. If the achievement of European economic solidarity were to depend on compromise formulae worked out by the various administrations concerned, the result would very probably be weakness and conflict.
>
> So the over-riding political interest must prevail. Above all, we must be guided by the need to build Europe so as to ensure peace, prosperity and social justice...
>
> You see: we can already speak of deciding to build a Political Community without being labelled utopian.

Fine, brave words. But although the Ad Hoc Assembly approved a draft political Treaty on 10 March 1953, it aroused scepticism and hostility – all the more so since the fortunes of EDC remained uncertain. Germany ratified the EDC Treaty on 19 March 1953, and the Netherlands, Belgium and Luxembourg soon followed. In Italy and France, however, a series of government crises delayed the vote. In Italy's June 1953 elections, De Gasperi failed to secure the 50 per cent of the poll he would have needed to win two-thirds of the seats; and after failing either to reconstitute the coalition with the lay parties or to establish a purely Christian Democrat Government, he retired from office to become Secretary-General of his party and then its president in May 1954.

By that time EDC, and the political Treaty with it, had almost reached the end of its life. So had Alcide De Gasperi. He died, aged 73, on 19 August 1954, at Sella di Valsugana, not far from his birthplace. Soon afterwards, as I remember reporting, the streets of Rome were filled with crowds paying him their last tributes – while government offices were echoing with the gloomy obsequies of EDC. On 30 August 1954, the French National Assembly had rejected it, on a procedural vote, by 319 votes to 264, with 43 abstentions. The triumphant opposition from the twin extremes of Left and Right sang the *Marseillaise*. Two months later, when Jean Monnet announced that he would not seek re-election as President of the ECSC High Authority, the prospects for Europe seemed suddenly grim. That they revived within a year was thanks to Monnet among others. It was also, and especially, thanks to Paul-Henri Spaak.

Paul-Henri Spaak

Paul-Henri Spaak was born on 25 January 1899, in the Brussels suburb of Schaerbeek, to the north-east of the city centre. Unlike both Robert Schuman and Alcide De Gasperi, he came from a family already distinguished in politics. His father was a teacher, translator, poet and playwright, who also helped to run the Brussels Opera.

These artistic pursuits were continued by Spaak senior's two younger sons, Charles and Claude, who made their careers in the cinema and the theatre. It was Paul-Henri who carried on the family's political tradition. This came from his maternal grandfather, the Belgian Left-wing Liberal Paul Janson – himself the grandson of a 1789 French revolutionary from Paris. From his earnings as a Brussels barrister, Janson had bought a small *château* in France, just across the Belgian frontier; and here Paul-Henri Spaak spent many of his school holidays. Spaak's uncle, Paul-Emile Janson, was also a politician, several times Minister of Justice and once, briefly, Prime Minister; while his mother, Marie Spaak, was the first woman to enter the Belgian Parliament, as a Socialist member of the Senate in 1922.

By then, Paul-Henri Spaak had already gone into politics: he had determined to do so while still at school. He had still not finished school when, at the age of 17, in 1916, he tried to escape from occupied Belgium to join the Belgian troops who were fighting on the Yser in the north-west corner of the country. He was caught and sent to prison in Turnhout, to the east of Antwerp, where he spent four months, two of them in solitary confinement, before being shipped to a prisoner-of-war camp near Paderborn in Germany.

Once released at the end of the First World War, Spaak began reading law – one traditional preparation for a political career. By sheer hard work, he got his degree in two-and-a-half years instead of the usual five. Soon after graduating, he began work as a lawyer, and by the age of 23 felt secure enough to marry the daughter of a Liberal Senator. The rest of his spare time he divided between tennis and bridge.

Despite – or perhaps because of – his bourgeois background, Spaak at that time espoused firmly left-wing ideas. In 1921, after a brief flirtation with the Liberals, he joined the Belgian Socialist party: Liberalism, he had decided, was no longer ahead of the times as it had been in his grandfather's day. But even the Socialist party, it began to seem, was too hidebound. In July 1925, in a coalition Government of Socialists and left-wing Catholics, Spaak was offered the post of deputy *chef de cabinet* to the Socialist Minister of Labour and Industry. For a young man of 26 it was a tempting appointment, and Spaak gave up his law practice to accept it.

Yet within nine months he had resigned. A run on the Belgian franc had triggered a government crisis. Reviving a wartime expedient, the leader of the right-wing opposition had formed a 'Government of Sacred Union' composed of Catholics, Liberals and Socialists. Such a compromise was too much for the fiery Spaak. Retiring to his law practice, he founded a fortnightly called *Bataille Socialiste*, in which he thundered against 'reformism' and demanded 'a radical, total transformation of existing society'. In later life, Spaak dismissed these and other remarks as 'stupidities'; but, rather than youthful folly or Marxist dogma, they sprang from his generous, impetuous nature. It was this that made him march, in 1934, with an angry crowd through the streets of Brussels, breaking the windows of right-wing newspapers, and again, in July 1950, in a procession to the royal palace at Laeken on the outskirts of the city to demand the abdication of King Leopold III. Excesses? Misjudgements? Perhaps. But it was also Spaak's emotional nature that made him an outstanding orator.

His skill developed only slowly. For two years after resigning his political post he went on addressing local meetings and breathing fire in print in *Bataille Socialiste*. It folded in 1928; and in that same year Spaak made his first, unremarkable speech to the Socialist Party Congress. Two years after that, in the courtroom, he suddenly discovered his powers.

It was in September 1930. Spaak was defending an Italian anti-Fascist who had fired two wildly ill-aimed shots at Crown Prince Umberto, in Brussels to marry Princess Marie-José. The night before his final plea, Spaak sat down after dinner to compose his text – and faced writer's block. At midnight he got up and tried again, with the same result. He set his alarm-clock for 4.00 a.m. but slept through it, and was only just in time for court. When he rose to speak he had nothing on paper and nothing in his head. Then the miracle happened. He spoke, dazzlingly, for an hour. The accused got a light, five-year sentence, commuted to one year at Umberto's request.

Spaak's oratory could be spell-binding: on occasion, it reduced me to tears. When he was finally elected to Parliament in 1932 he admittedly made a poor maiden speech. Then in May 1933 he spoke so powerfully that he nearly brought down the Government. In the same year he started a new weekly, *Action Socialiste*. Yet, despite violent words and sometimes violent actions, he himself was beginning to change. In July 1934 he wrote: 'In the present state of the world it is childish to imagine that we can achieve integral Socialism'. And although in February 1935, when the Government banned a Socialist rally, he resigned in protest, some two weeks later he accepted a post in a new Government, many of whose members he had previously attacked. 'I used to think,' he confessed, 'that by practising an intransigent Socialism we could galvanise our troops into winning a majority. Ten years of action have shown me I was wrong'. Spaak duly served first as Transport Minister, then, from 1936 onwards, as Foreign Minister under the former banker Viscount Paul Van Zeeland. In 1938 he even became Belgium's first Socialist Prime Minister, before reverting to the Foreign Ministry in Hubert Pierlot's 1939 Government, which was in exile during the Second World War from 1940 to 1945.

Spaak said later that his shift away from extremism had been influenced by the veteran Belgian Socialist Henri de Man, author of *Beyond Marxism* (1926). 'It was he who made me realise that in sticking to the Socialism of 1848 I was not exactly ahead of my time'. Later, however, Spaak and de Man fell out over domestic policy, and more especially when in the Second World War de Man resigned himself to a Nazi victory and was repudiated by his party.

Belgium's and Spaak's position before and during the Second World War was at first equivocal and confused. Having been part of Europe's battlefield in the First World War, the country was anxious to avoid that fate if at all possible; and so, while re-arming, it had long since declared itself neutral. In the winter of 1939-40 it resisted French and British pressure to send troops in. But early on 10 May 1940 Nazi parachutists attacked the fort of Eben-Emael on the eastern frontier, and an air-raid over Evere aerodrome in the north-eastern suburbs of Brussels not far from Spaak's birthplace destroyed half the nation's air force on the ground. Four hours later, a Nazi ultimatum demanded to occupy Belgium 'to forestall imminent invasion by Britain and France'. The Belgian army fought gallantly; but the situation soon became hopeless. Most of the Cabinet took refuge in France: only Spaak and Pierlot, with the Ministers of War and of the Interior, stayed on. Their position was ambiguous: the administration was under siege and King Leopold III was Commander-in-Chief of the armed forces. As defeat or an armistice loomed closer, they tried in vain to persuade the King to continue the struggle in exile as the Queen of Holland was doing. Instead, when Leopold at last sued for peace on 27 May, he determined, no doubt courageously but perhaps unwisely, to 'stay with his people' as a virtual prisoner in his palace at Laeken. The decision was fiercely attacked at the time, and long afterwards, although Leopold refused to set up a Quisling-style government and rejected Pierlot's suggestion that the absent Ministers should return to Brussels to negotiate an armistice. For Pierlot and Spaak, it was as well that he did so: such a negotiation would surely have tarred them with a Vichy brush. In the event, 74 Belgian deputies and a number of Ministers withdrew their opposition to negotiating with Hitler. But Spaak, Pierlot and their few remaining colleagues stayed in exile in France, first in Poitiers, then in Bordeaux, and finally in the ignoble maelstrom of Vichy. At length, after much debate, they left on 27 August 1940, for the Spanish border; and despite countless further hold-ups, bureaucratic squabbles, and a long wait under police surveillance in Barcelona, they were smuggled into Portugal in a secret compartment of a small truck. On 24 October 1940, they finally arrived in London, and stayed there for the next four years.

If the fearful summer of 1940 had re-emphasised, for Spaak, the fragility of Europe's internal frontiers, his time in London broadened his horizons still more. In a slightly bemused Gallic way he was fond of the British: 'They like animals better than people and do not stare at lovers'. After the war, his son Fernand went to Trinity College, Cambridge, and his daughter Marie Marguerite married a British diplomat. Spaak himself was no great linguist: 'I am often told,' he conceded in later years, 'that I look like Winston Churchill and speak English like Charles Boyer. But I wish it were the other way round'. He was a heavy but discriminating eater, with a particular fondness for profiteroles: 'We dig our graves with our forks,' he ruefully admitted. Even by 1940 he had lost his tennis-player's lissome shape and become a burly bulldog, pleased to be likened to Churchill, whom he greatly admired.

As Foreign Minister of the Belgian Government in exile, and often its voice on the radio, Spaak had the time as well as the incentive to think about the future of Europe and the wider world. Already in 1939 he had told a French politician 'something that will probably surprise you coming from someone who was the initiator of Belgium's neutrality policy. I believe that in the future the Western powers – France, Great Britain, Belgium and Holland – will have to seek their security in a common defensive system'. Now, he concluded, 'the events of the last twenty months in Europe have shown that its countries must unite'. That he wrote in 1941. 'By 1942, my thinking had become more specific. "There can be no political solution without an economic solution, and vice versa.".' As a first step, he and his colleagues envisaged a customs union linking Holland, Belgium and Luxembourg. On 5 September 1944, a few days before returning to liberated Belgium, they announced its establishment as Benelux, 'to take effect provisionally when the Governments are in place once more'. But back in Brussels, many civil servants objected and the agreement hung fire. Spaak, in any case, was busy – attending the San Francisco Conference in 1945 to help draft the United Nations Charter, chairing the first UN General Assembly sessions in London and New York in 1946, as well as facing domestic upheavals, including a further short spell as Prime Minister, and the continuing problem of relations with the Crown. In April 1946, however, Spaak determined to revive Benelux. He went to see the Dutch Prime Minister, and together they told their officials to settle the remaining technical problems within six months.

> They at once protested and attempted to show that what we wanted them to do was impossible since we had grossly under-estimated the difficulties involved. They raised every conceivable objection... We did not give an inch and just went on reiterating our instructions. Six months later, the difficulties had been overcome... These events helped me to crystallise my ideas about the relationship that should exist between a minister and his experts. Ministers who do not know how to deal with a problem tend to set up a committee. The experts, left without directives, discuss endlessly, produce objection after objection, stubbornly defend their respective points of view, and end up by confusing the whole issue. They are often completely negative. But they are not to blame. The guilty party is the minister who is trying to dodge his responsibilities. But when, on the other hand, a minister is courageous enough to make a decision and then turns to his experts to discover how his political decision can be implemented in practice, they will apply all their technical knowledge, all their intelligence and imagination to find a solution.

The Benelux customs union – and Spaak's brisk method of dealing with it – both set precedents for the future.

His impatient drive and decisiveness, in particular, greatly hurried along the growing efforts to unite Western Europe. In January 1948, when Britain proposed the defensive Brussels Pact, it was Spaak who urged that it should be a collective regional arrangement, economic, social and cultural, as well as military. In May of that year he took part in the great Congress of Europe in The Hague, which he called 'a key moment in the history of Europe'. In 1949, when the Council of Europe was set up in Strasbourg (and he was again free of Government responsibilities), he was unanimously elected President of its Consultative Assembly. At the end of its first session he declared: 'I came to Strasbourg convinced of the need for a United States of Europe. I leave with the certainty that union is possible'. Two years later he resigned. 'If a quarter of the energy spent here in saying "No",' he thundered, 'were used to say "Yes" to something positive, we should not be in the state we are in today'. Looking back on his experience of the Council's Committee of Ministers, he wrote: 'Of all the international bodies I have known, I have never found any more timorous or more impotent'.

By that time, of course, Jean Monnet had initiated the Schuman Plan and the Pleven Plan for EDC; and Spaak was a strong supporter of both. When the Ad Hoc Assembly was formed in 1952 to draw up a Constitution for the European Political Community Spaak was elected to preside over it – 'a forum,' wrote Monnet, 'worthy of his European convictions and his great oratorical gifts'. He doggedly defended EDC and EPC throughout their troubled gestation. Handing to Ministers the draft EPC Treaty on 9 March 1953, he reminded them:

> Less than ten years ago, the countries represented here were at war with one another... Each of us had only one thought, one aim: to destroy each other as completely as possible.
>
> In the immensity of our misfortune, in the ruins that we have made, in our weakness and poverty, in the threats we face and the uncertainty that reigns, we have suddenly realised the mortal danger to which our disputes and quarrels were exposing the way of life we share and the thousand-year inheritance that each of us has helped to increase and enrich.
>
> We have come to our senses and, without forgetting the past – which would be a sacrilege – we have decided to embark on this great adventure. If it succeeds – and it will succeed – it should enable us to save the best and finest of what we share.

Even in the summer of 1954 when EDC was facing probable defeat in Paris, Spaak (who was once more Belgian Foreign Minister) argued lengthily with the new French Premier Pierre Mendès-France, who wanted EDC watered down. 'We shan't agree,' said Mendès-France finally; 'I'm convinced of it'. And when at the end of August he presented the EDC Treaty to the French National Assembly, he neither endorsed it nor demanded a vote of confidence. The result was predictable. All Spaak's eloquence had failed.

But it was now that stubborn persistence triumphed – Spaak's and Jean Monnet's. Two days after the defeat of EDC in Paris, Monnet began a series of consultations with a view to further progress. They continued for months. 'To enlarge what had begun,' he wrote, '– or in other words, to delegate more power without reviving still smouldering disputes – that was the difficulty; and I discussed it on more than one occasion with Paul-Henri Spaak against the background of the Ardennes, white with winter snow'. In February 1955 Mendès-France's Government fell, and a new, perhaps more amenable administration took office under Edgar Faure. In April, Spaak proposed a meeting of the Community countries' Foreign Ministers 'to re-launch the European idea'.

By now, his and Monnet's thoughts had begun to crystallise around two main proposals: the pooling of peaceful atomic energy (which greatly appealed to Monnet and the French) and completing the coal and steel 'common market' with a general common market for all goods (whose chief advocate was Monnet's assistant Pierre Uri and whose major political support came from Germany). As Monnet wrote:

> I had Spaak's agreement on the proposal, which was already drafted in the form of a declaration. He made every effort to convince his Benelux colleagues, in particular Johan Willem Beyen, the Dutch Foreign Minister, who on his side was pressing for full economic union...

> Finally Spaak reached an agreement with Beyen, who was delighted to see new scope for his own ideas. Under the name of the 'Memorandum from the Benelux Countries to the six ECSC countries', Spaak drafted a four-page proposal which his *directeur de cabinet* Robert Rothschild sent me on 6 May 1955, with the simple message 'Herewith your child'. It contained, in fact, the essentials of our draft declaration. If the words 'United States of Europe' were no longer included, the notion of an 'Economic Community' was nevertheless more sharply defined; and a procedure was proposed. The treaties were to be prepared simultaneously by a conference comprising the Six, the ECSC, and the British Government.

Meeting in Messina on 1 and 2 June 1955, the Foreign Ministers of the Six considered three proposals: the Benelux Memorandum, a paper from Germany calling in particular for a European University, and a proposal from Italy especially stressing social and economic development. The resultant agreement was a patchwork of all three; but to see how to implement the various proposals the Ministers set up a committee of national representatives, assisted by representatives from the High Authority and other bodies, and chaired by Paul-Henri Spaak.

His imposing presence, warmth and dynamism ensured that the Committee stuck to its task – to study methods, not debate principles. It held its first meeting, on 9 July 1955, at the Ministry of Foreign Affairs in Brussels. Thereafter it met in the Château de Val Duchesse, in a wooded park on the outskirts of the city. To Spaak's great regret, and despite his repeated pleas and explanations, the British Government soon decided that 'Britain cannot join in such a project' and withdrew the Board of Trade representative it had sent to Val Duchesse. Barring this major disappointment, progress was rapid. On 13 March 1956, Spaak presented his Committee's draft conclusions to a special meeting of the ECSC's Common Assembly held in the Belgian Senate chamber. On 21 April he submitted them to Ministers, who in Venice on 29 April adopted the modest-looking white paperback that came to be known as the Spaak Report. The Spaak Committee then became, *mutatis mutandis*, a treaty-making conference, which held its first meeting on 26 June 1956. Again, Spaak forced the pace. On one occasion that became famous, experts haggled endlessly about the tariff to be applied to banana imports. Deliberately, Spaak lost his temper. 'I give you two hours,' he told them. 'If it's not settled by then, I shall call the press in and announce that Europe won't be built after all, because we can't agree about bananas'. Then he walked out. When he came back two hours later, the problem had been solved. Under Spaak's energetic chairmanship, the negotiations were completed in less than a year. On 25 March 1957, Belgium, France, Germany, Italy, Luxembourg and the Netherlands signed the two Rome Treaties setting up Euratom and the European Economic Community. Europe had been re-launched.

It was perhaps Spaak's greatest achievement, but it was not his last. He went on, almost at once, to become Secretary-General of NATO. In 1961 he returned to Belgium and European politics as Deputy Premier and Foreign Minister, weathering the two Community crises – of 1963, when General de Gaulle vetoed British membership, and 1965, when France pursued the hazardous policy of 'the empty chair'. In 1966 Spaak finally retired from politics to work in private business. He died six years later, on 31 July 1972.

Conclusion

If Robert Schuman, Alcide De Gasperi and Paul-Henri Spaak were all men of the frontier, this was true in more than a geographical sense. The other frontier they spanned was that dividing the urgent present from the archaic past. All three were born in the late nineteenth century, when gaslight was still common, motor vehicles were rare, and the telephone was a novelty, while tanks, aircraft, radio, television, atomic energy and electronic computers were unknown. In their lifetime they saw old certainties questioned – the class system, the role of women, the position of the Church and the monarchy, the legitimacy of Empire, the supremacy of Europe, the unfettered sovereignty of the nation-state. All three witnessed the senseless slaughter of the First World War. All three opposed Fascist and Nazi dictatorship. All three saw and survived the resultant horrors of the Second World War.

When they came to wield political power and influence, they were determined to start afresh and build better. Today, some of their language – 'federation', 'a central political authority', 'the United States of Europe' – may jar on ears lulled by comforting clichés: 'independence', 'national sovereignty', 'the special relationship'. But those like Schuman, De Gasperi and Spaak, who had had a drastic, rapid and enforced education in realities, were naturally impatient to put some sense into international relations, and were not afraid to say, boldly, what they meant. As Europe continues to debate its future, we can rely on the experts to point out the difficulties and on the cowards and bigots to use them as excuses for inertia. It will take people with Schuman's vision, De Gasperi's determination, and Spaak's energetic eloquence to give Europe the stature its responsibilities demand.

Jean Monnet – Pragmatic Visionary

François Duchêne

Jean Monnet is the hardest of all the eminent Europeans to fit into a pigeonhole. He has left a much bigger imprint on history than most, but somehow the credit washes off him because he was not an elected politician and lacked the politician's public talents. Knowing this, critics are inclined to dismiss him as a technocrat, but he hated administration and left school at the age of sixteen. So was he the self-made man in politics? His business career seems to have been at its best when he tried to make it a kind of public service; he was no tycoon by temperament and he died comparatively poor. Perhaps he was above all a talented man of affairs who grew into a political strategist. He might in another era have made an outstanding chief minister to a pliant autocrat. But even this analogy is very imperfect. Monnet, unlike de Gaulle, was not a man of state. His impulses were much closer to those of the honest citizen of his native Cognac than of any ornament of a ruling class. One of the sources of his originality and magnetism was that he tended to conceive his plans with the instincts of an outsider and to carry them out with more than the average insider's flair and precision. He appealed to the romantic streak in people by idealistic aims anyone could understand and to the expert by the tireless discipline with which he reshaped even familiar ideas to the needs of a new situation. Like many remarkable men, he really only fitted a category of one.

Jean Monnet was small, stocky without being fat, in old age vaguely round – a moustached and tonsured moon-face, a barrel body and even a hint of bandy legs. In appearance he was so caricaturally French of the pre-1914 period – he was, after all, born in 1888 – that the British journalist, Anthony Sampson, could not help thinking of Hercule Poirot. It tickled Monnet's fancy to be called a peasant, but though his father had undoubtedly started life as one, the description did not really fit the son. Monnet senior had become chairman and main shareholder of a middle-ranking Cognac brandy firm initially set up as a cooperative to compete with the Hennessys, Martels and their like, but which duly ended up as J. G. Monnet & Co. Jean was brought up in a large house which was as much a company headquarters as a family home: it had two Corinthian columns in the hall. Though he had financial ups and downs and informal tastes, his simple life was always expensive.

Cognac played quite a part in shaping the politician. The Cognac firm gave Monnet a modest financial independence all his life. Also, Cognac was provincial yet wide open to the world. On leaving school at sixteen, he went not to Paris and the *grandes écoles* that train the French establishment, but to the City of London to learn English with a family acquaintance. As his *Memoirs* put it at the end of his life, 'between Cognac and London, there were direct links that by-passed Paris ... At Cognac, one was on equal terms with the British; in Paris, one was somewhat under their influence'. Before 1914, in his early twenties, he was already making deals on behalf of the family firm in Sweden, Russia, Egypt and above all North America. In 1912, annoyed at failing to book a berth, he narrowly missed drowning on the maiden voyage of the Titanic. The English-speaking world was to be Monnet's arena more than France until late into his 50s. All this made him, though very French in his basic make-up and culture, far more internationalist than most of his fellow countrymen and at times raised a barrier between him and them.

The later Monnet began to emerge clearly from the young one during the First World War. He was declared unfit for military service because of nephritis, but was immediately active as an official. He had dealt for Monnet brandy with the directors of the Hudson Bay Company (HBC) in Canada. He now proposed that the HBC should become the French government's agent for all war purchases in North America. This may be why, aged 25, he was able to get through to the French prime minister, René Viviani, at the height of the battle of the Marne. Monnet suggested to Viviani that the French and British, each of them carrying on the war virtually on its own as in the Crimea, must make the most of scarce resources by planning purchases together. This was a message from outer space at the time and Monnet was not really able to put his idea into practice until a politician of talent, Etienne Clémentel, who was also a friend of his father, became minister of trade late in 1915. Jean Monnet became one of Clémentel's key aides and by the end of the war represented France on the Allied Maritime Transport Executive (AMTE) in London. By controlling the scarcest item, shipping, the AMTE in effect planned war supplies on behalf of the British, French, Italians and Americans. It was, Harold Nicolson wrote, 'the most advanced experiment yet made in international cooperation'. Clémentel and Monnet bitterly regretted the decision of the Americans and British to wind it up in the name of free trade as soon as the war was over.

After all that, it seemed natural for Monnet, though only 30, to be appointed deputy secretary-general of the League of Nations and for the British to give him an honorary knighthood. At the League, he was involved in several strenuous tests. There was fighting between German and Polish irregulars over Upper Silesia, a minor Ruhr, inhabited by both peoples and to which both countries laid total claim. Yet within six weeks, Monnet devised a 15-year League of Nations interim regime – the German Reichstag was draped in black for the ratification debate – which lasted the full term. The crucial body was an Arbitration Tribunal which was in Monnet's mind when he launched the first European Community (EC) thirty years later. Shortly after, a recovery programme was worked out for starving Austria. The main obstacle was the fear of Austria's partition by her neighbours. This made it impossible to raise loans. Monnet dreamed up a Protocol of Abstention signed by all the prospective predators, including Italy and Czechoslovakia, and a successful recovery programme followed. The Saar, however, was a failure. The French were determined to incorporate the German Saar, a sizable producer of coal and steel just across the border from French Lorraine, as a partial (very partial) makeweight against the Ruhr. Monnet thought it a serious error, but had no power to prevent the French takeover. The regime was temporary, though the French no doubt hoped to make it permanent; but when time ran out with a referendum in 1935, Nazi Germany duly reabsorbed the Saar on a tide of nationalist feeling. Here again, prewar memories influenced Monnet in 1950 when the Saar once more became a bone of contention between France and Germany. A major reason for launching the EC was to stop history repeating itself.

As with most founding fathers of the European Union (EU), the roots of Monnet's commitment to integration after the Second World War lay in the frustrated hopes of peace after the first. In retrospect, Monnet considered the League of Nations to be powerless because every country had a veto on decisions. But the same view of its working methods was built into his own views at the time. The young Monnet believed in cooperation between governments, like British civil servants after the Second World War. His federalist beliefs after 1945 were a direct reaction to his experiences with the League recollected in tranquillity. The scales dropped from his eyes, he claimed, when the League failed to stop Japan annexing Manchuria in 1932.

By then, Monnet had been away from Geneva for a full decade. He went in 1922, leaving a brilliant reputation behind, to save the family business in Cognac from bankruptcy. He succeeded in the next few years by jettisoning his father's policy of small sales of luxury spirits in favour of cheaper spirits for larger markets. He might well have failed without a loan on very easy terms from the HBC.

It was clear that Monnet's heart was by now no longer in the family business. In 1925, he became head in Europe of one of the leading investment banks on Wall Street, Blair & Company. Foreign loans floated in the US during the 1920s exceeded the total of similar loans floated in all the other capital-lending countries put together. Most of these loans went to Europe. They were one of the main motors of the vigorous growth on the continent in the late 1920s. They constituted, as John J. McCloy later put it, almost a 'mini-Marshall Plan'. Monnet negotiated, on behalf of Blair as part of American consortia, the 'stabilisations' of the Polish and Romanian currencies in 1927 and 1928. These put the two countries' economies on their feet (all too briefly before the Great Slump) rather as IMF loans are supposed to do today. In many ways, Monnet was carrying on in the private sector the kinds of politico-economic operations, stabilising the shakier parts of Europe, that had absorbed his energies at the League of Nations.

Then came a fateful flight of Icarus. Blair & Company merged with the Bank of America in a would-be 'world bank'. What happened instead was that the Great Depression slashed the new merger's share price by 99 percent, Blair's directors were worsted in a proxy fight in February 1932 and Monnet, briefly a shares millionaire, found himself winged, singed and grounded without a job. His friend, John Foster Dulles, then a leading Wall Street lawyer, found him a stopgap as a liquidator on behalf of American creditors of the assets of the famous Swedish swindler, Ivar Kreuger. But soon his friends at the secretariat of the League pointed him to a more congenial role, to launch a Chinese economic development programme as adviser to T. V. Soong, the arch-moderniser in the Nationalist government. Monnet also seems to have had a loan from Lazard's of London – whose leading figures were connected with the HBC – in the hope of profiting from his Chinese efforts.

The assignment was a very difficult one. For twenty years China had repaid neither principal nor interest on loans and her credit was zero. A development programme was a form of decolonisation plan and adamantly opposed by Japan, the implacable enemy of Chinese recovery. Monnet proposed a China Development Finance Corporation (CDFC) involving all the main Chinese private banks, with state backing, to launch joint ventures with Western investors. Joint ventures were almost unthinkable at the time, because of the prejudices of colonisers and colonised alike. But they mobilised Chinese self-interest against default and ensured that Western investors could not treat China as a colonial nobody. It looked at one time as if the CDFC might succeed in galvanising investment in Chinese railways as the core of a development strategy. But one event after another, and finally the Sino-Japanese war, scuppered it. Monnet was reluctant to admit this. Backed financially by the future secretary of state, John F. Dulles, he entered in 1935 into partnership with an American banker, George Murnane, in a small financial consultancy. Monnet brought little business to the partnership, clinging to the Chinese venture in preference to private deals.

That was still the position by the time of Munich in 1938. Immediately after that humiliation, the French prime minister, Edouard Daladier, sent Monnet as a secret emissary to Roosevelt to buy American warplanes. It was widely believed at the time that a war might be won in short order from the air without land battles, à la H. G. Wells, a view Churchill expressed to Roosevelt's envoy, Harry Hopkins, as late as December 1940. Daladier considered Monnet 'a friend' of Roosevelt because the influential American ambassador in Paris, William C. Bullitt, recommended him. In short, Monnet was returning home to France under American auspices. When war broke out in Europe in September 1939, Monnet, by joint decision of the British and French prime ministers, was appointed the coordinator of the two countries' international arms purchasing, the kind of work he had carried out at a slightly less exalted level in the First World War. His office was in London, though he commuted to Paris. When the fall of France came, he was one of the prime movers behind the ill-fated offer put by Churchill to the French premier, Paul Reynaud, for an Anglo-French Union. Notions of that kind had been circulating in London for some months. At the critical juncture even de Gaulle was involved; the first time he and Monnet met. To have both Churchill and de Gaulle on board for a plan of Union suggests that federalism was not foremost in peoples' minds at the crisis. Monnet himself said it was not in his. The aim was simply and desperately to keep France in the war. It would be wrong to see in the plan some sort of precursor of today's European Union. It was only premonitory in showing that national boundaries laid no fences across Monnet's imagination even then.

After the fall of France, although an effectively stateless Frenchman, Monnet, at his own request, was despatched to Washington on a British passport signed by Church-ill in person, to work in effect as the strategic planner in the British Supply Council (BSC) buying war supplies from the US. Already after Munich, Monnet had hoped to bring in the New World to redress the balance of the Old by masses of aircraft. Now, in Washington, he took the same line that 'ten thousand tanks too many are better than one too few' and gradually came to exert an extraordinary influence on people like John J. McCloy, the number two at the War Department, and Harry Hopkins, Roosevelt's *alter ego*, who were at the heart of American war production planning. One official in the BSC said that Monnet 'usually saw long before anyone else what was the move after the next one on the board'; and another that 'if the British had some insoluble problem with the Americans, it was always Monnet whom they briefed and sent in to see Harry Hopkins: the trick never failed'. It is well attested that Monnet, the unlikely lone Frenchman, was one of the main driving forces behind the struggle to get the United States to establish a 'Victory programme' to overwhelm the Germans by sheer mass of *matériel* while still a neutral country with strong isola-tionist instincts. This programme was just about ready when the Japanese obligingly attacked Pearl Harbour on 7 December 1941. Roosevelt was able, in a month, to enumerate incredible targets of '100,000 airplanes' and other weapons to scale, which were actually achieved. After the war, Keynes said that Monnet 'had short-ened the war by a year'. Monnet was a member of a team, but it was an incredible feat for a Frenchman at the heart of Anglo-American war planning. All the more so because a small number of top American and British officials actively queried his *bona fides*.

After that, it may not seem wholly surprising that once the Allies landed in North Africa, Monnet re-established contact with his fellow countrymen as a *de facto* em-issary of Roosevelt to Algiers. Roosevelt wanted his nominee, General Giraud, to lead the French authority in exile in Algiers and to exclude de Gaulle, seen as less than a democrat but also *in petto* as too assertive a Frenchman for Roosevelt's post-war purposes. However, plans based on the idea that Giraud, a stupid man, could stand up to a leader of de Gaulle's stature, were doomed from the outset. Monnet, who on leaving Washington told American friends that his aim was French unity, soon began to play the honest broker in setting up a French government in exile; inevitably this was led by de Gaulle, but Monnet worked hard to ensure democratic restraints on any temptation to play the Bonaparte. That done, at the end of 1943, Monnet returned to Washington as the head of the new French Supply Council and stayed there until 1945. His main achievements were to persuade the invading Allies not to administer France as an occupied country in line with the wishes of Roosevelt, hostile as ever to de Gaulle; and to negotiate a Lend-Lease agreement (for the same reason very late) in February 1945, only seven months before the end of the war. However, the deal included a strong injection of investment funds for postwar reconstruction, a novelty that aroused strong opposition in Congress.

When the war ended and Monnet, aged 57, returned to France, this time more or less permanently, he had lived twenty years (as he did until his mid-eighties) a highly mobile life in which his headquarters were primarily the United States. This was partly where business led him. But from 1934, his marriage in the Kremlin (*sic*) to the Italian wife of one of his own former Italian employees at Blair & Co gave him personal reasons for doing so too. His wife had a daughter from her first marriage and as custody belonged to the husband in countries of Roman law, she could not have kept her if she had lived in France, Italy or Switzerland. She obtained custody in New York but her daughter had to stay in America for her to enjoy it, and so Monnet did too. During these two primarily American decades, Monnet had become much admired by many of the Americans who collectively were to shape the postwar world. Monnet first met Dulles at the Paris Peace Conference in 1919 and Dulles thought him 'one of the most brilliant men that I know'. Monnet also met around or before 1930 'Jack' McCloy, Dean Acheson, Donald Swatland, Henry Stimson, Averell Harriman and many more. To move in such circles at the heart of the American establishment meant that he would be passed on effortlessly to all the other people on the revolving circuits. It was one of Monnet's main sources of political strength after the war. His postwar influence in Washington bemused Europeans. It seemed vaguely incredible, a mystery. Yet it was simply that few appreciated in his later days the depths of Monnet's immersion and acceptance in America long before. Interestingly in view of Monnet's close links with Britain – collecting a knighthood as early as the First World War and working as a senior British civil servant in the second – he was never accepted there in quite the same way. Monnet's relations with America were in every way unique. Even they probably became as strong as they did only in the special conditions of the war.

The other legacy of Monnet's career by 1945 was his conviction, not at all special at the time, that some new political system must replace the balance of power between nations that had twice broken down in world war. At the League of Nations, as we have seen, he had simply believed in cooperation of an intergovernmental kind. The tragedies of the interwar period showed this was totally inadequate. Stronger political medicine was needed. Monnet expressed himself on these matters quite frequently – and variously – in the later days of the Second World War. Paul-Henri Spaak remembered a lunch in Washington in 1941 where Monnet outlined a scheme in which French and German steel, the sinews of war, should come under a common authority. In 1943 in Algiers, Monnet showed a colleague, Etienne Hirsch, a map in which the same areas were shaded in pencil and argued that they should be extracted from the two countries. On 17 October 1943, in Algiers, in a conversation with de Gaulle and others, Monnet spoke in favour of a Europe united 'as a single economic entity with free trade'. On 7 July 1944, he told Harold Macmillan that the future of Europe turned on Germany and that, although a full United States of Europe was out of reach, a strong League of Nations enhanced by interstate trade and monetary arrangements might be feasible. England, he thought, should take the lead, backed by France. In August, he told *Fortune* magazine that there would have to be 'a true yielding of sovereignty' to 'some kind of central union, a big European market without customs barriers', to prevent the nationalism 'which is the curse of the modern world'. 'But where to begin? And how far to go? And could England be brought in? For without England ... the concept of a unified Europe turns all too quickly into a Germanised Europe all over again'.

Monnet and the Plan Commissariat

Monnet's return home was not, however, for a European but a national purpose: to reconstruct and above all to modernise France. This sounds ordinary enough in the 1990s. At the time it was the dream of a brave new world. France had suffered in the 1930s from an economic decline that seemed in retrospect all too typical of her paralysis in the face of Nazi Germany and of the humiliating collapse of 1940. 'Modernisation or decadence' was Monnet's slogan after the war. Monnet's *Memoirs* say he told de Gaulle in Washington in 1945: 'You speak of greatness ... but today the French are small. There will only be greatness when the French are of a stature to warrant it ... For this purpose they must modernise – because at the moment they are not modern'. De Gaulle duly sponsored what came to be known as the 'Monnet' Plan of massive investments to make the country a true industrial power. It was launched at the end of 1945 by the two of them together. It was the first and last time they really sang in tune.

Interestingly, Monnet launched his plan when the idea, almost a cliché a few months before, was on its last legs. Pierre Mendès-France had tried to launch a plan as minister for the Economy in the first de Gaulle government after the liberation of Paris, in the winter of 1944. But he presented it as part of a radical general overhaul, which ironically fell foul of the allegedly radical Socialists and Communists, with their peasant clientele; and he wanted authority over all the economic ministries, which put all his colleagues' backs up. Plans proposed by other politicians failed for similar reasons, all typical of the centralising, authoritarian French administrative tradition. Monnet, the outsider, approached the task in a completely different spirit.

Monnet's first novelty was to avoid grand principles. He presented his plan as a piece of crisis management, to persuade the Americans to cough up the massive dollar loans of which the ruined French stood in desperate need now that the end of the war had cut off Lend-Lease. He asked for no authority over anyone. He agreed with the authors of the plan for steel that 'however carefully a plan has been worked out, it will be effective only to the extent that it has been thought through and adopted as their own by a broad enough swathe of the people involved'. Great pride was taken in elaborate consultations in 'modernisation commissions' bringing together civil servants, industrialists, labour unions and independent experts. This approach was quite novel in France where the civil service regarded itself as the authority to which all others should defer. In case all this sounds too good to be true, and seems to leave out all scope for leadership, the answer is that Monnet guarded vigilantly his access to the top ministers and to the funds.

This sounds easier in theory than it was in practice. The French Fourth Republic that took over from de Gaulle when he resigned in 1946, was deliberately designed to be a regime of weak governments which on average lasted about six months at a time. Monnet had to pay constant court to premiers and ministers of finance. He succeeded on the whole because ministers had little time to spare from their game of musical chairs, while he had stable tenure, a formidable reputation and was a constant source of practical ideas. Also, though the personnel rotated from ministry to ministry the same faces tended to turn up again and again in slightly different combinations of jobs, and he knew them all. Confident in his capacity to think ahead of his political customers, Monnet was less interested in formal powers than in easy access to the top. He had to fight for this on many occasions, but he rarely if ever lost touch.

The other problem was the control of funds. At first, Monnet hoped to achieve this by obtaining large amounts of dollars and by keeping them out of the reach of Parliament with its ineradicably short-term ways. Unfortunately, the Americans failed to provide funds in 1946 on the scale Monnet had expected and he launched the plan at the end of the year without its really being funded. It was a huge gamble but it was a start. Monnet always believed in making a start; he said even of the Marshall Plan that it was really the first year that mattered. The key was to gain momentum. Crisis duly followed in 1947. But Monnet was lucky. The crisis was so general in Europe that it led to the Marshall Plan. Now the money began to flow in the broad stream Monnet had worked for. Better still, Monnet's close alliance with Marshall Aid officials, both in Paris and in Washington, ensured that his investment plan would get the lion's share of dollars. He was aided in this by the glaring contrast between his clear strategy and the usual fecklessness of the Fourth Republic. This made powerful civil servants in the ministry of Finance as well as the Americans collude in Monnet's purposes.

Little by little, between 1945 and 1950, Monnet himself, the Monnet Plan and the Monnet Plan administration imposed themselves as a source of creative action in a country that felt sorely starved of any such thing. Monnet was a master of discreet publicity, again aided by the fact that he had results to which he could point. His small but talented administration at the *Plan Commissariat* – never more than 100 staff down to the last cleaner and driver (a matter of great pride) – gradually became a centre of hope and perceived success in a country generally regarded as the sick man of Europe until the end of the Algerian war in 1962. In retrospect, and in comparison with some of the other West European countries, France's record of growth in the 1950s was not outstanding. But by comparison with France in the disastrous 1930s, the first Monnet Plan from 1946 to 1952 (the only one in which Monnet was involved) was an inspiration. The Fourth Republic was short-termist in its very essence. The Monnet plan was the one exception with long term goals. To defend them against short-termism was, in the context of the politics of the day, an achievement in itself. The Monnet Plan in effect gave France the infrastructure to profit from the economic 'miracles' of the mid and late 1950s, which it had been lacking before. It was, from this point of view, the centre-piece of France's recovery postwar from a moth-eaten great power in the old style to a 'modern' medium-sized industrial state in the mode both Monnet and de Gaulle had recognised to be necessary in 1945.

Monnet and the Schuman Plan

In 1950, the wartime 'European' suddenly re-emerged in Monnet because of the resurgence of the new Germany. The German policy of France's first postwar governments resembled the later Cold War *boutade* of the novelist, François Mauriac, that 'we love Germany so well, we prefer to have two'. The postwar governments wanted as many German regional states as possible, along with an international (i.e. non-German) regime for the Ruhr, a form of divide-and-rule that worked well for France between Richelieu and Bismarck. They also started, once again, to annex the Saar 'economically' as a tame source of coal and steel. But once the Marshall Plan was launched in 1947, it became evident that the Americans were not going to lend massive sums to promote Western Europe as a bastion of the Cold War and leave out Western Germany, the economic heart of the region. Backed by the British, they made it plain they were determined to create a new West German state whether the French liked it or not. The French, partly inspired by Monnet, then fell back on a policy of international controls over coal deliveries from the Ruhr. The Ruhr must not be allowed, as prewar, to withhold coal supplies from France, raise the production costs of French steel and, so the argument ran, cripple French manufacturing in general. All this was coming unstuck by early 1950. First, the Federal Republic of Germany had come to life in September 1949, with Konrad Adenauer as Chancellor asserting that 'the Germans want to become good Europeans but as equals not slaves'. Second, the Saar was predictably poisoning Franco-German relations. Third, the USA was visibly about to lift the controls on the Ruhr so dear to the French. In fact, the US secretary of state, Dean Acheson, had virtually warned the French foreign minister, Robert Schuman, in September 1949 that this would be the case unless he formulated a French policy for the new Germany that the Americans and British could endorse. The basic flaws of French postwar policy towards Germany, that it relied on the Americans who had few reasons to pursue French goals, and that it roused all the old ill feelings with the Germans, were coming home to roost.

Monnet had been worrying about these matters since the Marshall Plan. On at least two occasions, in 1949 and early in 1950, he held discussions in Whitehall on some kind of joint policy towards Germany. 'Neither England nor France', he was reported as saying, 'had any positive policy to Germany. ... Unless they soon developed a common one, they would find themselves disputing about the line to be taken'. But the British, determined not to be more involved across the Channel than the Americans, had no interest in a European as against an Atlantic policy towards Germany. By early 1950, virtually every leading politician or official, including many who were later to take a vital part in European integration, assumed that the British veto made such integration impossible to achieve; and that some Atlantic solution with the United States, however limited, would have to be worked out. It was at this very moment that Monnet sold to Schuman the scheme that was to achieve fame as the Schuman Plan. Once again, as in 1945, Monnet achieved a breakthrough when the strategy he brought to life seemed to be in its last throes.

The French had to put forward a positive policy on Germany when Schuman met Acheson and the British foreign secretary, Ernest Bevin, in London in May 1950 or else lose all control of events. The date of birth of the Schuman Plan, announced on 9 May 1950, and so of European union, was no accident at all. Nor were the terms of the scheme. It proposed that France and Germany and any other countries ready to join them (in the event Italy and the Benelux trio) should set up a federal body, with its own powers (i.e. no national vetoes) to make policy for, and administer, their coal and steel industries. This was Monnet's old wartime idea and it also covered the ground of French attempts to internationalise the Ruhr. But the key difference from the latter was that internationalism was not to be imposed on the Ruhr from the outside. It applied equally to all participating states, including France, whose coal and steel were included in the pool on the same terms as any others. This made France's neighbours take the Schuman Plan seriously. But by the same token, it was why the French foreign office failed to produce it and the author had to be an outsider like Monnet. The heirs of the great power tradition, in France as in Britain (and there lies a lasting bond between the two), were viscerally incapable of producing a scheme to tie France's hands. It was anathema to the diplomats. They could not launch the Schuman Plan, so Monnet had to.

The Schuman Plan had two aspects, variously expressed by Monnet's memoranda to the two leading lights in the French government of the day. In writing to the prime minister, Georges Bidault, who was no federalist, Monnet stressed the dangers the French economy would face if all controls on the new Germany were to disappear and France to have no say in the Ruhr. Writing to Robert Schuman, a 'European', Monnet underlined the need to reconcile France and Germany to establish the long term peace. Both elements were present in the Schuman Plan, but the more important by far was the second, more political theme. French postwar aims in the Ruhr and Saar have become irrelevant in a cooperative system – they only made sense in an adversarial one – and have been largely forgotten, but the European Union, for all the problems it has always faced, goes marching on.

The Schuman Plan made key strategic choices which have underlain European integration ever since. Many are characteristic of Monnet's approach, and are personally as well as politically significant. One of the most important was to hone the proposal to the practical possibilities of the day. Previous plans, such as for a Council of Europe with the institutions of a union but national vetoes all along the line, or for a customs union between France and Italy, the two most protectionist countries of a highly protectionist region, had no political roots. But the Schuman Plan addressed a critical problem for the French government which could ruin leading politicians whether they acted or not. This made them listen to proposals with more attention than usual. The scheme gained a hearing because it met an urgent need (again, as did the Monnet Plan before it).

Further, while the Schuman Plan waved the grandiose banner of a united Europe, it confined the specifics to French and German coal and steel at a time when strategic choices in this area had to be made anyway. Monnet realised that union in Europe could not resemble the United States of America because the European countries differed too much from one another. The Schuman Plan, restricted to a fairly narrow sector of the economy, raised the issue of sovereignty but not in decisive areas like foreign policy, defence or money. The idea was to create a federal prototype. Once 'a practical community of interests' had been created, mentalities would change, other steps would become possible, a new dynamic would begin to operate and finally, step by step, lead to a federal destination. Of course, in such a pragmatic approach, federalism was a favoured, but not predestined outcome. There has always been something open-ended about the European Community. Yet this very pragmatism has made possible the progress so far towards a European Union. Here again, the parallel is striking with Monnet's falsely modest audacity in launching the French investment plan.

Monnet's strategic choices in the Schuman Plan also settled some of the basic issues central to European integration ever since. The decision taken to go ahead with Germany even if that meant casting off from Britain has had at least two results. The first is that since Britain did not accept a federal approach in 1950, the French in effect dropped the *entente cordiale*. This was unthinkable for orthodox French diplomats, but it was not as rash as it seemed. The Americans now offered the insurance Britain could not provide. The Schuman Plan solved the American dilemma of promoting the new Germany as a western bastion in the Cold War without undermining it from the rear by creating a disaffected France. The Americans were able to referee relations between France and Germany as Britain could never hope to do. Monnet admitted that the negotiations on the Schuman Plan which finally produced the first European Community, for coal and steel (ECSC), in August 1952, would never have been completed without determined American intervention. The necessary and sufficient condition for the EC in the 1950s was the triple alliance of the US, France and West Germany. Britain was sidelined because it was neither willing to join in nor central to the action.

The process by which France and Germany went ahead with Italy and the Benelux countries to negotiate the ECSC in 1950 had a second consequence. A minority acted without waiting for the abstentionists, though the latter accused them of 'dividing' Europe. Without that, nothing would have happened. The decisiveness of the minority soon proved the locomotive for the rest. Most countries joined later for fear of being marginalised and losing influence, in Europe and in relations with the US. The 'two-speed' approach to integration has been one of the prime sources of the relatively rapid progress to European Union. Little by little, more and more countries have sought to join the Community. It began with six founding members, had fifteen by 1995, with another twelve waiting to enter and an unknown further number waiting in the wings. The length of the queue is such as to give new meaning to Raymond Aron's aphorism that 'nothing fails like success'. Debating points about 'little Europe' have been left far behind by the clamour to join the club.

From the outset, then, the Schuman Plan contained in embryo most of the strategies which have led integration, in Monnet's words, from utopia to reality. However, it was one thing to launch the themes, another to work them out. The major achievement of Monnet in the following five years was probably to implant the new and in many ways alien body of the EC into the intergovernmental circuits.

This began with the negotiation of the Schuman Plan by the founder states in 1950. The European federal agency Monnet had in mind at first was a transposition of the Monnet Plan Commissariat to a European level, a quite inadequate idea when six governments had to be integrated into a single process. There was an intense dialogue with the Dutch in July 1950. From this confrontation there soon emerged a system inspired by the classical principles of a federal balance of powers. Relations between the institutions have changed over the years, but evolved naturally from that beginning. The Dutch, in this as in other phases of integration, played an important part. But without Monnet's initiative, tenacity, flexibility and relations with the Americans, the EC would never have been born. In the words of Miriam Camps, a State Department official who later became a distinguished commentator on European integration, Monnet was 'the driving force ... the philosopher and generally accepted leader of the movement for creating unity in Europe by the method of which the Schuman Plan was the prototype'.

When the ECSC was set up, Monnet was the obvious choice to lead its executive, the High Authority. The three years of his tenure were overshadowed by the political crisis over the European Defence Community (EDC) project which he, once again, had persuaded the French government to launch in October 1950. This was a less than welcome by-product of the Korean war that broke out without warning the Sunday after the Schuman Plan negotiations had opened on 25 June 1950. The Europeans, concerned about the political effects that might be caused by fears of a Korean-style attack on West Germany, called for American troops to stop any rot in Europe. The Americans agreed only if the Europeans would help themselves, meaning that Germany should rearm with the others. It was a tall order only five years after Hitler. The EDC was proposed by the federal faction in France as, from their point of view, the most constructive alternative to a German army in NATO. Monnet in particular felt that if the Germans were offered national sovereignty through rearmament they would lose any incentive to accept collective controls on coal and steel in the Schuman Plan, so that the European policy would be still-born. However, by late 1952, it became evident that a steadily growing proportion of French parliamentarians would refuse to ratify the EDC treaty, now signed. French governments wavered and prevaricated and postponed for as long as possible and, on 30 August 1954, on a tide of nationalist feeling, the French National Assembly refused to ratify the treaty though Germany and the Benelux countries had already done so. Thus, the whole of Monnet's tenure of the presidency of the High Authority from August 1952 to his resignation in June 1955 was overshadowed by the EDC crisis in France and by its aftermath.

In these tense circumstances, it is not surprising that Monnet lost the struggle between the High Authority and European coal and steel cartels led by the Ruhr. To that extent, the initial high hopes of creating a new kind of European government were foiled. Ironically, however, the ECSC succeeded in more important ways. The common market for coal and steel eliminated several forms of discriminatory treatment between member states. The ECSC had the luck to preside over a long boom in which the restrictive behaviour for which the steel cartel had become proverbial pre-war was irrelevant. Above all, the ECSC locked the governments in constant negotiation under a set of rules. In intergovernmental organisations, governments tended to inform their partners of their moves after the event. In the ECSC, they normally negotiated ahead of them. This was a major step forward to cooperation in depth. It also led to the ECSC being accepted, warts and all, as a more effective model of international government than the alternatives on offer.

This was a factor in the European revival after the EDC fiasco. The European idea retained enough strength in all six founding countries, despite the nationalist upsurge in France, to make further economic, as opposed to defence, integration a feasible prospect. Monnet and the Belgian foreign minister, Paul-Henri Spaak, determined early in 1955 to relaunch European integration along economic lines by proposing (mainly) a European Nuclear Energy Community (Euratom). It was a time of visions of nuclear energy so cheap that domestic users would get it free. However, the Dutch foreign minister, Johan Beyen, and the Germans considered sectoral integration of the Monnet type too narrow and thought that future integration must be based on a general Common Market. This was far from popular in France. Monnet feared the French Parliament might reject it like the EDC. He also feared that a real Common Market would require a dose of supranationality far beyond what any government would contemplate and that anything less would amount to free trade without European overtones. Thus, though Monnet had a period of considerable influence over the government of Guy Mollet in Paris which pushed through both the Common Market and Euratom treaties in 1957, he marginalised himself to some degree by promoting Euratom, which most politicians sooner or later regarded as much the junior of the two schemes. In short, Monnet is the father of the European Community, not of the Common Market, its decisive application. Ironically, his achievement, as opposed to his reputation is political rather than economic.

Despite this misjudgement, Monnet's influence would probably have remained very great had the Fourth Republic survived. In the event, it collapsed in May 1958 as a result of a coup by the European settlers in Algeria as soon as they saw the Fourth Republic about to negotiate independence with the Moslem rebels. General de Gaulle returned to power, the incarnation of France and enemy of 'stateless' Europe. Monnet and de Gaulle agreed on some issues – both favoured more consultation between heads of government – but in essence they remained the personifications of two rival policies. Monnet lost his influence in Paris. He could still see almost any head of state he wished, could still get governments to treat his schemes seriously, and still had the ear of many leaders, notably in the US, Germany and the Netherlands. He still had a hand in a surprising range of acts, such as (oddly enough) the establishment in 1959 of the forum of the industrial powers, the OECD; the decision of Britain in 1961 to seek to enter the EC; and even the proposal of president Giscard d'Estaing of France in 1974 (when Monnet was 85) for a European Council of heads of government.

However, for these and many other activities, Monnet ceased to make the impact of his heyday between 1945 and 1955. The underlying strategies he was pursuing after 1958 were either ahead of their time or beside it. Two were particularly ambitious. The first was the desire for a 'partnership of equals' between the US and the uniting states of Europe to which Kennedy responded in his famous Atlantic partnership speech of 1962 but which de Gaulle short-circuited. With it disappeared Monnet's hopes that he might get the European Commission accepted as the 'single voice' of the EC countries in economic cooperation with the United States, a notion which was anathema to de Gaulle. The second was to move beyond the Common Market to the 'political' dimension the EC still lacked. He proposed monetary union through a European Reserve Fund as early as 1959; and tried to bring the heads of government together through the European Council. Although the latter was a Gaullist expedient, Monnet, as a realist, felt the priority was to get the heads of government involved. All in vain. There were no decisive moves beyond the Common Market till he died in 1979 aged 91. In fact, the issue in the EU today is still how far there will be a 'political' union through a single currency or joint action in defence and diplomacy. The Community method has brought one to the gates of political union as Monnet calculated, but since the Community's very existence was based on the need to finesse the core problems of political union and national sovereignty, it is evident that they will have to be addressed in different terms.

Despite his disappointments, Monnet's last active period, from 1958 to 1975, was far from empty because he consolidated his view of European union as the orthodox one. In October 1955, soon after he left the presidency of the High Authority, he formed a public lobby of the leaders of the political parties and labour unions of the Six founding countries of the EC to back supranational integration. Its title was a programme in itself – the Action Committee for a United States of Europe. The Communists and Gaullists alone stayed outside. Even during the years in the wilderness when de Gaulle was attacking the federal aspects of the EC – putting a veto on majority voting in the Council of Ministers – the Action Committee attracted new members, such as the 'Nenni' Socialists in Italy emerging from the shadow of their alliance with the Communists. With broad and active backing, and because he was the only leader who looked beyond the tactical issues of integration to the deeper purposes behind, Monnet in effect made his vision of Europe the received version. He is the tutelary deity of Brussels (and devil of Eurosceptics) today.

Monnet was a practitioner and his views evolved with his practice: the older he grew and the more the EC developed, the more he stressed the vital role of institutions. In his eyes, they were 'the real pillars of civilisation'. This is very much the outlook embedded in the EU. The EU is often viewed simply as a state in the making or an economic great power; both are true as far as they go. But if one regards it as a reform of international relations, it takes on more original qualities. By setting up common rules and institutions to formulate them, it ensures that the democratic standards of domestic politics in most European countries begin to apply across frontiers. Frontiers cease to pose threats to those standards. The political dynamic is reversed as civil politics begin to cover over the traditional balance of power. This has no doubt been a factor in the relative ease with which Germany's reunification has been accepted by her neighbours. Within the new system also, rules tend to restrict the directorates of great powers that marginalise smaller nations. Probably the most significant single feature of the EU is the influence it has given to smaller countries which had no voice before. The desire of eligible ones to join the EU reflects the magnetism of a rule-based system. The larger states now complain, understandably, that the crowd of smaller states (21 out of 27 in an enlarged EU) could have a majority of votes although the few large states contain a big majority of the population. That such a complaint is even possible is a tribute to the creation of an international legal order. The rather hypocritical charge of some opponents that the EU is not democratic enough is also a back-handed compliment. It demonstrates that the norm is now domestic politics not the great power hegemony. It is a basic change.

The role of personality in politics is difficult to determine. Without the existence of an opportunity there can be no achievement, and all political achievement is more or less collective. It can always be claimed of any outcome that collective forces lay behind it. On the other hand, many opportunities exist which leaders fail to seize.

The gap between latent possibility and active innovation is the area within which leadership can be exercised. There is little doubt that without Monnet the French would have been outflanked in 1950 by American policy on Germany as they were on other occasions. The difference that time was Monnet's creative opportunism, 'turning a need into a policy'. Twice, with the Monnet Plan in 1945 and the Schuman Plan in 1950, he took up and made a success of an idea which was on its last legs. This suggests he was a better strategist and tactician than most. But his creative power went deeper than that. It had scope because his attitude was closer to that of the ordinary citizen than to those of the establishments he moved among. Few Frenchmen could have mustered the inner conviction to forge ahead with a European policy that violated all the habits of the French state. Monnet never tried to seem a rebel but had a rarer quality, an original political temperament.

Though de Gaulle and Monnet were utterly unalike and the one hugely outshone the other in their lifetimes, people who knew both at close quarters, like René Pleven, twice premier under the Fourth Republic, tended to bracket them together as historic figures rising above the crowd. In fact, and odd as it may seem in the light of their conflicts, their achievements were to a great extent complementary. De Gaulle saved France after the nadir of 1940 in his first period of rule and in his second, as the father of the Fifth Republic, freed her from the neuroses of lost empire and gave her a badly needed political stability. Yet it was the Fourth Republic, of considerable importance and too little reputation in history, which founded a new economy at home and a new Europe abroad. In both cases, Monnet was the architect and driving force of innovation. He was in many ways the major statesman of the Fourth Republic without having ever been one of its conventional politicians. And in the case of the European Union, the potential goes far beyond that of any single European nation in the third millenium that is about to open.

Selected bibliography

Primary source material comes from the following archives:

FNA (1946) – French National Archives, CG au Plan, 80 AJ 11, *1er Rapport Commission Modernisation Sidérurgie*, Nov.1946.

PRO (1949) – UK Public Record Office, FO 371/77933, Edwin Plowden-Roger Makins, 10th March 1949.

HBCA (1922) – Hudson Bay Company Archives, Winnipeg, A.1/265, meeting Governor and Committee, 28th March 1922.

Other works consulted include:

Camps, Miriam (1964) *Britain and the European Community 1955-1963*, London: Oxford University Press.

Davenport, John (1944) 'M.Jean Monnet of Cognac' in *Fortune Magazine*, August 1944.

Duchêne, François (1994) *Jean Monnet: the First Statesman of Interdependence*, New York: Norton.

Fursdon, Edward (1980) *The European Defence Community*, London: Macmillan.

Hirsch, Etienne (1988) *Ainsi Va La Vie*, Lausanne.

Lisagor, N. and F. Lipsius (1988) *A Law Unto Itself: the Law Firm Sullivan and Cromwell*, New York.

Macmillan, Harold (1967) *The Blast of War*, London: Macmillan.

McCloy, John J. (1981) Interviewed by L. Tennyson, 15th June 1981, Lausanne: Fondation Jean Monnet pour l'Europe.

Monick, Emanuel (1970) *Pour Mémoire*, Paris.

Monnet, Jean (1955) *Les Etats-Unis d'Europe ont Commencé*, Paris.

(1978) *Memoirs*, translated by Richard Mayne, London: Collins.

Nicolson, Harold (1935) *Dwight Morrow*, New York.

Rieben, H., ed. (1985) *L'Europe une Longue Marche*, Lausanne.

(1987) *Des Guerres Européennes à l'Union de l'Europe*, Lausanne.

Salter, Arthur (1961) *Memoirs of a Public Servant*, London: Faber and Faber.

Sampson, Anthony (1971) *The New Europeans*, London.

Spaak, Paul-Henri (1969) *Combats Inachevés*, Vol.2, Paris.

In Their Own Image –
The Americans and the Question of
European Unity, 1943-1954

John L. Harper

Background: The 'labyrinth of conflict'

In late 1942, Count Richard N. Coudenhove-Kalergi, the half-Hungarian, half-Japanese advocate of a strong federated Europe including Germany, sought an appointment at the White House. He had been turned down at a previous attempt in December 1940. When the president's secretary, General Edwin Watson, was asked this time if he wanted to see Coudenhove-Kalergi, he replied: '*No*, if I can avoid it'. This reflected Franklin Roosevelt's own view. Compared to what it later became, the idea of European unity was not an especially popular one in Washington at the time.

Indeed, if Coudenhove-Kalergi had managed to have a frank talk with Roosevelt, he would have learned that the president's vision of postwar Europe was, if anything, the opposite of his own. Like his predecessor Woodrow Wilson, Roosevelt embodied an old American antipathy toward the system of European power politics, and a desire to reform it. But Roosevelt was a more coldblooded statesman than Wilson and – understandably in view of 1930s developments in the Old World – even more Europhobic. In May 1942, Roosevelt told Soviet Foreign Minister Molotov that, after the war, four essentially non-European powers, the United States, Britain, the Soviet Union, and China would be 'the policemen of the world'.

On the main postwar problem, FDR wrote to Queen Wilhelmina of the Netherlands in August 1944, 'There are two schools of thought – those who would be altruistic in regard to the Germans . . . and those who would adopt a much "tougher" attitude'. He continued, 'Most decidedly I belong to the latter school'. This was amply demonstrated when he approved the famous 'Morgenthau Plan' in September 1944. Charles Bohlen's 1943 appraisal of Soviet postwar aims was a fair rendering of what FDR himself had in mind:

> Germany is to be broken up and kept broken up. The states of eastern, south-eastern and central Europe will not be permitted to group themselves into any

federations or associations. France is to be stripped of her colonies and strategic bases beyond her borders and will not be permitted to maintain any appreciable military establishment. . . The result will be that the Soviet Union will be the only important political and military force on the continent of Europe. The rest of Europe will be reduced to political and military impotence.

Roosevelt's reaction to a British scheme for a 'Supreme World Council' and several regional councils sheds more light on his thinking. According to Churchill's scheme, Supreme Council members would 'sit on the Regional Councils in which they were directly interested' – making the United States a member of the European council. This posed a dilemma for Roosevelt. On the one hand, he favoured the idea of great-power regional hegemony, and such councils might facilitate the regional policeman's work. As he remarked in 1942: 'Russia would be charged with keeping peace in Europe. The United States would be charged with keeping peace in the Western Hemisphere. The US and China would be charged with keeping peace in the Far East'. On the other hand, Roosevelt feared Churchill's plan as a device to entangle the United States in Europe. Reflecting Congress and the US electorate, Roosevelt wished to have his cake and eat it: a final settlement of the European problem but one that did not require American soldiers to stay on hand to enforce it. Indeed Roosevelt 'doubted if the United States Congress would agree to the United States' participation in an exclusively European Committee which might be able to force the dispatch of American troops to Europe'. At most he 'envisaged the sending of American planes and ships to Europe' with Britain and Russia providing the land armies 'in the event of any future threat to peace'. But a European council to which the United States did *not* belong presented another set of problems: it might be beyond US influence, or evolve into an anti-American bloc. On balance, a European regional body was not a good idea.

FDR's rejection of regionalism in 1943 represented a victory for Secretary of State Cordell Hull. Like Roosevelt, Hull and his advisers wanted to put an end to the destructive pattern of European power politics but theirs was a purer, more evangelical Wilsonianism than his. They argued – with regrettable accuracy from FDR's standpoint – that public opinion would support only a 'general international organisation based on the principle of sovereign equality'—as opposed to a cabal of the big powers. Hull, who hailed from the Tennessee hills, and his lieutenant William L. Clayton, a Texan and founder of the world's largest cotton export company, were part of an old free trade tradition associated with the Democratic Party, agriculture and the South. Their 'One World' programme had a crucial economic component: an end to rival blocs and a return to an open, multilateral system along pre-1914 lines.

If Roosevelt was indifferent, even hostile, to European economic unity – for him Europe's geopolitical demotion always took precedence over its economic reformation – the idea found favour in State Department and business circles. It was assumed that integration would lead to greater efficiency, higher incomes and increased demand for surplus American production. In other words, opening the European market would help to avoid a new depression. For Hullians the elimination of barriers within Europe was never an end in itself. Rather, it was a stepping stone to an integrated world economy. This was also the view of the New York-based Council on Foreign Relations (CFR). According to a 1942 CFR report:

> The United States would favour economic unification of Europe only if steps are taken to avoid the creation of an autarkic continental economy. Positive American policy should aim at the interpenetration of Europe's economy with that of the rest of the world, as well as a lowering of economic barriers within Europe.

Hull, not surprisingly, did receive Coudenhove-Kalergi and no doubt took an interest in his schemes. But it seems that the crusading count had a real meeting of minds with two other officials: Adolf A. Berle, member of FDR's original Brains Trust and Assistant Secretary of State, and William C. Bullitt, the flamboyant former ambassador to the Soviet Union and France. Berle and Bullitt were disillusioned Wilsonians who had warned against US intervention in Europe after 1919 to uphold a peace settlement that reflected the triumph of European selfishness and myopia, or, as Berle wrote to Roosevelt in September 1938, 'to maintain a situation which was untenable from the time it was created by the treaties of Versailles and Saint-Germain'. This message had endeared them to FDR – although their deep anti-Communism had not. The influence of both declined during the period of US-Soviet entente.

Berle and Bullitt thought the break-up of Austria-Hungary had been a serious mistake and hoped for a territorial unit in Central Europe of sufficient stability, cohesion, and economic scale to ensure peace and to stem the tide of Bolshevism without outside help. They saw the restoration of German power as unavoidable and necessary, though they wished this to happen in the context of peace with France and overall European union. 'The root of the problem,' Bullitt said in November 1936, 'is still – as it has been for so long – reconciliation of France and Germany'. He was prepared to concede Austria and Czechoslovakia to Germany, but argued in November 1937: 'The only way that I can see that the growth of German strength, which I regard as inevitable, can be used for constructive instead of destructive purposes is by a general effort to make the giving of these concessions to Germany a part of a general plan of unification for Europe'.

At the time of the Czech crisis in September 1938, the young Soviet expert George F. Kennan commented:

> the break-up of the limited degree of unity which the Habsburg Empire represented was unfortunate for all concerned. Other forces are now at work which are struggling to create a new form of unity... To these forces Czecho-

slovakia has been tragically slow in adjusting herself. . . . The adjustment – and this is the main thing – has now come.

Like Berle and Bullitt, Kennan believed that a process of reconsolidation was at work; Hitler, willy-nilly, was its agent; the result, on balance, was positive for the West. In this view there was no sympathy for Nazism; rather the sense that German strength – in some sort of larger container – had to be pitted against Russia in order to create an inherent European balance. Without such a balance, it was feared, the power and resources of Germany and Russia might be combined under a single political authority – the nightmare of Anglo-Saxon geopoliticians since the days of Halford Mackinder. Or else the task of maintaining the balance would fall on an unlikely and unsuitable candidate: the United States.

In January 1943, Bullitt warned Roosevelt that 'Europe cannot be made a military vacuum for the Soviet Union to flow into'. In March 1943, he sent the president a Coudenhove-Kalergi memo calling for a European federation. His views spurned, Bullitt – in a typical theatrical gesture – offered his services to General Charles de Gaulle and was made an officer in the French army for the rest of the war. (Bullitt's break with FDR was also linked to his role in the plot to oust Undersecretary Sumner Welles, the President's favourite in the State Department.) In 1944, after writing several critical memos on the administration's Soviet policy, Berle was sent as ambassador to Brazil. In June 1944, Kennan – still a junior official – declared his dissent from 'the general lines of thinking. . . with respect to future policy' – meaning FDR's design to weaken Europe and accommodate the Russians. On the same occasion he expressed his belief that 'some degree of federation for Central and West Europe . . . seems to offer the only way out of this labyrinth of conflict'.

Creating something new

The desire of Americans, embodied by FDR, for some kind of 'new world order,' including a definitive solution to the problem of Europe, survived the president's death in April 1945. The notion that the new order would be based on a US-Soviet partnership did not survive Roosevelt – at least not for long. That idea, discredited during the 1945 Polish controversy, was laid to rest by Kennan in his famous 'long telegram' of February 1946. It was an utter waste of time, Kennan wrote from Moscow, to try to be friends with people 'committed fanatically to the belief that with the US there can be no permanent *modus vivendi*'. This struck a responsive chord in the Truman administration at the time. Another part of Kennan's message, that 'gauged against the Western World as a whole, the Soviets are still by far the weaker force,' did not, or only to a limited degree. This was in part because during the next twelve months relations with Moscow seemed to go from bad to worse.

Soviet pressure on Iran, Turkey, and Greece, along with Britain's inability to play the role of 'containing power,' – a role which Brook Adams had predicted would be taken over by America – called forth the Truman Doctrine in March 1947. Historians have done well to debunk the claim that by that time, 'the life of Europe as an organised industrial community had come well-nigh to a standstill, and with it, so had production and distribution of goods of every sort'. But to Washington, bombarded with pleas for help from Europe and reports of punishing winter weather, that is how it seemed. The presence of strong Communist parties in France and Italy was a particular concern. Those economies that were on the upswing in 1946-7 faced an imminent 'dollar gap' – the lack of means to pay for the imports of food, raw materials and capital goods needed to avoid slipping back. In Germany, an indispensable market and source of production for the rest of Europe, recovery had not yet begun. When Secretary of State George C. Marshall returned home from Moscow in late April 1947 after fruitless negotiations over Germany with the Russians and the French, he told a radio audience, 'The patient [Germany] is sinking while the doctors deliberate'. He told Undersecretary of State Dean Acheson and Kennan, now head of the Policy Planning Staff, to start to prepare a systematic aid programme to include Germany, what became the European Recovery Program (ERP), or Marshall Plan.

If, as Acheson has claimed, Americans since Wilson had believed that 'something new' had to be created in the Old World, it was only natural for them to insist – once they had decided to make an unprecedented financial commitment – that the 'something' resemble the United States. It is hard to separate the element of vanity from the considerations of self-interest. Certainly America's federal political system, combined with its single continental market, looked like a dazzling success compared to Europe's divided sovereignties and separated economies. According to a 1948 Congressional report on aid to Europe, 'every effort should be made now to lay the sound foundation for a more far-reaching economic federation'. The optimistic assumption was that this would 'produce a considerable degree of political federation' as well. Resolutions had already been introduced into both Houses of Congress in March 1947 calling for a 'United States of Europe'. Congress kept up the pressure on the administration to link US aid to progress toward European integration. Prominent figures like Allen Dulles (brother of John Foster) and Senator J. William Fulbright formed the 'American Committee on United Europe'. They believed, in the words of Senator Alexander Wiley, that the US was 'selling something besides [its] goods and merchandise' in Europe, namely an American formula for prosperity and peace.

This is not to say that the administration itself was of one mind about how or to what end Europe should be united – aside from agreement that the Europeans should take the initiative, and would have to be weaned off American aid soon. Kennan saw the Marshall Plan as primarily political, its goals being to defeat communism in France and Italy, reintegrate Germany, and hasten the Soviet withdrawal from eastern Europe. Undersecretary of State for Economic Affairs Clayton did not disagree but thought the basic purpose of the plan was to bring about an integrated world economy. He wanted the Europeans meeting in Paris during the summer of 1947 to do away with a 'morass of bilateralism and restrictionism' by committing themselves to remove all tariffs within ten years. General Marshall lent his name and enormous prestige to the ERP legislation but kept an Olympian distance from the details. President Truman himself, faring badly in the opinion polls, was modest and shrewd enough to give Marshall credit for the plan.

In his discussion of the ERP Michael Hogan makes a distinction between the free traders' and the planners' views of European integration. The former were the classical liberals like Clayton; the latter, concentrated in the agency set up to run the Marshall Plan, the Economic Cooperation Administration (ECA), were also influenced by New Deal and Keynesian ideas. They emphasised restoring production and creating a supranational organisation that would allocate aid according to a Europe-wide plan. Both the free traders and the planners were utopians of a sort. Clayton looked back to the nineteenth century. Paul Hoffman, head of the ECA, believed in the potential of twentieth century US capitalism to transcend the business cycle and the class struggle: 'capitalism not for the capitalists but capitalism for everybody'.

Hoffman was a lowly salesman who had risen to the top of Studebaker Motors but his method was 'stark sincerity' rather than the hard sell. Walter Lippmann, not known for dispensing praise, wrote: 'He was patently not angry and not frightened, not envious and not scheming, not playing a game and not hiding his meaning. The air was fresh and clean, as if the windows had been opened'. Though handpicked by Republican Senate leader Arthur Vandenberg, Hoffman believed that government had a role to play in maintaining high real wages and employment. At the heart of his message was that Europe must redeem itself by creating a vast American-style integrated market permitting low cost production, rising productivity, and increasing living standards. *The New York Times* noted that in a speech given in Paris in October 1949, Hoffman used the word 'integration' fifteen times.

Hoffman's agency spent much of its time trying to fulfil Congress's wish that the Organisation of European Economic Cooperation (OEEC; founded April 1948) become a strong, supranational body – Washington's interlocutor in Europe and embryo of a federal state. Spearheading this effort was ECA Special Representative W. Averell Harriman, the heavyweight financier and former ambassador to London and Moscow. But Harriman and his large staff, installed in Paris at the *Hôtel de Talleyrand*, soon ran foul of the British. Although Americans and continental Europeans alike looked to them as the natural leaders of Europe, the British blocked all progress toward a supranational organisation. While paying lip-service to unity, London had no intention of handling aid and political matters with Washington through the OEEC, rather than on the 'special' bilateral basis to which it had become accustomed during the war.

The battle of Paris pitted Harriman, described by the American journalist Theodore White as 'a tank crushing all opposition,' and his assistant, the brilliant Yale economist and future CIA official Richard Bissell, against Sir Edmund Hall-Patch, the agile chairman of the OEEC's Executive Committee, and Sir Stafford Cripps, the Labour Government's uncompromising Chancellor of the Exchequer. In October 1948, the OEEC approved the first annual division of aid and a plan for a new intra-European payments scheme, victories for the ECA. But the British, having been burned when they returned to convertibility in 1947, dragged their feet on the payments scheme and were able to postpone the creation of a strong director general-ship for the OEEC. What the British called the 'Harriman problem' flared again when the Special Representative insisted on attending meetings of a new Consultative Group (of member country ministers) to the OEEC. The British refused on the grounds that the Americans, who did not belong to the OEEC, were trying to control it in alliance with the smaller and more supranationalist members. For a time the British were able to fend off Harriman but eventually he managed to meet with the Consultative Group and to advance the payments project designed by Bissell and his assistants.

An alternative approach

Britain's refusal to play the role to which the Americans had appointed it was a serious setback, and prompted the search for an alternative approach to European unity. George Kennan represented one such approach. Basically a conservative and admirer of traditional European culture, Kennan deplored what seemed to him to be the reigning policy assumptions after 1947 – that the western half of Europe should be Americanised while the eastern half was written off. In May 1947 Kennan had insisted that the offer of participation in the Marshall Plan be extended to the eastern Europeans and the Soviet Union because he thought this would sow the seeds of discord between Moscow and its satellites. Kennan explained after Tito's break with Moscow in 1948:

> By forcing the Russians to permit the satellite countries to enter into a relationship of economic collaboration with the west of Europe which would inevitably have strengthened east-west bonds and weakened the exclusive orientation of these countries towards Russia or to force them to remain outside this structure of collaboration at heavy economic sacrifice to themselves, we place a severe strain on the relations between Moscow and the satellite countries.

His colleagues, by contrast, had seen the invitation more as a device to place the onus of dividing Germany and Europe on the Russians.

Kennan and his fellow Soviet expert Charles Bohlen did not think the Soviets intended to attack and opposed the idea, launched by Foreign Secretary Ernest Bevin, of a formal alliance between Western Europe and the United States. After the US, Britain, and France agreed in mid-1948 on the 'London Programme' for a separate West German government, Kennan prepared an alternative plan for the creation of a single German government and the withdrawal of all occupying forces to seaside garrison areas. In November 1948, Kennan wrote that the Atlantic alliance 'would amount to a final militarisation of the present dividing line'. By then most of the State Department believed that Europe needed the psychological reassurance of a formal treaty, regardless of the Soviet threat. The new Secretary of State, Dean Acheson, signed the North Atlantic Treaty in April 1949.

Kennan's concern about the division of the continent and the Europeans' failure to move toward federation nonetheless led him to insist on an alternative approach. In mid-1949, he advanced the idea of two distinct federal groupings: the United States, Britain, and Canada, on one hand; France, Germany, and the smaller European countries, on the other. It was obvious from their attitude that the British constituted a basic obstacle, or 'ceiling', to European federation. To advance that project, and to prevent new burdens from falling on the United States, Britain's limited resources should be used to defend Western interests outside Europe. The US would have to underwrite and gradually liquidate the sterling system but this was seen as a price well worth paying if it meant 'the continental countries would be free of the greatest barrier to rapprochement between themselves'. Kennan acknowledged that if the United States and Canada were to join a European federation, the British would go along. But such an entity could not extend to Eastern Europe. The Russians would never allow their satellites to join something organised and dominated by the Americans, while the notion of a federation 'extending from San Francisco to the eastern Carpathians and the Pripet Marshes' was absurd. Kennan's 1949 design sprang naturally from his prewar Germanocentric view. He saw no point in denying that Germany was the magnet around which the smaller central and eastern European raw-material-producing countries would cluster. Indeed in 1949 he said, 'The Germans are natural leaders and the only potential unifiers in Europe. I am afraid our solutions are ignoring these basic facts'. Germany had to be the brawn, even if not necessarily the guiding brain, of a self-reliant federation. The alternative was a continent subordinated to the big outside powers – the belated triumph of FDR's Europhobic line.

Though Kennan's influence was in decline, the American stance during the US-British-Canadian talks of September 1949 appeared to reflect his view: Kennan had prepared Acheson's briefing paper for the talks. Britain agreed to devalue the pound as a step toward the liberalisation of intra-European trade; the United States agreed – in Kennan's interpretation – 'that an attempt should be made to link the United Kingdom more closely to the United States and Canada and to get the United Kingdom to disengage itself as much as possible from Continental European problems'.

But Kennan spoke too soon. The general State Department reaction to the September 1949 talks was anything but favourable. This reflected the fear of the French that they were now to be abandoned by the Anglo-Saxons. Bohlen, minister in Paris, lectured Kennan: 'We must again permit no grounds for the continental Europeans believing that we have any special understanding with Great Britain and Canada'. According to Bohlen, the failure of the Anglo-Saxons to back France had been a basic cause of French appeasement in the past. That this could not be allowed to happen again was an article of faith to Bohlen, ECA Special Representative Harriman and Ambassador to France David K. E. Bruce. Top US officials meeting in Paris in October 1949 reaffirmed the view that Britain was a necessary part of a united Europe. For Harriman the British were simply not cooperating and should be told so 'bluntly and immediately'.

Secretary of State Acheson himself adopted a compromise position on Britain, but one somewhat closer to Kennan's view than to Harriman's and Bohlen's. In late October 1949, he told Foreign Secretary Bevin: 'Any suggestion that the UK's integration with Western Europe should impair her relations with the Empire and the Commonwealth or undermine her position as a world power would be as unfortunate for the US alone as it might be disastrous for the whole Western world'. Acheson added: 'this did not imply that there were not steps of a more far-reaching character than any so far taken by the UK and the participating countries toward economic commonality'. When Harriman tried to appoint a strong European director general of the OEEC – the Belgian Paul-Henri Spaak – Acheson agreed, but he was unwilling to impose Spaak on the British and told them that the importance of the position was essentially 'symbolic'.

A first generation British-American – his father emigrated to Canada and thence to the US, while his mother came from a prominent Anglo-Canadian family, the Gooderhams – Acheson once compared Anglo-American relations to a 'common law marriage,' something that seemed to him 'the very heart of what we must do to try to hold the world together'. As an admirer of the nineteenth century world economy and former Assistant Secretary under Hull, he strongly supported the liberalisation of trade. Though sceptical of a 'United States of Europe,' he was also open to the idea of applying supranationalism to specific problems, as he said in October 1949, 'a method of progressing without being sure where you want to go'. Acheson was not in touch with him at the time, but this sounded much like Jean Monnet. Acheson had a natural affinity for Monnet (whom he knew from the war), the English-speaking offspring of Cognac merchants whose great market was the Anglo-Saxon world and who had named a street in their town in honour of Richard Cobden.

Above all, Acheson's late 1949 position on European integration was pragmatic. A seasoned lawyer, he respected the facts of the situation, including what his European 'clients' could and could not be made to do. Thus, he said, 'our position here should be to encourage, to help, to constantly remind, to urge all the speed that is possible, but basically to understand... We have to have an attitude of forbearance in watching, helping, encouraging the Europeans to greater economic and political unity'. The 'Britain must lead Europe' thesis faced mounting evidence to the contrary, while Kennan was virtually alone in desiring German leadership and the rapid integration of the East. Isolated on this and other issues, he resigned as head of the PPS at the end of 1949. To Acheson the conclusion was inescapable. He told French Foreign Minister Robert Schuman in September 1949: 'The best chance and hope seems to us to be under French leadership. It doesn't work for us to take the lead. We are too far away'. In late October 1949, he told Schuman that French leadership must 'integrate the German Federal Republic promptly and decisively into Western Europe'.

Breaking the impasse

In recent years historians have cast doubt on the relevance of the Marshall Plan. It has been calculated, for example, that local resources accounted for 80 to 90 percent of capital formation in the major economies during the first two years of the plan. Most students of the subject would agree, however, that without the plan the recovery of production and progress toward multilateralism would have been much slower and more difficult than was the case. During the ERP as a whole (1948-52), Western Europe's aggregrate gross national product increased by over 32 percent and industrial production was up by 40 percent compared with the prewar level. The ECA project of a European Payments Union finally went into effect in mid-1950, with American financial backing. Around the same time the OEEC countries eliminated quantitative restrictions on sixty percent of their private imports from each other.

Even so, in assessing what might be called the 'heroic' phase of US efforts to promote European unity – mid-1948 to mid-1950 – Hogan, the ERP's chief defender in recent years, himself emphasises the 'central failure of American Marshall Planners'. This refers to the overly ambitious attempt to create a single market and to transform the OEEC into a supranational body. Harriman, tired of arguing with the British and thinking about a US political career, left the ECA in June 1950. Hoffman, unhappy about the shift in US policy from economic to military aid, resigned in October. Already at the beginning of 1950, six months before the outbreak of the Korean War, Washington was mainly preoccupied with the problem of defence. The campaign for European unity seemed dead in the water—pending a positive answer to Acheson's invitation.

The panicky American mood of early 1950 grew out of the unity impasse, combined with the fall of China and the end of the US atomic monopoly the previous autumn.

At this time, too, Senator Joe McCarthy began his vicious attacks on the Truman administration. With no American army in Europe, Washington wondered how its allies would react to the shrinking credibility of its promise to protect them. For Bohlen, Europe was 'showing decided tendencies to drift back to its former bad habits of disunity'. From London the Embassy reported tendencies leading to 'the resurgence of the neutrality complex'. The Germans, of all people, respected strength and despised weakness. From Bonn, US High Commissioner John J. McCloy noted a 'growing sense of fear that has been permeating the country for the last six months or so,' due in part 'to what the Germans consider a lack of power in the West'. The NSC-68 re-evaluation of US strategic needs in April 1950 observed:

· The risk that we may... be prevented or too long delayed in taking all needful measures to maintain the integrity of our system is great. The risk that our allies will lose their determination is greater. And the risk that in this manner a descending spiral of too little and too late, of doubt and recrimination, may present us with ever narrower and more desperate alternatives, is the greatest risk of all.

NSC-68 recommended an unprecedented peacetime military build-up, one of whose main purposes was to restore European confidence in the United States.

With Europe seemingly adrift, the Americans began to favour a tighter Atlantic relationship. This was all the more necessary since Washington had concluded that German 'manpower and industrial capabilities' would have to be used in order to retain German loyalty and to strengthen Western Europe, although this did not mean the creation of German military forces, something the State Department still opposed. Accepting this in principle, the French and British were ambivalent about the kind of European unity that might one day leave them facing their former enemy alone. At the tripartite meeting in London in May 1950, Schuman told Acheson that 'it was necessary for some more lasting relationship between the US, Canada and Western Europe to be established' before the ERP ended in 1952. For the British, European morale could recover only under an 'Atlantic umbrella'. Ambassador Bruce had concluded that if the British were not interested, the idea of 'purely European integration' was without a future. As an alternative he recommended 'a broadening of the conception of an Atlantic Treaty Community that will comprise most of Western Europe as well as the US, UK and Canada and eventually Western Germany'. (The result of the London meetings was the creation of a permanent council of deputies to the North Atlantic Council, responsible for defence planning.) It may have occurred to Bruce that such a community was also insurance against a European 'third force' that might defy America – however remote a possibility that might have been. If, as Acheson later put it, the choice was between Kennan's vision of a detached America and the closer Atlantic solidarity urged by the Europeans, it seemed to him 'that we had to do the latter, whether it was right or wrong'. For Acheson the spirit behind this was not so much 'our opportunity has finally arrived,' as 'our friends demand it and leave us little choice'.

Something like the Schuman Plan, announced on 9 May 1950, had been in the air for several years – Clayton had suggested to Monnet in 1947 that there should be an overriding international authority (for the Ruhr) of which Germany should be part – but the proposal for a European Coal and Steel Community (ECSC) took Washington by surprise. Indeed, the Americans did not appreciate the extent to which they themselves were responsible for Monnet's move. Monnet had worked closely with Americans for years, most recently with Bruce and William 'Tommy' Tomlinson, the energetic young financial attaché who had ably supported Monnet's efforts to gain ERP financing for the earlier Monnet Plan. But Monnet's 1950 move seems to have been essentially a *reaction* to the recent thrust of US policy and an attempt to contain its negative effects. Monnet was 'exasperated with the American pressure' in early 1950. This had to do, as François Duchêne suggests, with the ECA's importuning of Europe on free trade, but also with other pressures. After 1947 the Americans had blocked France's initial postwar policy of detaching the Rhineland, extensive dismantling, and strict limits on German industry. When Acheson met Adenauer for the first time in November 1949, he gave his personal blessing to the Chancellor's policy of integration into the West on the basis of equality. The Americans were 'pressing relentlessly' to expand German production by early 1950. An increase in German steel production endangered the Monnet Plan of 1947, which assumed that a greatly expanded French steel industry would take over German export markets and supplies of coking coal. Once again Germany would eclipse France.

But there was even more at stake. In his confidential memo for Schuman on the ECSC, Monnet expressed dismay with Washington's drive to integrate the Federal Republic into 'the Western political and military system,' something the Russians would oppose 'by every means at their command'. Monnet denies in his memoirs that he was a neutralist (although he sometimes sounds like one), seeking a way for France and Germany together to opt out of the cold war struggle, but there is no doubt that he was groping for an alternative to the American solution to the German problem – that is, one that would not provoke World War III. He was also trying to preserve the idea of an essentially European entity, with its own dignity and identity – as opposed to the single, all-encompassing, US-dominated entity that Bruce, for example, had in mind. Thus in August 1950, Monnet spoke of a 'structured Atlantic free world, accommodating the diversity of its three constituent parts, the United States, the British Empire, and continental Western Europe federated around an expanded Schuman Plan'.

High Commisioner McCloy, a former Wall St. lawyer and Assistant Secretary of War, emerges as a kind of *deus ex machina* at this point. Having warned Monnet – whom he had known since the 1930s – that the US was determined to revive German industry, he now helped to persuade Adenauer and Acheson to support the Schuman Plan. Acheson seems to have been awed and puzzled by Monnet's brilliant, somewhat inchoate proposal. Only half facetiously he said, 'The most terrible preparation for diplomatic life is the training in Anglo-Saxon law. That gives you a spurious desire for the specific: you try to find out categorically what things mean. People who have really great constructive ideas don't really know what they mean'. Understandable or not, the French move broke the unity impasse and suggested an unexpected degree of European political vitality. Most important, the coal and steel pool was a means of advancing Franco-German reconciliation and German integration into the West. This is what the Americans wanted to accomplish without knowing exactly how. When Bevin, who had not been consulted, began to give Schuman 'absolute hell,' Acheson reminded him that the French had not been consulted before the devaluation of sterling. Schuman told Acheson, 'You have a large deposit in my bank'.

Having set the stage, the Americans became 'a major force behind the scenes' during the negotiation of the ECSC treaty. Tomlinson and Raymond Vernon of the State Department encouraged a strong High Authority and a commercially open Community. McCloy's adviser Robert R. Bowie, an anti-trust lawyer, worked closely with Monnet in drafting the treaty's provisions on monopolies and cartels. By that point in late 1950, however, both the ECSC treaty negotiations and relations between the United States and Western Europe in general had been greatly complicated by the war in the Far East.

Acheson's dilemma

If the Schuman Plan initiative had suggested that something short of a full-scale US protectorate would suffice to counter the negative trends feared by Washington, Korea dashed those hopes. The war brought dramatically to the surface the mutual mistrust that had preoccupied Washington since early 1950. The fear animating American policy was not so much that the Soviet Union would attack western Europe directly; rather that European doubts – by late 1950 the US had suffered a major military disaster in Korea – would translate into neutralism or worse. Reinforcing that tendency were European fears that the American decision to create a German army would provoke a war in Europe. Mixed with fear was animosity arising from raw material shortages, higher taxes, inflation and falling living standards – the by-products of general rearmament in Europe.

The decision to rearm Germany grew out of the fear that East German forces would attack following the North Korean example. McCloy warned that if Germany was not to be lost politically, it must be convinced both that the United States could defend it and that 'some opportunity would be afforded' the Germans to defend themselves. The Pentagon and Congress demanded no less in return for their reluctant assent to the European request for US help in defending the continent east of the Rhine. The French had told the Americans in July 1950 that they would not 'support the major share of the burden of land war in Europe, unless they were assured that massive mutual support from their allies would be on the spot upon the outbreak of hostilities'. The Pentagon's 'one-package' proposal on 8 September 1950 called for increasing of US troop strength in Europe from about two to about six divisions, an integrated Western army including German contingents, and a US supreme commander. When the objective of deterring and meeting an attack had been achieved, it was hoped that the Europeans would take 'the primary responsibility, with the collaboration of the United States, of maintaining and commanding such a force'.

Acheson supported the individual elements of the 'package deal' but thought that linking them together was a tactical disaster. With public opinion in France bitterly opposed, trying to force Paris to accept the immediate creation of German units would 'delay and complicate the whole enterprise'. Conscious of his leverage, Adenauer had offered German contingents – accompanied by a request for the restoration of full sovereignty. Just as the French government demanded Anglo-American involvement on the frontlines as a condition of its own indispensable contribution, the German government insisted, 'If Germans are to make sacrifices of every kind then the road to freedom must be open to them just as it is to all other Western European peoples'. Acheson's dilemma was how to propitiate Paris and Bonn at the same time, while salvaging Franco-German rapprochement.

Acheson's reaction to the Pleven Plan of October 1950 – permitting mere German battalions only after an elaborate supranational political structure had been set up – was sceptical: 'Aside from the minimal accretion to European defense... the second-class status accorded Germany was all too plain'. But he was intent on reassuring France. Bruce suggested endorsing the underlying principle of the French plan, 'as long as deliberations to create an integrated army did not delay the raising of German contingents and the force would be within the NATO chain of command'. A December 1950 compromise allowed for negotiations aiming at a modified version of the Pleven Plan – eventually called the European Defence Community (EDC). In the meantime, steps would be taken to raise German forces, and a US supreme commander would be sent without delay. The German units were to be regimental combat teams comprising a total of 6,000 men; this represented a compromise between the divisions of 12,000 men which the Pentagon wanted and Pleven's battalions comprising only 1,000 men.

Partly to sweeten the rearmament pill, Washington undertook a major effort on behalf of the Schuman Plan. After September 1950 the French had tried to tie agreement on German rearmament to the successful outcome of the treaty negotiations. Those talks reached an impasse over the question of decartelisation. The Americans now told Adenauer that progress toward the so-called contractual agreements returning German sovereignty would be heavily influenced by the outcome of the current ECSC as well as the forthcoming EDC negotiations. Working together, McCloy and Monnet conducted what Gillingham has called the 'bashing of the Ruhr,' the use of heavy pressure to break down the resistance of Bonn and local business magnates to 'law 27' requiring the reduction of vertical integration in the steel and coal industries and the breakup of the coal industry's combined sales agency, the DKV. Even if its terms were never really carried out, agreement on those issues allowed for the signature of the ECSC treaty in April 1951, a milestone in the history of European integration.

In mid-1951 the State Department also decided, as Acheson later put it, 'to make a bet on the EDC'. This was indeed a gamble, even in light of the ECSC success. The Pentagon, British and Dutch were opposed, while the Germans were even less enthusiastic about something they considered politically discriminatory and militarily useless. The main State Department backer of the EDC was Bruce, whose position was generally close to that of the French government. His allies were Tomlinson, McCloy and Bowie, the US officials who were personally closest to Monnet at the time. McCloy and Bowie arranged for Monnet to meet General Dwight Eisenhower, NATO supreme commander, in June 1951. Eisenhower's much-publicised conversion to the EDC had to do with the need for 'some spectacular accomplishment' to shore up sagging public support in the US for the commitment to Europe, but also with a geopolitical outlook that linked Eisenhower to Coudenhove-Kalergi, Berle, Bullitt, and Kennan: the purpose of a federation was to allow Europe to counterbalance Soviet Russia without having to rely heavily on outside help. Once the Europeans had built up an adequate force with trained reserves, Eisenhower said, the Americans could come home. He told Truman that US forces could begin to come home in four to eight years.

Acheson had wanted to separate the raising of German forces from the supranational aspect of EDC – backing the latter, but not letting it stand in the way of the former objective. Bruce made what seemed an eminently practical argument: setting up the supranational structure would actually be the *fastest* way to obtain German soldiers. The Germans refused to rearm until the 'contractual agreements' had been negotiated, but the French were sure to delay them until their security concerns had been met. Within a European army framework, Bruce argued, France would allow the 'contractuals' to go forward and would accept larger German military units. The result was a State-Defence recommendation on 30 July 1951 calling for the settlement of three questions by 1 November 1951: the creation of a European defence force under NATO; a specific plan for raising German forces; and arrangements for restoring German sovereignty. The US position was that 'support of point no. 1 would be contingent upon the three points being treated simultaneously and within the indicated time period'.

One has the sense that the real complexity of the European venture on which the Americans had embarked began to dawn upon them only at this point. German and general European rearmament had become essential to disarm Republican Party critics who charged that the Europeans were not doing their share, and also to reduce the risk of a Soviet attack that rearmament itself entailed. But the Europeans had reached the end of their financial tether. Adenauer's political survival was linked to his capacity to deliver the contractuals, but this depended on successful negotiation of the European defence force. The 1 November deadline came and went. Frenchmen feared that without the Anglo-Saxons Germany would either dominate the EDC – the flower of the French army was dying in Indochina – or else abandon it to pursue a revanchist course. The Germans demanded equality of treatment – McCloy spoke of their 'almost hysterical attitude' on the subject – across the board. The German government feared US isolationism, also that the German public might prefer a deal with Moscow to integration with the West. Once the United States had embraced the EDC, Italy followed suit but requested revision of the 1947 peace treaty and backing for territorial claims against Yugoslavia in return. The Dutch and Belgian governments feared that an EDC without Britain would lead to German domination and a more detached United States. The new British Conservative government was ready to give political support to the EDC but aimed to refurbish a semi-exclusive relationship with Washington. The thread running through these interconnected European anxieties, grievances and ambitions was that only the Americans – or so it seemed – could put things right.

By early 1952 the Americans had other complications. As Truman told Prime Minister Churchill, it 'was going to be a very political year'. Truman's foreign policy had little to show for itself after 1949 without the EDC and contractual agreements. In a presidential election year, such agreements had to be before the Senate by midsummer to ensure ratification. If the Europeans had never needed the Americans more, the converse was almost as true.

A diplomatic grand finale

Acheson's reserves of stamina and skill were put to their great test during the first half of 1952. In meetings in London and Lisbon, he brokered a compromise on Germany's financial contribution to Western defence and security controls (in effect, the military items that Germany would not be able to manufacture). Though excluded from NATO, Bonn gained a semblance of equality through a formula permitting it to call joint sessions of the North Atlantic and EDC councils, and NATO approved a protocol extending protection to all members of the EDC. At Lisbon the French received the promise of a statement reiterating US resolve to keep troops in Europe and abiding interest in the integrity of the EDC. They also got a pledge of American aid that would help them to pay for an EDC force (twelve divisions) on a par with Germany's while at the same time pursuing the Indochina war.

After Lisbon, the Truman administration survived the 'battle of the notes' with the Russians, oversaw the conclusion of the EDC Treaty and contractual agreements, and obtained Senate approval of the latter on 1 July 1952. (The Soviet note of 10 March challenged Adenauer's policy of *Westintegration* by proposing a reunited and non-aligned Germany. After a series of exchanges and dilatory tactics by the Allies, Eden declared the 'battle of the notes' won.) McCloy and the State Department obtained concession after concession from France and Britain to Germany on the contractuals while Acheson personally negotiated with Adenauer, Schuman and Foreign Secretary Eden the outstanding issues, including the German defence contribution and the question of the international rights and obligations of a future unified Germany. On 27 May 1952 Acheson was in Paris to witness the signing of the EDC Treaty. Keeping that appointment required an eleventh-hour *tour de force*. The French made last-minute demands, including a promise from the United States and Britain to augment their forces in Germany should the latter withdraw from the EDC, to be included in a tripartite declaration accompanying the EDC Treaty. Acheson and Eden implored the French to accept the declaration as it stood (stating, *inter alia*, US, British, and French interest in the integrity of the EDC) and a separate presidential declaration reiterating the US interest in keeping troops on the continent. With time running out, the French accepted a face-saving change of wording in the declaration. The treaty was ready for the formalities – held, appropriately, in the Clock Room of the Quay d'Orsay.

Looking back, Acheson said, 'I think there was a momentum going forward which everybody... believed would result in EDC being ratified by the end of 1952'. Unfortunately, 'the American government went out of the business of being a government for a year,' from the summer party conventions until the time the new Eisenhower administration had spent six months getting settled. What this suggestive thesis fails to take into account is that Washington probably would not have achieved the May 1952 agreements *in the absence* of the US electoral deadline and the temporary leverage that it afforded. The midyear deadline hastened agreements that created the impression of progress but which had exhausted the administration's capital and were of a patched-together nature.

Only four days after Lisbon, the government of Edgar Faure fell over the issue of a tax increase to pay for French military commitments made during the conference. His replacement, Antoine Pinay, hoped to neutralise the economic effects of rearmament, but to do so he had to go cap-in-hand to the Americans and promise to rearm to their standards. Those standards were almost impossible to satisfy and the Americans, in any case, had nearly run out of money. After the May 1952 agreements the whole complex of French objections to the EDC – fear of German domination, preference for negotiations with Moscow, resentment of France's second-rate status *vis-à-vis* the Anglo-Saxons, anger that French sacrifices in Indochina were not appreciated, outrage over the loss of the national army and the supranational features – came to the fore. Inevitably Pinay and his successors tried to tie their support for parliamentary ratification of the EDC to new US aid and political guarantees against Germany. The ink on the treaty was hardly dry when the US Embassy reported: 'The fact that the EDC represents the fulfilment of French policy for which France has obtained US support has been almost entirely lost from sight'. The EDC had become an American policy forced upon the French.

The thrust of Acheson's approach after 1949 was to assist the initiatives of America's European 'clients'. Even as the United States responded to invitations to entangle itself in Europe's affairs, Acheson continued to believe that American power was no substitute for local strength. If February-June 1952 had indicated what US aid and mediation could achieve, the second half of the year gave rise to a different view. When Monnet told him of progress in setting up the ECSC in December 1952, Acheson replied:

> I was glad to be encouraged because the situation had seemed to me most depressing indeed. Last June, I had hoped and believed that there was a spirit and momentum toward European unity, including ratification of the EDC, which would in the year 1952 carry all of these matters so far along the road that neither Soviet obstructionism nor the natural hesitancy of nations to take such far-reaching steps could prevent the accomplishment of something almost unparalleled in history. However, it had seemed to me that the momentum had been lost, retrogression had set in, and that we might now be on the verge of complete disaster. ... I did not see that there was very much, if anything, that I could do now.

Dénouement

No doubt there was an element of hubris in Acheson's June optimism, just as there was an element of (uncharacteristic) self-pity in his December gloom. When Acheson saw Monnet at the end of 1952, he and Truman had only a few weeks left in power. His parting view, in any event, was of a Western Europe too divided, dependent, and vulnerable to be trusted, but too important to be let go. In effect, the only way not to lose it was for America to hold it fast within the kind of 'Atlantic Treaty Community' foreseen earlier by Bruce. Ironically, other US officials were concerned at the time about the possible implications of European cohesion. One stressed the importance of a strong Atlantic framework that would preclude 'the possibility of the European union becoming a third force or opposing force'.

The contrast between this and the view of the incoming Eisenhower administration is rather striking. Few people were more single-minded about the idea of a self-reliant European federation than President Eisenhower and Secretary of State John

Foster Dulles. 'In the long run,' Eisenhower had said, 'it is not possible – and most certainly not desirable – that Europe should be an occupied territory defended by legions brought in from abroad'. Taking office in the wake of the huge NSC-68 Korean War build-up, Eisenhower and his advisers were convinced that the United States was overextended and must return to a solvent policy. Accordingly:

> In Western Europe a position of strength must be based mainly on British, French, and German cooperation in the defence of the continent... The United States must continue to assist in creating and maintaining mutually agreed European forces, but should reduce such assistance as rapidly as United States interests permit.

The idea of a European third force did not bother Eisenhower any more than it had bothered Kennan. Even after the rejection of the EDC by the French parliament in August 1954, Eisenhower emphasised on 21 November 1955 'the desirability of developing in Western Europe a third great power bloc'.

Dulles, an international lawyer, Republican Party foreign policy spokesman and friend of Monnet, whom he had met in 1919 and with whom he worked closely in the 1930s, had called for a 'federated commonwealth' of Europe in 1941. As Secretary of State, Dulles was sure that there was no option other than the EDC. He believed that a peripheral strategy, which would have meant giving up the idea of trying to defend Europe east of the Rhine, would be 'disastrous,' while bringing Germany into NATO independently would not be permitted by the French. He saw the EDC's failure as tragic but was heartened at least when the British and French displayed some initiative in finding an alternative: 'We need not feel too badly about this since one of our great objectives has been to get the Western European States to stand on their own feet'. Later in the 1950s Dulles was prepared to live with a more protectionist and independent European community because 'the resultant increased unity would bring in its wake greater responsibility and devotion to the common welfare of Western Europe'.

Dulles's determination to save the EDC seems remarkable in view of the circumstances he faced. With the death of Stalin and end of the Korean War in 1953, East-West tensions began to relax. Churchill did little to conceal his preference for the Germany-in-NATO solution. Alexander Werth may well be right that, 'The fundamental fact of all these tortuous negotiations spreading over nearly four years is that... all the French governments from the end of 1950 till the actual rejection of EDC in 1954, knew that *at no time* was there a majority in the National Assembly or in the country, to sanction EDC'. Not the least of the obstacles facing the Eisenhower-Dulles policy of European self-reliance through unity was that by 1953 it was probably too late to break the paradoxical pattern of trans-Atlantic relations that had developed during the previous few years. If for the Americans the overriding purpose of unity was to end Europe's internecine struggles and allow it to 'stand on its own feet' *vis-à-vis* the Soviet Union, it was clear that the Europeans would not move very far in that direction, if at all, unless they were given the type of political and military guarantees that would tie the United States down on the continent for many years to come. As Foreign Minister Georges Bidault told Dulles in December 1953 when trying to make EDC and German rearmament dependent on the presence of specific numbers of US and UK troops: 'With you, yes, without you no'. In other words European unity without the American umbrella was worse than no unity at all.

While basically sympathetic to the idea of withdrawing troops from Europe, Dulles had to warn Eisenhower and the US military that it could not be done 'at this time [October 1953] without great injury to NATO and the prospects of EDC'. While wishing to foster greater European autonomy, Dulles had to promise the French and Germans that if the EDC were ratified American troops would stay in Europe – rather than go home. By the same token, he warned in December 1953 that failure to ratify the EDC 'would compel an agonising reappraisal of basic United States policy'. In other words, if Europe did not build up its inherent strength, the US might withdraw. This was a natural reaction to French foot-dragging and equivocation, and accurately reflected the feelings of public opinion and of the US military who were not willing to make sacrifices in order to help those who did not seem to want to help themselves. But it was also a self-defeating position in light of the administration's long-term goals.

A balance sheet

August 1954 marked the end of an era with respect to the United States and the process of European integration. Never again would the Americans find themselves involved in the day-to-day political manoeuvering to the degree that they had been during the previous seven years. The balance sheet of American policy for that period is a positive one, despite the disappointments. In 1947, the Truman administration replaced Roosevelt's policy of weakening and dividing Europe with a policy of promoting its cohesion and independence. America's incessant pressure on the question of integration, its provision of dollars and advice on an unprecedented scale, the sheer power of its example – all of these factors contributed to rapid progress toward the liberalisation of European trade and payments. America's direct pressure on France to take the initiative, its rather brutal determination to reintegrate Germany on the basis of equality, its energetic diplomatic and technical interventions during the actual negotiations—all of these factors were crucial in the timing and success of the Schuman Plan. During the delicate early phase of Franco-German reconciliation neither Paris nor Bonn was prepared to become friends unless it was sure that it could count on Washington for protection. Only Washington could provide the guarantees.

US policy did not work solely to the benefit of European integration. Though it is hard to see how else the US could have responded to European requests for help in defending Europe east of the Rhine, the American drive for German rearmament endangered the Schuman Plan itself in 1950, and called forth the premature effort to apply supranationalism to defence. Having adopted this policy as their own, the Americans – partly because of their domestic electoral considerations – decided to accelerate the diplomatic pace. The unravelling of the agreements reached in 1952, while probably inevitable, led to scepticism and disillusionment in the US. As Dulles and Eisenhower discovered, probably even more than the Russian threat it was the decision to rearm Germany only five years after the the war that led to European demands for the kind of permanent American protectorate which, over time, removed the incentive for the Europeans to move toward greater reliance on themselves.

In the end, the American postwar approach to Europe was a far cry from Roosevelt's Europhobic policy, but neither was it the opposite sort of policy, as represented by Eisenhower or Kennan. What became known as 'American hegemony' in Europe could be seen as a kind of compromise between the former policy, which had aimed to restrict Europe's independence, and the latter, which had desired to restore it. After 1954, US policy-makers were for the most part sincere supporters of European integration but they had reason to doubt the willingness of the European states themselves to enter into arrangements leading to greater autonomy, or likely to impair their sovereignty or bilateral channels of influence with the United States. Along with scepticism about 'purely European integration' came a general preference for the Atlantic Community framework. The Hullian strain in US policy had always been concerned with economic exclusion, but the deeper preoccupation was a loss of political control. Experience in the early 1950s and subsequently suggested to many Americans that, with or without the Soviet Union, the European states, left to their own devices, were incapable of organising an effective political-military coalition and that the European state system tended, as Wilson and Roosevelt had believed, towards egoism and war. Tacitly or otherwise many Western Europeans came to accept this view.

After the launching of the European Economic Community in the late 1950s – and again in the late 1980s – many Americans also believed that if the Europeans did succeed against the odds in organising a relatively autonomous third force, there was little reason to believe that it would see eye to eye with the United States. NATO therefore came to be viewed as a way to promote a desirable degree of European unity – the Europeans themselves had been the first to argue that the American umbrella was indispensable to that end – but also a ceiling beyond which 'purely European integration' could not go. Henry Kissinger wrote in the 1960s that American policy had become 'extremely ambivalent,' urging 'European unity while recoiling before its probable consequences'. He might of course have added that America's ambivalence about European integration had for many years reflected, and been reinforced by, Europe's own.

Selected bibliography

Primary material comes from the following archives:

FDRL – Franklin D. Roosevelt Library

FRUS – Foreign Relations of the United States

GKP – George F. Kennan Papers, Seeley Mudd Library, Princeton, N.J.

Other works consulted include:

Abramson, Rudy (1992) *Spanning the Century: The Life of W. Averell Harriman, 1891-1986*, New York: William Morrow.

Acheson, Dean (1969) *Present at the Creation: My Years at the State Department*, New York: Norton.

Adams, Brooks (1947) *America's Economic Supremacy*, New York: Harper Bros.

Ambrose, Stephen (1983) *Eisenhower, Vol. 1: Soldier, General of the Army, President Elect, 1890-1952*, New York: Simon and Schuster.

Ball, George (1982) *The Past Has Another Pattern*, New York: Norton.

Beloff, Max (1976) *The United States and the Unity of Europe*, Westport, Conn.: Greenwood Press.

Bohlen, Charles (1973) *Witness to History, 1929-1969*, New York: Norton.

Bullitt, Orville H., ed. (1972) *For the President, Personal and Secret: Correspondence Between Franklin D. Roosevelt and William C. Bullitt*, Boston: Houghton Mifflin.

Douglas, Paul F. (1954) *Six Upon the World: Toward an American Culture for an Industrial Age*, Boston: Little, Brown.

Fontaine, François (1991) 'Forward with Jean Monnet' in Douglas Brinkley and Clifford Hackett, eds, *Jean Monnet and the Path to European Unity*, New York: Macmillan.

Fossedal, Gregory A. (1993) *Our Finest Hour: Will Clayton, The Marshall Plan and the Triumph of Democracy*, Stanford, California: Hoover Institution Press.

Gillingham, John (1991) *Coal, Steel and the Rebirth of Europe, 1945-1955: The Germans and the French from Ruhr Conflict to European Community*, Cambridge: Cambridge University Press.

Harper, John L. (1994) *American Visions of Europe: Franklin D. Roosevelt, George F. Kennan, and Dean G. Acheson*, Cambridge: Cambridge University Press.

Hogan, Michael (1987) *The Marshall Plan: America, Britain and the Reconstruction of Western Europe, 1947-1952*, Cambridge: Cambridge University Press.

Hull, Cordell (1948) *The Memoirs of Cordell Hull*, London: Hodder and Stoughton.

Joffe, Josef (1984) 'Europe's American Pacifier' in *Foreign Policy*, No.54, Spring 1984, pp.64-82.

Kaplan, Lawrence (1984) *The United States and NATO: The Formative Years*, Lexington: University of Kentucky.

Kennan, George F. *Memoirs, 1925-50.*

(1968) *From Prague after Munich*, Princeton, N.J.: Princeton University Press.

Kimball, Warren, ed. (1984) *Churchill and Roosevelt: Their Complete Correspondence*, Princeton: Princeton University Press.

Kissinger, Henry (1969) 'What Kind of Atlantic Partnership?' in *Atlantic Community Quarterly*, Vol.7, No.1.

Mackinder, Halford (1962) *Democratic Ideals and Reality: With Additional Papers*, New York: Norton.

Maier, Charles (1981) 'The Two Postwar Eras and the Conditions for Stability in Twentieth-Century Western Europe' in *American Historical Review* Vol.86.

McClellan, David (1976) *Dean Acheson: The State Department Years*, New York: Dodd, Mead.

Milward, Alan S. (1989) 'Was the Marshall Plan Necessary?' in *Diplomatic History* Vol.13.

Miscamble, Wilson D. (1992) *George F. Kennan and the Making of American Foreign Policy, 1947-1950*, Princeton, N.J.: Princeton University Press.

Pisani, Sallie (1991) *The CIA and the Marshall Plan*, Lawrence, KA: University Press of Kansas.

Pruessen, Ronald (1982) *John Foster Dulles: The Road to Power*, New York: Free Press.

Roosevelt, Elliott, ed. (1950) *FDR: His Personal Letters, 1928-1945*, New York: Duell, Sloan and Pearce.

Schwarz, Jordan (1987) *Liberal: Adolf A. Berle and the Vision of an American Era*, New York: Free Press.

Schwarz, Thomas A. (1991) *America's Germany: John J. McCloy and the Federal Republic of Germany*, Cambridge, Mass: Harvard University Press.

(1992) 'Dual Containment: John J. McCloy, the American High Commission and European Integration, 1949-1952' in Francis H. Heller and John R. Gillingham, eds, *NATO: The Founding of the Atlantic Alliance and the Integration of Europe*, New York: St. Martin's Press.

Werth, Alexander (1966) *France, 1945-55*, Boston: Beacon Press.

Winand, Pascaline (1993) *Eisenhower, Kennedy and the United States of Europe*, New York: St. Martin's Press.

The Great Betrayal – Tory policy towards Europe from 1945 to 1955

Julian Critchley

The Great Betrayal

> The federated action of Europe, if we can maintain it, is our sole hope of escaping from the constant terror and calamity of war, the constant pressure of the burdens of an armed peace, which weigh down the spirits and darken the prospect of every nation in this part of the world. The Federation of Europe is the only hope we have.

How strange it is to read this statement made by Lord Salisbury, Tory Prime Minister in 1897 at the time of Queen Victoria's Jubilee, the apogee of British Imperialism, made when surveying the European scene. How different this nineteenth century speech sounds from the anti-European rhetoric of the twentieth century in England.

Yet, England (I make no apologies for using the proper term) has, since the end of the war, aspired 'to lead Europe', regardless of the fact that we refused to sign the Treaty of Rome in 1957, strove to build up the European Free Trade Area (EFTA), a rival trading organisation without political content, and dismissed out of hand the notion of a British contribution to the EDC, the European Defence Community. The younger Tories of the 1950s were reminded of the three interlocking circles: the Atlantic Alliance, the Commonwealth and Europe. Britain stood at their centre; three horses but only one fit to ride. How ridiculous we were!

In the autumn of 1942, a few days before the battle of El Alamein, Churchill wrote a minute of extraordinary foresight to Anthony Eden:

> I must admit that my thoughts rest primarily in Europe – the revival of the glory of Europe, the parent continent of the modern nations and civilisation. It would be a measureless disaster if Russian barbarism overlaid the culture and independence of the ancient States of Europe. Hard as it is to say now, I trust that the European family must act unitedly as one under a Council of Europe ... I look forward to a United States of Europe in which the barriers between the nations will be greatly minimised and unrestricted travel will be possible. I hope to see the economy of Europe studied as a whole.

The Council of Europe which Churchill foresaw came into being on 28 January 1949 (despite Bevin's resistance). On 18 March they invited five other states – Italy, Eire, Norway, Denmark and Sweden – to join. All consented. The first meeting of the Council proper was held in Strasbourg in September 1949; it consisted of twelve countries (all democracies) and 101 participants. The British delegation consisted of eleven Socialists, six Conservatives and one Liberal. The Socialists included Hugh Dalton and Herbert Morrison (both ministers), William Whiteley, the Government chief whip, Maurice Edelman and Kim Mackay, both ardent Europeans, Fred Lee and Lynn Ungoed Thomas. The Tory team consisted of Churchill, David Maxwell Fyfe, David Eccles, Bob Boothby, Ronald Ross and Harold Macmillan. Duncan Sandys (who was still a prominent member of the British delegation when I became a member in the 1970s) took part in his capacity as chairman of the European Movement.

The Council of Europe in 1949 was a serious business. Successive additions included the Federal Republic of Germany, Turkey and Greece. The process degenerated, culminating in the late 1970s when members of the Conservative delegation, then led by Sir Frederic Bennett, the Tory MP for Torbay, seriously promoted the admittance of Liechtenstein into the comity of European nations; an event which led to the distribution of 'funny' medals by a 'funny' Grand Duke. The Council of Europe waned slowly in influence as the European Parliament waxed, despite managing to share representation with the Assembly of the Western European Union, set up in 1954, in order to buttress the member countries of the Treaty of Brussels. There is a third body active today, the North Atlantic Assembly, which includes American senators and Congressmen.

Sir Gilbert Campion, the former Clerk to the British Parliament, was responsible for the physical lay-out of the Council of Europe Assembly. It was not to be confrontational, as is Westminster. It was a hemi-cycle, but not divided into parties. The progression from left to right, when viewed from the President's chair, was simply alphabetical. Members spoke from their places, unless they were committee chairmen or officers of the Assembly. Then they addressed the hall from the rostrum. Paul-Henri Spaak, the former Prime Minister of Belgium, was elected the first President of the Assembly; the Vice-Presidents being Jacini of Italy, de Menthon of France, Kraft of Denmark and Layton, who beat Whiteley for the fourth place. It was the first defeat for Herbert Morrison, who had urged Whiteley's election upon the Assembly. Churchill promptly went to the Place Kléber where he addressed that famous meeting of 20,000 enthusiastic people.

There was another reason why Churchill was so popular in the city. In the winter of 1944, at the time of the German offensive in the Ardennes, Eisenhower wanted to pull back the American and French troops covering Strasbourg – which had been recently liberated. Churchill persuaded Eisenhower to stand firm. The Strasbourgeois were saved from Nazi retribution. Thus, holding no political office, Churchill lived off his reputation, and, in Strasbourg, he clearly dominated events. A villa was put at his disposal, amply stocked with food and drink by a grateful populace.

In the 1970s, the Tory party whips appointed me as a delegate to the Council of Europe and the Western European Union. It was a consolation prize for lack of office. Thirty-six MPs from the three parties would travel to Strasbourg three times a year, and twice to Paris. We went always by a charter-air. We were, as a delegation, drawn from the *deuxième crû* of the Conservative party, in marked contrast to the late 1940s and early 1950s, when Churchill, Sandys, Eden and Macmillan, among many such others, boarded the express at la gare de l'Est, a six-hour journey bound for the delights of Strasbourg.

They would have been pulled by a great, black, pacific steam locomotive, and having taken their places among the snow-white napery of the dull-green restaurant car, they would have gathered speed through the darkening industrial suburbs of Paris, lulled by the gentle tinkling of ice on glass. And how well they must have dined, those great men, cosseted by the best chefs of the SNCF, and comforted by a noble claret! They would have arrived at Strasbourg at a late hour, those mellow visitors of Hitler's war, to be met by Le Préfet, the Mayor and the city's band. Vive Churchill! Vive l'Angleterre! Vive la France!

In the early 1970s, the Council of Europe was still housed in a pre-fabricated two-storey building in the northern suburbs of the city, opposite a park with a sad zoo, a lake and a large building used frequently for *les vins d'honneur*. The dingy building was torn down in 1978 and replaced by a spectacular new Palais. The yellowing photographs of the great men of the 1940s – among them Churchill and his two sons-in-law, Sandys and Soames, standing beside the well-upholstered figure of Bob Boothby, their faces flushed by *les vins d'Alsace* – were ceremoniously moved to the new building. They stand in the congenial company of those 'fathers' of Europe, Robert Schuman, Paul-Henri Spaak and Alcide De Gasperi. All the photos of the 1940s were transferred to remote corridors of the new multi-coloured building where they hang to this day: fading reminders of what was once a great idealism.

Were we British sincere in our much rehearsed oratory in favour of a United Europe? That was the impression given in Europe by the frequent speeches of these great men. Or was it all a genial act of deception in which France was encouraged to make an alliance with the Federal Republic of Germany, the *rapprochement* disguised by 'European' oratory and encouragement given to Italy and the Benelux countries to join the club. After all, the idea of a United Europe pre-dated Hitler who had himself attempted the unification of continental Europe by force of arms. Even the German conspirators, the anti-Nazis like von Stauffenberg, Beck and von Trott, looked beyond Hitler's war to a Europe united in peace. Norman Angell, Nobel Peace Prize winner in 1933, advocated a United Europe well before the Second World War.

How genuine were Churchill, Eden and Macmillan? Was it just 'conference oratory' designed for Blackpool and Brighton, used to draw the distinction between the Tory party's positive position and Attlee's suspicions of a capitalist Europe, and his Government's refusal to join the Coal and Steel Community? It was not enough for the Foreign Secretary, Ernie Bevin, to proclaim Strasbourg the new capital of Europe. Was he not surprised to discover that its inhabitants spoke German at home and French between 9 and 5? If so, it was because Sir Frank Roberts, at that time his private secretary, had had to tell him so.

What role did the British play? Was Churchill's 'support' for a United Europe no more than a sentimental gesture towards the building of a monument to his greatness? Anthony Eden harked back to the pre-war balance of power in Europe, with Britain playing its time-honoured role. He backed Churchill's vision and his sentimentality. Only Harold Macmillan spoke at the time with something approaching sincerity. In *Tides of Fortune* he quotes from a response he made to a questionnaire on war aims in October 1939:

> Many people are asking what kind of Europe one could hope to emerge out of the chaos of today. The picture could only be painted in the broadest colours. But if Western civilisation is to survive, we must look forward to an organisation, economic, cultural and perhaps even political, comprising all the countries of Western Europe.

In the 1960s, when Prime Minister, he was to become a convert to the idea of Britain in Europe. In the late 1940s, Boothby would have had Britain join, but he carried little weight. He and Sandys, who was to become Macmillan's defence minister and Soames, who was the father of John Major's junior defence minister, were in general sympathetic to Britain's entry. The bulk of the Tory party was not. It found the idea outrageous. But, before reaching any conclusions, we must first examine the record.

In *Tides of Fortune*, Harold Macmillan quotes from a speech he made in the House of Commons on the future of Germany. It was 1949. Paper guarantees were useless, thought Macmillan:

> ... the only guarantee is if the soul of the German people is won for the West. If Germany enters a Western European system, as a free and equal member, then indeed German heavy industry can be subjected to control; but not an individual control directed against Germany alone, but to exactly the same regulations as to quantity, planning, development and so forth, as the coal, iron and steel industries of Belgium, Holland, Luxembourg, France, Italy *and Britain* (emphasis added).

The Euro-optimists of the late 1940s might well have read Duff Cooper's famous paper to the Foreign Office delivered in 1944. In the months leading up to D-Day in 1944, Eden and Cooper quarrelled bitterly with Churchill over the course of postwar British foreign policy, with Cooper, a career diplomat with the rank of Ambassador, arguing strongly for a united Europe as a bloc between American power and Russian imperialism. Churchill, who disliked de Gaulle intensely, took sides with Roosevelt, and would do nothing that would increase Soviet suspicions. De Gaulle and Churchill met in a stationary train on the South Coast where the British Prime Minister made it plain to the Free French leader that, were Britain faced with a choice between an alliance with America and some rival European arrangement, Britain would always choose America. So dogmatic a statement made a great impression on de Gaulle (who had also quarrelled with Roosevelt), and was to be returned with interest in 1963 when de Gaulle exercised his veto against Harold Macmillan's attempt to take Britain into Europe. It was the veto, not Profumo's love affair, that brought about the fall of the Macmillan Government in 1963.

Churchill, whose reputation stood higher in Europe than that of any other political leader, in or out of office, was a Liberal Unionist with Imperialist leanings. He was a Victorian, determined to preserve what was left of England's greatness. He deplored the two European civil wars of the twentieth century and was determined to avoid a third. But he was also a nationalist who saw a United Europe in terms of British leadership. The same was true of Anthony Eden for whom European relationships were bilateral, as at Suez when he connived with the French and Israelis against Nasser. He was also a believer in the 'special relationship' with America, which revisionist historians like John Charmley have argued never existed, and which, if it ever did, Eden's Suez adventure swiftly succeeded in destroying. Neither Churchill nor Eden saw clearly the hostility with which Americans like Roosevelt, Dulles and Kennedy regarded 'British Imperialism'. Eden, from the wartime coalition until 1955 the heir apparent, was obsessed with detail; Churchill with the larger picture; Duff Cooper was, of the three, by far the most far-sighted.

Lord Moran's diary entry of 1 October 1954, at the time of the agreement on revisions to the Brussels Treaty (the treaty creating the Western European Union) highlights the ambiguity of Churchill's relationship with Europe:

> ... the PM's fear that America might withdraw from Europe and 'go it alone' was not without reason. When the nine power conference met on Wednesday, Mr Dulles spoke of a great wave of disillusionment which had swept over America after the European Defence Community had been rejected (by France); there was a feeling, he said, that 'the situation in Europe is pretty hopeless'. It was in this bleak atmosphere that the delegates were asked to find some means of re-arming Germany that would be accepted by a majority of the French Assembly. Round the table they sat, doodling, mumbling, despairing...

> ... Then Mr Eden rose and told the representatives of the nine powers that if the conference were successful, Britain would undertake to keep on the con-

tinent the forces now stationed there; that she would not withdraw them without the consent of a majority of the Brussels Treaty Powers, including West Germany and Italy, as well as France and the Low Countries. Mr Eden called this 'a very formidable step to take', since it committed Britain to the defence of Europe. The delegates sat dumbfounded. The silence was at last broken by M. Spaak, who, turning to M. Pierre Mendès-France, said, 'You've won'. Everyone felt that the situation had been transformed and that Mr Eden's pledge saved the conference when it was bound to end in fiasco...

... I brought him back to Anthony Eden's pledge. 'It can be cancelled at any time,' he went on with a mischievous smile. 'It does not mean anything. All words. Of course, I shall not say that,' he added hastily. 'But what is all the fuss about? No-one in their senses thought we would bring our forces back from the Continent'. He paused, spoke of the Russian threat and concluded, 'Now they are going to do exactly what I suggested at Strasbourg in August 1950. Never,' he said, smiling broadly, 'was the leadership of Europe so easily won'.

The Attlee Government of 1945 to 1951 had been a government of national reconstruction. Labour had adopted Lord Beveridge's plan for a welfare state, and the country was on the verge of bankruptcy. Attlee looked to Truman to save Britain, as Churchill had to Roosevelt, and General Marshall duly obliged. The thrust of British politics was aimed at 'low' rather than 'high' politics. The truth was that the British Labour party, with the exception of Ernest Bevin, was insular and reluctant to join what it saw as a 'capitalist club'. Its concern was to build the welfare state. Aneurin Bevan was against diverting money for rearmament at the expense of the National Health Service, which he regarded as his creation, brought about despite the opposition of the doctors. Ernest Bevin was a patriot and a great foreign secretary. He recognised Soviet ambition for what it was, and was determined to see Western Europe rearm. But the idea of a United Europe, however vague, was left to the Tories, and to a lesser extent to the Liberals, as their particular province.

Hence the importance given by people living on the continent of Europe to speeches such as Churchill's in 1949 in the Place Kléber in Strasbourg. Twenty thousand people filled the square; every hotel window was filled, save for Ernie Bevin's. Eden never shared Churchill's transitory enthusiasm for a United Europe. It was left to less senior Tories like Macmillan, Boothby, Sandys and Soames to march behind the blue and gold starred banner.

When Churchill, old and sick, had returned to Downing Street in 1951, the Empire had vanished with Indian independence, and the Commonwealth, which was to take its place, had little influence or power. Canada, pro-British, was bound closely to the United States; Australia was also still pro-British; the idea of a 'Republic of Oz' was then unthinkable. New Zealand sent us her soldiers (the best in the world) and her lamb, all of which was frozen stiff. The African territories, including South Africa, were awaiting Harold Macmillan's 'wind of change' and Iain Macleod's act of liberation.

The choice became increasingly obvious to those who could see it: isolation or Europe? Macmillan set out to convert his party to Europe. But what kind of Europe was on offer?

The concept of a united Europe was almost as old as Europe itself and 'Europe' has long meant different things to different peoples. For many centuries, statesmen and philosophers have dreamed of the day when the countries of Europe, conscious of their common heritage, could forget their animosities and rivalries and join together for peace and prosperity. The Roman Empire, the Roman Catholic Church and Charlemagne had shown the way. The barbarian invasions from the East, Luther and the rise of nationalism with Napoleon the Great, had stood in its path.

By the 1950s, the Dutch had out-lived their period of greatness, and were content to ally themselves closely with their neighbours. Dutch 'nationalism' was long since dead. Belgium was a relatively modern state, the Walloons being pro-French, the Flemings, or many of them, pro-German. There was a Flemish SS Division raised during the war. But there was no such thing as Belgian nationalism, in fact the opposite was true, there was a desire for internal harmony and external friendship. Together with Luxembourg, they made up a community of their own – Benelux – and were in the vanguard of progress towards Europe unity from 1944.

France was still deeply nationalistic, despite her defeats, and the corruption and inefficiency of the Fourth Republic. Her principal aim was to enlist a divided Germany in friendship, duality of powers roughly equal in strength and population. France was developing the bomb; Germany had the industrial potential and the distant prospect of re-unification. France, too, wished 'to lead Europe', and has, in many ways, succeeded in doing so. For the Quai d'Orsay, the Franco-German alliance was the key; for de Gaulle, the exclusion of England.

Italy, a relatively recent creation of the 1860s, had rejected the Roman ambitions of Mussolini, and was content to play host to the signatories of the Treaty of Rome. Agriculturally and industrially, it had much to gain. An independent Italian foreign policy smacked of fascist illusions of grandeur, of Abyssinia, Tripoli and the unhappy invasion of Greece. A country that had lost the war and changed sides, besides fighting a civil war, had had its fill of nationalism. It was enough to invent and export the Vespa scooter and set up a fashion and film industry to rival that of France.

West Germany under Adenauer was eager to bury the past. German nationalism had died in the fires of 1918 and 1945, and politicians of all parties used Germany's place in the new Europe as a substitute for re-unification and nuclear rearmament. In the period after 1945 Adenauer sought the goodwill of the rest of Europe together with the creation of the Bundeswehr as the substitute for the rejected European Defence Community. Germany was to be the good neighbour and the power-house of

Europe, its economic miracle the envy of Europe. The closeness of its relations with France under the Fifth Republic went a long way to limit the effect of France's withdrawal from the military side of NATO which took place in the early-1960s.

Thus England was, with France, the only European country to preserve its national-ist pride. Had we not emerged victorious from two world wars? Were we willing to sacrifice our sovereignty and lose our identity to a bunch of unreliable foreigners? Everyone thought not, save for some of the far-seeing younger members of the Tory party. The British monarchy served as the symbol of our national independence, and the acquisition of nuclear weapons by Attlee served to disguise our decline in power relative to both friend and foe. Our coal was as cheap as our fish, and we had no wish to share either commodity with our continental neighbours.

Only in Britain was the Left, in the guise of Clement Attlee's Labour party, anti-European and nationalist in outlook. The French, Dutch, German and Italian social-ist parties were pro-European. Communists of every nationality were opposed to a movement that could only serve to create a European identity, and recruit the power of the Federal Republic to the defence of the Continent against Soviet ambition. The British Tory party held the highest cards. Its leaders had defied Hitler, and Church-ill had 'won the war'; but its attitude towards Europe was equivocal. Did it go much beyond dinners with De Gasperi, Schuman, Adenauer and Jean Monnet? How per-fidious was Albion? Was British oratory fuelled only by *les vins d'Alsace* and the genius of the head chef of *Le Crocodile*, that luxurious Strasbourg restaurant? There were many abroad who feared so.

If the bulk of the post-war Tory party held no view about Europe, the handful of enthusiasts were balanced by a group of antis that included Lord Hinchingbrooke, Angus Maude and Sir Derek Walker Smith. The traditional right of the party were suspicious of Winston Churchill whom they regarded as a Liberal Unionist at heart (Lady Churchill remained a Liberal until her dying day). Eden was no friend of integration with the Continent; R. A. Butler was regarded as 'wet' and devious; while Harold Macmillan was thought of as 'pink' (indeed, Attlee once said that Macmillan would one day lead the Labour party) and more liable than any of his peers to adopt 'unsound' policies. They were correct: by 1957, Macmillan, having restored the country's prestige after Suez, was moving towards Europe and colonial independence. But the bulk of the party concentrated its fire upon the Labour Gov-ernment, whose social revolution was running out of steam, and whose majority had been drastically reduced in the election of 1950. Only the Tory 'Young Turks' were in favour of closer ties with Europe, and they were, not unreasonably, all Macmillanites.

The high point of the Council of Europe lay between 1949 and the signing of the Treaty of Rome in 1957. After Britain's entry into the Community under the premiership of Edward Heath (who had been Harold Macmillan's chief whip and confidant) in 1973, the European Parliament came gradually to replace the Council of Europe in power and influence. At first unelected, and therefore an 'assembly', the Parliament attracted the more able among the European politicians; when elected, the process continued at a faster rate, although the national parliaments resisted any transference of power to it. Although both bodies shared the same buildings in Strasbourg and Luxembourg, the European Parliament looked increasingly towards Brussels, where resided the Council of Ministers and the Commission – the two bodies over which the European Parliament strove to win control.

The visits to Strasbourg, Luxembourg and Brussels had a great effect upon those MPs of both parties who were lucky enough to be included as delegates to the Council of Europe and the Western European Union assemblies. Strasbourg was the most beautiful of the three rival cities. A black and white centre with its one-spired cathedral, carefully re-created after the ravages of wars, and encircled by canals connected to the Rhine, the heart of Strasbourg was surrounded by suburbs: French towards the railway station; German in the administrative and university quarter built under the Kaisers. The food, after England's post-war privation, was unbelievably good: French in flavour, German in quantity. The cafés and Bierstuben were packed by the Strasbourgeois eating quiche lorraine, onion tart, knuckle of pork and river fish served in a cream sauce. The wines were a discovery in themselves. Riesling that had none of the cloyingness of the German equivalent, Tokay, Pinot Gris and the ubiquitous Gewürztraminer with its scented sweetness. The delegates to the Council of Europe would spend the spring and autumn sessions sitting with a bottle of a local apéritif outside cafés, gazing towards the blue line of the Vosges like so many Frenchmen deprived of their two provinces after Prussia's victory in 1870. 'Speak of it rarely; think of it often' had been their watchword. In 1945 Strasbourg was once again French, and, what was more, the putative capital, if the French Government had its way, of the new Europe.

Conservative MPs were not alone in becoming enamoured of Strasbourg, *les routes des vins* and the black and white villages of the Vosges which looked so much like parts of Herefordshire. Roy Jenkins returned from Strasbourg to make a series of compelling speeches in favour of Europe to MPs of all parties and influential opinion beyond Westminster. He certainly carried me with him when I was elected to the House in October 1959. Maurice Edelman, the suave Labour MP of Jewish origins, became a 'European'. So, too, did Shirley Williams and many other Labour politicians who were later to form the SDP. We were romantic idealists who, *en route* for Strasbourg by car, had viewed the battlefields of the Franco-Prussian War, Mars la Tour and Vionville, but had paused at Verdun, where we gazed through the dusty windows of l'Ossuaire, surely the most ugly building in the world: a long, low, lizard-like edifice with a stump of a tower inside which were piled the bones of 200,000

French and German soldiers who had no known grave. 'Europe' was about putting an end to the civil wars that had devastated the Continent and cut down the flower of German, French and British manhood. It was not, as it was to become at the prompting of later Europhobe Tory MPs like William Cash, Christopher Gill, Teresa Gorman and Sir Teddy Taylor, a matter of the straightness of bananas.

When the Tories were returned to power in October 1951, Churchill, no longer the man he had been, re-entered 10 Downing Street, his attentions absorbed by the Cold War, the conflict in Korea and the rebuilding, as he saw it, of the 'special relationship' with the United States. Anthony Eden, brittle and *fin de race*, waited impatiently for the Old Man to retire, his Eurosceptic views shared by the Foreign Office. Sir David Maxwell Fyfe, who had spoken up for Europe at Strasbourg, was given the Home Office. Harold Macmillan was given the choice between the Board of Trade and the Ministry of Housing, with a party-conference-led task of building 300,000 houses a year. Thus he was removed from the international scene.

Sandys and Soames were both given junior office and from then on the delegation of the Conservatives to Strasbourg was drawn increasingly from the *deuxième crû* of its MPs. In my day the delegation came to be led by Sir John Rogers, who never missed a party, Sir Simon Wingfield Digby, whose idea of Europe was Antibes, and Sir Frederic Bennett, who collected foreign decorations. Europe was put on the back-burner.

In *Tides of Fortune,* Macmillan writes:

> The return of Churchill to power was hailed throughout Europe and America as likely to mark a wholly new approach towards the question of European Unity. His great prestige, unrivalled since the days of Marlborough, and the energy with which he had thrown himself into the founding and promotion of the European Movement, not unnaturally served to raise widespread hopes. Now, at last, after so many hesitations, Britain might be expected to give a definite lead. If what followed was to prove a sad disillusionment – almost a betrayal – it is right to recall some of the difficulties, internal and external, with which Churchill was faced...

But 'betrayal' it most certainly was.

The external 'factors', such as Soviet ambition, Korea and then Suez, were all eventually to solve themselves. Britain's economic problems waxed and waned, with a more general prosperity replacing the days of Labour austerity. But, among the internal factors which curbed any enthusiasm Churchill might have had for a diminution of our sovereignty and closer European integration, the situation remains much the same today. Macmillan describes it as 'an ambivalence if not a division within the ranks of the Conservative party over Europe'. The traditional right of the party was imperialist in tone; the Suez Rebels, with the possible exception of Julian Amery, were every bit as keen to defend concepts such as 'identity' and 'sovereignty' as Mr

James Cran *et al* are today; the party's 'ballast', the so-called 'Knights of the Shires', were more inclined towards loyalty than are their equivalents, the Knights of the Suburbs, today. Labour had lost power after six years in which a social revolution had taken place; today the Tory party has endured 17 years of power, during which the wear and tear of the Thatcher years, her overthrow, and the unsuccessful attack by the Right, helped by Messrs Murdoch and Black, on the premiership of John Major, have combined to increase the fragility of the party. The Eurosceptics include several from among the cleverer of the new Tories and their numbers, combined with the narrowness of John Major's majority, have severely restricted the Prime Minister's freedom of action. In the forty years that have elapsed since the return of Churchill to Downing Street, great progress has been made towards a more united Europe, but Labour has been converted to a kind of Europeanism which governance must sorely test; the Liberals are still in favour of Europe, but count for little; and the Tory party remains racked by its own internal divisions.

Selected bibliography

Churchill, Winston (1951) *The Second World War Vol.IV*, London: Cassell.

Macmillan, Harold (1969) *Tides of Fortune*, London: Macmillan.

Moran, Lord (1966) *Winston Churchill: the Struggle for Survival*, London: Constable.

Konrad Adenauer and Walter Hallstein – the Basis of Trust

Thomas Jansen

Konrad Adenauer has survived in public memory as one of the founding fathers of European Union and has already been the subject of several important biographies. Walter Hallstein on the other hand is in danger of slipping into oblivion, despite the important contribution he made to the early development of the European Community. For ten years from 1958 to 1967, Hallstein was in office as the first President of the European Economic Community, just as long as Jacques Delors (1985-94) who is the only one of his successors to equal him in political and historic importance.

Without Adenauer, however, Hallstein is unthinkable, at least the Hallstein who grew to be such an eminent personality on the European political scene. He came into his job with and because of Adenauer since he had no political base of his own. But he became pre-eminent as a protagonist of European integration through his own merits and in his own fashion.

In 1950, shortly after the founding of the Federal Republic of Germany – Adenauer had become Chancellor on 15 September 1949 – the two men met for the first time and during the following decade together they shared in establishing – each according to his calling and in their different ways – the role of Germany in Europe.

But where did they come from? What conspired to ensure they had such historic effects? What motivated them and from where did they derive the principles that underlay their actions?

There are no indications that they ever met in person before 1950 when the Chancellor gave the former Frankfurt Professor of Commercial and Social Law the task of leading the German delegation at the negotiations to set up the European Coal and Steel Community (ECSC). If history played tricks they might have met each other at the end of the 1920s at some social event or another in Berlin. Konrad Adenauer, then Mayor of Cologne, was frequently in the capital as President of the Prussian State Council. At that time Walter Hallstein was a researcher at the Kaiser Wilhelm Institute for International Law. But such a meeting never took place. The working spheres and the interests of the two men were too far apart.

Different careers, different characters

Hallstein was still a completely unknown young man at the start of his career. In 1925 he had just been awarded the degree of Doctor of Law; in 1929, aged 28, he qualified as a university lecturer.

In 1926 Adenauer was already fifty and at the peak of his professional and political career. He had been Mayor of Cologne since 1917. Since 1921 he had been President of the Prussian State Council, the second chamber in Prussia. His name was often in discussion for a national post, but he did not want to be either Chancellor or a Minister. The centre of his life was Cologne, the major city on the Rhine. It was here that he had established the strong position that gave him a reputation and role at national level. That was what had earned him the chairmanship of the Prussian State Council. As a particularly successful and respected Mayor with responsibility for a major city with an important cultural image and considerable industrial strength, with world-wide economic and trade relations, Adenauer was closely interested in and well informed about major national and international questions of his time.

What could the established and successful politician and the young academic lawyer have discussed if they *had* met then? Perhaps Adenauer might have asked Hallstein's opinion about the proposal he had put forward in 1923 for a 'Franco-German Economic Community'. Hallstein understood business law and Adenauer had referred publicly to his proposal on several occasions. He had also called it a 'European Common Market' and even a 'Coal and Steel Union'. But such a meeting remained purely hypothetical. Hallstein was unknown and his area of law gave Adenauer no cause to consult him.

Hallstein, born in 1901 in Mainz, was a Protestant. Although he saw himself as a man from the Rhineland – his schooling and childhood were spent in Mainz, ending with the Abitur in 1920 – after early studies in Bonn and Munich he went on to Berlin and in 1930 he became Professor at the University of Rostock on the Baltic.

Adenauer, born in Cologne in 1876, on the other hand, was a Catholic. In his heart he was always in sympathy with the West. His childhood and youth were uneventful; he attended the German School in Cologne and with a scholarship from an educational foundation he studied law at the Universities of Freiburg, Munich and Bonn. In 1902 he joined a respected legal practice whose senior partner was Chairman of the Centre Party in Cologne City Council and carried considerable political influence. It was thanks to this contact that he found his first political post, coopted into the Cologne city administration in 1906, and this served him as a springboard for a career that led him to the post of Mayor.

Their personal characters were also different. Hallstein stayed a bachelor all his life. Adenauer, on the other hand, was a committed family man. He married his first wife, Emma, in 1904 and they had three children. She died in 1916 and three years later he married again. Gussie, his second wife, was nearly twenty years younger than him and they had four children.

As a politician Adenauer was always open to new ideas and generated many himself. He was interested in people, their strengths and weaknesses, and he knew how to bring everything and everyone to bear on a situation in order to achieve his goals. He was interested in practical solutions to problems. He appreciated administration as an unbroken chain of decisions and for him it represented a real pleasure. He understood how to use laws and administrative regulations for his own political purposes and he knew ways and means not to be constrained and frustrated by them.

Hallstein on the other hand was interested in theory. Even in his later years as a politician, the cast of his mind remained academic, seeking a system in everything. What was important for him was to develop and create order, to lend permanence to his aims and achievements through law making and through administrative structures.

All these differences notwithstanding, both men shared one essential characteristic: a discipline in their appearance, their bearing and presence which lent them the added advantage of authority. Adenauer, however, exercised this discipline from a position of strength and in a relaxed manner, mixed with a Rhineland sense of humour, enlivened with a touch of spontaneity and in particular a quickness of mind which showed in his delight in the ridiculous. Hallstein's discipline, on the other hand, was much drier, more tense, more contrived. He, too, was quick and could use irony, but it always seemed the result of intellectual effort, the expression of inner constraint.

Surviving the Third Reich

Thus the two men at the beginning of the 1930s, just before Hitler and the Nazis seized power in Germany. How did these two men, who were later to play such fundamental roles in the construction of the Federal Republic and the European Community, survive the Third Reich and the Second World War?

Our knowledge of Walter Hallstein's life before he entered politics is extremely sparse. A substantial biography remains to be written and, in contrast to Adenauer, Hallstein left no autobiographical writings. What we know of him up to the end of the War can be briefly summarised.

His dissertation, 'Contemporary Commercial Law: a Comparative Presentation of Drafts and Statutes' was completed in 1929 and published in Berlin in 1931. On the basis of this work Hallstein was offered a professorship in law at the University of Rostock.

Eugen Gerstenmaier, who was studying theology in Rostock at that time, has left a record of Hallstein's character and reputation. Gerstenmaier was later to be Speaker of the Bundestag for many years (1954-1969) and exercised considerable influence on the history of the Federal Republic. But in 1934 he was already in difficulties because of his criticism of the Nazi regime. Disciplinary proceedings began against him with a view to excluding him from the university and the possibility of further study. But he was acquitted and in 1981 wrote in his memoirs, *A Time for Quarrels, a Time for Peace*:

> The result was thanks to the young Rostock Professor of Commmercial Law, Walter Hallstein. ... He had a reputation as an unusually bright lawyer, as an exceptional negotiator and as a man who had no sympathy at all with the regime. He played a major role in the University Court. Not that it was difficult for him, since none of the members of the Disciplinary Courts was a fanatical supporter of the Führer.

Hallstein continued to teach in Rostock until 1941 when he was offered a chair at the University in Frankfurt-on-Main. Alongside this he became Director of the Institute for Comparative Law, International Economic Relations and Company Law. Together with Wilhelm Kalveram he published in 1942 a volume on 'Social Equity and Company Capital'. But finally he could evade military service no longer. His artillery unit was captured by the Americans near Cherbourg during the Allied invasion in 1944. In a prisoner-of-war camp in Como, Mississipi, he organised a camp university.

Adenauer was a prominent member of the Centre Party, the Catholic political grouping detested by the Nazis. Along with the Social Democratic Party it was regarded as a typical product of the Weimar Republic which was to be swept away by Hitler's revolution. When the Nazis seized power he was bound to face difficulties if he stood by his principles. With his concern for legality and as the democratically elected city leader he acted courageously and objected to the illegal demands of the new regime. But he could not hold out long as Mayor. In March 1933 he was deposed and had to reckon indeed with the prospect of being incarcerated or possibly murdered. He tried to hide, or at least not to draw attention to himself, first in Berlin, then in the monastery Maria Laach. With his large family, which he did not want to desert and which he needed near to him, that was no easy task. Hitler used the so-called 'Röhm Putsch', which was stage-managed by the Gestapo, to rid himself not only of opponents within the Nazi Party, but also of opponents of the regime. In the wave of arrests that followed the putsch, Adenauer was taken into custody, subsequently released, and then for weeks he was on the run.

And yet – one of the extraordinary paradoxes of the Third Reich – he managed to ensure that the Interior Ministry continued to pay him a regular pension as former Mayor and obtained compensation into the bargain for his two houses in Cologne which the Nazis had seized. With the money he bought a plot of land in Rhöndorf on the Rhine, near Bonn, and built a comfortable house of considerable size into which his large family moved in 1936. There he stayed quietly, not drawing attention to himself, until the end of the War, always hoping and indeed reckoning that Nazi Germany would lose. He was of course on the Nazi 'black list' and was kept under surveillance. But the Nazis considered that this 60-year-old, who now counted as old and retired, was no longer dangerous, given his current good behaviour. Even so, when Count Stauffenberg's plot failed in July 1944 and the regime ruthlessly hunted down all its enemies, Adenauer, too, was arrested and held in jail for some months. He was fortunate to escape a worse fate.

The foundations of new political thinking

This deeply felt experience of impotence when faced with political dictatorship, along with a sense of gratitude for their rescue by the western democracies which had stood up to Hitler's war machine and had defeated it, formed the basis of political thought and action by the men and women who – like Adenauer and Hallstein – took over responsibility for rebuilding their country in the postwar years. Added to that was the memory of all those who, politically motivated as democrats or for ethical reasons as Christians, had been killed in active resistance to the regime. Guilt and gratitude combined to commit the survivors to political and moral action, since those who had died had taken it upon themselves to bear witness to history and to the world of 'another Germany'.

But there were still more elements to these foundations. On the one hand there was the sense of 'collective guilt' for the crimes against humanity committed in Germany's name, in particular the systematic extermination of millions of Jewish citizens and the Jewish population of almost all of Europe. The experience of these crimes, which flowed directly from a racist ideology which made an absolute of a single race and a single nation, gave those Germans who accepted responsibility in Germany's 'zero hour' a certain immunity against the ideological temptations of communism and of nationalism. On the other hand, concerned reflection on the weaknesses and failure of the first attempt to establish a democratic state in Germany – the Weimar Republic – led those same Germans to a fundamental review and a redefinition of their understanding of the state and of the concept of democracy.

Both Walter Hallstein and Konrad Adenauer, despite their differing personal development and the very different roots from which they sprang, articulated this common experience and helped to make it public, each in his own domain, immediately after the war. And this must also count as the decisive motive which led them, along with the majority of Germans, to decide in favour of the unification of Europe and for a federal and democratic structure for that enterprise.

In spring 1945, immediately after the liberation of the Rhineland by the Americans, Adenauer was installed as Mayor of Cologne by the military government. The city had been destroyed to an extent scarcely imaginable. Public services did not function; the bridges lay broken in the Rhine. It was an enormous task and Adenauer attacked it immediately with energy and with his sense for practicalities. But before he had time to get far he was again dismissed, in autumn 1945, this time by the British military authorities. The Americans had handed over control of the Rhineland to the British, and the officer responsible for Cologne, Brigadier John Barraclough, considered Adenauer incompetent. It was a judgement and a decision that was to have considerable consequences.

Adenauer was now free to devote his energies to a task which went far beyond a limited concern for the devastated city of Cologne and the Rhineland to a larger concern for what was left of Germany. Since he was no longer allowed to concern himself with solving the immediate problems of his own city, he turned his mind to preparing the future of his country and its citizens. He threw his energies into the founding of the Christian Democratic Union (CDU) and soon assumed a leading role. His first task in the face of the collapse of all state structures was to build up a consensus on objectives and to create an organisation with the material means and a system of communication able to put forward a political programme.

In a certain sense the CDU was the successor to the Weimar Republic's Centre Party, but with the key difference that the CDU aimed to unite Christians of all denominations, not just the Catholics, in joint political action. This was the result of two quite specific lessons: firstly, the realisation that the Weimar Republic had been destroyed in part because democrats, including those of Christian persuasion, had not stuck together, and secondly, the realisation by Christians, born of their insight in the years of resistance to the Nazis, that the essentials of their faith were more important than distinctions between Protestants and Catholics.

The CDU was to leave a deeper mark on the history of the Federal Republic than any other political force. It is not a conservative party in the Anglo-Saxon sense of the word. Like other Christian Democrat parties which assumed political leadership in various continental European countries after the war, it saw itself as a popular party, aiming to integrate the differing interests and concerns of all social classes and groups by developing consensus. Encouraging consensus, continually seeking balance and understanding between divergent tendencies and principles, is an underlying element of the political aims of Christian Democrats. At the centre of their philosophy stands the individual personality, who – in explicit contrast to the group ideology of the Nazis which despised the individual – is morally responsible before God and politically responsible before society. For this reason Christian Democracy is equally concerned with the individual, with human society and with the state as a whole and hence not with the interests of a specific class or the concerns of a specific group.

The concept of the social market economy springs from this principle. It was developed by Christian Democrat academics and politicians in Germany in an attempt to reconcile economic efficiency with social justice, to reconcile the laws of the market with the requirements of social responsibility.

Such a philosophy has practical consequences for the political attitudes and actions of those who represent it. It requires a willingness to understand and a patient attempt to reconcile antagonistic positions. That is why the CDU in Germany, and Christian Democrats in the other continental countries where their parties were successful, aimed to assume the middle ground in the political spectrum, trying to reconcile the contradictions which mark human existence in social and political life, preferring moderate solutions and a balanced, incremental approach rather than radical prescriptions.

Adenauer as Chancellor discovers Hallstein

The CDU was the basis of Konrad Adenauer's personal power when it came to leadership of the new West German state which the western allies now decided to set up. He had assumed the formal chairmanship and the practical direction of the Party as a matter of course, helped by respect for his age. He had greater authority and greater experience than others. Above all, he knew what he wanted.

In the first free elections at local level in 1946 and 1947 the Christian Democrats emerged as the second political force, just behind the Social Democrats. In 1948 a constituent assembly – the Parliamentary Council – was called into being and Adenauer assumed the role of President. The Social Democrats allowed him to do this, putting up no opposition, not only because of his age but because they thought such a post was purely representational and thus unimportant. But Adenauer knew how to make political capital out of the representational nature of the office. He was already thinking of the national elections which would soon have to take place and he profiled himself early as a politician, indeed a statesman, well placed at the head of the Assembly, a man who knew what had to be achieved.

The first federal elections took place in September 1949. The CDU won the elections and had a relative majority in the new Parliament. Adenauer, now 74, was elected Chancellor. The vote for Chancellor was close, with a majority of only one. Apart from members of his own party he rallied support from the Liberals and various smaller bourgeois parties which he included in his government. He won over those members of his own party – and they were numerous – who wanted a coalition with the Social Democrats. The CDU had 139 seats, the SPD 131. A coalition of these two, the biggest parties in Parliament, would have produced a solid majority. And faced with the immense tasks to be tackled, there were good reasons to plead in favour of the stability to be expected from such a broad coalition. But Adenauer feared – and rightly – that working together with the Social Democrats, and particularly with their leader, Kurt Schumacher, he would not have been able to follow the policies which he had decided were necessary.

In the years immediately following the war Walter Hallstein reached the peak of his career as an academic. In 1946, aged 45, he came back to Frankfurt from America. He had been able to make good use of his time – nearly two years – as a POW. He had organised education courses for his fellow prisoners and taught the law courses himself. In this way he prepared for the role that was awaiting him back in Germany. And in the cooperation between POWs and the camp administrators and guards he came face to face with examples of American generosity and fairness which made a deep impression on him.

In 1946, the year of his return, he became Rector of his university in Frankfurt, a post which he held for two years. The speech he gave on assuming office dealt with 'the reestablishment of private law'. He also became chairman of the Conference of Southern German University Rectors. He attended as a representative of his university the Congress of the Hague in 1948, which was where the active politics of European integration began, although he had no particular role to play there. With Karl Geiler he co-edited the *South German Lawyers' Journal* from 1946 to 1948 and was heavily involved in university reform, both practical and legal. At the invitation of Georgetown University he spent 1948-9 as guest Professor in Washington and made many contacts with American academics there, learning more, too, about the United States. In May 1950 he became Chairman of the German Unesco-Commission.

What led Hallstein to the tasks which he was soon to take over and what drew him to Adenauer's attention? Hallstein had never played a political role and had made his career exclusively as a university lecturer and academic administrator. He had published little, certainly no major work which might have given him a reputation as an intellectual force in circles beyond the universities. Yet wherever he had been he had made his mark through the clarity of his thought and the precision of his speech. Through that alone he earned the natural authority which made him appear the right man for tasks requiring leadership and negotiating skills.

Professor Wilhelm Röpke, the economist whose important works (among them *Civitas Humana*, published in Switzerland in 1944) exercised considerable influence in the postwar years on the West German non-socialist political elite, pointed Hallstein out to Adenauer. At the beginning of June 1950 Adenauer invited Röpke to advise him on the Schuman Plan which had become the centre of political debate. Röpke was somewhat sceptical about the economic aspects of the plan to merge control over France and Germany's coal and steel production since he recognised socialist planning tendencies at work in it. But he underlined the positive political importance of the initiative and suggested Walter Hallstein as a particularly suitable candidate to conduct such negotiations since he combined 'exceptional economic and legal knowledge with considerable psychological gifts in dealing with foreigners'.

We owe this observation to Herbert Blankenhorn, Adenauer's foreign policy and diplomatic adviser. He felt Adenauer had made a good decision in putting Hallstein in charge of the German delegation to the conference in Paris on the Schuman Plan since – as he wrote in his political diary:

> Hallstein combines an excellent understanding of the legal matter in hand, timeless energy at his work and that important ability to feel his way into the psychological position of his partner in any negotiation and thus to create trust. Jean Monnet and Walter Hallstein quickly discovered a particularly fruitful and mutually trustful way of working together. They complement each other in a most fortunate manner: the Frenchman is full of ideas, passionate for a new Europe, rich in knowledge and experience gained on the international scene – so much so that sometimes he underestimates political difficulties – and the German, who is more cool, with a deep knowledge of law and economics, his lawyer's gift for exact expression, his doggedness in pursuing his goal, his controlled passion when it came to winning friends or convincing opponents.

Robert R. Bowie, a Harvard Professor who shadowed the negotiations as chief adviser to American High Commissioner McCloy, had a similar impression: Monnet and Hallstein 'developed a remarkable rapport' he wrote, and François Duchêne quoted him in his biography of Monnet, '[Hallstein] was intellectually very honest. At bottom, so was Monnet. He could dissemble, but basically, he really did want to get down to what the reality was ...Obviously, [Hallstein] had to represent the German point of view and Monnet to bring along the French, but both were coming at it like people trying to create something'.

In fact Hallstein proved himself admirably. The Chancellor quickly grew to trust him and to value his many talents. In October 1950 he made him Secretary of State in the Chancellery and gave him responsibility for developing the embryonic German Foreign Ministry.

The direction of foreign policy

What were the aims of those in charge – above all the Chancellor and his Secretary of State – as they shaped the foreign policy of the young state, Federal Germany's relations with its neighbours?

Regaining sovereignty for the state and freedom in external relations were certainly among their first aims, since the sovereignty of the Federal Republic was still limited by the conditions laid down by the Occupying Powers, despite the revisions of 1951. 'External Affairs, including international agreements concluded by Germany or in its name' remained the preserve of the Allies, but following the revisions the reserved responsibility 'should be carried out in such a way that the Federal Republic should be allowed to pursue relations with other countries in as full a range of matters as remains consonant with the requirements of security, with other reserved responsibilities and with the engagements of the Occupying Powers in respect to Germany'.

Once this revision was agreed, the way was open to set up a Foreign Ministry. Walter Hallstein moved across from the Chancellor's Office into the new Foreign Office. Adenauer kept political responsibility for foreign affairs himself, taking on the post of Foreign Minister in addition to that of Chancellor, and he kept both posts with the re-establishment of the Federal Republic's sovereignty in 1955 when the Statute of Occupation came to an end. But the day-to-day execution of business in the Foreign Ministry was Hallstein's responsibility.

Vis-à-vis the Chancellor, who was now also his departmental Minister, Hallstein was clearly in a position of dependency, service even. As he himself put it in an essay in 1976, Adenauer was 'My boss'. But the initial trust between them was complete, and that was far from the normal relationship the suspicious 'Old Man' developed with his colleagues. In this, as in other cases, Adenauer knew his man. He saw and knew that Hallstein was personally devoted to him and that, in addition, they thought as one when it came to the concepts behind policy, their appreciation of what was necessary, desirable and possible. Hallstein was no rival; he owed his position and the possibilities it gave him entirely to Adenauer and the trust he placed in him. On top of that he was the sort of man who was primarily – indeed entirely – interested in the task in hand. He had no family and he lived simply. His interests outside his work were essentially intellectual, indeed spiritual. Adenauer had recognised and noted that.

And Hallstein had for his part found in Adenauer his ideal boss. What mattered for this Chancellor was no longer satisfying some personal ambition and not even enjoying the exercise of power. For that he was both too old and too wise. What drove him was concern for Germany and for Europe, the worry that the propitious moment for thorough-going reconciliation with Germany's neighbours, particularly France, might be wasted and that, faced with the Soviet threat, the unification of Western Europe might not be realised in time.

That was Hallstein's concern as well, though his optimistic nature led him to speak less of the worries and more of the opportunities and possibilities which he saw in the application of federal ideas to the labile European situation.

Given the tense international situation, exemplified by the Korean War, there was a considerable convergence of interests in security questions between the Occupying

Powers and the Federal Republic. That contributed to the generous manner in which the Allies applied the remaining restrictions of the Statute of Occupation and to the fact that the Germans did not consider them particularly onerous. Adenauer and Hallstein worked systematically and successfully to remove what discrimination these remaining restrictions implied. And eventually in May 1955, the Federal Republic gained formal sovereignty as a state, and hence its freedom to act in foreign affairs, with the entry into force of the Treaties of Paris signed the preceding October, which formally ended the occupation status.

The story of the re-establishment of the Federal Republic's sovereignty cannot be separated from efforts to resolve the question of how to involve Germany in attempts to organise the defence of the Western World. The Federal Republic regained its freedom and equality as a state in a process that ran parallel to growing interest in a German contribution to that defence, and Germany's readiness to offer that contribution. Sovereignty in 1955 – like the creation of the Federal Republic in 1949 – was a function of wider Western policies, and both were determined by the expectation that West Germany, given its economic potential and its geographic position, would be the cornerstone of a construction that contained Soviet expansion.

But the aim of attributing such a role to the Federal Republic was initially frustrated to a considerable extent by mistrust of the Germans. While the Western Allies wanted the new German state to make an effective defence contribution, they were also concerned that one day this capacity could be turned against those who were currently helping Germany to become strong and powerful.

How were the Western Allies to behave? They were prepared to end discrimination against the Federal Republic. They were strengthened in their resolve by the moderate and trustworthy behaviour of people like Konrad Adenauer and Walter Hallstein. But at the same time the Germans, who according to popular opinion in their home countries were still not to be trusted, were to be kept under control.

The path of European integration offered the method by which this problem could be solved. The idea of European unification had many supporters and to many politicians and to the public it appeared as the most attractive way of shaping the future. It was no longer just a utopian vision but had become an actual and a practical necessity, for only in this way could the continent be reconstructed and at the same time its security and defence be assured. The European 'idea' offered precisely the guarantee required that Germany present and future would pose no threat since it tied the Germans into a framework of obligations and interdependence which made a dangerous, individual foreign policy impossible.

Adenauer and Hallstein saw the situation no differently from their partners in neighbouring Western states. They, too, were frightened by the prospect of any special or separate role for Germany. Their systematic rejection of any new discrimination through the rules of a 'European Security System' or through disarmament measures or armaments control were motivated essentially by their fear of this danger.

Belonging to a tightly-knit alliance, or indeed to a community of states, eliminated above all else the danger of neutrality. Neutrality implied isolation and hence either domination by the Soviet Union or a common policy by the superpowers at the cost of Germany. The main interest of German foreign policy was therefore to avoid isolation, since, in the light of all historical experience, German isolation led to unpredictability in European relations and encouraged uncertainty both in Germany itself and among its neighbours. Like Bismarck, Adenauer had a *cauchemar des coalitions* and his was called Potsdam. 'The danger of a common policy between the superpowers at the cost of Germany has existed since 1945 and continued even after the founding of the Federal Republic. The foreign policy of the Federal Republic was from the very beginning aimed at escaping from this danger zone. Germany is lost if it ever falls between these millstones'.

What this meant for the manner of execution of German foreign policy, its style and its methods, was above all the need to gain the trust of other states and to strengthen and maintain that trust. Hence aims and goals had to be clearly defined. Unambigious actions, always in credible harmony with official declarations, were vital. Theory and practice had to be identical; consistency was essential.

Adenauer, Hallstein and their collaborators conducted international negotiations with that clearly in mind: the Schuman Plan (1951-2), the projected European Defence Community (1952-4), the German Treaty (1952) and its revision in the framework of the Paris Treaties (1954). There was to be no doubt in anybody's mind about West Germany's refusal to countenance any form of neutrality or any 'separate role'. Western partners had to be convinced – and were eventually convinced – that the Federal Republic wanted the closest possible relationship with the community of Western democracies and was ready to commit itself definitively to them, to bind itself in.

The German question and the European answer

Hallstein stayed on as Secretary of State at the Foreign Office when Adenauer appointed Heinrich von Brentano to succeed himself as Foreign Minister in 1955. He stayed to ensure continuity and to see that German diplomacy under its new leader kept to the course that had been set. Brentano, with his high estimation of his own qualities of leadership, had no problem with that arrangement. As leader of the CDU/CSU group in the Bundestag and a notable foreign policy specialist, he had already worked closely with Hallstein. Like him, he was a lawyer by training and keenly interested in all constitutional questions. As a member of the Constituent Assembly in Hesse and of the Parliamentary Council he was one of the founding fathers of the Federal Republic.

He was just as convinced as Hallstein and Adenauer about European unification and threw himself with just as much commitment into the struggle. He was a member of the Consultative Assembly of the European Coal and Steel Community and Chairman of the Ad Hoc Assembly to draw up a Statute for the European Political Community, a project which failed, along with the European Defence Community, when the French National Assembly voted against it in on a procedural motion in August 1954.

Relations between the new Foreign Minister and his State Secretary were correct. Both were completely loyal to the Chancellor, who continued to be intensely concerned with foreign policy. Any friction, misunderstandings or quarrels about areas of competence were not paraded in public. They were settled in bilateral conversations and left their traces in the many letters which Brentano addressed 'Dear Chancellor'.

German foreign policy now had some room for manoeuvre. In international law the Federal Republic was now a sovereign state. It was a member of the Council of Europe, the European Coal and Steel Community, the Western European Union and NATO and it began to play a specific part in the councils of these organisations. But Germany was still divided and a great deal of energy had to be deployed in foreign affairs to keep 'the German question' open. Nothing was to be allowed to happen, to be written into international law, which would confirm the division of Germany. Everything was to be kept provisional in the hope and expectation that one day it would be possible to negotiate reunification.

Hallstein himself did not play an active role in policy regarding the German question despite his name being given to the so-called 'Hallstein Doctrine'. He was not particularly concerned by the complex of issues around that question. He devoted his energy and attention to European issues. Policy on Germany he left to the Head of the Political Department, Professor Wilhelm Grewe, a specialist in international law, who explained this division of labour thus:

> Just like Adenauer, he [Hallstein] was convinced that the reunification of Germany was not an issue on which Federal foreign policy could hope to achieve any results, let alone successes.

> From this he drew the conclusion that he should devote himself completely to the topic which in any case attracted him most and whose prospects he felt were more promising – Europe. This division of labour presupposed agreement on the basic direction of policy regarding German affairs.

> And that was given, since I shared Adenauer's and Hallstein's conviction that a serious chance for reunification could only present itself when the political balance at global level changed, in particular the balance of power in Europe, and above all when the overwhelming predominance of the Soviet Union faded away.

The 'Hallstein Doctrine' implied a policy which was based on the claim of the Federal Republic to represent Germany in its entirety and therefore actively tried to prevent recognition of the German Democratic Republic (GDR). Ironically, Hallstein had little to do with its formulation. It emerged from a process of consultation and, as State Secretary, Hallstein was of course involved in it, but essentially in a formal role while Grewe led on both the concept and the content of the policy.

As far as European policy was concerned, the earlier efforts at unification, begun with the Schuman Plan and the resulting Coal and Steel Community, needed to be revived after the failure of the European Defence Community (EDC) project in autumn 1954. Hence, in June 1955, only a few days before Heinrich von Brentano took over as Foreign Minister, Hallstein represented the Federal Republic at the Conference of Messina, which was to be crucial for the further development of Europe. Here negotiators succeeded in preparing the '*relance européenne*' which was to lead within two years to the setting up of the EEC. Learning from the experience of the Coal and Steel Community, which had dealt with that specific economic sector, they developed a new method: the goal was the full range of economic activity and the conditions in which it should take place, and clear objectives and timetables were set to bring about the desired Common Market. There was an inner logic to economic integration and it was put to good use: more and more sectors of the economy would have to be organised in common as success spilled over from one sector to another.

To ensure the success of this method, responsibility for the way it functioned was entrusted to a supranational institution, the Commission, to act as an independent authority. The Commission was to put forward proposals for common policies based on an analysis of the common European interest. There was to be a dialectic between the common interest as formulated by the Commission and the interests of the member states represented in the Council of Ministers. This dialectic was to create the dynamic tension necessary to solve the tasks of future integration. The voice of Europe's citizens was to be represented by the European Parliament, composed initially of national MPs and later to be directly elected. The Parliament was to stimulate and encourage this dialectic process of integration.

Such a concept was not uncontested inside the Federal government. The Ministry of Economics under the popular and successful Ludwig Erhard preferred the liberalisation of world trade to any European organisation in which it suspected dirigiste and protectionist tendencies. In discussions between the Foreign Ministry and the Economics Ministry, the Chancellor supported Brentano and Hallstein against Erhard. The differences went deep and even later, when the success of the Common Market was clear for everyone to see, Erhard would not be convinced of the ideas that were written into the EEC and Euratom Treaties.

On 25 March 1957 the Treaties were formally signed in Rome. A few days previously the Chancellor and the Foreign Minister had left it to Hallstein as State Secretary to explain the outline of the agreements in the Bundestag. It was a clear sign of recognition for his achievement as negotiator in delivering the final text. Strong in the knowledge that he enjoyed the trust of both the Chancellor and his Minister, Hallstein had taken responsibility on behalf of Germany for these Treaties. The fact that he also became the first President of the European Economic Community set up by the Treaties testifies also to the trust and recognition he achieved among partners in the member states' capitals.

Germany, France and Europe

In the autumn election of 1957, a few months after the Treaties of Rome were signed, Konrad Adenauer at the head of the CDU won an absolute majority in the Bundestag. At the age of 81 it was the greatest electoral success of his years as Chancellor. It was essentially a personal victory for him and it confirmed his policy on Europe along with his internal, social and economic policies. The 'economic miracle' was in full swing.

But two short years later the Chancellor's position was decidedly worse. It had turned out harder than expected to govern with a majority drawn entirely from his own party. Conflicts inside his party were considerable and now they had free rein. In 1959 Adenauer toyed with the idea of being a candidate for the post of Federal President. When he decided against it, he disappointed not only those who had hopes of succeeding him as Chancellor but also many of his loyal party supporters. They took it particularly amiss that he openly opposed the choice of Ludwig Erhard to succeed him, since the successful author of the 'economic miracle' was exceptionally popular and the CDU had high hopes of his leadership following Adenauer, not least because he was a very effective campaigner on the election trail. But Adenauer did not trust Erhard's judgement in foreign and European policy. He was afraid that the inheritance he was leaving would be wasted: reconciliation with neighbouring states, especially France, binding Germany into the European Community and the Atlantic Alliance, the commitment of the Western Allies to keep open the prospect of eventual German reunification.

Since 1959 security issues had moved back to centre stage. Unpredictable scenes and threats by the Soviet party leader Nikita Khrushchev, particularly during a visit to the United States, had caused confusion. General Eisenhower's time as President was drawing to a close and there was a lame-duck administration in Washington. Adenauer had good reason to be worried about the strength of American commitment. His fears were confirmed by the lukewarm response in August 1961 when the Berlin Wall went up and international relations became critical. There was a Presidential campaign in the United States which John F. Kennedy won – and that, too, was a cause of concern for Adenauer, since the new President and his advisers were largely inexperienced.

In France, General de Gaulle came to power in 1958. His personal authority and the constitution he gave the Fifth Republic, with presidential powers designed specifically for him, had a powerful stabilising effect on France and an exceptionally positive effect on the young EEC. During its early years the EEC had developed at an astonishing pace under Hallstein's strong leadership, but for the French President the Brussels Commission was now dabbling too much in politics and claiming functions and competences which did not belong to it. On the other hand de Gaulle wanted Europe to be organised as more than just an economic community. Faced with the insecurity engendered by Soviet policy and with the dependence of Europe on American protection, over which the Europeans had no influence, he aimed to create a political union and one that would naturally subsume the EEC.

The negotiations for such a political union became a tug-of-war between opposing views of the future of the Community. In de Gaulle's mind the new Union should put cooperation between the member state governments on a regular basis. The Dutch, the Belgians and the Italians were particularly opposed to the Gaullist vision of the Union and strongly supported a supranational authority. Adenauer tried to take a conciliatory position, not only because 'Atlanticists' and 'Gaullists' were both to be found inside his government and on this it was not united, but also because agreement with France was for him more important in the long term than pushing through a specific conception of organising Europe, even if he considered a particular model to be right.

In addition he had been able to rely on de Gaulle, especially during the Berlin crisis. Adenauer and de Gaulle found broad areas of agreement in their historical assessment of relations between France and Germany and of the role of Europe in the world. It therefore hardly came as a surprise when, after the ups and downs of negotiations on Political Union and its final rejection in April 1962, de Gaulle and Adenauer quickly agreed on the Franco-German Treaty which contained important elements of the previous treaty text and set up a 'Union of Two'. At the end of his time as Chancellor, Adenauer considered this his most important political achievement. By creating the institutions which embodied Franco-German reconciliation and cooperation he had built an indestructible basis for stability in European affairs. Binding together the two central member states, whose perceptions and interests were so often opposed, was intended to guarantee that their dialogue would never again be broken off, not even during the crises which inevitably would again and again characterise this complex relationship in the future.

By the time the Franco-German Treaty was ratified Adenauer was already politically weakened at home. The Liberals had made gains in the 1961 elections. They had won with the promise that they would go into coalition with the CDU only on condition that the 'Old Man', now in his 85th year, would not head the government. The CDU had lost its absolute majority and Adenauer had to concede that after just two more years at the helm he would step down. In autumn 1963 Konrad Adenauer retired after fourteen years as Chancellor.

Hallstein as President

There is plenty of evidence which shows how Hallstein set about making the Commission in practice an instrument that amply fulfilled the potential outlined in the Treaties. He did it with enthusiasm and with skill, viewing it as a challenge which responded to his own Euro-federalist ambitions. He acted with finesse and precision, always with the status and prestige of the institution in mind. In his view the Commission, the new institution most directly identified with the Community, had above all to gain recognition and respect in the eyes of the member states' governments, in political and social circles and in public opinion.

The Treaties of Rome were milestones on the road to European integration but they were far from being the desired destination. As President of the EEC Commission in Brussels, Hallstein set about the task of breathing life into the Treaties. He had no illusions about the opposition he would face in this task. He knew very well how rigidly governments and administrations thought in categories of national sovereignty and how fiercely they defended their special interests.

Walter Hallstein shared the underlying conviction of European Christian Democracy which was embodied in the early postwar years in personalities such as Adenauer, Schuman and De Gasperi. They saw in federalism the most appropriate means of reconciling necessary unity with the protection of diversity. Unity was necessary because almost all the social, economic and political problems of the individual states of Europe had taken on a transnational character and could now only be solved by joint efforts. But the protection of diversity was and remains the basic rule by which Europeans can live together: whenever this basic rule has been transgressed it has led to crises, conflicts and wars.

In the European Community – as in the parallel concerns of Euratom and the Coal and Steel Community – the essential task was to organise the unifying factors while respecting diversity. For Hallstein, European integration was not a process of centralisation or a levelling down, but the very opposite. He believed that the historical conditions of the age following the two world wars demanded close cooperation between neighbouring states and their membership of a larger community. At the same time the identity of the different nations and peoples had to be preserved and developed. The drive to establish the Community would simultaneously encourage the diversity that made up Europe's rich heritage.

In the book he wrote on leaving the Commission, *Der unvollendete Bundesstaat*, Hallstein described the Community as a 'dynamic organism that already carries the seeds of the future within it, a work-in-progress' which required continuous application to bring it to perfection, like the great cathedrals of the Middle Ages. In a speech in 1970 he said:

> We speak of the dynamic nature of integration. The Community lays a requirement upon us, the requirement to bring it to perfection. Integration is not a static state; it is a process, a 'continuous creation'. It is not a condition but a development: becoming, not being. Each new solution gives rise to new requirements which in turn demand a European solution. There is nothing automatic about it. Nothing in politics is automatic; everywhere the human will plays a role. But it is progression. All the time new situations arise, new questions are thrown up which – so long as reason rules – find European answers. The European 'challenge' is continuous. And this progression is the underlying, lasting element.

The relationship between Adenauer and Hallstein was changed fundamentally by Hallstein's assumption of his new institutional role. From the early 1950s they had worked as chief and assistant, master and journeyman. When Adenauer took leave of his former State Secretary he asked him, as he now assumed the role of President, to continue his goodwill toward the Federal Chancellor. Hallstein replied – and we have his own testimony to this effect – 'Chancellor, I learnt from you how to deal with those who represent the constitutent parts of the state, the Länder'.

That was almost certainly a humorous observation, yet it does reflect very accurately the picture Hallstein had of the relationship between the President of the European Commission and the Heads of Government of the member states. Given this approach, and also because of his formal sense of what was and was not correct, Hallstein was never tempted in his new function to give preference to the interests or viewpoints of the German government and to seek instructions from Bonn. He could always assume that the Chancellor and his Foreign Minister Brentano shared his fundamental convictions and therefore understood when, in the interests of the Community, he took up a different position from that of the Federal government. In any case they made no attempt in Bonn to 'direct' him. It would have been a lost cause.

Hallstein's relationship with the Minister of Economics, Ludwig Erhard, was more difficult. A little later, at the end of 1963, Erhard succeeded Adenauer as Chancellor. Erhard represented a different philosophy. What always mattered for him as a first priority was lifting all kinds of restrictions which might otherwise prevent fullest development of economic activity. To this aim he subordinated all political points of view. The policy of the EEC – indeed the whole EEC project – was therefore for him fundamentally flawed. He considered that what Brussels stood for was extending French planning to the European level, that is to say a sort of planned economy which he rejected in all its forms, as much for its theoretical basis as for its practical expression.

Hallstein also had difficulties with Adenauer's last Foreign Minister, Gerhard Schröder, who held this post from 1961 and kept it under Erhard until 1966. Hallstein no longer enjoyed the substantive and trusting identity of views which had characterised his relationship with Brentano. Instead of the Community mechanisms which Hallstein defended, Schröder favoured the classical procedures of intergovernmental diplomacy. In the debate concerning the conditions for enlarging the Community, for instance, Schröder, like Erhard himself, inclined to a very large extent to accept the arguments put forward by Britain. He was also a convinced Atlanticist and for defence and security reasons gave priority to relations with the United States of America over relations with European neighbours.

Success and defeat

Hallstein served as President of the Commission from 1958 to 1967. Completely independent of instructions from the German or any other government he pursued a consistent line: strict adherence to the Community treaties, their full application, speedy construction and development of the Community institutions, comprehensive fulfilment of the mandate to shape and implement specific Community policies. In that he was in complete agreement with his eight colleagues in the Commission and, what is more, also within the framework of expectations *vis-à-vis* the Commission shared by the majority in the European Parliament and the Council of Ministers.

This line was so successful that it was not long before it conjured up opponents who for ideological reasons did not wish to see this success and for political reasons feared it. Among them was the most redoubtable opponent of Hallstein's policy, Charles de Gaulle.

During its earliest years de Gaulle had agreed with the development of the EEC and supported it, in particular because it helped ensure that France enjoyed stability after many years of confusion. But soon the development of the EEC went too far for him. It was not that he was against an organised community of Europeans: quite the contrary. He, too, aimed at the unity of Europe, most clearly with his insistence on a statute for political union in 1961-62. In his view, however, it was in foreign and security policy that unity should manifest itself, and, what was more, it was to rest exclusively on the cooperation of the governments of the nation states. They alone were the representatives of national sovereignty.

The General thought that the direction the Commission had taken under Hallstein was absurd. It pursued unrealistic plans, the proposals of 'a technocratic, stateless Areopagus responsible to nobody' as he said in 1965. Such ideas, he felt, were designed to undermine the dignity and honour of the nation states which had set up the Community. It was bound to come to a clash. De Gaulle was pressing for a revision of the whole concept of the Community and was looking for an opportunity to deal a death blow to the '*finalité politique*' of the EEC. He wanted to set aside the Community method and above all to limit the role of the Commission.

In June 1965 de Gaulle found the opportunity for an attack. The negotiations for long-term financing of the agricultural policy had run into difficulties. A few months previously the Commission had come forward with a proposal to give the EEC the power to create its own financial resources, among them customs duties raised at the external borders. For de Gaulle this was the *casus belli*. He must have been particularly disturbed by the increased opportunities for control and codecision by the European Parliament and the strengthening of the Commission's executive functions that this represented.

From July 1965 to January 1966 France took no part in the work of the European Community. That was a breach of the treaty. The French government aimed to emasculate the Commission by pursuing this 'empty chair' policy and to establish quite clearly that without France's agreement there could be no decisions, and hence no EC policy.

Hallstein was at the apogee of his political career when the crisis broke. He had major successes to his credit. But they lay already some distance in the past: decisive, historical achievements, but clearly historical. The European administration he had established had begun its work and already developed a certain routine. In the quarrel with de Gaulle, Hallstein may well have had the better arguments but he did not have the power to see they won the day. It also became apparent that he could not rely on a Chancellor like Adenauer to support his views in talking to de Gaulle. Adenauer was no longer in office. Hallstein was not alone – indeed the governments of Italy, the Netherlands, Belgium, Luxembourg and the Federal Republic were on his side; so were the parliaments and public opinion in these countries, as well as the European Movement and the European Parliament. But de Gaulle's determination, his insistent opposition and his ability to ignore the treaties were stronger than the power of the others to stop him.

In a formal sense the crisis was settled in January 1966 with the 'Luxembourg Compromise'. In fact it was not a compromise at all but rather the confirmation that everyone agreed they could not agree on the key issue: majority voting in the Council of Ministers. The French wrote a declaration in the minutes of the Council of Ministers to the effect that they would not accept being outvoted on questions of vital national interest. Life in the Community carried on, but little by little the injury done to the Commission and its President became clear. For the remainder of his mandate Hallstein was denied further successes in the construction of Europe, despite the achievements of earlier years.

Despite support for Hallstein from the governments in The Hague, Luxembourg, Brussels and Rome the French President finally had his way in 1967 and blocked the renewal of Hallstein's mandate as President of the Commission. That was made possible only by the new German government's failure to support him. Under Kurt-Georg Kiesinger as Chancellor and Willy Brandt as Foreign Minister the Federal Republic hoped to win over de Gaulle with such a gesture. The General saw it simply as a sign of weakness.

Konrad Adenauer died on 19 April that year. During the last years of his life and until shortly before his death he had remained active in politics. He was still a member of the Bundestag and his speeches at CDU party conferences and on many other occasions were noted in the media and had an effect on public opinion. Many visitors, both from overseas and from Germany, sought his advice and appealed to his judgement. And he had written his memoirs, clearly setting out his policies again in detail, explaining and justifying them.

After Brussels

Walter Hallstein was in his sixty-seventh year when he left the Commission at the end of 1967. He was at the height of his powers, respected and honoured, if not always loved, throughout Europe. He had enormous experience of European administration and enjoyed extensive contacts with those who wielded power in the economy and in politics. How could the potential that he embodied be put to best use?

The International European Movement was quick off the mark and on 20 January 1968 elected Hallstein as President. It was an ideal platform for the man who was a founding father of the Economic Community and in an exemplary manner during the first ten years had driven forward the cause of European unity, guided the integration process in the Community and shaped the construction of the EEC.

Hallstein expressed his own view about the role of the European Movement on the occasion of his re-election to this honorary post in February 1970. He was speaking to the Federal Council in Rome:

> The European Movement is a private initiative. Its source of strength is the initiative of private, European citizens and the direction of its efforts reflects this. Positioned on the margins of the organised process of integration, the European Movement is a constant source of warning, encouragement and enthusiasm for Europe. Its structure is transnational. The men and women who share this commitment and work for the common cause within the framework of the European Movement form a transnational society; in that they foreshadow as in a model a federal European populace whose loyalty, interests and political consciousness are focused on the European Community we are in the process of constructing.

People looked to a President of the European Movement such as Walter Hallstein for guidance and encouragement. And Hallstein responded by writing down his experiences and insights in a book as soon as he left Brussels. In its title – *Der unvollendete Bundesstaat*, translated in 1972 as *Europe in the Making*, although literally meaning *The Incomplete Federal State* – he coined a phrase which both summarised his view of the construction emerging from the three European Communities – the Coal and Steel Community, Euratom and the EEC – and encapsulated the purpose he gave to the task of establishing the Community with a federal perspective. In this book he wanted to show not only that the basis of a federal structure with all its necessary attributes was already in place in the European Community but also in what way and with what means these bases were to be developed to complete a federal state. In it Hallstein laid out systematically and with great clarity the principles and elements of the European construction, insisting for good reasons on the decisive role of the institutions which give this construction its necessary durability and reliability.

The book enjoyed considerable success. There were several reprints and translations. A second edition – revised and considerably enlarged – appeared in 1973 with a new title: *The European Community*. Without a doubt the changed title reflected Hallstein's realisation that, to describe what was developing at 'supranational' level and was necessarily a federally-structured common entity, the concepts and terminology of classical political science were no longer adequate. All attempts to use the old terminology led to misunderstandings and were thus unhelpful. Only a close analysis of what was actually happening, what was developing in practice, would lead to an understanding of this new political system and its characteristics and would make it possible to formulate suitable terminology to explain it. The concept of 'community' was, according to Hallstein, at the heart of what he had laboured to achieve politically and what he was now describing.

In the Federal elections in autumn 1969 Walter Hallstein was invited to put his name forward as a candidate for the Bundestag by the Chairman of the Christian Democratic Union in Rhineland-Palatinate, Helmut Kohl. Hallstein was an attractive candidate: he was famous as a 'European' and his name carried echoes of the successful policies of the former and well-remembered Chancellor, Konrad Adenauer. But quite apart from that, this invitation was certainly also intended as a gesture of reconciliation to Hallstein as the symbolic figurehead of Adenauer's European policy. In the last analysis it was Chancellor Kiesinger who had allowed Hallstein to fall in the struggle with General de Gaulle over the correct course for European policy. Kohl was already preparing his climb up the greasy pole to the leadership of the CDU and by giving Hallstein this prominence he was putting down a marker that pointed in the direction of continuity with Konrad Adenauer's federally-oriented European policy towards the Community.

The CDU's hopes of forming a government after the elections were not fulfilled. Willy Brandt and Walter Scheel put together a coalition of Social Democrats and Liberals. As an opposition spokesman in Parliament Hallstein was not cast in the right role. His career and his own assessment of himself pointed in another direction. He was – quite literally – a secretary of state; better still, a statesman, a servant of the state, a man who had learnt to use the range of instruments of the executive and who thought in governmental categories. He would have qualified that simply to add that he had never ceased also to be an academic and a teacher and thought also in an academic mode and with a passionate desire to pass on his knowledge.

In the Bundestag Hallstein concerned himself almost exclusively with foreign policy issues and in particular with issues to do with Europe. The parliamentary leadership made him spokesman on Europe, a post shared with two other deputies with whom he formed a 'steering committee': Erik Blumenfeld, who concerned himself with the Council of Europe, and Carl-Ludwig Wagner, who dealt with the European Parliament. Hallstein himself dealt with institutional questions. Hallstein's prestige and natural authority ensured that his colleagues gave him precedence whenever he insisted for substantive reasons on taking a particular initiative. On the other hand Hallstein was not one to push himself into the limelight to the detriment of his colleagues. He was well past that and had no need to do so.

He intervened only seldom in debates and then only on special occasions relating to European policy – for instance following Willy Brandt's governmental declaration on 24 June 1971 on the conclusion of negotiations for the accession of the United Kingdom to the EEC. Speaking for the CDU/CSU parliamentary party, he declared: 'This is a victory for the idea of a single Europe. It is a great success for the European Community, and that means a success not only for the specific, current efforts in the negotiations which have just been concluded, and we ought to thank those who were engaged in them on all sides. It is also a success for determined, long-term efforts'. And in this context he thanked Willy Brandt, who had added him a few moments earlier to the list of European pioneers – Robert Schuman, Jean Monnet, Konrad Adenauer and Alcide De Gasperi – saying 'I think I have done no more than my duty'.

Walter Hallstein finally stepped down from the political stage when he relinquished his parliamentary mandate in autumn 1972 and subsequently resigned as President of the European Movement in summer 1974. But as long as his health permitted he remained active. He was much in demand as a speaker on formal occasions. He was invited to ceremonies by the European Community. He remained true to the European Movement and took part, regularly invited and always welcome, as guest and adviser at numerous events. He busied himself revising and extending his book for its fifth edition in 1979 and collaborated on the publication of his *European Speeches*.

Walter Hallstein died on 29 March 1982 in Stuttgart.

Adenauer and Hallstein

The 'Adenauer years' did not end when the man who had shaped the state left office, but when he died. Even out of office Adenauer's presence was felt everywhere in politics, reinforced by the talks he had with numerous visitors, through his speeches, both official and private, in Germany and abroad, and through his *Memoirs*, of which three volumes appeared before his death.

It was not by chance that Hallstein's time at the head of the EEC Commission came to an end shortly after Adenauer's death. Hallstein was another incarnation of the 'Adenauer years' to which he, too, gave typical expression. Apart from the 'Old Man' he was their most distinguished representative although – or perhaps because – he was so very different from him. Some essential characteristics of Konrad Adenauer's political personality which left their mark so clearly on the 'Chancellor's Democracy' can be seen quite clearly in Hallstein: a certain authoritarian characteristic and the discipline that goes with it, a spartan rigour in personal life-style and in his approach to work, a strong sense of impatience in pursuing the goals identified as central, a strong sense of history and an unshakeable self assurance based on personal integrity. These characteristics – one could call them principles – bound the two men together, despite the very different careers they had pursued before they met. And, once together, they worked to enhance the effect and influence they had during a decisive period of German and of European history.

More than a century elapsed between the year of Adenauer's birth and the year of Hallstein's death. In less than one hundred years Germany had reached such heights and plunged to such depths as Empire, Weimar Republic and Nazi dictatorship, only to collapse in defeat. In the last third of this period it re-emerged as the Federal Republic and developed as an integral part of the European Community, working hand in hand with the Western democracies with which it had previously been locked in mortal combat. At roughly the same age Imperial Germany collapsed at the end of the First World War.

The new Germany now also has nearly fifty years of history behind it and has reunited with its Eastern Länder. Federal Germany today is in good economic and political order, enjoys a stable constitution and has plenty of potential for growth and development, in large part thanks to being anchored in the European Union. These conditions exist thanks essentially to Konrad Adenauer and to Walter Hallstein who together ensured that the lessons of German and European history not only were learnt for the ephemeral political life of their day but, laid down in institutional form at national and at European level, continue to exercise their effect up to the present.

Translated from the German by Martyn Bond

Selected bibliography

Adenauer, Konrad (1965-8) *Erinnerungen (I-IV), 1945-1963*, Stuttgart: Deutsche Verlags-Anstalt.

Baring, Arnulf (1974) *Sehr verehrter Herr Bundeskanzler! Heinrich von Brentano im Briefwechsel mit Konrad Adenauer 1949-1964*, Hamburg: Hoffmann und Campe.

Blankenhorn, Herbert (1980) *Verständnis und Verständigung. Blätter eines politischen Tagebuchs 1949-1979*, Frankfurt-am-Main: Propyläen.

Dehio, Ludwig (1961) *Deutschland und die Weltpolitik im 20. Jahrhundert*, Frankfurt-am-Main: Fischer.

Duchêne, François (1994) *Jean Monnet: The First Statesman of Interdependence*, New York and London: Norton.

Gerstenmaier, Eugen (1981) *Streit und Frieden hat seine Zeit. Ein Lebensbericht*, Frankfurt-am-Main: Propyläen.

Grewe, Wilhelm G. (1995) 'Hallsteins deutschlandpolitische Konzeption' in Loth, Wallace and Wessels.

Hallstein, Walter (1969) *Der unvollendete Bundesstaat: Europäische Erfahrungen und Erkenntnisse*, Düsseldorf: Econ Verlag. (Published in English as *Europe in the Making*, London: Allen and Unwin, 1972).

(1976) 'Mein Chef Adenauer' in Dieter Blumenwitz *et al*, eds, *Konrad Adenauer und seine Zeit. Politik und Persönlichkeit des ersten Bundeskanzlers. Beiträge von Weg- und Zeitgenossen*, Stuttgart: Deutsche Verlags-Anstalt.

(1979) *Europäische Reden*, ed. Thomas Oppermann, Stuttgart: Deutsche Verlags-Anstalt.

Loch, Theo M. (1969) *Walter Hallstein: Ein Portrait*, Freudenstadt: Lutzeyer.

Loth, Wilfried, William Wallace and Wolfgang Wessels, eds, (1995) *Walter Hallstein: Der vergessene Europäer?*, Bonn: Europa-Union Verlag.

Ramonat, Wolfgang (1981) 'Rationalist und Wegbereiter: Walter Hallstein' in Thomas Jansen and Dieter Mahncke, eds, *Persönlichkeiten der europäischen Integration. Vierzehn biographische Essays*, Bonn: Europa-Union Verlag.

Schwarz, Hans-Peter (1986) *Adenauer: Der Aufstieg 1876-1952*, Stuttgart: Deutsche Verlags-Anstalt.

(1991, Vol.2) *Adenauer: Der Staatsmann 1952-1967*, Stuttgart: Deutsche Verlags-Anstalt.

von Hassell, Ulrich (1946) *Vom anderen Deutschland. Aus den nachgelassenen Tagebüchern 1938-1944*, Atlantis Verlag, Zurich, with a Foreword by Hans Rothfels, Frankfurt-am-Main, 1964: Fischer-Bücherei.

From De Gaulle to Mitterrand – conflict and continuity in French European policy

Jean-Louis Bourlanges

French European policy, as it developed from the Schuman Declaration of 9 May 1950 calling for the creation of a European Coal and Steel Community, has been marked by a strange paradox: on the one hand, it has been the centre of the most lively controversy, dividing political parties and public opinion on at least four significant occasions – in 1954, 1965, 1979 and 1992. On the other hand, it has been characterised by impressive continuity through a succession of regimes, majorities and leaders, surviving the collapse of the Fourth Republic and the arrival of de Gaulle, the sworn enemy of any attempt to abandon state sovereignty, surviving also the testing change to socialism in 1981 and a striking but short-lived change in national economic policy. Disagreement and yet continuity in France's approach to Europe, or – put another way – agreement on European action despite the discontinuity of regimes and majorities: that appears to be the strange course of events for close on half a century. But, like all paradoxes, further analysis can throw some light on its hidden constituent parts.

From Robert Schuman to Charles de Gaulle

From the time of the Schuman Declaration in 1950 to de Gaulle's return to power in 1958, France endured weak government characterised by the absolute power of the National Assembly, fragile governing majorities and growing instability of executive authority. The Republic was faced with a double challenge: on the extreme left, the Communist Party, and on the right, the Gaullists within the RPF (Rassemblement du Peuple Français). Then, from 1956, there were the Poujadists, small businessmen and skilled workers in revolt against the tax authorities and the bureaucracy; soon to be followed by nationalist agitators attacking the institutions of the state in the name of 'Algérie française'. The Republic, which had survived the revolutionary strikes of 1947, overcome the Gaullist surge of 1951, and marginalised the Poujadists in 1956, collapsed nonetheless in 1958 under the weight of contradictions inherent in the Algerian issue.

Yet it is remarkable that a political construction with such weak institutions as the Fourth Republic could have produced such an impressive record in the area of European affairs. The Coal and Steel Community following the Schuman Declaration, the European Defence Community and the project for European Political Union (although these two failed), the Messina Conference in 1955 leading to the Treaty of Rome and the establishment of the Common Market and of Euratom: this series of successes as well as failures is an impressive record of activity and achievement.

It is the result of a series of battles between two groups of actors on the French political stage. On the one hand, placed at the core of the system, there were the parties of the 'Third Force', Christian Democrats grouped within the MRP (Mouvement Républicain Populaire) and Socialists in the SFIO (French Section of the Workers' International), sharing with each other, and some others, the main responsibilities of office, and sharing, despite divergences of view on many other issues, the same European enthusiasm. It was, for instance, governments dominated by the MRP which led the European dance from 1950 to 1955 and then Socialists who played a leading role in negotiating and concluding the Treaty of Rome. Outside this core, on either side of the parties in power, were two strong nationalist movements, the Gaullists and the Communists, who, while theoretically in the minority, could from time to time encroach enough on the moderate right and on the non-Communist left to cause difficulties for the fragile pro-European majorities of the Fourth Republic – as happened, for instance, on 30 August 1954 when the Chamber refused to ratify the texts establishing the European Defence Community.

The arguments of the anti-Europeans at that time ran along two distinct tracks. Firstly, there was the fear of Germany, which led Communist MPs, for example, to call the Foreign Minister, Robert Schuman, 'Boche' when he rose to speak, because he came from Lorraine and was born inside the German Empire before the First World War. Secondly, and less hysterically, there was the line of argument that led the Gaullist MP, Gaston Palewski, to denounce the logic of the European Defence Community on the 'only known example of the conqueror demanding and obtaining parity with the conquered'. More fundamentally, opposition to the process of European integration was based on the defence of national sovereignty, and this coincided with an essential component of the French mindset, a way of thinking which, in both Republican and Poujadist guise, had been in many respects the dominant ideology of the nation since 1792. It was in the name of just such a popular identification of the power of the people and the sovereignty of the nation that Pierre Mendès-France abandoned the project for the European Defence Community to its sad fate in Parliament in 1954 and that, three years later, he opposed the ratification of the Treaty of Rome.

In 1958 everything was turned on its head. As the Fourth Republic gave way to the Fifth, the President was given pre-eminence over both the government and the parliament. Then de Gaulle, vigorously opposed to the European treaties during the Fourth Republic, decided without hesitation and without delay to endorse them. This *volte-face*, which surprised many observers though not Jean Monnet, sprang from two sources. Born in Lille, de Gaulle was a man from the north of the country, from the frontier traditionally exposed to the invader. Like Charlemagne and like Robert Schuman, he was a child of the old Frankish region. He spoke German, learnt at military college at Saint-Cyr, where they taught the language of France's 'hereditary enemy', and he chose a military career because he knew better than most that the historic problem of the Gauls has always been to keep the peace on the eastern border. Keeping faith with the spirit of the Treaty of Westphalia, he was in favour of breaking Germany into several smaller states after 1945, but when he returned to power thirteen years later he could not fail to see that this project was impractical in the contemporary situation. As far as the French and the Germans were concerned, there could be no mid-point between relations based on mistrust, intimidation and domination on the one hand and confidence, friendship and solidarity on the other. This is in marked contrast to British perceptions: the closeness, intensity and permanence of the German threat persuade the French to practise a policy of 'all or nothing' in relation to their neighbour across the Rhine. Across the Channel, however, there is a tendency to balance the German threat against the French threat, to fear too close an agreement between the enemies of yesterday's war and to prefer the balance of power, however temporary or fragile, to the ever closer union of the peoples of the continent. With this brutal but logical reversal from being opposed to being in favour, the General set about energetically wooing the Germans, claiming for himself the mantle of the previous Republic in this respect. The friendship between elder statesmen as personified in his own relations with the German Chancellor, Adenauer, embedded Franco-German reconciliation in popular support.

Gaullism was also characterised by another feature: the desire to modernise, a profound sense of movement, innovation and competition, which led it to despise the tradition of French protectionism and the excessive claims for protection by economic actors. De Gaulle put it like this: 'The French are strong, but they do not know it'. He decided, therefore, to play the card of opening the frontiers to international competition. His sense of nationalism encouraged him to accept the constraints and opportunities offered by of the Common Market, a modernising nationalism which substituted the logic of economic development for that of territorial gain. He preferred the prospect of dynamic economic change on the American or German model to an out-dated grandeur based on administrative and military control of extensive colonies. France's European commitment was, and is, in many respects a sort of 'ersatz', a substitute designed to help the French forget the loss of a colonial empire which de Gaulle himself had the courage to wind up.

Hence, while his predecessors had resigned themselves to postponing the date of entry into force of the Treaties because of the financial crisis, the new Head of State decided that the Treaties, which he would certainly never have signed, should be applied without delay. De Gaulle's complex character escapes all simplistic assessments, despite his emotional sense of history which seems to encourage uni-dimensional interpretation. His actions suggest the conclusion that he was at one and the same time both the most and the least pro-European of the leaders of his time.

He was without doubt more European than his partners in as far as he saw himself in the 1960s as the most committed supporter of deepening the European project politically, a fact which explains his no less ferocious opposition to widening the Community to include the United Kingdom and the EFTA states. Sensing immediately one of the underlying ambiguities of Jean Monnet's project, de Gaulle refused to the end to reduce the European project simply to its economic dimension and to exclude from the field of joint endeavour any attempt to create what we call today a common foreign and security policy. Doubtless the Founding Fathers of the Community could argue that political and military pre-occupations were not wholly absent from the initial project, since the Schuman Declaration had clearly presented economic integration as a step along a path which would lead, thanks to patiently organised shared experience – *solidarités de fait* – to a real political federation. The European Defence Community had also underlined this ambitious European perspective as far as security and defence were concerned.

But de Gaulle was right to point out that Monnet's method over-estimated the possibilities of a gradualist approach towards European Union and underestimated the difficulties. Those difficulties are inherent in moving from the sphere of economics, which is susceptible to rational discussion of the means leading to joint development and common prosperity, to the political domain which demands what are inevitably more difficult agreements on aims and objectives, hence on popular perceptions of legitimate interests. The General had no difficulty in demonstrating that the European Defence Community, at least in its early years, could hardly be more than a military instrument politically controlled by the mighty American ally. It would have clashed with the elementary principle of Clausewitz that 'war is nothing more than the continuation of politics by other means.' De Gaulle's conclusion was that a European military instrument must necessarily be subordinated to a European political authority. Anything else was unimaginable and unacceptable.

The Fouchet Plan, which was designed to reflect Gaullist political ambitions in this area, aroused opposition, outright or covert, from all of France's partners. Perhaps this was less because of its inter-governmental character, which bears in fact a striking resemblance to the second pillar of the Maastricht Treaty, than because it sinned against one of the fundamental principles of the European construction, the separation of economic affairs from security and defence issues. The former were the province of the Community; the latter were to remain the province of the Atlantic Alliance, that is to say, the United States of America. None of France's five partners in the Community at that time was prepared to countenance the affirmation of a European defence identity which might have had a de-stabilising effect on solidarity across the Atlantic. It was left to the Dutch, in the person of Joseph Luns, to remind everyone of this situation. They and he did it with a firmness and determination that could only come from a state with four hundred years of history, as firmly convinced of its national interests as France was of its own. In the end it was the machiavellian de Gaulle rather than that disciple of Saint-Simon, Jean Monnet, who placed the vital necessity of giving the old continent its specific political dimension most firmly at the centre of his pre-occupations.

A series of events in the early 1960s at the end of his first period in office served to turn the General's attention to some extent away from the immediacy of France's European neighbours towards the Soviet Union and a diplomatic offensive reflecting solidarity with the Third World: the failure of the Fouchet Plan in the spring of 1962, the moral break between the General and his European partners following his veto of the British application in January 1963, the succession of the Atlanticist Erhard as Chancellor in the Federal Republic eight months later, taking over from the Europeanist Adenauer, the deteriorating situation of the war in Indo-China, tensions with the United States and, finally, new possibilities offered to French diplomacy by the end of the Algerian conflict. Yet it is significant that, even while this opening to a wider Europe 'from the Atlantic to the Urals' and to the developing world was in progress, de Gaulle put his energy into pleading the case for a specific organisation for Western Europe, confirming the pre-eminence of the largest states in the Community above the others. In his view, a larger Europe should not be allowed to raise the spectre of instability, with potential advantage for the East, unless the Western part of the old continent could present a united front *vis-à-vis* the Soviet Union. In this dual movement – opening to the East and strengthening ties in the West – it is tempting to see a political pre-figuration of the 'hard core' dear to Karl Lamers and of the 'Europe of concentric circles' proposed by Edouard Balladur.

But one can argue that if de Gaulle was in many ways a courageous European, he was not equally or always correct in the approach he took to the issues and challenges he faced. In as far as his conservatism *vis-à-vis* the European institutions and his implacable hostility to all forms of supranational integration slowed down the building of Europe, it also paralysed his own grand design for a 'European Europe' by undermining his attempts to give it durable form. Between 1958 and 1969 there are innumerable episodes, both amusing and dramatic, which illustrate the Gaullist phobia concerning anything which symbolised the effort of Europeans to go beyond the 'concert of nations' and purely inter-governmental practices. There was the famous quarrel with Walter Hallstein, the first President of the Commission, caricatured as the 'red carpet quarrel'; the resignation of MRP ministers in the first

Pompidou government when de Gaulle ironically cast doubt on European integration at a press conference on 19 March 1962 at the Elysée; and the crisis of the 'empty chair' in mid-1965, designed to block moves to qualified majority voting in the Council of Ministers as foreseen in the Treaty. This crisis was resolved at the start of 1966 by the so-called Luxembourg Compromise by which France unilaterally declared that it refused to submit to a majority vote whenever it deemed that its vital interests were threatened by a proposed decision.

With the benefit of hindsight, what is a fair assessment of de Gaulle's dramatic step? From the point of view of the European project, the quarrel of the 'empty chair' and the Luxembourg Compromise without a doubt cost the enterprise nearly twenty years, and in the 1970s it did nothing to prevent the growing risks of paralysis inside the Community as the number of members increased. But, from the point of view of French interests as de Gaulle appreciated them, the balance sheet is hardly any more favourable. In order to protect himself from a danger which was to a large extent imaginary – being put in a minority on a vital issue which other member states could not in any case override – he strengthened unanimity as a rule for decision-making and blocked greater progress towards continental integration. In the end this made the accession of the United Kingdom inevitable, since she was happy to see the Community falling back once more into inter-governmental ways, and it contributed in no small measure to the collapse of the grand 'neocarolingian' design with which the General and the Chancellor had been credited a few years previously. In short, the crisis of 1965 caught France in a contradiction which, thirty years later, it had still not resolved. France must choose between her proclaimed ambition to create a strong Europe and her tenacious attachment to weak European institutions.

For de Gaulle it was probably true that tactical considerations did not have sufficient weight when put in the balance against considerations of principle. The latter were sufficiently important in his eyes to lead him to ignore – with a gesture of disdain – any negative consequences resulting from his decisions. What was at stake was the sovereignty of France: nothing could justify it being insulted, questioned or even shared in common with the sovereignty of France's partners. What de Gaulle refused in 1965 was the sharing of power. He refused to recognise the right of others to have a say in French affairs in exchange for France's right to have a say in theirs. And this is at one and the same time the central thesis and the essential limit of the Gaullist enterprise: the assumption that sovereignty is defined in the last resort in a negative way, by not being dependent on others, and not in a positive way, by a state's capacity to influence and guide others. There are numerous phrases used in the French political debate which express this protectionist, introverted, even anguished concept of sovereignty: 'national independence', 'a nation with its hands free', 'territorial integrity' – all phrases related to the nightmare of 1940 and repeated in an attempt to prevent its recurrence. What they all have in common is their concentration on an effort to safeguard France from any form of external influence, to preserve France jealously like a sanctuary from the risks of contamination brought by increased exchanges and mutual participation which would result from putting sovereign powers in common.

A psychoanalyst might well have much to say about this excessive cult of sovereignty guarded like virginity. It is not easy to distance it from the Marian imagery with which, like a halo, the General illustrated his devotion to France.

But it would be unwise to press too far along this particular track and more profitable to compare the Gaullist view of sovereignty to that of a property owner surveying his estates. Alas, it reflects a completely outdated view of political organisation. Modern states simply are not like a series of fields, laid out one beside the other and each separately owned and subject to a distinct and exclusive sovereign authority. Paradoxically, this view, which assimilates the nation to one vast estate, protected from its neighbour by a frontier as impenetrable as possible, is the very opposite of the General's strategic vision, for he was the greatest critic of the static Maginot line, an expert in mobile warfare and a master of psychological and political manipulation within complex systems. Sovereignty conceived as independence is a legally archaic concept, descended directly from a nineteenth-century view of rural France. Sovereignty conceived as influence is what is required when post-modern societies share power in complex relationships. The outdated concept could not be more opposed to the strategic and economic modernity of view of a man such as de Gaulle, who pursued further than any before him the policy of opening the national frontiers, accepting the challenge of international competition and the inevitable interpenetration of national economies in finance, industry and trade.

From Georges Pompidou to François Mitterrand

After years of tension between France and her partners, the two successors of General de Gaulle – Georges Pompidou (1969-1974) and Valéry Giscard d'Estaing (1974-81) – both pursued these goals in different, indeed opposite, ways. For Pompidou, it was by enlarging the Community to bring in the United Kingdom, Denmark and Ireland; for Giscard d'Estaing it was – despite the accession of Greece – through deepening the Community's responsibilities and strengthening the institutions. The presidential term of Pompidou, cut short by his death, seems in some respects a parenthesis in French European policy. The early 1970s were marked by the President's evident reserve *vis-à-vis* Germany and by his concern to open the Community to include the United Kingdom. In contrast to de Gaulle, Pompidou came from the Midi and typically for this leader from the south of France relations with Germany were less emotional, more distant than those of his illustrious predecessor. By an unfortunate twist of fate, this southern conservative, steeped in classical notions of moderation, found himself matched with Willy Brandt as Chancellor, the most romantic, northern and the most left-wing of post-war German statesmen. There never was a personal rapport between the French President and the German Chancellor, and the *entente* between the two peoples was put on hold.

Franco-British *rapprochement* took place in this context without any illusions, allowing Britain and her two EFTA partners into the Community. Apart from the tactical advantage of renewing contact with the existing members of the club, Pompidou counted on two further gains following Britain's accession: an insurance against German hegemony, which otherwise seemed to him the inevitable result of the evolution of the balance of forces between the two countries, and a shield against any temptation towards a supranational development of the Community. Both these objectives were essentially negative, and they marked the moment when French policy towards Europe was closest to that of her new British partner.

But it was only a relatively brief moment, since Giscard d'Estaing, who was only forty-eight when he was elected President in 1974, speedily renewed the continental tradition of French European policy. The young President was the product of two particular political experiences. Under the Fourth Republic he made his parliamentary début in a moderate, liberal grouping committed to European integration and this led him to assume the inheritance of the Founding Fathers, joining Jean Monnet's Committee for the United States of Europe. Under the Fifth Republic he made a personal commitment to General de Gaulle, voting against the majority of his party colleagues in Parliament, and subsequently worked with the government. Nobody was in a better position than he was to relaunch attempts to deepen the Community, bringing together Robert Schuman's federal dream and the Gaullist plan for a 'European Europe' under the leadership of France and Germany. Thanks to his personal relations with Helmut Schmidt, the Franco-German dialogue revived, and Giscard d'Estaing pushed the Community forward on two fronts: economic and institutional. On the economic front, he established the European Monetary System, extending the Community's responsibilities and linking the currencies of participating states. On the institutional front he established the European Council, the regular meeting of Heads of State or Government, thus satisfying his Gaullist supporters, and he pressed for the direct election of the European Parliament, a move which pleased his supporters in more integrationist circles. The elections themselves led to a powerful challenge from within the majority by followers of Jacques Chirac, hostile to a 'talking shop' with a 'party of foreigners'. Pro-Giscard candidates were led by Simone Veil, who subsequently became the Parliament's first elected President, her group having been more successful in the largely pro-European atmosphere of the time. But the European issue continued to create discord inside the majority in Paris and it played a far from negligible role in the Presidential elections of May 1981.

By the time he came to power in 1981, François Mitterrand was already over sixty years old, with a character formed over many years by successive experiences, each laying down a different stratum, one on top of the other, memories and friendships creating a bizarre and often labyrinthine construction to which he alone held the key, of which he alone knew all the secrets. His years in the Elysée Palace completed this masterpiece by adding to an already complicated construction several more layers. So many different and often opposing elements were reconciled in his personality by an idiosyncratic syncretism that his life and oeuvre escaped definition, shimmering with ambiguity. In his own person he reconciled service to the Vichy regime and to governments of the Fourth Republic; campaigning for Pierre Mendès-France and saving socialism in the SFIO; demonising capital and rehabilitating market forces; virulent opposition to Gaullism and a discreet imitation of Gaullist policies: it was a personal tour de force.

Allied to the Communists when he came to power, and because of this alliance determined to concede nothing to them, François Mitterrand at first seemed a straightforward inheritor of the French Socialist tradition, flowing from the inter-war years and Léon Blum, with Atlanticist and pro-British assumptions. Despite ideological opposition to the Reagan-Thatcher line, he had no qualms in supporting the British cause in the Falklands War, in pursuing a prudent and consistent policy of small steps to bring France closer to NATO, and, above all, to press strongly for the installation of Cruise and Pershing missiles in West Germany.

But Atlanticism was only one component among many in Mitterrand's personality. Where de Gaulle was Cartesian to excess, Mitterrand did not accept the principle of contradiction. He loathed having to make choices, because choices imply excluding and rejecting. He wanted to add and collect, not to refuse and reduce. For him, there was no contradiction between continental solidarity and Atlantic solidarity, and – fortunately – his German counterpart, Helmut Kohl, felt similarly: the two concepts could complement and reinforce each other. Mitterrand's famous speech to the Bundestag on 20 January 1985 – 'The pacifists are in the West but the missiles are in the East' – illustrates his method perfectly. On the other hand, he links up with an Atlantic tradition that de Gaulle had treated roughly, and on the other he licks the General's boots by underlining defence solidarity with France's German neighbour, just as in the good old days of the Berlin crisis in 1959. The Schengen Agreements between a limited number of EC states on abolishing frontier controls and on police co-operation illustrate it again, building a continental arrangement for increased co-operation from a Franco-German initiative, and promising more.

At the start of his presidency, Mitterrand was not concerned by the prospect of weakening national sovereignty in joint institutions, and, aware of the necessity of reform, he moved rapidly to make progress with France's relations with Europe. From 1983, France gave up the false Luxembourg Compromise and escaped from the easy paralysis it had induced. Three years later, France signed the Single European Act, and thus took a major step along the federal road, considerably extending qualified majority voting, reinforcing the powers of the Commission and associating the European Parliament more closely with the legislative procedures of the Community. In substance, the Single European Act managed to reconcile François Mitterrand and Margaret Thatcher by combining her economic liberalism with his concern for regulatory harmonisation: a single market under common rules.

But the political timetables – national and European – did not coincide. In 1981, the President changed while Europe continued as before; in 1988, Mitterrand was re-elected, but Europe was soon after in turmoil. With the collapse of the Berlin Wall, the reunification of Germany and the fracturing of the Soviet system, Germany lost a nightmare. But France lost the threat which had given her added value in relation to Germany, and Europe lost the stimulus to federate. The situation was completely novel: power relations between France and Germany were transformed, European public opinion demobilised by removing its favourite bogeyman, and a serious risk of diluting the European Union through enlargement appeared. President Mitterrand, drawing on the diverse resources of his multiple personalities, reacted both as a nationalist, as a European and as a Head of State. As a nationalist, he had read Charles Maurras, whose pre-war essay, 'From Kiel to Tangiers', extolled the Russian alliance against Germany. Mitterrand, too, did not hesitate to see in Russia a counterweight to a re-emergent Germany. The benefits of such a policy – Germany's recognition of the Oder-Neisse frontier and her acceptance of monetary union in exchange for reunification – were easily seen, and the costs – a serious blow to the underlying Franco-German contract – were even more quickly perceived. In the first months of 1990, it was already clear that France would be playing with fire if she seriously tried to renew countervailing alliances, such as Delcassé had made before the First World War and Louis Barthou before the Second. Mitterrand the European then re-emerged and, together with Chancellor Kohl, took the most important European initiative since the original Treaty of Rome: they launched the project for a single currency, managed independently of national governments by integrated common institutions. And Mitterrand the Old Monarch was not far behind. With a lasting taste for the solitary exercise of supreme power, he recalled the fact that Europe is really a club of princes and that it should stay that way. The timidity of political union set up at Maastricht is in stark contrast to the audacity of monetary union. It can be reduced, in fact, to strictly inter-governmental co-operation conducted by a coterie of Heads of State or Government deciding by consensus. Applying one of General de Gaulle's subtle distinctions, what we are dealing with here is less the 'taste for power' exercised in common than a 'jealously guarded power of individual decision' – placed within the remit of titles five and six of the Treaty on European Union and referring to the famous – or infamous – second and third pillars.

Like a Janus standing where the two Republics meet, François Mitterrand looks out from the one which saw him grow to political maturity and the one which called him to rule. At the end of his life he underwrote this most disconcerting of treaties, the monetary section of which could have been written by Jean Monnet and the political section by Charles de Gaulle. With good faith on both sides, protagonists can declare that it is and is not federal in design. It is a Treaty which reflects the tenacious lack of clarity of the French as to the institutional model they really want for the European Union. The European career of François Mitterrand, as indeed the whole of his career and his life itself, is played out under an immense question-mark.

Maastricht and its divisions

The continuity of French policy towards Europe from 1951 to 1995, and the long series of political battles which have marked the development of this policy, are both indicators of a relatively strong consensus within French society about the objectives of the European project and the limits set for it by history, geography and ideology. The best guide to distinguish the various factions within this consensus, to show up the particularities of one group or another, is the referendum on 20 September 1992 on the ratification of the Treaty on European Union. With elections to the European Parliament, European and domestic politics are inextricably mixed; with the Maastricht referendum, the debate and the division of public opinion were almost exclusively related to the issue of Europe.

Analysis of the results shows two divisions among the electorate, one social and one geographical, which – as Emmanuel Todd has shown convincingly in an article in *Le Nouvel Observateur* – are closely related. Socially speaking, Europe is attractive for elites, the well established, better-off groups, but it is frightening for those who are weak, economically precarious or socially excluded. The reason is simple: the European construction is identified with liberal economic change; it is seen as modernising by its supporters and as de-stabilising by its opponents. Support for Europe correlates very largely with each person's degree of self confidence and confidence in the future. For the first time, the two groups who opposed each other throughout the nineteenth century – urban workers and rural peasants – found themselves very largely together in the *No* camp; and for the first time this exceptional combination found themselves – just – in the minority. It was an indication of the magnitude of the social transformations of the last forty years and of the irresistible rise of the salaried middle classes. In late twentieth-century France, the 'people', the 'masses' no longer form a majority.

From a geo-political viewpoint, the lessons to be drawn from the referendum are even more fascinating. Voting *Yes* to Maastricht were the elites in major urban areas, foremost among them Paris and its economically fortunate suburbs. Then came a circle of peripheral provinces, distant France with Alsace and Brittany, mountainous France with the Pyrenees and Savoy and including the neglected heart of the country, the Massif Central. In short, these are the parts of the country that have best resisted the secularising process of centralisation, the levelling of local culture, first by the monarchy, then by the Jacobins, the subjection of the Church to the Crown, and then revolutionary atheism. Emmanuel Todd has demonstrated it convincingly: the *Yes* map for Maastricht is largely identical to the map showing those areas where the clergy refused the constitutional oath in 1791. And the *No* map is equally clear: the strongest positions are in traditionally republican areas, lay and anticlerical, such as the Paris basin, an area which has been central for the administrative organisation of the state since Clovis. Modern France spread out from here, often by conquest, and this area is often identified with what is quintessentially modern France. The religious division has roots which go even deeper into the past than the revolutionary divide; it points back to the quarrel between Jansenists and Jesuits, Gallicans and Ultramontanes, which poisoned the last hundred years of the monarchy. It is, to say the least, curious to note that *Yes* voters in 1992 came more from the ancient papist areas used to following a foreign order, the rule of Rome, while the *No* voters came more from the heart of France which, since the time of Philip the Fair, asserted the pre-eminence of the sovereign over the Holy See and the Holy Roman Empire.

The way these two strands of analysis come together is clear: those in France who still had faith in intercession and had maintained the habit of obeying elites who think for them, tended to vote *Yes*. Those who had gained the right to determine their own fate without, and indeed despite, these elites tended to vote *No*. Cultural factors overlay social factors: small farmers, victims or beneficiaries of the same reforms of the Common Agricultural Policy, voted *Yes* in Île-et-Villaine, and *No* in Yonne and in Seine-Maritime. Cultural factors also overlay the power of elites: Paris voted *Yes* but did not sway the Paris basin, because Paris is a city-elite in the centre of an area which has lost the habit of obeying anything other than the power of the state, that splendid fiction created for the specific purpose of allowing everybody to obey an abstraction rather than a living person.

To make the picture even clearer, compare Republican Yonne, which voted *No*, and Catholic Brittany, which voted *Yes*. On the one hand lies the France of Paul Bert, an important lay preacher of the Republican school, a department more permeated than any other by Jansenism in the eighteenth century, and then, by a furious wave of atheism which decapitated hundreds of statues of the saints in its churches, a land of closed families, submitting directly to the state and its institutions, with no mediating aristocratic or religious class. On the other hand lies the France of humble folk who attend Mass or parade in religious processions (or at least remember having done so), large families with their structures intact, often uncontestedly patriarchal, a trade union movement inspired by Christian origins (CFDT), farmers trained by a Christian rural youth organisation (JAC), a powerful regional daily (*Ouest-France*) with the biggest circulation of the whole French press, and whose editorial team took on the task of encouraging a *Yes* vote as a spiritual duty.

The imperfect consensus

Could one deduce from the preceding analysis that the 'European' party is the direct descendent of the clerical and counter-revolutionary party, and that Maastricht marks the belated revenge of the *Ancien Régime* over the Revolution, or even of the Jesuits over the Gallican Jansenism of the eighteenth century?

Clearly not, or else we should have to admit that, due to a staggering, indeed providential, reversal of the balance of power within French society, those who had repeatedly lost every struggle during the preceding two hundred years had suddenly won this battle. Even if the results of the referendum on the ratification of the Treaty on European Union allow one to distinguish two large matrices from French history operating against each other – Catholic, Ultramontane France on the one hand, Republican, Jacobin France on the other – they in no way allow one to identify the 'European' party with the former and the national party with the latter. The victory of the *Yes* vote in September 1992, narrow though it was, was doubtless due to many voters from numerous, different groups of the Jacobin tradition voting *Yes* as well. Geographically speaking, this was clearly true of the big towns, led by Paris, and, socially speaking, equally true of the liberal professions, managers and many representatives of the middle classes. At the other end of the spectrum, the most traditionalist groups at the periphery of France, led by Philippe de Villiers from the Vendée, were prepared to join with the Jacobin tendency in voting *No*. They could go thus far in concert with Philippe Séguin and Charles Pasqua, leaders of that tendency, but they could never have sung with them the Marseillaise, the revolutionary anthem abhorred by their clerical tradition.

The balance sheet shows that these various political desertions and betrayals were not enough to prevent the partisans of ratification from winning. The effect of de Villiers's campaign in wooing away some voters from the mainstream Catholic tendency was more than compensated by the number of *Yes* votes drawn from the Jacobin camp. Maastricht split what one could call the 'State' party from top to bottom, the top resolutely for *Yes*, the base strongly for *No*. A strong pro-European group emerged, led by Jacques Chirac and Edouard Balladur, similar to the movement led by Charles de Gaulle in 1958. There are then two different pro-European sensibilities at work in French society and their basic solidarity with each other has proved crucial for the continuity of France's European policy. Their periodic quarrels have been the cause of the recurrent conflicts observed since 1950.

First there are the 'passionate' Europeans, those who see in the European project an end in itself and who see in federalism a way to have done with the Jacobin state once and for all, substituting the rule of law for administrative despotism. Then we have the 'thoughtful' Europeans, those for whom Europe is an instrument by which a state like France, which no longer has the means to be great as before, can become so again. Europe is for them what General de Gaulle called 'Archimedes' lever', the instrument which would again allow France to exert influence in the world. While the first group clearly remains a minority, they dream of a federation of peoples, strongly decentralised, which would undermine the state both from below and from above by re-organising power both at the regional and at the supranational level. The second group is considerably more numerous and looks to a confederation of states which should give each of its members – and above all France, which they imagine more important than all the others – the collective force which they each lack on their own. The Maastricht Treaty, with its federalist aspects regarding monetary union and its confederalist aspects regarding political union, had the special quality of being all things to all men, equally capable of satisfying or disturbing 'passionate' as well as 'thoughtful' Europeans.

What characterises the European debate in France, and distinguishes it from the debate in the United Kingdom, is primarily the fact that the European idea, in its many and diverse forms, not all of them consistent, is supported by the vast majority of the French people. The number of those voting *No* in the referendum who described themselves, or even thought of themselves, as anti-European was extremely small. Among the diverse groups in favour, there is a fundamental consensus on the political, economic and social principles which should guide the European Union, even if there is a real disagreement about the institutions required for it to function satisfactorily. Among the points of agreement, there is also a certain doubt about indefinite enlargement, a concern to contain any trade liberalisation, both within and outside the Community, with rules to ensure its fair operation, a desire to keep existing common policies, starting with the CAP, and to develop new ones, and an ambition to have a truly European foreign policy and the military means to underpin it. Among the points of disagreement there is an extreme reluctance on the part of some of the 'thoughtful' Europeans to accept the collective institutional disciplines and the more fully integrated of the European institutions themselves; qualified majority voting, political responsibilities for the Commission, the powers of the European Parliament, the role of the Court of Justice, and the supremacy of Community law over national law, these are all questioned repeatedly.

One could maintain, with little exaggeration, that there is no authentically and consistently anti-European party in France, with the sole exception perhaps of the extreme right, and that everyone on the southern side of the Channel wants a strong Europe. There is nothing comparable to what we see in Great Britain where numerous political figures and ordinary citizens actively press for a European Union reduced to a free trade zone, shorn of those useless and costly common policies and organised in a strictly inter-governmental framework. Even the champions of the anti-Maastricht movement in France, Philippe Séguin or Philippe de Villiers, are diametrically opposed on ideological grounds to their British counterparts. They criticise nothing in the Community more fiercely than its slipping into free-trading à *l'anglaise*, its subversive effects on the foundations of established societies, its destruction of hundreds of thousands of industrial and agricultural jobs and its questioning of the sacred principles of public service à la française. In short, there are no supporters in France for the British view of a 'minimalist Europe'.

That is not to say that the European project is free from criticism in France, any more than in Britain. Indeed, it is loathed and criticised by many, but not for the same reasons as in Britain. The hallmark of British Europhobia is a refusal to countenance a strong Europe. The hallmark of French Europhobia is the self-contradictory fear of a weak Europe and of European institutions which are too strong. What distinguishes pro-Europeans from anti-Europeans in France is that the former, in their desire to be consistent, do not separate their definition of aims – a strong Europe – from the means of achieving it – efficient and democratic institutions; the latter accept unthinkingly the contradiction between stigmatising the structural weakness of the Union and at the same time rejecting proposals to strengthen the institutions. Torn between their almost religious reverence for the 'State' and their painful awareness of the economically subversive forces of a minimal Europe, active campaigners against Maastricht in France seem less and less like spokesmen for an alternative project – l'autre politique, much heralded at the time of the referendum, has still not taken on a clear form – than like the depository for all sorts of frustrations in modern society; reacting against the Brussels technocracy, financial discipline, international competition, the opening of frontiers and rising unemployment. Quick to anger, slow to offer proposals, unable to replace government, the anti-Maastricht forces in France appear to be more a reservoir of protest than an alternative force. What distinguishes them from their pro-European opponents is essentially what distinguishes an opposition, free from the constraints of real politics, from a government, careful to ensure compatibility between means and ends. Where the pro-Maastricht forces are consuls, the anti-Maastricht forces are tribunes.

These reflections lead one to conclude that there is a broad consensus in France on the aims of European Union and, at the same time, to play down the elements of disagreement which are limited to the institutional question. That has not stopped this limited disagreement from weighing heavy in the debate from time to time: in 1954 , on the issue of the common army; in 1965, on the issue of qualified majority voting; in 1979, on the issue of direct elections to the European Parliament; in 1992, on the issue of the European Central Bank; and in 1993, on the issue of the role of the Commission in the Uruguay Round. The poison of this institutional disagreement has a double action: directly, by arousing bitter argument about the institutions and their procedures, and indirectly, by weakening the structures of the Union and making them incapable of keeping the promise of strong, independent, efficient action whose tangible results would convince public opinion of the benefits of strong institutions. In the face of unemployment, war and insecurity, Europe is seen to languish in endless negotiations, impotent to act – and Europe gains no credit from delay and impotence. The French consensus is thus attacked from two angles, blaming Europe for failing to achieve results, and refusing Europe the necessary means to achieve the desired results.

On the threshold of the third stage of economic and monetary union, and of major enlargement of the European Union to the states of Central and Eastern Europe, can France remain satisfied with the imperfect compromises of the past between confederalists and federalists, between partisans of an 'instrumental' Europe serving the sovereign states and champions of structures as in Germany or America, a real federal state which would relegate the nation states to the level of secondary, subordinate actors? It does not seem sufficient for today's circumstances. One side must admit that the Union's continuing enlargement will undermine de Gaulle's unbalanced compromise between a strong Europe and weak institutions. The other side cannot be blind to the fact that their federal project cannot rally sufficient support in as far as it is attacking the very nation states which have been the principal actors in the European construct from the beginning. Both sides must also be concerned at the risk of the dilution and weakening of the Union which would result from indefinite enlargement without deepening.

The time has doubtless come for a lasting reconciliation between the two dominant strands of pro-European opinion in France. What is needed is a new institutional synthesis able to guarantee the nation states the central role which is theirs in the European project and, at the same time, submitting each and every one of them to collective procedures and disciplines borrowed from federalism. Fifty years ago, Robert Schuman and Jean Monnet dreamed of a federation of the peoples of Europe. General de Gaulle, firmly believing in the legacy of fifteen centuries of history, looked for a simple confederation of European states. François Mitterrand decided to let the logic of federalism and the logic of confederalism co-exist, the rule of states beside the emergence of the peoples of Europe, without, however, seeking to resolve any of the contradictions. Today the time has come to go further and construct a synthesis which guarantees at the same time the pre-eminence of the states and the efficiency of their joint actions. This synthesis will clearly be a federation of nation states.

Translated from the French by Martyn Bond

Brandt and Schmidt – Germany's View of Europe

Roger Morgan

Introduction

Willy Brandt and Helmut Schmidt will always be remembered as two sharply contrasting personalities: the former a charismatic figure with an instant appeal to mass audiences, the latter much more reserved and more pragmatic in his statesmanship. Between them, as the Federal Republic of Germany's first two Social Democratic heads of government, they held office from 1969 to 1982, Brandt handing over the Chancellorship to Schmidt in 1974. Brandt's election victory in 1969 was accompanied by great expectations of change and reform. He was Germany's first Social Democratic Chancellor since 1930, and the 'Social-Liberal' coalition which he headed (his party's partner being the Free Democratic Party of Walter Scheel, who became Brandt's Foreign Minister) promised the modernisation and rejuvenation of Germany after 20 years of Christian Democratic rule.

Although the Brandt-Schmidt period did see some important reforms in Germany in such fields as education, public administration, and technology policy, their thirteen years in office were heavily dominated by changes in the world outside Germany and by the Federal Government's attempts to respond to them and shape them.

There were many external forces which influenced the policies both of Brandt and of Schmidt towards the European Community: the breakdown of the Bretton Woods world monetary system in 1971, the economic recession which followed the oil crisis of 1973 and worsened as the years passed, and a number of dramatic fluctuations in East-West political relations. Both men were convinced that the unification of Western Europe had a vital role to play in relation to these and other complex problems and their commitment to the development of the EC forms a continuous thread running through their period of office.

It is perhaps important to stress the European commitment both of Brandt and of Schmidt, because even by the late 1960s their party had still not fully shaken off its reputation for hostility to Western European integration as a process which might block Germany's chances of national unification. This line had been passionately advocated by the Social Democrat Kurt Schumacher as leader of the opposition in

Adenauer's early years, and even Helmut Schmidt, like many in his party, had re-fused to vote for Germany's ratification of the Treaty of Rome – though the reason he gave for this was that the European Community without Britain was incomplete. Even though after 1960 the Social Democratic Party formally renounced this view, and was in fact committed to Adenauer's policy of integrating the Federal Republic into Western Europe, some suspicion lingered on. Willy Brandt was criticised, as Chancellor, for giving so much influence to his adviser Egon Bahr, a Berlin journal-ist who had worked closely with Brandt during his years as Mayor of West Berlin, and then served as Head of the Foreign Ministry's Planning Staff when Brandt be-came Foreign Minister in 1966; Bahr was known to be sceptical about the European Community and a believer in re-emphasising German national interests, particu-larly the goal of national unification. Could a man with these views, the critics asked, be trusted to maintain Bonn's full commitment to the West at the same time as masterminding the revolutionary developments in *Ostpolitik* which became the most prominent element of Brandt's foreign policy?

A few years later, after Brandt had been replaced by Schmidt, questions about the Bonn government's commitment to European integration were of a different kind. Schmidt, whose down-to-earth Hamburg background gave him a more practical image than that of the extrovert and easy-going Brandt (and whose rough debating style had earned him the nickname of 'Schmidt the Lip'), did not hide his impatience with what he called 'the bloated bureaucracy of Brussels'; and as the recession of the mid-1970s put increased pressure on the German budget, he scornfully queried whether Germany should forever be expected to be 'the paymaster of Europe'. Both Schmidt's political opponents and – still more – his European partners asked whether language of this kind indicated a weakening of Germany's commitment to European unity.

The answer to such doubts, both about Brandt and about Schmidt, is that their party, by the time they took office, had thoroughly overcome its earlier hesitations about Europe. Neither the Eastern designs of Brandt, nor the budgetary impatience of Schmidt, signified more than minor undercurrents in a German policy line which quite unambiguously saw Germany's national interest as lying in the consolidation and development of the European Community. This was, at least, the view they repeatedly stressed in public statements, both while they held power and later, after the constraints of office had been removed.

Brandt, in a volume of memoirs published in 1976, shortly after he left office, re-called his regret that when he became Foreign Minister the Community was still suffering from effects of the 'Luxembourg Compromise' of 1966, but stressed his determination to move things forward:

> In April 1967, when for the first time I led the German delegation to the Council of Ministers ... I promised that the Federal Government would make all possible efforts to achieve the aims of the Treaty of Rome. What was needed

was to push forward from a customs and agricultural union to a full economic union ...

Among the many eloquent statements on Europe made by Brandt as Chancellor, from the Hague Summit Meeting of December 1969 onward, the most dramatic was his address to the European Parliament on 13 November 1973, at the height of the Arab-Israeli War of that autumn:

> The move towards European Union is indispensable... the unification of Europe is not merely a question of the quality of our existence. It is a question of survival between the giants and, in the rugged world of the young, the old nationalisms. The aim of our policy for European integration remains clear-cut. It is, as I have put it from time to time, a sensibly organised European Government, which in the fields of common policies will be able to take the necessary decisions and will be subject to political control. The European states will transfer to that government the sovereign rights which in the future can only be effectively exercised together; the remaining rights will stay with the Member States. In this way we shall both preserve the national unity of our peoples, which is the source of their strength, and add the European identity from which fresh energies will ensue.

Looking back on his Chancellorship in a further volume of memoirs published in 1989, Brandt recalled his role (together with Monnet and others) in preparing the way for the European Council, the institutionalised summit meetings of EC heads of government. This began formally under Schmidt and Giscard d'Estaing in 1974 but had a precursor in the Copenhagen summit of December 1973; in Brandt's words, the idea was 'to give the Community a political top authority through an institution representing the heads of government, and to put a brake on the influence of the feuding ministerial bureaucracies'. He claimed that the new institution did not reduce the role of the Commission, and actually enhanced that of the European Parliament, but recorded his regret that 'the democratic basis of control of the Community's work remained underdeveloped and highly unsatisfactory'.

If Brandt's declarations on European integration sometimes have a high-flown quality, reflecting the enthusiasm of a reforming Chancellor aiming at great things, those of his successor often reflect not only the more practical nature of Schmidt as a person, but also the more prosaic and problem-ridden period in which he was Chancellor. Schmidt's statements often reaffirmed Germany's vital interest in consolidating a European Union based on democracy, trust and equality of rights among its members. Sometimes he stressed – as he did for instance in a speech to Germany's leading Catholics in September 1978 – a broader perspective:

> Europe is more than a one-purpose grouping for raising the standard of living. The European Community contributes to the securing of freedom, peace, and

democracy as well as economic and social equilibrium; to serve these aims in a lasting way, and better than each individual state can do it alone, gives the Community its specific moral and political legitimacy.

Schmidt also welcomed the EC's decision in 1976 that the European Parliament should be directly elected by Europe's voters: speaking to the Executive Committee of his party, he characterised this step as 'one of the most important possibilities of bringing Europe forward a bit', notably by giving the Parliament a better chance to develop its own possibilities. Schmidt was, however, more guarded in his assessment of the chances of the EC's collective development at the time of the Genscher-Colombo initiative of late 1981 (the work of Schmidt's Foreign Minister and his Italian counterpart): the Chancellor released a statement which, while stressing his government's desire to develop the EC 'as a factor in the world political balance', went on to emphasise that 'Bilateral relations with our EC partners remain an important element of European cooperation', and, even more explicitly, 'German-French cooperation continues to be of particular significance'.

Schmidt's statements about European integration only became really warm, sometimes even emotional, after he had left office. Writing in 1992, ten years after his Chancellorship ended, he stressed the vital importance of the Community for the newly-united Germany:

> Only through a deepening and consolidation of the EC, and only through an indissoluble linking of Germany with the EC, can we Germans hope for lasting understanding and goodwill on the part of our neighbours. Our neighbours have to be made to feel safe from future domination by 78 million Germans.

On 12 May 1995, when Franco-German tension appeared likely to increase after the election of President Chirac, and German enthusiasm for economic and monetary union (EMU) was clearly waning, Schmidt fired a public broadside in the Hamburg weekly *Die Zeit*:

> Without a common currency the 'common market' is in fact impossible; it would degenerate into a free trade area with some marginal institutional accompaniment. Even more important: without monetary union the D-Mark would become, within one or two decades, the currency which dominates Europe, and German financial institutions would rule Europe's financial markets. This would be against the cardinal strategic interests of both countries (i.e. France and Germany).

In September 1995, when EMU was being discussed with growing scepticism by the German Finance Minister, the Bundesbank, and even some leaders of Schmidt's own Social Democratic Party, he went further, again in *Die Zeit*:

The progress of European integration is not a mere object of German idealism, but corresponds to Germany's vital long-term strategic interest in peace
– if she really wants to avoid an anti-German coalition coming about for a
third time. This view was axiomatic for every Chancellor from Adenauer to
Kohl. We must not lose it now.

Thus both Brandt and Schmidt indicated their commitment to pursuing policies
designed to enhance the integration of Western Europe. What were the concrete
circumstances in which their successive governments had their chance to work towards this end?

The context of Germany's European policy

When Willy Brandt moved from the Bonn Foreign Ministry to the Chancellor's Office in 1969, West Germany's foreign policy was dominated, as it had been for 20
years or more, by 'the German question'. For Germans, this meant essentially the
question of whether Germany's division into two mutually hostile states could in the
long run be ended, and whether in the short run the consequences of this division for
the German people could be made less intolerable. In some ways, the problem was
harder to bear in 1969 than it had been in 1949, after the Soviet blockade of West
Berlin. By the late 1960s the population of East Germany was firmly shut in behind
the Berlin Wall built in 1961; foreign travel was a privilege rarely granted to East
Germans, and then only to one member of a family at a time; West Germans were
only allowed to visit their Eastern relatives on payment of a substantial entry fee in
Western currency; and the Russian occupying forces were able to make clear Moscow's displeasure at West Berlin's links with the West by occasionally blocking traffic on the Autobahn to the city, or by 'buzzing' the Reichstag building in West Berlin
when West German parliamentary events were held there.

Brandt, like his predecessors in office, resisted any temptation to seek a deal with
Moscow which might reunite Germany in exchange for her shifting into international
neutrality, and out of NATO and the European Community. Now that his party had
abandoned its earlier inclination towards such a policy, Brandt saw Germany's membership of the EC, as of NATO, as part of the policy of 'negotiation from strength'
which would one day give Germany a chance of reunification in a reorganised Europe. Meanwhile, Brandt's Federal Republic benefited from a number of concessions which her European partners had made in earlier years. Ever since 1957 the
EC had regarded trade in goods between the two German states ('inner-German
trade') as domestic rather than external trade, so that East German exports were
freely admitted to the West: these East-West German economic links, even though
they led to occasional complaints from Bonn's EC partners, certainly helped to maintain what Brandt was to call 'the substance of the German nation'. So did the special

arrangements by which West Berlin, though not fully a *Land* of the Federal Republic, was regarded as being in every way covered by the Treaty of Rome: this meant that Berlin benefited from European financial subsidies, and that West Berlin members of the Bonn parliament were included in the Bundestag's delegation to the European Parliament (which was, of course, not yet directly elected).

Brandt was thus able to take for granted the Federal Republic's integral and unquestioned membership of the EC, as well as of NATO, as he embarked on the new *Ostpolitik*, or Eastern Policy, which was to bring a major change in relations between the two German states, and with their neighbours, by the time he left office in 1974. Indeed he repeatedly emphasised, to forestall disquiet in Germany and among her Western allies, that his *Ostpolitik* was rooted in *Westpolitik*. As he negotiated treaties with Poland and the Soviet Union, and established a formal relationship between the Federal Republic and the German Democratic Republic (GDR) (without giving the latter full diplomatic recognition), he made sure that Bonn's acceptance of Germany's existing frontiers and the new working relationship between the two German states had the backing of his Western partners. An important element in the process of change was the 1971 four-power or Quadripartite Agreement on Berlin, by which the Russians and the three Western allies responsible for Berlin (the US, the UK, and France) agreed to respect and to stabilise the existing situation in the divided city, including West Berlin's strong links with West Germany.

The European dimension of these agreements became clearer by the time Brandt handed over to Schmidt, as the 35-nation Conference on Security and Cooperation in Europe (CSCE) worked out its Helsinki Final Act of 1975. In this document, states from the US to the Soviet Union committed themselves to cooperate in military confidence-building measures, trade, and questions of human rights. Germany was to ensure that the European Community was fully included in this comprehensive attempt to move Europe forward from the Cold War.

As these positive developments in East-West relations in Europe were accompanied by the first SALT (Strategic Arms Limitation Talks) agreement between Washington and Moscow, and by general negotiations on conventional disarmament (Mutual and Balanced Force Reductions) between NATO and the Warsaw Pact, Brandt's Chancellorship and his policies in EC affairs occurred at a time when Europe's political prospects, as a whole, looked brighter than for a decade or more.

In international economic affairs the general context soon came to look less promising. Even though the European economy at the end of the 1960s looked prosperous enough, the difficulties brought on by the global monetary crisis of 1971, and still more the drastic impact of the 'oil shock' of 1973, made the prospect much bleaker. Brandt's optimistic hopes of increasing the EC's budget to allow more spending on regional development policies, on social welfare provision and on technological research and development were thus to be fulfilled only in a small measure.

As far as the EC itself was concerned, the most important issue facing Germany and the other member-states when Brandt took office was that of enlarging the membership beyond that of the original group of six countries. Britain, Ireland, Denmark and Norway were moving towards formal negotiations about joining, and the question of the terms of their membership became linked with that of the Community's future 'deepening' in institutional and policy terms, as well as the question of the completion of the arrangements for existing policies, notably in agriculture.

If the general setting for Brandt's policies towards Europe was the broadly promising one of East-West détente and a range of questions now ripe for solution, the context in which Schmidt took over the leadership of Germany in 1974 looked distinctly less bright. In the first place the economic situation continued to worsen, leading to general international instability, in particular in monetary relations. The annual summit meetings of the Group of Seven, inaugurated at Rambouillet in November 1975, were designed in large part to provide a top-level forum for coordinating national economic policies so as to counteract these negative trends. By the end of the decade Chancellor Schmidt and the French President, Valéry Giscard d'Estaing, were agreed on the need to promote a closer and more binding form of monetary cooperation in Europe. Thus the European Monetary System, designed to ensure that Western Europe at least would become an area of monetary stability in an uncertain world, was launched at the Bremen meeting of the European Council in July 1978: the EMS was the successor of an earlier attempt at Economic and Monetary Union launched during Brandt's Chancellorship, which had foundered in the monetary storms of the mid-1970s.

The creation of the European Council itself was a further sign that the turbulence in the world's economic and political relations required additional attempts at collective management. This new institutional device was promoted by Schmidt and Giscard d'Estaing, who had taken office almost simultaneously and whose close partnership was based partly on their earlier cooperation as their countries' Finance Ministers. The Council which they developed from the EC's earlier system of occasional summit meetings (The Hague 1969, Paris 1972, Copenhagen 1973) became a regular thrice-yearly meeting of the EC's top political leaders, designed to give the Community a clearer sense of direction at a time when it faced increasing difficulties.

These difficulties included renewed friction between Schmidt's Germany and the US administration of President Jimmy Carter. Whereas Brandt's period as Chancellor had been characterised by generally good relations with the Washington of Richard Nixon, even while both governments had been conducting delicate détente negotiations with the East, the Schmidt and Carter administrations seriously failed to understand each other. Differences arose over monetary policy, over military doctrine (especially the US proposal to develop the 'neutron bomb') and over the question of how to deal with human rights issues in the Soviet bloc.

At the end of Schmidt's period of office, in 1981-82, he was faced with an American régime he found even less congenial, that of Ronald Reagan. Whereas Schmidt's priority, as East-West relations worsened, was to maintain contact with Moscow and with East Berlin, Reagan saw the Afghanistan crisis, developments in Soviet missile power, and the imposition of martial law in Poland as evidence that Russia was 'the Evil Empire'. He responded by pressing for economic sanctions and the stationing of more American missiles in Western Europe. Although Schmidt personally supported the last-mentioned policy, the majority of his party deserted him on the issue: this, and the defection of Genscher's Free Democratic Party (FDP) into a new coalition under Helmut Kohl, provoked the fall of Schmidt as Chancellor in October 1982.

It was against this turbulent international background that Schmidt had struggled for eight years to promote the development of the EC in the sectors where this was possible. The challenges he faced included trying to hold together the currency 'snake' set up in the early 1970s, and developing it into the much more effective EMS from 1978 onwards; giving the EC the institutional strengthening of the European Council in 1974 and the directly-elected Parliament in 1979; keeping the United Kingdom as a member of the EC when the Wilson government's referendum in 1974 might have gone either way; and preparing the way for further enlargement when Greece, Spain and Portugal emerged from dictatorship in the 1970s and Greece proved ready for EC membership by 1981.

The policy record: the Brandt years

In assessing the policy of the Brandt administration towards the affairs of Europe, one factor of fundamental importance must be kept in mind. The years from 1969 to 1974 represented the first occasion in the history of the Federal Republic when the Bonn government could undertake serious negotiations, and expect to achieve serious results, with its Eastern as well as its Western neighbours. A combination of circumstances at the turn of the decade, including the effects of de Gaulle's ostentatious pursuit of détente during the 1960s, President Nixon's proclamation of an 'Era of Negotiations', and a new flexibility in Moscow, allowed Bonn at last to pursue a real *Ostpolitik* as well as a real *Westpolitik*.

Chancellor Brandt, as he embarked on the talks with Moscow and Moscow's allies which were to produce a *modus vivendi* with the GDR, a stabilisation of Bonn's links with Berlin and the chance of unprecedented influence on the countries of the Warsaw Pact, was in a radically different position from that of his predecessors over the previous two decades. Adenauer, at the head of the Federal Republic created by the Western powers under the shadow of the Berlin blockade, could achieve only one concrete agreement with Moscow during his whole thirteen-year term of office: his single visit to Moscow, in 1955, led to the return to the Federal Republic of several thousand German prisoners of war and the establishment of formal diplomatic relations with the Soviet Union – but the value of these relations was strictly limited. Adenauer's successors between 1963 and 1969 had even less success with any kind of *Ostpolitik*. Erhard made little pretence of even trying to talk with the East, and the tentative attempts made by Kiesinger towards the normalisation of Bonn's relations with Eastern Europe (the partial relaxation of the Hallstein Doctrine) appeared to come to a brutal full stop with the Warsaw Pact's intervention in Prague in August 1968. The achievements between 1969 and 1974 of Willy Brandt (who had been Kiesinger's Foreign Minister) are all the more remarkable when they are considered against the sterile history of Germany's Eastern relations during the preceding two decades – not to mention the horrors of 1941-45. It is thus not surprising that the diplomacy of Brandt's *Ostpolitik* – covering the transformation of Bonn's relations with Moscow, Warsaw and East Berlin, and the parallel reassurance of the Western allies at a time when they, too, were active in East-West negotiations – overshadowed Bonn's more prosaic involvement to the West, in the development of the European Community.

In this central aspect of *Westpolitik*, however, things also began to move fast. The EC's critical summit meeting in The Hague in December 1969 (the first of Brandt's period as Chancellor) was called on to take decisions on the enlargement, deepening and completion of the Community. Progress was rapid, at least under the first and third of these headings. Negotiations for the EC's enlargement, meaning the projected admission of four new members (the UK, Ireland, Denmark and Norway) were approved at The Hague, and formal negotiations began in April 1970. These resulted (after perhaps being made easier by Harold Wilson's replacement by Edward Heath two months later) in the Community being joined in January 1973 by the UK, Ireland and Denmark. Although this marked a success for Brandt's policy, he felt deep personal regret that the fourth applicant, Norway – his adoptive country during the Nazi period – voted in October 1972 by a narrow majority not to join: as Brandt ironically recorded in his memoirs, rural voters were swayed by propaganda saying that the Common Agricultural Policy would impose compulsory wine-drinking throughout Norway and that Norwegian girls would be seduced by 'dark-haired Southerners'.

As for the 'completion' of some of the EC's unfinished business, this was partially achieved by an agreement of the Council of Ministers shortly before Christmas 1969 (under the direct impact of the momentum established by Brandt and his colleagues at the Hague Summit) on the Community's 'own resources', including the financing of the Common Agricultural Policy by taxes on external trade. This resolution of an issue which had been a source of discord for at least five years was due in large part to a personal commitment given by Brandt to Pompidou in the course of the Hague Summit: Brandt wisely made a concession on a point of critical importance to France, in order to ensure Pompidou's agreement to Germany's plan that the Community should be enlarged.

The third heading of the Hague agenda, 'deepening', inevitably posed bigger problems. Significant progress was indeed made in some important policy sectors. The project to accompany the EC's commercial and agricultural achievements with progress towards full economic and monetary union (already pressed by Brandt in the Council of Ministers in 1967) took a big step forward with the plan produced by the Werner Committee (named after its Luxembourg chairman) in late 1970. Simultaneously, and again following guidelines laid down by Brandt and his colleagues in The Hague, the process of systematic consultation between the Foreign Ministries of the Six was formulated for the first time in the Davignon Report (named after a senior official of the Belgian Foreign Ministry, later a European Commissioner). This attempt to move towards a common foreign policy for the EC, soon to be institutionalised under the name of 'European Political Cooperation', was of particular importance to Brandt and his Foreign Minister Walter Scheel, at a time when the foreign policies of the EC's member states ran a serious risk of diverging under the pressure of dramatic events in world politics.

It was more difficult to make real progress on another aspect of 'deepening' which was of special importance to Brandt as a Social Democrat. This was the area of policy which came to be known as 'the social dimension': the idea that the Community should concern itself not only with economic growth but also with the living and working conditions of its citizens. Concretely this implied among other things the redistribution of resources from richer to poorer European regions through economic development funds; concern for the harmonisation of working conditions and industrial relations; and measures to provide better opportunities for women, migrant workers, and other disadvantaged groups. Brandt's concern with these matters may be explained partly by his wish to give Europe's citizens more concrete motives for identifying with the Community: it was to take the form of a memorandum on a 'European Social Union' which he submitted to the EC's Paris summit of October 1972, but, as he regretfully noted later, Europe's economic and financial situation by then did not allow increased spending on the scale he had hoped for.

Much of the attention of Europe's leaders, indeed, had to be devoted to monetary problems, as the successive crises in exchange rates and waves of currency speculation swept over the Western world from 1971 onwards. Brandt and his colleagues clearly saw that Economic and Monetary Union was in theory an important element in the economic consolidation and development of the EC, and the Werner Plan of 1970 provided a fairly detailed blueprint for movement towards this objective. The Brandt government was originally inclined to commit a significant part of Germany's monetary reserves to a European Reserve Fund, which was an important element of the European monetary arrangement set up in 1971-72. This was the so-called 'snake', which limited exchange-rate fluctuations between the participating currencies. Unfortunately for Brandt's optimistic designs, the continuing uncertainties of world monetary affairs led to the early disintegration of the 'snake': the pound sterling, which had joined the system in 1972 in anticipation of Britain's membership of the EC, left it again by the end of the year; the French franc did so early in 1974; and frequent revaluations of the D-Mark proved necessary to maintain the system. It was by now unrealistic for large-scale German reserves to be committed to the proposed European Reserve Fund: attempts at monetary unification in the EC had to wait, essentially, until a new attack on the problem was mounted with the establishment of the European Monetary System in 1978 under Helmut Schmidt's Chancellorship.

Other aspects of Europe's integration, however, were being pressed actively by Brandt and his ministers. In connection with the entry of the UK, Denmark and Ireland, a redefinition of the Community's long-term political and institutional objectives was necessary as the first two of these states were particularly sensitive about the question of national sovereignty. An essential part of this redefinition, or reaffirmation, of the rules of the EC game was an agreement reached on 21 May 1971 between President Pompidou and Prime Minister Heath that 'the identity of nation states in the framework of the developing Community will be maintained, and in practice decisions of the Community will be taken unanimously, when vital interests of the member states are at stake'. This reaffirmation of the 'Luxembourg compromise' of January 1966, which explicitly indicated the limits of British and French readiness to pool their sovereignty, was communicated to Brandt a few days later (significantly by Heath, whose relations with Brandt were by now close and effective): it confirmed that progress towards a supranational European Union could only be slow, and would always have to strike a balance between the national interests of the member states and the sense of common purpose of the Community as a whole.

Although Brandt's own preference would have been for quicker progress towards a more comprehensive and more supranational European Union, he was in practice content to settle for the gradual bringing-together of national viewpoints and standpoints which was clearly preferred by Paris and London. His own day-to-day diplomacy in Europe, indeed, also required a good deal of bi-lateral government-to-government negotiation with partners both inside and outside the Community.

Brandt should not be accused of inconsistency for committing himself in 1972 to the goal of 'European Union' by 1980 (Pompidou and Heath did so, too), or for appealing for a 'sensibly organised European Government' during the energy crisis of autumn 1973. Rhetorical flourishes of this kind indicated the long-term or maximalist objectives of European unification: they served as signposts to indicate the overall direction or framework for the pragmatic decisions which Brandt, like all heads of government, had to take on a day-to-day basis.

Overall, the Brandt administration's achievements in relation to Western Europe's unification were very considerable. There were, it is true, disappointments for Brandt in the limited degree to which the EC developed its programmes for regional development, social policy, or the coordination of energy resources; there was also the unsatisfactory experience of the attempt at monetary integration, taken at a time when economic turbulence in the outside world and the resulting monetary fluctuations set up pressures which were too great for the embryonic European monetary union to handle.

On the other hand Brandt could look back, as he left office in 1974, on a number of substantial achievements, not least the enlargement of the EC from six states to nine (involving a difficult adjustment of the interests of Britain and France, among others), and the stabilisation of Western Europe's relations both with the North Atlantic world and with the Soviet bloc at a time when both Western and Eastern stability and dialogue were very far from being guaranteed.

The view westward from Europe, in Brandt's period of office, was troubled by conflicts of various kinds. At the level of economic relations these included the perennial problem of agricultural protectionism, which was so intractable that it had been excluded from the Kennedy Round of trade negotiations conducted by the GATT in the mid-1960s: both the EC and the US accused the other of providing unacceptable protection for its farm producers, in defiance of the principles of fair trade. Parallel with this endemic conflict there was the huge problem of monetary relations after Washington's virtual ending of the Bretton Woods system in August 1971, and the weakness of the dollar over the years which followed contributed to strains and stresses in the world monetary system which required strenuous efforts of management by Europeans and Americans alike. Furthermore, overshadowing even these massive economic and monetary problems, there was the whole question of the political relationship between the United States and the evolving European Community, at a time when NATO's *raison d'être* was being thrown open to question by what President Nixon called 'the Era of Negotiations'. In a sense NATO had, as Brandt knew from his time as Foreign Minister, been here before. In response to the flurry of experiments in East-West negotiations attempted in the mid-1960s (most spectacularly by de Gaulle), NATO had, in 1967, adopted the Harmel Report (named after the Belgian Foreign Minister of the time), which committed the alliance to the pursuit of détente as well as the maintenance of deterrence. Brandt had taken the leading part, together with his European colleagues, in bringing about this early redefinition of the purposes of NATO, which was in some ways a precursor to the more controversial 'dual track decision' of 1979.

Thus Brandt as Chancellor showed great mastery in maintaining good relations with Washington (as well as with London and Paris) during the hectic period of his *Ostpolitik* negotiations with Moscow, Warsaw and East Berlin. By 1973, following the conclusion of the Eastern treaties (and Brandt's own re-election as Chancellor at the end of 1972) and after the enlargement of the EC, there was a new situation in West European-American relations. When Henry Kissinger in the spring of 1973 proclaimed the 'Year of Europe' in American foreign policy and invited – or challenged – the new Europe to step forth as a major actor in a five-polar global system, Brandt, like other European leaders, was not sure how to respond. The nine member states of the EC were in the process of trying to develop a European voice in world affairs through the consultative mechanism of European Political Cooperation, and one of the declared aims of this was to give the European members of the Atlantic Alliance a more effective and more collective say in its affairs – perhaps to give NATO the kind of two-pillar, or dumb-bell, structure envisaged by Kennedy ten years earlier.

Coming at a time when the EC's member states were struggling to define a 'European identity' in this context, Kissinger's proposals of 1973 for a 'new Atlantic Charter' to provide for systematic political and strategic consultations at the Atlantic level received a very mixed reaction in Europe. In Paris, predictably, this apparent bid for American 'hegemony' went down very badly indeed: in Britain, by contrast, the prospect of close and systematic consultations with Washington appeared on the whole welcome and normal. It was greatly to the credit of Willy Brandt, as a European statesman whose international stature was by now greatly enhanced through his successful *Ostpolitik*, that a way was found to reconcile the conflicting designs and perceptions of Washington, Paris and London (not to mention the emerging EC institutions in Brussels).

Even after the further transatlantic storms caused by the 'oil shock' of late 1973 – when the US reacted by threatening the oil producers with confrontation and force, while the EC on the whole opted for a policy of cooperation, including the so-called 'Euro-Arab Dialogue' – Brandt's diplomacy was able to achieve its aim of reconciling the aspiration for a 'European identity' with the pragmatic development of consultation between the EC and the United States. A declaration expressing the nature of the 'European identity' was issued by the EC's Copenhagen summit conference in December 1973, partly thanks to Brandt's tactful mediation between the viewpoints of Pompidou and Heath; and four months later Europe's leading diplomats, now increasingly versed in the habits of European Political Cooperation, complemented this by the so-called 'Gymnich Formula' (named after the German Foreign Ministry's guest house near Bonn), which provided for systematic consultation between the new European grouping and the US.

Brandt and his colleagues should thus be given credit for stabilising the relationship between an expanded EC and its major partner in the West; but we should not forget the equal importance of ensuring that the EC was also embedded in the transformed landscape of Europe's and Germany's new relationship with the East – where lay the origins of the new East-West dialogue which Nixon labelled 'the Era of Negotiations'.

From the late 1960s onwards hopes began to grow in the Federal Republic that real negotiations with Germany's Eastern neighbours might at last be possible, and there arose a vague but widespread feeling that the sterile confrontation of the Cold War might after all give way to something new. Willy Brandt expressed many of these hopes when he declared, in one of his first statements as Foreign Minister: 'We need an orientation which will place the German question in its European context, and for this we need a conception that contains the essentials of a European peace order'.

Brandt's aspiration for a 'European peace order' certainly expressed the spirit of the times – it was incessantly quoted in the debates and controversies which followed – but it was not at first clear how this 'order', with its emphasis on East-West détente, would relate to 'the construction of Europe' in the sense in which this had been promoted by Monnet, Schuman, Adenauer and Hallstein. Indeed, there were strong suspicions that Brandt's 'peace order', if it took the form apparently envisaged by his close adviser Egon Bahr, would involve a Europe of nation states, including a German nation state oriented towards the East, and abandonment of all that Adenauer had stood for. In the event, the Brandt administration was to remain true to the principles laid down by Adenauer: that the Federal Republic's place in NATO and in the EC, its relations with Washington and Paris, were not negotiable, and that any new relationship with the East must be built on these foundations rather than supplanting them. Brandt, a perceptive observer put it, wanted to be not only 'the Adenauer of *Ostpolitik*' but also 'the George Washington of Europe', and his efforts to develop the EC into a European Union as a fixed element in the European peace order were sustained and sincere.

The very fact that the EC was so important to Brandt and his Western colleagues made it all the more suspect in the eyes of Moscow. The Soviet Union refused to give formal recognition to the Community until the late 1980s, but – partly thanks to the priorities laid down by Willy Brandt at a time of decisive changes in Europe – the Community was to remain as a central pillar of the European order after the Soviet Union itself had disappeared.

Germany's policy in the Schmidt years

An assessment of Helmut Schmidt's role in European unification, in comparison with Willy Brandt's, has to take account of the great contrasts between the periods of time in which they held the Chancellorship. Brandt held office in an exceptionally optimistic period characterised by economic growth, East-West détente and the deepening and widening of the EC, whereas Schmidt had to face a time of recession, renewed Cold War tensions and hesitations about European unification in many quarters. Another important factor was the personal contrast between the two men, in terms both of temperament and experience. Brandt came to the Chancellorship after years of highly publicised political campaigning, and his main public responsibilities had been those of Mayor of Berlin and Foreign Minister: both of these posts, while they entailed a heavy burden of decision-making work, also implied an important role for charismatic leadership, either to boost the morale of the West Berliners closed in by the Wall or to build international support for the modest innovations in German foreign policy during the late 1960s. Brandt was a glamorous figure, with a physique which was described as Kennedyesque: the comparison between the two was often made, particularly after Kennedy's famous visit to Berlin in 1963.

Schmidt's experience had been rather different, and his temperament was very different: while Brandt had spent the war years as a political exile in Norway, Schmidt had served with the Wehrmacht in Russia and elsewhere. After the war, and after studying economics at the university of his home town, Hamburg, he began a political career in which he attracted attention as a promising Bundestag debater in the 1950s, and above all as an efficient 'Senator' for home affairs in Hamburg in the 1960s. After serving as the SPD's parliamentary whip during the Kiesinger-Brandt 'grand coalition' – *par excellence* a job for a political fixer with a gift for detail – he held the key ministries of defence and finance during Brandt's period as Chancellor. Schmidt thus came to the Chancellorship with extensive experience of the problems of international security and finance, both of which remained at the top of the agenda throughout his period in office. Like his friend and counterpart Dennis Healey, Schmidt enjoyed a reputation for a businesslike approach to politics and a rough style in political arguments, whether these were on parliamentary or private occasions.

The complementary talents of Brandt and Schmidt – one the charismatic socialist orator, the other the down-to-earth man with a reputation for getting things done – produced a natural partnership which for a time gave great strength to their Social Democratic-led government. In 1974, when Schmidt succeeded Brandt as Chancellor, the latter kept his post as party Chairman – which indeed he had assumed in 1964 and was to hold until 1987. Thus, while Brandt during the exciting years since 1969 had been both Chancellor and party leader, the roles were separated during the more difficult period of Schmidt's Chancellorship. It was in many ways a source of strength that, while the no-nonsense Schmidt adopted policies designed to reassure the business community or Germany's NATO allies, the party guru Brandt was available to persuade the often reluctant left wing of the SPD to overcome its aversion to policies of this kind. However, Schmidt himself, after his fall from office in 1982, argued that he had made a mistake in not combining the two offices, as Brandt had done: Schmidt felt that if he had been able to speak to the party as its own leader as well as the head of the government, he might have been able to win Social Democratic support for the policies of economic retrenchment and military rearmament which the party in the end rejected.

When Schmidt took over from Brandt in 1974 – almost simultaneously with the arrival in office of Valéry Giscard d'Estaing and Harold Wilson – the European Community had more or less settled down after the incorporation of its new members: from the point of view of Germany's interests, it now offered a mixed range of advantages and potential burdens.

For Germany, the advantages of the EEC – which left no doubt that Schmidt would continue to support and develop it – included first and foremost the fact that Germany's firm incorporation in a West European group of democracies gave the best guarantee of peace and security both for Germany and for her neighbours. This remained true even though Brandt's *Ostpolitik* had begun the process of stabilising Germany's relations with Europe's eastern part as well. Schmidt fully shared Brandt's view that a process of changing the Soviet Bloc through getting nearer to it ('change through *rapprochement*', as Egon Bahr had called it) offered the best hope of moving towards the distant goal of national unification, but he also saw that this could only be achieved if the Federal Republic remained firmly anchored in the West.

On this basis Schmidt worked out a German strategy towards the East with his Foreign Minister, Hans-Dietrich Genscher, the leading Free Democratic minister who took Walter Scheel's place when the latter was elected Germany's Federal President in April 1974. Genscher was temperamentally somewhat similar to Schmidt, as Scheel had been similar to Brandt. A pair of pragmatic and calculating politicians now took over from a pair of more flamboyant predecessors. The central theme of this Eastern policy was that the breakthrough achieved by Brandt should now be followed up and consolidated by the 'Europeanisation' of *Ostpolitik*, which would imply that the Eastern and Western blocs in Europe would come together in a more businesslike relationship, as the two German states were beginning to do. Schmidt and Genscher brought this objective nearer in 1975, after hard negotiations in the mid-1970s between a total of 35 states, with the signature in 1975 of the Helsinki Final Act of the Conference on Security and Cooperation in Europe. This impressive artefact of multilateral diplomacy, signed by heads of government from Washington to Moscow, codified the basic principle of a more secure and cooperative Europe. The signatories committed themselves to develop 'confidence-building measures' in the field of international security (including a pledge not to change international frontiers by force), to promote trade and economic cooperation generally, to respect such basic human rights as the right to travel freely, to receive publications and other information from foreign countries and to be united with other members of one's own family.

For Schmidt's government the link between this ambitious pan-European programme and the consolidation of the EC in Europe's Western part was very clear. In the first place, the Community had a natural role in the economic agenda laid down in the second main chapter of the Helsinki document (known as 'Basket 2') since Germany and the EC's other member states had transferred responsibility for foreign trade policy, including tariffs, to the Community when they created its Common Commercial Policy. More generally, the negotiations leading to the Helsinki Agreement in 1973-5 and the ensuing review conferences convened at two-year intervals to monitor progress in implementation provided a perfect forum for the embryonic common foreign policy known as 'European Political Cooperation'. The diplomats of the EC's member-states, with Germany playing a leading part on these issues of East-West relations, developed great skill at arriving at shared assessments of East European and Soviet developments and working out common positions on the various points to be negotiated.

This development of an *Ostpolitik* for the EC, encompassing and carrying forward Germany's own actions in the direction of what Brandt had called a 'European Peace Order', represented an important element in the Schmidt administration's policies in relation to the Community.

Turning to the internal policies of the EC, particularly its central economic objectives, Helmut Schmidt and his colleagues faced a difficult dilemma. On the one hand the competitive German economy had everything to gain from the liberalisation of the EC's internal market, and also, by the end of the 1970s, from an extension of its frontiers which would add further regions of Europe to the area that was secure for German trade and investment. On the other hand, the level of economic development of the Community was so diverse (even before the question of membership for Spain, Portugal and Greece became realistic) that the only way to create an open market, let alone a unified currency area, was for the richer member states, especially Germany, to transfer resources into building up the economic infrastructure of the Community's peripheral regions. Schmidt complained that Germany could not forever be 'the paymaster of Europe'; but he accepted, in effect, that in order to achieve the 'negative integration' of the removal of barriers to free movement of goods and investment, Germany had to accept 'positive integration' in the form of a European Regional Development Fund managed from Brussels. He complained, in this connection, that the Fund should not spray its resources indiscriminately over Europe 'like a watering can', but should be concentrated on specific infrastructure projects: once this argument was taken into account, his government was in the end willing to pay the lion's share of the necessary budget.

Another aspect of the Community's economic policy where Germany had specific interests was that of external trade. The temptation to pursue protectionist policies, which had been characteristic of France and some other member states since the EC started, was strengthened by the recession of the 1970s. However, Schmidt's government, together with the United Kingdom, took the lead in fighting for a more liberal trade policy. The results of this were shown, for instance, in the outcome of the Tokyo Round of GATT negotiations (1973-9), which significantly reduced the barriers to world trade: the fruits of this agreement, fortunately, included the containment at least of one source of friction between the EC and the United States, at a time when their relations were going through a difficult period for other reasons.

As early as the end of 1974, when Schmidt had been Chancellor for just over six months, an EC summit in Paris took important decisions on many of the policy issues just mentioned. The formal establishment of the Regional Development Fund was accompanied by a commitment to try to maintain Economic and Monetary Union; the transformation of the EC's occasional summit meetings into the institutionalised European Council, which was basically inter-governmental, following the wishes of France, was balanced by the decision to proceed with direct elections to the European Parliament, potentially a strong supranational institution, as Germany desired; and a budgetary adjustment mechanism was established, ensuring a fairer deal to all member states, and partly with an eye to winning a pro-European result in the British referendum due to be held after the Wilson government's renegotiation of the terms of British membership. In all of these measures, designed to consolidate and advance the process of Europe's integration, the hand of Helmut Schmidt could be detected. Indeed, on the issue of the UK referendum, he played an active individual role by appearing at the Labour Party's special conference on the subject to make an emotional appeal for a 'yes' vote because, as he put it, 'your German comrades need you in'.

There were other issues to be taken into account in Schmidt's assessment of how Germany should work to develop and to use the EC. These included a specifically German problem, that of the complicated interactions between the EC and Berlin. This, of course, was not a matter which the Chancellor had to handle on a daily basis: the complex set of issues affecting Berlin was managed not only by the Chancellor's Office but also by the Foreign Ministry under Genscher as well as the Ministry of Inner-German Affairs, and sometimes others, too. However, the link between the Berlin question and the development of the EC did have distinct implications for high politics, and thus was often an issue to be considered by the Chancellor personally.

The links between the EC and Berlin had a long history. West Berlin – both for economic and for political reasons – had been included since the beginning in the geographical area covered by the provisions of the Treaty of Rome. However, the Federal Republic's three Western allies with responsibility for Berlin and for 'questions affecting Germany as a whole' had always refused to recognise the *Land* of West Berlin as an integral part of the Federal Republic: to do this, they argued, would open the way for the Soviet Union to integrate East Berlin formally into the GDR, and thus to weaken the West's chances of influencing Germany's future. Over the years, West Berlin's involvement in the EC's economic development programmes, and the application of EC laws and regulations there, raised occasional minor difficulties with the Western allies, but the situation became potentially much more strained in the 1970s. The four-power agreement on Berlin, signed in 1971, explicitly prohibited the location of Federal Government agencies in Berlin, and Bonn's insistence shortly afterwards on placing the new Federal Environmental Agency there led to a major diplomatic row with the Russians, and consequent recriminations between Bonn and the Western allies. The Federal Government, now strictly forbidden to do anything of this kind again, but still concerned to reinforce Berlin's links with the West, began systematically to use West Berlin's status in the European Community to encourage EC institutions to hold important events there, and even – as with the European Centre for Vocational Training, established in 1977 – to choose Berlin as their location. This very understandable line of German policy was hotly denounced by the Soviet and East German governments, which claimed that European links of this kind represented an attempt to incorporate West Berlin in the Federal Republic by indirect means. These accusations were redoubled when it was announced that three Berlin parliamentarians were to be included among the 81 German members of the directly-elected European Parliament, for which elections were scheduled for 1979. The fact was that the three West Berliners – at the insistence of the Western powers – were indeed *not* to be directly elected, but were to be nominated by the Berlin City Assembly. However, this was not enough to still Russia's complaints that West Berlin was being illegally absorbed into a West European superpower – moreover a superpower whose leaders were beginning to hint, by the late 1970s, that its power might one day be military as well as economic.

As things turned out, by the time this larger project was seriously debated within the EC at the Inter-Governmental Conference which produced the Maastricht Treaty at the end of 1991, the Soviet Union had relinquished its authority in Berlin to a united Germany. This particular Berlin conflict was thus, quite unexpectedly, resolved. However, the experience of the interactions between Berlin, Bonn, the EC and the outside powers, particularly during the 1970s, demonstrated how carefully Schmidt and his administration had to tread in trying to promote a legitimate German interest – that of links with West Berlin – by means of Germany's involvement in the EC.

Perhaps the European issue most closely identified with Helmut Schmidt, however, is the establishment of the European Monetary System at the end of the 1970s. The currency 'snake' established in Brandt's time had run into difficulties as the international financial situation became more uncertain: Britain and Italy left the system after only a brief period of membership, and even France, after leaving it and then rejoining in 1974-5, left again in March 1976. The French policy of financial austerity, introduced by Giscard d'Estaing in the wake of this event, coincided with Helmut Schmidt's determination to establish a zone of monetary stability in Europe: it was this convergence of French and German interests which made possible the creation of the EMS. Schmidt and Giscard were both alarmed by the precipitous decline in the value of the dollar from early 1977 onwards (matters were not improved by the very poor personal relations between Schmidt and US President Jimmy Carter), and they worked actively on plans to counteract the disruptive effects of the dollar's decline on Europe. The discussions between world leaders at the Group of Seven summit in Bonn in 1978, under Schmidt's chairmanship, confirmed the need for action, and at the European Council in Brussels at the end of that year the creation of the new European Monetary System was agreed.

The EMS was in fact only to come into operation three months later in March 1979 because of a dispute over reforming the system of financial payments connected with the Common Agricultural Policy – a cause to which Schmidt attached great importance. In the EMS the main characteristics of the new monetary regime were the establishment of fixed but adaptable exchange rates, the permissible variations being no more than 2.25 percent; the European Currency Unit (the ECU) as the common denominator for currency parities; and the establishment of a system for settling balances and providing credit, the European Fund for Monetary Cooperation. Schmidt was heavily involved in the establishment of the new structures, believing as he did that common European action to promote price stability was essential to prevent the existing Common Market from falling apart. The objectives of the EMS, in his mind, were: firstly, to keep Europe's exchange-rates as stable as possible, in order to promote the value of European currencies and to develop the EC through increased internal trade; secondly, to ensure that if changes in exchange rates did become essential, such revaluations or devaluations were only carried out after due consultation, so as to further the long-term convergence of national monetary and economic policies and thus the development of economic integration; and thirdly, to develop the ECU into a single European currency capable of exercising world influence in the same way as the dollar and the yen.

Schmidt had the satisfaction of seeing the EMS give Europe a decade or more of stable exchange-rates and growing economic integration, before a new set of pressures – arising partly from German unification – raised new difficulties for the whole enterprise. Schmidt's hopes for progress in Europe's monetary affairs suffered disappointment from the fact that Italy hesitated before joining the EMS and that the UK, while joining the EMS as a whole, remained outside one of its central institutions, the Exchange Rate Mechanism. However, by 1990 enough remained of what Schmidt and Giscard had created to give some hope for a further advance in economic and monetary union after the Maastricht Treaty, an opportunity his Christian Democrat successor as Chancellor, Helmut Kohl, seized decisively.

Schmidt's last few years in office were dominated by storm-clouds of a different kind: the threat to European peace which arose from the Soviet invasion of Afghanistan in 1979 and the imposition of martial law in Poland in 1981. Schmidt was among the most vocal of Europe's leaders in urging the two superpowers not to allow these conflicts to damage the prospects of a peaceful order in Europe. He was particularly concerned when the new American administration under Ronald Reagan threatened an escalation both of political and of military confrontation with the Soviet Union. Schmidt was alarmed at this prospect, even though he was personally in favour of an increase in NATO's resources in Long-range Tactical Nuclear Forces

(Pershing II and Cruise missiles), as long as the Soviet Union's superior strength in this category of weapons was not reduced. By stressing the concept of a distinct military balance for the 'European theatre' – controversial though this was, not least in his own party – Schmidt was drawing attention very clearly to the fact that Europe's strategic position was not identical with that of America, and that Europe's specific interests and problems should be more directly taken into account.

There was an ironical element in the decline and fall of Helmut Schmidt as Chancellor. It was ironic for some that the fall of Brandt's predecessor, Ludwig Erhard, in 1966 had been provoked by failures in economic policy, of which Erhard was thought to be a master; and that Willy Brandt, the great impresario of East-West détente, should have been forced to resign in 1974 after the discovery of an East German spy in his entourage. In the same way Schmidt's own fall in October 1982 was due at least in part to the unwillingness of his party to support him on the issues on which he was an outstanding expert, those of international security.

After the problem of an imbalance in 'Long-range Tactical Nuclear Forces' had become a central issue in East-West strategic relations (partly thanks to Schmidt's London lecture of October 1977), NATO moved towards its 'dual track' decision of December 1979: this implied in essence that if the number of Soviet SS20 missiles targeted on Western Europe was not reduced by negotiation, NATO would redress the balance by stationing Pershing II and Cruise missiles in Germany and elsewhere in Western Europe. East-West exchanges on this issue ground forward during 1980 and 1981: it would be too much to call them 'negotiations', and their slim chances of success were further reduced by the escalation of East-West tension resulting from the crises in Afghanistan and Poland. Schmidt's political position was seriously weakened by a public split in his party, in which the party Chairman Willy Brandt became the leading spokesman of the opposition to Schmidt's policy on nuclear weapons.

At the same time that Schmidt's position was being weakened, his Foreign Minister was having some success in brightening his own image as a promoter of European integration. He did this by launching in January 1981 the initiative which became known as the 'Genscher-Colombo' plan and led indirectly to the Single European Act of 1986 and the Treaty on European Union of the early 1990s. Genscher's proposal for a consolidation and continuation of European integration under the new title of 'European Union' was thus to bear fruit only after a number of years – by which time Genscher was the Foreign Minister of another coalition, under Helmut Kohl. It could certainly be said that, given the great popularity of the idea of European unity in Germany, Genscher's strong public identification with this theme helped to enhance his political standing and with it the attractiveness of the FDP as a coalition partner for Kohl's Christian Democratic Union (CDU).

Schmidt's reaction to the Genscher initiative was less than enthusiastic: he was more interested in the concrete development of Germany's collaboration with France on such important issues as defence and economic policy. In both these areas Schmidt made significant progress with Giscard d'Estaing and continued it with his successor Mitterrand after the change of presidency in 1981. Schmidt's increasingly close cooperation with France was not due to innate Francophilia but grew from his developing sense of where the priority interests of Germany and of Europe lay. As he explained in an interview with *The Economist* in 1979: 'I grew up as an anglophile, then became up to a point an americanophile, and have now, in the course of my ten years in government, developed into a francophile'. Under Schmidt's Chancellorship the partnership between Bonn and Paris grew stronger: despite their differences on many issues, they were prepared to work hard and consistently at their joint goal of making Europe more united.

Despite the election victory of his coalition in 1980 Schmidt's position was undermined by the divisions in his party and, to an increasing degree, by disagreements with the FDP about economic and budgetary issues. Finally, in the early autumn of 1982, the FDP ministers in his government resigned and shortly afterwards their party agreed on the terms of a new coalition pact with Helmut Kohl's CDU. The new parliamentary majority then voted Schmidt out of office, replacing him by Kohl on 1 October 1982.

This short survey of Helmut Schmidt's record in office confirms his commitment to the goal of a united Europe: he believed that this offered Europe the best hope of economic prosperity, political stability, and international security. Even though Schmidt did not often express himself with the political passion of his predecessor, Brandt, his feelings on the subject were very strong and they were expressed with force and eloquence. Examples of this have already been quoted, in the writings and declarations he made in the years after his retirement. A further testimony to his European convictions may be found in a speech he prepared for delivery to the Social Democratic Party (SPD) Mannheim Congress of mid-November 1995. (Schmidt did not in fact deliver the speech. He decided not to attend the congress after learning that it had deposed Rudolf Scharping as party Chairman in favour of Oskar Lafontaine, but he had the text printed in *Die Zeit* on 24 November 1995). Schmidt's peroration includes these words:

> Peace on our little continent depends on the progress of European integration ... the progress of European integration is a fundamental interest of the German people! Adenauer knew that, Brandt and Schmidt knew that, and Kohl knows it too. So I say to you, Rudolf, and to you, Gerhard Schroeder: will you also please make sure you know it, and take it to heart ... And take good care of our friendship with France, which is the most precious blessing that we have received in the twentieth century ...

Schmidt's retrospective flourish of 1995 is certainly accurate in including both Brandt and himself among the German postwar leaders who recognised the fundamental importance for Germany of promoting what some people call 'the construction' and others 'the Europeanisation' of Europe. Of course there was an element of rhetoric in the statements they made, as well as an element of German national interest in the policies they pursued; but most observers would conclude that both Brandt and Schmidt interpreted this national interest in a broadminded and forward-looking way, and worked to develop economic policies and political structures designed to serve the interests of both Germany and of Europe.

Selected biblography

Bracher, K-D, *et al* (1986) *Geschichte der Bundesrepublik Deutschland, Band 5, Republik im Wandel I. 1969-1974, Die Ära Brandt*, Stuttgart: Deutsche Verlags-Anstalt.

Brandt, Willy (1976) *Begegnungen und Einsichten, Die Jahren 1960-1975*, Hamburg: Hoffmann und Campe.

(1989) *Erinnerungen*, Frankfurt-am-Main: Farenczy.

Carr, J. (1985) *Helmut Schmidt: Helmsman of Germany*, London: Weidenfeld and Nicolson.

Everling, Ulrich (1983) 'Die Bundesrepublik in der Europäischen Gemeinschaft' in R. Bieber and D. Nickel, eds (1988) *Das Europa der Zweiten Generation, Gedächtnisschrift für Christoph Sasse*, Baden-Baden: Nomos.

Federal Government, (1988) *European Political Cooperation (EPC)*, Bonn: Press and Information Office, 5th edn.

Jäger, W *et al* (1987) *Geschichte der Bundesrepublik Deutschland, Band 5, Republik im Wandel II. 1974-1982, Die Ära Schmidt*, Stuttgart: Deutsche Verlags-Anstalt.

Ludlow, Peter (1982) *The Making of the European Monetary System*, London: Butterworths.

Morgan, Roger (1974) *The United States and West Germany, 1945-1973. A Study in Alliance Politics*, London: Oxford University Press for the Royal Institute of International Affairs and the Harvard Center for International Affairs.

and C. Bray (1986) 'Western Europe and West Berlin' in R. Francisco and R. Merritt, eds (1986) *Berlin Between Two Worlds*, Boulder and London: Westview Press.

Peters, S. (1990) *The Germans and the INF Missiles*, Baden-Baden: Nomos.

Schmidt, Helmut (1992) *Menschen und Mächte, Band 2: Die Deutschen und ihre Nachbarn*, Berlin: Siedler.

Britain's indecision –
from Macmillan to the Referendum

Dick Leonard

Harold Macmillan, Hugh Gaitskell, Edward Heath, Harold Wilson, James Callaghan, Roy Jenkins and Tony Benn were the main British political actors in the turbulent period between July 1961, when the first British application for entry into the European Economic Community was tabled, and June 1975, when membership was endorsed by a two-to-one majority in a referendum. They are all entitled to be considered as 'Eminent Europeans', though not all of them would be admitted into a pantheon of whole-hearted labourers in the cause of European integration.

The most ambivalent figure in this list is perhaps Macmillan. He was the prime minister who made the first approach to the EEC. He showed great skill, and no little ruthlessness, in marshalling his own party behind the cause. Moreover, he showed good judgment in appointing Heath as his chief negotiator with the six founder members of the Community, and the detailed negotiations were pushed to the brink of success before they were aborted by de Gaulle's veto in January 1963. Yet Macmillan cannot escape part of the responsibility for provoking this veto, and throughout most of his earlier ministerial career he shared the debilitating illusions of national grandeur which prevented most of his countrymen from viewing the European adventure in a realistic light. He himself later acknowledged his error when, writing in the Prologue to his autobiography, he confided: 'I shall never cease to blame myself' for not having stood out against the consensus of postwar Labour and Conservative governments in their opposition to Britain becoming a founder member of either the European Coal and Steel Community or the EEC.

Indeed, much in Macmillan's earlier life might have suggested a stronger and earlier commitment. His American mother insisted that he should become a competent French linguist, he spent two years in the trenches of the First World War fighting alongside French comrades, in the Second World War he was Minister-Resident in North Africa, working with de Gaulle and gaining insight into the views of the French and other European allies. He was closely associated with the European Movement in the late 1940s and was a delegate to the Council of Europe. His record as a rebel Tory MP in the 1930s showed that he was unafraid of challenging party orthodoxy in causes in which he strongly believed, such as the need for a planned economy to combat the effects of the Depression and the necessity of standing up to fascist dictators.

Yet, as a minister in the Churchill and Eden governments from 1951-7, hardly a flicker of his earlier independence and wide-ranging vision was seen to survive. In their place appeared a rather world-weary figure, increasingly cynical in his approach, and appearing to be more concerned to curry favour with fellow Conservatives than to question the validity of their prejudices. He gave every indication during this period that he fully subscribed to Churchill's famous analysis of the three interlocking spheres of influence within which British foreign policy should operate, with Anglo-US relations in first place, the Commonwealth in second, and Europe definitely in third place.

At the time of the Messina conference in June 1955 he was already Foreign Secretary and, with Prime Minister Eden, must have been mainly responsible for the decision that Britain should not be represented. Instead, a middle-ranking civil servant, Russell Bretherton, was despatched as an observer. Later, when the six governments represented at Messina wanted to give Britain a further chance to climb aboard before the final negotiations for the Treaty of Rome were concluded, Macmillan was sent an invitation to attend talks. 'I don't want to go. Tell them I'm too busy dealing with Cyprus,' was the insouciant instruction he gave to one of his top Foreign Office officials, Nicholas Henderson.

It was the Suez War, in which Macmillan earned the dubious distinction of being 'the first in and the first out', which stripped the wool from his eyes. Having been one of the strongest advocates of military intervention against Egypt, he abruptly changed tack when, as Chancellor of the Exchequer, he had to cope with a terrifying run on Britain's currency reserves only a few days into the action. He had to reconcile himself to the fact that Britain – even in alliance with France – was no longer a major player on the world stage. Even then he failed to draw the logical conclusion that membership of the European Community would be the best hope of making British influence felt. He promoted instead the essentially spoiling tactic of creating the European Free Trade Association (EFTA), the unavowed purpose of which was to neutralise, or at least provide a makeweight to, the EEC.

It was another four years before, after endless hesitation, he at last took the plunge and decided to apply for British entry. This was a full year after an interdepartmental committee of senior civil servants had concluded that 'on political grounds – that is, to ensure a politically stable and cohesive Western Europe – there was a strong argument for joining the Common Market'. In the meantime the bulk of the serious press – the *Financial Times, The Economist, The Guardian, The Observer* and *The Times* – had concluded that this was the only feasible option. Strong pressure from the new Kennedy administration was reinforced by evidence that de Gaulle was pressing to turn the EEC from a purely economic organisation into an instrument for political co-operation, from which Britain's exclusion threatened to undermine her influence on the world stage further. Moreover, Britain's dwindling standing, even within the Commonwealth, was underlined when, following the Sharpeville massacre, South Africa was effectively forced out against the wishes of the British government.

Macmillan compounded his hesitation by the lukewarm nature of his statement to the House of Commons announcing the British application. This provoked a perceptive comment in the following day's edition of *The Guardian*:

> The plunge is to be taken, but, on yesterday's evidence, by a shivering government ... All that Mr Macmillan said is correct. But his approach is so half-hearted that it must diminish the chances of success in the negotiations. He has made a depressing start ...We must show that we believe in the ambition of a politically united Europe. This is just what Mr Macmillan has not done.

One reason for Macmillan's snail-like approach was undoubtedly his fear of trouble within the Conservative Party. In particular, he was concerned that his rival, and deputy, R.A. Butler, would use the issue as a pretext to try to unseat him from the leadership. In the event his fears proved unfounded and his speech to the Conservative conference in October 1961, in which he argued with much greater enthusiasm than he had shown in the House of Commons, was an overwhelming success. By December 1962 the negotiations had been all but concluded, and the French Foreign Minister, Maurice Couve de Murville, told Edward Heath that 'nothing can now prevent their success'.

On 15 December Macmillan hastened to a meeting with President de Gaulle at Rambouillet, from which he returned mistakenly confident that the French president accepted Macmillan's decision to seek Polaris missiles from the Americans rather than to develop an Anglo-French missile, but apprehensive, as he later told his biographer Alistair Horne, 'that de Gaulle would, if he dared, use some means, overt or covert, to prevent the fruition of the Brussels negotiation'.

Three days later Macmillan met Kennedy at Nassau, where he was informed that the United States was to cancel development of the Skybolt missile, on which the British government had depended as a delivery system for its so-called independent nuclear deterrent. As Horne relates, a reluctant Kennedy acceded to Macmillan's humiliating plea to supply Polaris instead, while privately describing Macmillan's cherished deterrent, which had caused all the fuss, as 'a political necessity but a piece of military foolishness'.

At the time, the Nassau Agreement was widely blamed for the veto which de Gaulle announced three weeks later. In retrospect, the judgment of Anthony Verrier, the historian, seems more plausible:

> In 1963 de Gaulle would probably have vetoed the British government's application to join the EEC whether or not the Nassau deal had been made. De

Gaulle detested this apparent revival of the special relationship, but his opposition to Britain joining the EEC was mainly based on his determination
that France should dominate it. However, Macmillan, by making the realisation of
a British nuclear deterrent a political priority and reducing Britain's application to join the EEC to second place, provided de Gaulle with a pretext.

Horne, who usually gave Macmillan the benefit of any doubt, shared Verrier's view,
but frankly posed the question of whether the failure of the first British application
was 'Macmillan's fault?' He wrote:

> A criticism with hindsight more difficult to counter is that Macmillan failed
> to use his vast majority of October 1959 and the national support he still
> maintained over the next two years with audacity to sweep the British elector-
> ate into Europe. Instead, as has been seen, he delayed ... when a show of less
> hesitation could have convinced Europe, if not France, of Britain's new deter-
> mination ... So valuable time was lost, until de Gaulle himself became strong
> enough to turn what looked like pusillanimity against Macmillan, and then to
> impose his one-man veto over the rest of Europe.

Macmillan's record is open to criticism on at least one other score. As Philip Williams,
Hugh Gaitskell's biographer, commented:

> To some leaders such a great historic decision, about which alarm and enthu-
> siasm both cut across party lines, might have seemed appropriate for an at-
> tempt at bipartisanship. Macmillan never made the smallest gesture in that
> direction, for he was planning a crusade to carry the great decision into his-
> tory – and the Conservative Party back to power.

Perhaps Gaitskell would have scorned any such approach, but everything in his
previous career suggests that this would only have been after a thorough and consci-
entious consideration of the issue on its merits. Certainly he was suspicious of
Macmillan, understandably so in view of the sharp practice which he believed he
had employed before and during the 1959 general election campaign. Williams quotes
a letter which Gaitskell wrote to one of his constituency supporters in Leeds shortly
before Macmillan announced his application:

> Macmillan is a very crafty man. This is one reason why I am determined not
> to let the Party get committed on the Common Market. If we try to reach a
> decision ourselves I am pretty certain we would remain hopelessly divided
> while the Tories reluctantly decide to unite behind whatever Macmillan de-
> cides to do.

Gaitskell undoubtedly subscribed to the view that the link with the United States,
and the NATO alliance, was the most important factor in Britain's foreign relations.
He also attached enormous importance to the Commonwealth, though his sympa-

thies lay more with the Asian and African members than with the former White Dominions which had so strong an appeal to the 'kith and kin' Tories. Yet he was by no means hostile in principle to the notion of British membership of the EEC. Williams asserts that 'Commentators and colleagues all believed that he was privately a cautious supporter of entry'.

Gaitskell's own appreciation of his position, which he retrospectively analysed in a candid memorandum to President Kennedy in December 1962 is quoted at some length by Williams:

> From the start not only the Opposition but the Government as well were *not* in favour of *'going in and trying to get the best possible terms'* but only for *'going in if certain conditions were fulfilled'*...
>
> It may be said that in reality the Government had decided to go in whatever the terms and that they only laid down conditions in order to make their new policy acceptable to their Party. I do not know whether this is the case ... As for the Opposition, we certainly took the conditions very seriously ... I myself and my leading colleagues all happened to believe and still believe that the arguments of principle were fairly evenly balanced for and against and that the balance would be tipped in favour of our entry only if our conditions were fulfilled. Secondly, this policy of making our final judgment depend on the conditions was the only one which could have been accepted by the Party as a whole. If I had urged [either] unconditional entry [or] ... outright opposition whatever the terms ... there would have been a major split in the Party, which, following the great dispute on defence which had only recently been successfully concluded, would have been fatal to our prospects. Both minorities, however, were willing to depend on the terms, nor was there any real disagreement about what the terms must be.

I myself can keenly recall the growing alarm with which Labour pro-Europeans, who had been among Gaitskell's closest supporters in his epic struggle against the unilateralists over the previous two years, noted Gaitskell's gradual hardening against EEC membership during the late summer of 1962. Nothing, however, prepared us for the shock of his speech at the October Labour Party conference when, in highly emotional terms, he rejected the conditions which the Macmillan government had so far obtained in their Brussels negotiations. The speech itself was a conference triumph, better received than any he had previously given, though as his wife, Dora Gaitskell, wanly commented: 'All the wrong people are cheering'.

Various people have been blamed for Gaitskell finally coming off the fence on the anti-EEC side, notably the Indian diplomat K.B. Lall, a formidable advocate of Commonwealth interests, and Peter Shore, then research secretary of the Labour Party, who later emerged as one of the strongest and most persistent critics of the EEC and of British membership. It is certainly true that Shore produced a series of background papers for Gaitskell which were uniformly negative in tone, but there can be little doubt that the Labour leader was already moving firmly in the same direction.

The decisive influence on him was the meeting of Commonwealth heads of government in London in September 1962, when one after another the prime ministers of Canada (Diefenbaker), Australia (Menzies) and New Zealand (Holyoake) – all fellow Conservatives – rounded on Macmillan, claiming that he had failed to protect their countries' interests in the negotiations and that British accession to the EEC would have disastrous effects on their export trade.

On the eve of this conference, Gaitskell met the leaders of the Commonwealth Socialist parties for three days of talks, and was profoundly impressed by the degree of their hostility to the terms. He became convinced that Macmillan had abandoned the original conditions he had set out at the time of the British application, and was determined to bring Britain into the Community on any terms he could get. As Williams put it, 'That discovery transformed his whole bearing; from being cool, rational and calculating, he became heated, emotional and passionate.'

This was no passing aberration, but rather part of a pattern in Gaitskell's political career. He was not quick to make up his mind on complex issues; he believed in making a careful study of what he regarded as the relevant evidence. But once he had decided, he was adamant, and presented his case with a passion and panache which delighted his friends and discomfited his opponents.

He had displayed these qualities when he opposed Aneurin Bevan in 1951 over health service charges, elevating what – in the context of his budget – appeared a difference over a trifling sum into a matter of high principle. Again in 1960, when in the face of imminent defeat over unilateralism at the Labour Party conference in Scarborough, he promised to 'fight, and fight and fight again to save the Party we love', galvanising sufficient support to narrow the margin of defeat and preparing the ground for a triumphal reversal the following year.

It was the same tune at the Brighton conference in 1962. He might have made a low-key speech, noting that while he personally found the arguments for and against entry evenly balanced, he regretted that he had to recommend rejection because the terms negotiated appeared to be too damaging to Commonwealth interests. Instead, he launched into a bravura attack on the whole enterprise, culminating in the words: 'We have a government of faint hearts trembling on the brink of selling out a thousand years of history, tradition, political independence and individual liberty for a mess of pottage.'

Many of Gaitskell's closest associates – pro-marketeers almost to a man – consoled themselves with the belief that his opposition was, in reality, confined to certain specific terms which were damaging to the Commonwealth and that if a future negotiation could obtain better terms he would support them. Indeed, they foresaw that he himself would conduct such a negotiation. Perhaps so; we shall never know. Just over three months after delivering the speech he was dead: three days later de Gaulle pronounced his veto.

Gaitskell's words may not have had any significant effect on whether, or when, Britain should accede, though it is conceivable that they may have encouraged de Gaulle to proceed to his veto, strengthened in the knowledge that the British government did not have bipartisan support. What is certain is that the legacy which he left the Labour Party on the EEC issue had a lamentable effect on the way in which it was handled in the future. He lent a cloak of respectability to the anti-EEC cause, and made it easier for its advocates to seize control of the Party.

When de Gaulle signalled his veto in January 1963, he also made a perceptive prediction. 'The Labour Party,' he said, 'will come to power for a short and disastrous period, to be followed by the Conservatives with Heath at their head. It is he who will enable Britain to enter Europe.' The Labour interlude was, in fact, not particularly short, lasting from 1964 to 1970. Nor would it be fair to characterise it as disastrous, though many of its brightest hopes were shattered by the crippling delay in deciding to devalue the pound. It launched a second application for EC entry in 1967, and Prime Minister Harold Wilson and Foreign Secretary George Brown made a pilgrimage to the Elysée Palace to see whether they could persuade de Gaulle to change his mind. In vain. Neither does it seem likely that Heath would, at that time, have had any greater success, despite de Gaulle's prediction. In fact, by the time that Heath was able to take such an initiative, de Gaulle was absent from the scene, having resigned in 1969 and dying the following year. His successor, Georges Pompidou, shared little of his distrust of British intentions.

Yet Heath had one inestimable advantage over the authors of the two previous British applications, Macmillan and Wilson. Unlike them, he was no reluctant convert, but a long-term and passionate believer that Britain's destiny lay in Europe. When he was first elected to Parliament, in 1950, he devoted his maiden speech to an appeal for European unity, strongly regretting the British decision not to subscribe to the Schuman Plan. Before the War, as an Oxford undergraduate, he had already acquired marked European tastes through holiday visits to several continental countries, including Spain, from which he returned with convinced pro-Republican sympathies, unusual for a British Tory. He also supported the independent Socialist candidate, A.D. Lindsay, in the famous Oxford by-election in 1938 against the pro-Munich Tory candidate, Quintin Hogg, later Lord Hailsham.

When he unexpectedly became Prime Minister in June 1970, Heath found that the outgoing Labour government was well advanced in preparations to launch a third application. It had designated George Thomson as the minister responsible for conducting the negotiation, and Labour's election manifesto indicated that if sufficiently favourable terms could be achieved the party would recommend their acceptance.

Heath lost no time in tabling the application and he relied extensively on the contacts he had made during the Macmillan application and as a member of Jean Monnet's Action Committee for the United States of Europe to hurry the process along. One of his contacts was Michel Jobert, Secretary-General of the French Foreign Ministry, who had met Heath while on holiday in Spain. President Pompidou asked Jobert if he could rely on Heath for straight dealing, and when he was told that he could he invited the British Prime Minister for one-to-one talks at the Elysée Palace. The meeting, which took place in May 1971, was a success and led to a bond of mutual confidence between the two men. Spurred on by the German Chancellor, Willy Brandt, Pompidou encouraged the EC negotiators to proceed in a co-operative spirit, and by late June the deal was done.

Four issues dominated the negotiation – sterling, the Commonwealth, agriculture and the size of the British budget contribution. On the first of these, the difficulty was removed when French Finance Minister, Valéry Giscard d'Estaing, accepted a British undertaking that the sterling balances would be rapidly run down and that sterling should no longer be an international reserve currency. On the Commonwealth, Heath managed to achieve a better deal than during the Macmillan negotiation, notably by securing guaranteed access for a period of years for New Zealand butter and cheese and Caribbean sugar. On the Common Agricultural Policy (CAP), Heath had to accept that the system could not now be fundamentally changed, and he concentrated instead on a achieving a satisfactory period for the phasing in of the full effects of the policy on prices, and on obtaining concessions on certain particularly sensitive items. On the British budgetary contribution, Heath recognised that it might eventually become unacceptably large in relation to the other member states, but judged that it would be easier to negotiate on this issue once Britain was a member. He therefore sought a long transitional period during which the British contribution would build up only gradually, trusting that the system of Community financing would be adjusted later.

In making relatively modest demands during the negotiations, Heath virtually assured that they would be successful and would be concluded within a fairly short period. Any other strategy would have risked a further rebuff, or at the very least would have stretched out the bargaining over an unacceptably long period. In pursuing this path, Heath proved himself to be a realist, showing that he accepted that there was a price to be paid for Britain missing the boat in 1951 over the ECSC, and again in 1957 over the Treaties of Rome, and that it was only over the longer term that it would be possible to recoup.

He was doubtless guilty of some tactical errors, and gave a hostage to fortune when he said that Britain should not become a member of the European Community 'without the full-hearted consent of the British Parliament and people'. The consent actually given was evidently less than 'full-hearted': the parliamentary majority in

October 1971 was a respectable 356 votes to 244 (thanks to 89 Labour MPs defying their party whip), but the population as a whole was deeply divided, and for most of the time between 1967 and 1974 opinion polls showed a clear majority against entry. It is uncertain whether Heath could have won a referendum on the issue had he chosen to call one in 1971 or 1972, as the Irish, Danes and Norwegians did.

Yet Heath deserves enormous credit for the leadership he displayed and his single-minded determination to drive through a policy the necessity for which he never for one moment doubted. His consistency on the issue is impressive: interviewed over twenty years later for Phillip Whitehead's remarkable television series *The Last Europeans*, he described the European Union, as it had now become, as 'The great success story of the modern world ...nothing to get anywhere near it'. Heath's tenure of the premiership was relatively short, his electoral record was poor, many of his projects ended in failure and he was repudiated by his own party. Macmillan, Wilson, Thatcher, even Major, all enjoyed longer periods at the top, and were conventionally more successful politicians, but none of them could rival his single achievement.

If Heath showed leadership qualities of a high order in 1970-2, the same could unfortunately not be said of his opposite number in the Labour Party, Harold Wilson. He had already altered his opinion once over the issue of British membership. In 1962 he had come down strongly against, declaring his position some time before Gaitskell's lurch into the anti-marketeers' camp. Yet in 1967, he launched the second British application, originally prompted by George Brown, but becoming progressively more enthusiastic as their joint reconnaissance to European capitals progressed. 'Harold is straining every nerve to get in,' the anti-EC Barbara Castle confided to her diary.

Not long after his unexpected defeat in the 1970 election, Wilson began to prepare the ground for a further shift of position. Nobody credited him then, or later, with having genuinely changed his mind; George Thomson's opinion, expressed on several occasions, that the terms obtained by Heath were compatible with the negotiating mandate he had been given by the Wilson government, and would have been acceptable to a Labour cabinet, was almost universally recognised as carrying conviction. Wilson's move to a hostile stance was attributed instead to two over-lapping motivations: the desire to prevent a damaging split in the Labour Party, and his fear of being challenged for the party leadership by an anti-EEC rival. Both these motivations are tracked assiduously by Wilson's first serious biographer, Ben Pimlott. Wilson was particularly sensitive to the risk of a challenge from James Callaghan. Two years earlier, as Home Secretary, Callaghan had undermined Wilson's and Barbara Castle's attempt at trade union reform by lending support to its opponents in clear breach of collective cabinet responsibility. In so doing, he had helped to build himself a new power-base, of unions and union-sponsored MPs, and Wilson was deeply suspicious of his intentions.

It is difficult to discern whether Callaghan had – at any time – strong views on the EC issue. In his autobiography, *Time and Chance*, he recalls writing as a junior minister in 1950 to Foreign Secretary Ernest Bevin, arguing in favour of British acceptance of the Schuman Plan. This was, however, the only sign that he ever gave of sympathy to, or interest in, European integration until the time he became Foreign Secretary in 1974. The judgment of Hugo Young, the commentator of *The Last Europeans*, that he viewed the issue purely in party terms is convincing.

In May 1971 Callaghan nailed his colours to the mast, making a speech which was highly critical of the EC and which even went so far as to suggest that the French language would supplant English if Britain became a member. The speech was believed to have been drafted by his son-in-law, Peter Jay, whose own father, Douglas, had long been known as the party's leading anti-EC rightwinger.

Callaghan was not the only former senior cabinet colleague of whom Wilson was leery at that time. Roy Jenkins, former Chancellor of the Exchequer, by then Labour's deputy leader, had for some years been regarded as his most likely successor. There was, of course, no risk that Jenkins would attempt to outflank him on the anti-EC side, but his very consistency on the issue, which equalled Ted Heath's, cast an unflattering light over Wilson's manoeuvres and tergiversations.

Jenkins had been at Balliol College, Oxford, at the same time as Heath (and Denis Healey), and although his conversion to the European cause came later, it was earlier than that of any other prominent Labour politician. He attributes it, in his autobiography *A Life at the Centre*, to the influence on him of a two-year spell as a delegate to the Council of Europe at Strasbourg between 1955 and 1957. The immediate consequence was that he opposed the creation of EFTA by the Macmillan government in 1958, which he describes as 'a foolish attempt to organise a weak periphery against a strong core, which could provide no satisfactory European strategy for Britain'.

I myself vividly recall a Fabian weekend school about that time, where Jenkins gave a brilliant exposition of the case for Britain making the EEC the prime focus of its international relations; he joined the Labour Common Market Committee (later the Labour Committee for Europe) shortly afterwards. Jenkins was at that time a rising, and evidently ambitious, young politician, already very close to the party leader, Hugh Gaitskell, but he put loyalty to the European ideal before considerations of party preferment. He resigned as a front-bench spokesman in 1960, after only seven months, in order to be able to speak freely on European issues, and after Gaitskell's Brighton conference speech took the lead in rallying Labour's pro-Europeans despite the cool wind blowing from the party leadership.

By 1970 Jenkins was universally seen as the most committed European enthusiast among Labour's leaders, and opinion polls indicated that he commanded a great deal of public respect. Though never close to Wilson personally, his influence with him during the last three years of the 1964-70 government was considerable, and in the early summer of 1971 he made a last attempt to dissuade him from drifting into an anti-EC stance. In *A Life at the Centre*, Jenkins recounts, as best he can recall, his words to Wilson during a frank talk early in June:

> I know it is a difficult issue for you. I know you have great problems with the party, which I in no way underestimate. I know you are genuinely much less committed on the issue than I am, and it would be silly to criticise you for that. But what you should be equally aware of is that what is most damaging to your reputation and position in the country is that you are believed, perhaps wrongly, to be devious, tricky, opportunistic. If you stick to the pro-European position which you took up in government, difficult though it will be with the party, you will kill that damaging reputation. If on a major issue of this sort you take the hard, difficult, consistent, unpopular line, it will do your long-term reputation an immense amount of good. You may be defeated at the party conference, although that is by no means certain, but if you swing your whole influence pro-Europe it will only at worst be a narrow defeat, and you could sustain that at least as easily as Gaitskell sustained his 1960 defeat. I therefore beg you, not so much in the interest of the committed Europeans, but in your own interest and that of the party as a whole, as well as that of the country, to take this line.

Jenkins continues that Wilson:

> ... received all this with perfect good temper and even seriously, half giving me the impression that he was still genuinely undecided. Yet when I left the room I had little doubt that, courteously though he had listened and even if his mind was not formally made up, he was slipping, gradually, inevitably, irrevocably (for a few years at any rate) ...into the anti-European camp. But I felt that I had at least tried, with all the arguments at my disposal, and that I had also secured a licence, almost a blessing, for the course that I intended to pursue, without any complaints against the propriety of my behaviour as deputy leader being raised.

The course Jenkins intended to pursue was to rally as many Labour MPs as possible to vote in favour of British entry on the terms negotiated by Heath, even if the party decided to vote against them. Working closely with Jenkins, his colleague William Rodgers organised periodic meetings of pro-EC Labour MPs throughout the year, partly in order to discuss tactics and exchange views, but mainly to keep up morale and to demonstrate to each individual that he was not alone in the awkward decision which he or she would have to make, but that there were a goodly number of colleagues in the same position. I attended nearly all these meetings and can testify that it had the desired effect on the majority of those who came.

The strategy proved highly successful. In May 1971, before the pressure began to build up, 100 Labour MPs (out of 287) signed an advertisement in *The Guardian* backing British entry. On 28 October, five months later, 89 of us still refused to vote against British entry in the decisive House of Commons vote, 69 voting in favour and 20 abstaining. This was despite the cumulative effect of hostile majorities in the party's national executive, the TUC, the Labour Party conference, the Parliamentary Labour Party and, in the great majority of cases, among the bulk of supporters in our constituency parties. The strongest pressure came from the imposition of a three-line whip, despite earlier promises from Wilson and the Chief Whip, Bob Mellish, that a free vote would be allowed.

No doubt we exhibited a certain priggish self-righteousness, and we under-estimated the sincerity of those who took a different view, but for the bulk of us it was not really a difficult decision to take. We would have had no self-respect if we had behaved differently, having told our electors during the 1970 campaign that we would support British entry if it could be obtained on satisfactory terms, and being convinced that the terms were indeed satisfactory.

For this reason I never regretted my own vote, though it probably led to the premature end of my parliamentary career, as my seat was being redistributed and it proved impossible to secure selection for another, after 'having voted with the Tories over Europe'. A few other MPs were in a similar position, but Jenkins's own loss was far greater. The likelihood is that he would have become party leader, and probably subsequently Prime Minister, had it not been for his stand at this time and for his later resignation from the deputy leadership when the party decided against his wishes to back a referendum on the issue.

Of this referendum, Tony Benn has the undoubted right to proclaim himself 'the onlie begetter'. As early as November 1970 he had suggested it as a means of 'taking the issue out of the hands of governments and parties' and putting it directly in the hands of the people. It would also have the advantage, Benn argued, of making it possible for Labour frontbenchers to avoid 'any outright personal commitment or contradiction of earlier positions – without loss of face'.

Wilson contemptuously rejected the idea, as Benn recorded in his diary, and when he proposed it at a meeting of Labour's national executive committee it was rejected with only his own vote in favour. But during the passage of the European Communities Bill, the small group of Tory anti-marketeers tabled an amendment calling for a referendum, and Benn proposed at the National Executive Council that Labour should back this amendment. Largely due to the fortuitous absence of Wilson, Callaghan and Jenkins, Benn was able to carry the day by the narrow margin of thirteen votes to eleven.

When the issue reached the Shadow Cabinet, Wilson – sensing that this amendment might lead to the defeat of the Heath government (it did not) – shifted his position, and the referendum was approved by a tiny margin, leading to the resignation of Jenkins and two of his supporters. Little did they think at the time that a referendum, mainly supported by anti-marketeers, would eventually prove their undoing.

The European Communities Bill – which incorporated the terms for British entry – needed to be passed without amendment if the accession treaty was to be ratified. Pro-EC Labour MPs, who had voted in favour of the principle of entry, allowed themselves to be constrained to voting against the principal clauses of the Bill in order to prevent sustained intra-party strife, which threatened to rip the party apart, and also to demonstrate that the prospect of overthrowing the Heath government on the issue was a pipedream. In practice, the number of anti-EC Tories who were prepared to vote against the government was very small, while a tiny group of mainly elderly Labour MPs absented themselves on a few crucial occasions. Thus the Bill was rather ingloriously passed into law, with less than the 'full-hearted consent' that Heath had promised.

In the process, the Labour Party was deeply split and the fault-lines then revealed largely foreshadowed the division ten years later when nearly 30 Labour MPs defected to form the Social Democratic Party. In the shorter term, however, the damage to the party's standing was perhaps less than many anticipated, as other – more domestic – issues came to the fore and a Labour government was unexpectedly elected in the general election of February 1974. This immediately threw open the question of whether Britain's accession to the EC was for good.

Wilson, recovering some of his balance and tactical skill, had managed to see off an extreme anti-EC resolution at the 1972 Labour Party conference and had, instead, been left with one instructing him to 'renegotiate the terms of membership'. Labour had accordingly gone into the election with a pledge to do so and that 'the people should have the right to decide the election through a [further] general election or a consultative referendum'.

As Labour had, in any case, to fight another general election in October 1974 in order to transform its status from a minority into a majority government (which it only just achieved), it soon became evident that the question of membership would in fact have to be settled by a referendum rather than in a third general election within less than two years.

But, before this could happen, a renegotiation had to be attempted. This was entrusted to the new Foreign Secretary, James Callaghan, whose previous attitude to the EC had been several degrees cooler than that of Wilson. It soon became evident, however, that Wilson was eager for the negotiation to succeed, and Callaghan – now resigned to ending his career as Wilson's chief lieutenant rather than his rival – loyally set out to achieve this objective.

He was helped by the new German Chancellor, Helmut Schmidt, who proved a useful ally during the negotiations and who gave excellent advice to both the British leaders. The Labour government sharply downgraded its demands and concentrated on obtaining significant concessions on four points only – access for Commonwealth products; freedom to give states aids to industry and to disadvantaged regions; reform of the Common Agricultural Policy; and limiting the size of the British contribution to the Community's budget.

Callaghan was able to secure undertakings on all four points, though they were of varying long-term significance. On the Commonwealth, the EC agreed to extend guaranteed access to New Zealand butter beyond 1977 and for a study to be made into the question of access for New Zealand cheese. Commonwealth countries were also able to benefit from inclusion in the Lomé Convention, signed in 1975. On state aids the issue was successfully subsumed in the creation of the European Regional Development Fund, of which it was anticipated that Britain (together with Italy) would be the major beneficiary. CAP reform was restricted to measures (which did not prove effective) to rein in the level of agricultural expenditure, while the formula – agreed at a summit meeting in Dublin in March 1975 – to safeguard Britain against excessive budget contributions proved totally worthless when it was put to the test some years later.

The verdict that the renegotiation was largely a cosmetic operation cannot, in retrospect, be seriously challenged, but at the time a fairly convincing case could be made that Wilson and Callaghan had significantly improved on the terms which Heath had obtained four years previously.

The two men, both of whom were regarded as arch party manipulators, were sufficiently confident of this to recommend acceptance of the terms to the British people, in spite of the fact that they were repudiated by a vote at a special Labour Party conference and by a narrow majority of Labour MPs.

It was a tricky situation, but Wilson showed incomparable skill in weaving his way through the numerous obstacles. He averted the possibility of ministerial resignations by waiving the principle of collective cabinet responsibility and allowing ministers to campaign on either side. Although both he and Callaghan came down decisively on the 'yes' side, they held themselves aloof from the day-to-day campaign, which was run by a cross-party umbrella organisation led by Roy Jenkins, with Edward Heath and the Liberal leader, Jeremy Thorpe, in strong support.

Although the 'no' campaign was also cross-party, the leading role was played by Labour cabinet ministers, notably Michael Foot, Barbara Castle and Tony Benn, who had resiled from the pro-market position he had taken as a minister in the earlier Wilson government. The leading non-Labour campaigner was Enoch Powell, by then an Ulster Unionist MP. The Conservative contribution to the 'no' campaign was feeble, only eight of the forty-one MPs who had voted against membership in the free vote which Heath had allowed Tory MPs in 1971 supported the 'no' campaign.

The voters largely followed the cues given by their own party leaders. According to the election expert Michael Steed, writing in *The Economist* on 14 June 1975, Tories voted 85 percent to 15 percent in favour, and Liberals 70 percent to 30 percent. Labour voters were cross-pressured, with the party machine advocating a 'no' vote and Wilson and Callaghan 'yes'. Steed estimates that, by the narrow margin of 52½ percent to 47½ percent, they, too, voted predominantly 'yes'. The only significant party whose supporters voted 'no' was the Scottish National Party.

The overall result was a two-to-one (67.2 percent to 32.8 percent) victory for the 'yes' campaign, the proportion remaining extraordinarily uniform across the whole country. All four nations of the UK voted 'yes', and so did every one of the 68 counties which were the polling areas, except for the Western Isles and the Shetlands.

It was the anti-marketeers who had called for a referendum, and in the event it destroyed them as an effective political force, at least until Margaret Thatcher took against the European Community in the late 1980s. To some extent, they were the victims of unfortunate timing: a referendum before entry would certainly have been much closer, though it is by no means a foregone conclusion that the 'noes' would have won.

It is emphatically not the case, as is often alleged, that the mass of the British people have consistently been opposed to British membership of the EC and that only an unrepresentative elite has been in favour. On the contrary, there is convincing evidence that only a small minority of the population have held strong views on the issue, one way or the other. Most people at most times have been relatively indifferent, but have been ready to respond to a lead from the politicians they most respect. When the leaders have changed their minds, or have emitted indistinct signals, they have created confusion in the minds of their supporters. This explains the extreme volatility of voters' views as recorded in opinion polls taken between June 1960 and the beginning of the referendum campaign. These were analysed by David Butler in an article in *Political Quarterly* in 1979, and, as he recalled, 'the picture of fickleness in the overall figures is impressive ... In addition to short-term wobbles there were long-term tides,' he wrote, 'with peaks in 1960, 1965, 1972 and 1975 and troughs in between'.

The main reason for the fluctuation was the reception of differing messages from party leaders. Thus, when a Labour government attempted to negotiate entry in 1966-7 it carried a large majority of its own voters with it, but a majority of Tory voters swung against. Precisely the opposite effect was seen in 1971, when a Conservative government was in charge of the negotiations. The overall picture is not one of simmering hostility, but of confused voters awaiting a vision from their leaders which was often not forthcoming.

Vision there was from Heath and Jenkins – and, to be fair, from their opponents such as Peter Shore and Enoch Powell who were consistent in their patriotic preference for a nation state, which in the eyes of pro-Europeans was fast becoming an anachronism. Other opponents, particularly at that time in the Labour Party, were less interested in the issues involved but were prepared to use them as power-ploys in an attempt to seize control of the party.

Without the men of vision, Britain would not have entered the European Community in the early 1970s. Yet vision alone was insufficient to secure that entry. It also needed the wiles of party strategists and manoeuverers, like Wilson and Callaghan, and the ingenuity of Benn to devise a means of confirming the entry though that was hardly his intention. Looking back in 1996, the year of the 200th anniversary of the death of Robert Burns, his oft-quoted verse is perhaps the most appropriate epitaph on the 1975 referendum: 'The best laid schemes o' mice an' men/ Gang aft a-gley'.

Selected bibliography

Butler, David (1979) 'Public Opinion and Community Membership' in *Political Quarterly*, vol 50, pp 151-6.

Callaghan, Jim (1987) *Time and Chance*, London: Collins.

George, Stephen (1990) *An Awkward Partner: Britain in the European Community*, Oxford: Oxford University Press.

Horne, Alistair (1989) *Macmillan Vol.2*, London, Macmillan.

Jenkins, Roy (1991) *A Life at the Centre*, London: Macmillan

Pimlott, Ben (1992) *Harold Wilson*, London: HarperCollins

Verrier, Anthony (1983) *Through the Looking Glass: British Foreign Policy in an Age of Illusions*, London: Jonathan Cape.

Williams, Philip (1979) *Hugh Gaitskell*, London: Jonathan Cape, and Oxford: Oxford University Press, (1982), paperback.

Spinelli and the Federal Dream

Richard Corbett

Few men have appeared and reappeared at so many different stages in the history of European integration, seeking to stimulate and influence the process from such a variety of vantage points as Altiero Spinelli. Propagator of the federalist idea from Mussolini's prisons, proselytiser thereof in the resistance movements, founder and long-time leader of the European Federalist Movement, adviser to successive Italian governments, academic, writer of numerous books and articles, member of the Commission, MP and finally MEP, Spinelli's European action spanned five decades and helped shape Europe as we know it. Spinelli was not only 'present at the creation', he was present at the conception, the birth and several turning points in the life of the European Community.

One characteristic stands out in all of Spinelli's actions: his belief that the decisive impulse in creating a European federation could only be given by an elected European assembly – national governments alone were incapable of finding the necessary political momentum in diplomatic negotiations dominated by the vested interests of Foreign Ministries. Two episodes, looked at in detail later, stand out in particular in this regard: the establishment of the Ad Hoc Assembly in the early 1950s charged by the governments of the member states with drafting the statutes for a European Political Community – a draft constitution that fell with the demise of the European Defence Community Treaty but which helped pave the way for the later EEC negotiations – and secondly the drafting in the early 1980s by the European Parliament of a treaty on European Union, which helped to trigger the Intergovernmental Conference through which member states negotiated the Single European Act (SEA).

Spinelli was born in Rome in 1907. When he reached adulthood, Italy was under Mussolini's fascist regime. In opposition to that, Spinelli joined the Italian Communist Party at a very young age and participated in clandestine activities until he was arrested in 1927. He spent ten years in prison and six in internal exile first on the island of Ponza and then Ventotene.

During this period, Spinelli displayed his independence of thought. On the one hand, he refused to take an easy option which would have made him a free man by simply signing a document presented by the fascist authorities in which he would recognised the error of his ways. On the other hand, during this period he broke with the Communist Party. He did have access to documents and literature and much of what he read led him to reassess his own ideological perspective. The Stalinist purges in the Soviet Union also contributed to this reassessment. His turning away from the Communist Party meant that he was ostracised by many of his fellow internees in Ponza and Ventotene, including a childhood friend, Giorgio Amendola, who, paradoxically, would many years later, as leader of the Communist Group in the European Parliament, invite Spinelli to join his group as an independent member – on Spinelli's own terms.

It was during his period of exile in Ventotene that Spinelli first turned his thoughts to the future of Europe. He was soon to reach the conclusion that the anti-fascist struggle taking place across Europe, if it were eventually to triumph (far from certain at the beginning of the war), would be a pyrrhic victory if it led to the re-establishment of a system of competing sovereign states in shifting alliances that would, inevitably, one day go back to war.

In his early reflections on this, Spinelli was influenced by some books by British federalists sent to him by Luigi Einaudi (a future President of the Italian Republic). These books were produced by the British organisation, Federal Union, which had enjoyed a spectacular, albeit brief, prominence in the last two years before the Second World War. Spinelli later explained why these writings had influenced him:

> Since I was seeking clarity and precision of thought, my attention was not attracted by the nebulous, contorted and hardly coherent ideological federalism of the Proudhonian or Mazzinian type, which throve in France and Italy, but by the polished, precise and anti-doctrinaire thought of the English federalists ... who proposed to transplant to Europe the great American political experience.

Together with a fellow-prisoner, Ernesto Rossi, Spinelli drafted, as early as 1941, the celebrated 'Ventotene Manifesto' entitled *Toward a Free and United Europe*. In this document, written on cigarette papers and concealed in the false bottom of a tin box, they argued that at the end of the war, 'the question which must be resolved, failing which progress is no more than mere appearance, is the definitive abolition of the division of Europe into national sovereign states.' Furthermore, they argued that 'the dividing line between progressive and reactionary parties ... falls along a very new and substantial line: those who conceive the essential purpose and goal of struggle as being the ancient one, the conquest of national power, and those who see the main purpose as the creation of a solid international state, which will direct popular forces towards this goal.'

In order to 'direct popular forces towards this goal', Spinelli, Rossi and some twenty others established, as soon as they were able to leave their internment camp, the *Movimento Federalista Europeo* (MFE). The founding meeting, held clandestinely in Milan on 20-28 August 1943, adopted a 'political thesis' which, *inter alia*, stated: 'If a post-war order is established in which each state retains its complete national sovereignty, the basis for a Third World War would still exist, even after the Nazi attempt to establish the domination of the German race in Europe has been frustrated.'

These arguments are, of course, part of a long tradition of federalism as a theory of international pacification, stretching back as far as the leagues of ancient Greek city states. Numerous plans and schemes were drafted over the centuries, becoming more precise once they could draw upon concrete federal experiences, notably that of the USA. The 'Federalist Papers' of Hamilton and Madison provided a major source and inspiration for European writers more than a century later. The experience of the First World War and the subsequent failure of the League of Nations to maintain international order and peace stimulated the first governmental initiative for a federation of European States, that of French foreign minister Aristide Briand in 1929, and the first movements such as Coudenhove-Kalergi's Pan-European movement. Intellectual contributions flourished. As we have seen, the writings of Federal Union, centred around Lionel Robbins, Walter Layton, William Beveridge, Barbara Wootton and Lord Lothian, are acknowledged by Spinelli as the intellectual source of his federalism.

In drawing upon these traditions, Spinelli and his supporters in 1943 hoped that the circumstances were about to arrive in which a European federation could be established:

> At the end of this war, in the midst of a short period of national and international crisis, when the structure of the national states will either partly or completely collapse, we must seek to lay the foundations of real peace. This time there must be no repetition of 1919; the peace settlement must not be the outcome of diplomatic intrigue and the ambitions of ministers as though it were no concern of the people how the peace is organised. It will therefore be necessary to give firm support to that country or those countries which favour the creation of a federal organisation and to mobilise within every nation all popular forces behind this demand for a federal solution. For only during such a revolutionary period, and so long as the memories of the horrors of wars are still alive, will the European Federation be able to withstand pettiness, treason and nationalist interests and become a reality. If we allow this decisive moment to go by, the progressive forces will have fought in vain...

The aim of the MFE was thus to draw up a federal constitutional framework for the whole of Europe at the end of the war and this found a ready audience among many of those active in the anti-fascist resistance movements. The Ventotene Manifesto was copied and circulated hand to hand, smuggled out of Ventotene by Ursula Hirschmann, wife of fellow-internee Colorni, who was not properly searched by the guards as she was German. Colorni died before the end of the war, and Ursula became Spinelli's wife and life-long companion.

The Ventotene Manifesto was crucial in the dissemination and propagation of federalist ideas at the end of the war and in the early post-war years. Of course, many across Europe had reached similar conclusions. Few had as great an impact as the Ventotene Manifesto did in Italy and in several other countries, and the MFE became one of the most active components of the wider European Movement.

By 1943, typewritten copies of the Ventotene Manifesto had reached the resistance movements of a number of continental countries. By this time, Spinelli and Rossi had been released from detention and were able to make their way to Switzerland as 'missionaries' of the recently founded MFE. Spinelli and Rossi were convinced that it would be necessary to organise a political movement across the continent pressing for a European federation if there was to be any chance of achieving that objective. In an 'open letter', they invited resistance movements to send representatives 'to discuss together the problems of the reconstruction of Europe, in which they will soon be called upon to take part, and to issue a solemn declaration of our common aims'. The meeting took place at the private home in Geneva of Visser't Hooft, the General Secretary of the World Council of Churches. Resistance fighters from Denmark, France, Italy, Norway, Holland, Poland, Czechoslovakia, Yugoslavia and even Germany were able to attend the first meeting in March 1944, and a second meeting in April. The first meeting adopted a declaration stating that 'all the sacrifices and suffering endured for the same cause have created ties of brotherhood among [the resistances movements] and have given birth to a new consciousness of European solidarity, the maintenance of which will be one of the essential guarantees of peace.' At the second meeting, they adopted a manifesto in six points, advocating unity 'in a single federal organisation' and that only a federal union would enable 'the German people to join the European Community without becoming a danger to other peoples'. A federal union would be 'in a position to protect democratic institutions'. These declarations were crucial in disseminating federalist ideas among resistance leaders across the continent.

A further meeting took place in Paris in March 1945, largely organised by Spinelli and Ursula Hirschmann. Its participants included many of the leaders of the French resistance. At this conference, Spinelli began to outline some key aspects of his federalist strategy: that it might initially be necessary to start with only some countries, leaving it open for others to join at a later stage; and the idea that the task of developing a federal constitution should fall to an elected European assembly.

But the course of history was different. The old nations and state structures re-emerged as countries were liberated one after the other, as traditional political parties re-surfaced, as the resistance movements began to divide along communist/non-communist lines and, as Spinelli later saw it:

> the federalist idea was completely eclipsed in the last year of the war and the first two years of the postwar period, because Europe was not brought to a

position where it was forced to raise the question of its new international status. Europe was entirely conquered by the Soviet and Anglo-American forces who restored the old national states as a matter of course, which were formally sovereign but in actual fact controlled by the conquering forces.

Spinelli felt that the opportunity to create a federal European structure had been lost. He was discouraged and withdrew from federalist activity for a short while. However, he was soon to display one of his strongest characteristics: his belief that the strength of an idea could be measured in its ability to survive after a serious defeat. Ideas and projects which failed to survive their first setback were doomed to the dustbin of history. Those that were capable of rising again after setbacks or defeats were serious and relevant.

From 1948 until 1962 Spinelli led the European Federalist Movement as its Secretary General. Under his leadership, the MFE was the principal advocate of the 'constituent assembly' approach to European integration, arguing that a European constituent assembly, representative of all European peoples and political forces, would be the only body capable of acting with the democratic legitimacy needed to draw up and propose a European constitution. Furthermore, a parliamentary body could reach decisions publicly and by a majority vote. In this sense, it was the opposite of the diplomatic intergovernmental method which Spinelli dismissed as being incapable of producing anything other than unsatisfactory compromises. Spinelli and the MFE regarded the partial step-by-step, so-called functionalist, progress towards European integration negotiated by the governments with a high degree of scepticism. Of course, many of those actively involved in the setting-up of the Coal and Steel Community and later the EEC, including Jean Monnet, were also federalists – but gradual federalists rather than supporters of the line advocated by the MFE. The tensions between federalists would, indeed, lead to the split of the federalist movement in the late 1950s, largely on this point.

Why then, did Spinelli and his colleagues persevere with the 'constituent' approach after their failure to create a new European order in 1945? The answer lies primarily in the fact that, despite the failure to create a new European order at the end of the war, several states of Western Europe did embark on a gradual and partial integration process, even if it was one which was, to many federalists, insufficient and unsatisfactory. Painstaking compromises among governments reinforced the conviction that governments were incapable of delivering the desired result. It was affirmed by the MFE at their Strasbourg Congress in 1950 that 'it is indispensable to ... call a constituent federal assembly made up of representatives of the people and not the governments'. They did not accept the received wisdom of the time that economic integration would automatically lead to political integration.

Thus reasons both of principle – that is, it was 'more democratic', indeed, the traditional way in several countries of preparing new constitutions – and of strategy –

that it would bypass national governments – led many federalists to continue to press for a constituent assembly to draft a European constitution. These federalists were convinced that the neo-functionalist dynamic was in itself not sufficient to produce the desired result. Not all of them were dismissive about the achievements of the European Community, indeed these were generally recognised, not least by Spinelli himself – but they were felt to be limited and incapable of developing beyond certain boundaries.

Of course, some federalists supported this approach as a tactic, believing that a small organised group such as the MFE/UEF should argue strongly for an ambitious but clear objective on its merits, knowing perfectly well that the governments would do no more than muddle through with half-baked compromises. But even to achieve this required some 'maximalist' pressure on the governments. Spinelli himself was fully aware of this consideration.

The constituent assembly approach continued to have a body of support. This has lasted right up to the mid 1990s. The Italian government accepted a resolution from its own Chamber of Deputies on 20 November 1990 'stressing the urgent need to transform the relations between the member states of the Community into a Union on a federal basis ... on the basis of a draft constitution drawn up by the European Parliament'. The constituent objective has, of course, never been achieved. Nevertheless, the impact of its supporters has been significant, not only in terms of constantly expounding and advocating federalism (in which they were not alone) but in particular in the emphasis they always gave to the role of an assembly or Parliament, preferably directly elected.

Meanwhile, Spinelli and the MFE sought to exploit any opportunities offered by the gradualist method that had been embarked upon by six governments in the EEC. Pressure from federalists (of all tendencies) and others had ensured that the early institutional structures in Europe all incorporated a parliamentary assembly. Starting with that of the Council of Europe, this brought together politicians of all of Europe's main political parties, providing a forum other than an intergovernmental one for debating and furthering the European idea and ensuring that the minimal infrastructure was in place to organise a parliamentary body – and potentially a constituent assembly – at European level.

The discussions surrounding the creation of a European Defence Community (EDC) in the early 1950s provided an opportunity which Spinelli seized with alacrity. The day after the publication of the Pleven Plan, Spinelli stated that the French proposal 'is nothing more nor less than a proposal for continental federation. The unification of defence and economic policies and the relationship between states within the Atlantic Treaty is hard to imagine without a corresponding change in foreign policies, and in the long run without the founding of legal bodies to protect individual rights for citizens'. In the EDC debate Spinelli advocated the creation of a common

European army, and not simply a military alliance, because this would be an instrument forcing the member states to adopt common policies and to establish the necessary political infrastructures at the European level to bring such a common army under democratic control. It would also require a European defence budget and legislative and budgetary measures at European level. Spinelli's strategy was to link to the EDC process the idea that the assembly should draft the appropriate political structures. His efforts led to the approval of a resolution by the Italian Parliament on 31 October 1950 calling upon the Italian government to promote the creation of a European political authority through a European constitution. Spinelli then worked closely with Italian Prime Minister De Gasperi and the Italian delegation to the EDC negotiations, and also submitted a personal memorandum to Schuman. His efforts resulted in Article 38 of the EDC Treaty, which provided for the EDC assembly to study and prepare a constitution and amendments which might eventually have to be made to the treaty, and in doing so to be guided by the following principles: 'the final organisation which will replace the present provisional organisation should be so conceived as to be able to constitute one of the elements in a subsequent federal or confederal structure, based on the principle of a separation of powers and having, in particular, a two-chamber system of representation.' The assembly's proposals would be submitted to the Council within six months of the start of the EDC for consideration in an intergovernmental conference.

Not content with these achievements, whose implementation would have to await ratification of the EDC Treaty, Spinelli pressed for its anticipated implementation by proposing that governments should ask the ECSC assembly, which was about to be established following the ratification of the ECSC treaty, to carry out this task already. Spinelli multiplied his contacts with the governments of the six ECSC States, and on 9 June 1952 De Gasperi, on behalf of the Italian Government, made such a proposal. On 10 August the Foreign Ministers of the Six, meeting on the occasion of the installation of the ECSC High Authority, fixed the date for the first ECSC Assembly meeting and unanimously approved the resolution which entrusted the mandate specified in Article 38 of the EDC Treaty to the Assembly of the ECSC. Chancellor Adenauer, as President of the ECSC Council, invited the Assembly on the day of its inauguration to draft within six months the treaty which was to found a new European Political Community.

Spinelli set about trying to influence the work of the Assembly, which had been rebaptised 'Ad Hoc Assembly' for this purpose.

Working in parallel with the Ad Hoc Assembly, and seeking to influence it, the European Movement set up a committee chaired by Paul-Henri Spaak, including Altiero Spinelli and a number of ministers from member states. It adopted nine 'resolutions' on different aspects of the creation of a European constitution which did much to shape the work carried out in the Ad Hoc Assembly.

On 10 March 1954 the Ad Hoc Assembly adopted a 'draft treaty embodying the statute of the European Community'. This statute provided for a European Community competence in the field of security and foreign policy, the protection of human rights and the economy. Legislation was to be adopted by a bicameral parliament – consisting of a first directly-elected chamber and a senate elected by national parliaments – and executive tasks were to be in the hands of an executive council with members appointed by its president who would himself be elected by the senate. The executive would require the confidence of both chambers. A Council of national ministers would harmonise the activities of the executive council with those of the national governments.

This statute was presented to the national governments who began to consider it at an intergovernmental conference. However, the vote in the French National Assembly of 30 August 1954, which led to the non-ratification of the EDC Treaty, brought the whole episode to a shuddering halt. Spinelli was again confronted with the challenge of picking up the pieces and starting again.

The creation of the EEC in the 'European relaunch' three years later again posed the dilemma of working within gradualist institutions while continuing to press for a global approach in a constituent assembly. The ECSC and the EEC treaties did go well beyond any previous form of international cooperation in Europe, containing strong elements of supranationality and consisting of institutions that could prefigure a future federal structure. Spinelli, who had resigned as Secretary General of the MFE in 1962, decided, after a period in academic life and as an adviser on European affairs to Pietro Nenni, Italian Minister of Foreign Affairs, from 1968 to 1969, to enter the institutions and work within them. In 1970 the Italian government nominated him to the European Commission.

Inside the Commission, Spinelli played a key role in initiating and developing nascent Community policies on industrial policy, research, environment and culture, none of which existed when he joined. He was also instrumental in ensuring – after a major battle with Commissioner Ralf Dahrendorf – that the EC took a tough line against the military regime in Greece. But in terms of development of the Community as a whole, his most significant contribution in this period was to the drafting of the Commission's report on the future of Europe, drawn up as a preparation for the Tindemans report. The Commission's report presented different models and variants but favoured the development of a federal style European union, without, however, using the word 'federal'. It proposed that these changes and commitments should be enshrined in an 'active constitution, in the form of a new treaty' and suggested that such a treaty could either be drawn up in the classic way under Article 236 of the EEC Treaty, or by an elected European Parliament which, on the basis of general guidelines laid down by the European Council, could prepare a constitution in treaty form which would be referred by the member states' governments to their national parliaments for ratification. Here is the hand of Spinelli, and the initial shape of his idea to make use of the European Parliament, once it became directly elected, as a *de facto* constituent assembly.

The Tindemans report did not take up the Commission's ideas in a significant way and remained very general. It led to very little in concrete terms, other than the long awaited implementation of direct elections to the European Parliament. Spinelli left the Commission in 1976 after negotiations with the Italian Communist Party under its reformist and increasingly European leadership. This led to him being elected to the Italian national parliament as an independent on the Communist Party list and subsequently to the European Parliament, standing again in the first direct elections in 1979. This springboard was to provide Spinelli with a new opportunity.

Spinelli considered that the role of an elected parliamentary assembly at European level was crucial to the integration process. However, the first elected Parliament in 1979 was not initially predisposed to taking radical initiatives. The battle for direct elections had only been won with difficulty, the European economy was in a period of 'Euro-sclerosis' following the second oil shock, and all recent attempts to relaunch the European Union project had foundered. Most MEPs preferred to exploit Parliament's limited existing powers, rather than embark on a battle to revise the treaties.

Spinelli nonetheless persevered, circulating a letter to all MEPs in June 1980 setting out his ideas for a European Parliament initiative. Only eight MEPs responded and he organised a dinner at the 'Crocodile Restaurant' in Strasbourg on 9 July 1980. They founded the 'Crocodile Club' and began to circulate a regular newsletter to all MEPs, arguing the case for Parliament to take the lead in preparing a project for institutional reform by means of a new treaty. Gradually, and especially as MEPs gained in experience and began to see that the possibility of incremental change within the treaties was limited, more and more Members began to show an interest in these ideas. By December 1980, nearly 80 MEPs had expressed interest in the Club's aims, and the Club prepared a motion for a resolution proposing the creation of a parliamentary organ to prepare proposals for reform which Parliament would then submit to national governments and parliaments. In July 1981 the resolution was adopted by the European Parliament by 164 votes to 24, and the Committee on Institutional Affairs was constituted in January 1982.

Spinelli had succeeded in welding together a cross-party majority to launch the initiative. His task was now to keep it together in the face of diverging national and party pressures. As he reminded the Parliament in the July debate: 'I beg you to remember that a project like this one demands the participation of all the great political families of our countries and that each one must contribute its legitimate claims to the final agreement.' Spinelli's hopes were clear: to use the elected Parliament as the meeting point of European-minded representatives of all of Europe's main political parties. If the MEPs could agree on a project and carry their parties with them, then, in Spinelli's words, the proposal would 'gather momentum in the debates of the Assembly, whereas it would lose in a conference of national diplomats'. In his view, 'if the final draft is accepted by a massive majority in the Assembly, it will have a political force behind it which no diplomatic conference could provide.'

Spinelli became the general rapporteur of the Committee on Institutional Affairs, leading a team of six co-rapporteurs covering different sectors and representing the main political groups. The Committee held public hearings and its drafts were circulated via party political networks. By September 1983 Parliament was able to approve a lengthy resolution specifying the contents that a new treaty should have. The Committee, with the assistance of a team of legal experts, then translated this political resolution into the legal language of a draft treaty which was approved by Parliament on 14 February 1984 by 237 votes to 31.

This huge majority reflected the careful work of compromise and consensus building that had taken place among the main groups. The task of cajoling and bargaining with the groups to reach such a compromise fell largely to Spinelli as coordinating rapporteur. His position as an independent member (albeit elected on the list of the Italian Communist Party and an 'allied' member of the Communist Group) and as a historical figure in the European Movement, helped him to play such a role. He was also at pains to ensure that the project was not simply identified with himself, but with the Parliament as a whole. In his words: 'If the ideas contained in this draft and the resolution had not been in the minds of the great majority of this Parliament, it would have been quite impossible for me to put them there. I have merely practised the art of maieutics, after the manner of Socrates. I am the midwife who has delivered the Parliament of this infant. Now we must nurture it.'

The draft treaty was presented as a new treaty which could *replace* the existing treaties, while assuming the *acquis communitaire*. As such, it would be possible, though legally complicated, for the new treaty to be ratified simply by a majority of the member states. Parliament's proposal was for a majority of states representing two-thirds of the Community population as the minimum necessary. This idea raised the possibility of embarking on a European Union without the support or the participation of all the member states of the Community – an important and profoundly divisive consideration in any future negotiations.

The main changes that the draft treaty would have introduced compared to the existing Community system at that time were threefold. First, Parliament sought to clarify, and where necessary strengthen, the competences and responsibilities of the EC, arguing that powers should be attributed to the Community on the basis of the 'principle of subsidiarity' – a term virtually unknown in the English language until Parliament incorporated it into the draft treaty. Second, Parliament argued that those responsibilities that were exercised at Community level should be carried out more effectively. This would require abandoning the practice of unanimity in the Council of Ministers (except, at least initially, in foreign policy matters) and reinforcing the powers of the Commission to carry out agreed Community policies. Third, Parliament sought better democratic control and accountability, envisaging a co-decision procedure whereby Council and Parliament would jointly adopt European legislation and the budget, and where there would be better provisions for the protection of human rights through judicial review in the Court of Justice.

Adopting a draft treaty was one thing: gaining support for it was another. Parliament pursued four main channels in trying to build up support. These were:

- directly to governments, both individually and collectively in the European Council;
- through national political parties which had to take a position on the issue in their policy statements and manifestos for the 1984 European election, and which would have to bear in mind how their MEPs had voted;
- through national parliaments which were invited to support the initiative and to each of which the European Parliament sent delegations, usually including Spinelli, to explain and seek support;
- through interest groups, non-governmental organisations and academia by supporting and responding to the considerable interest stimulated in these circles by the draft treaty.

Generally positive reactions were immediately forthcoming from Italy, the Netherlands, Belgium and Germany. By far the most significant reaction, however, was that of President Mitterrand, speaking as President of the European Council to the European Parliament on 24 May 1984. In a major turning point in French attitudes towards European integration, his speech culminated in an expression of support for the draft treaty, stating that: 'France, ladies and gentlemen, is available for such an enterprise. I, on its behalf, state its willingness to examine and defend your project, the inspiration behind which it approves. I therefore suggest that preparatory consultations leading up to a conference of the member states concerned be started up'. This speech placed the draft treaty firmly on the political agenda. It also gave credibility to the idea of moving to European Union, if necessary without all the member states of the EC. It is not without significance, perhaps, that Mitterrand had been visited a couple of weeks before by Spinelli and Piet Dankert, then President of the European Parliament.

At the subsequent Fontainebleu European Council, it was agreed to set up an ad hoc committee of personal representatives of the Heads of State or Government, modelled on the Spaak Committee which had paved the way for the negotiation of the

EEC Treaty in the 1950s. The committee was instructed to put forward proposals on institutional matters to the European Council. Some heads of government nominated MEPs or former MEPs to represent them on the committee. These included Enrico Ferri, former chairman of the Parliament's Committee on Institutional Affairs, and Fernand Herman who was still a member in 1996. The committee also had meetings with the President of Parliament (then Pierre Pflimlin) and Spinelli.

The work of the ad hoc committee finally led to the adoption of a report which agreed with Parliament on the need for a new treaty establishing European Union. It recommended that this treaty be based on the existing Communities, the Stuttgart Solemn Declaration, and be 'guided by the spirit and the method of the draft treaty voted by the European Parliament'. As regards the substance of this treaty, there were striking similarities between the proposals of the ad hoc committee and the European Parliament's draft treaty. However, three members of the ad hoc committee – the representatives of the UK, Denmark, and Greece – stated publicly that they did not accept the main conclusions of the committee's report, nor did their governments accept the need to change the treaties at all.

The report was considered at the meeting of the European Council in Milan in June 1985. By then, several national parliaments had lent their support to the European Parliament's draft treaty. In Italy and Belgium, the parliaments had adopted resolutions calling for it to be ratified as such. In Germany, the Netherlands and in the French Parliament's responsible organs, more general support was forthcoming, urging their respective governments to open negotiations on the basis of the draft treaty. Even in member states not noted for their enthusiasm, the proposals were taken seriously. The House of Lords set up a special subcommittee to consider the issue, which held public hearings, including one with Spinelli, and concluded that some treaty changes were desirable.

The Milan European Council decided by a majority vote to convene an intergovernmental conference (IGC) to revise the existing treaties in accordance with the procedures set out in Article 236 of the EEC Treaty (requiring, ultimately, unanimous support from the member states for any Treaty changes). During the autumn of 1985 the member states pursued negotiations which eventually led to the Single European Act. The three recalcitrant states were, in the end, willing to negotiate compromises rather than be isolated.

During these negotiations, Parliament monitored the work of the IGC carefully. On two occasions, its President and Altiero Spinelli were invited to ministerial meetings of the conference, but mainly informal contacts were used. The IGC had agreed to submit the results of its work to the European Parliament, and this was done in January 1986, prior to the signature of the text by the member states. Indeed, Italy had indicated that it would not ratify the Act if the European Parliament rejected it.

Parliament, although considering the results to be insufficient, nevertheless accepted them. The Single European Act was signed in February 1986. After national ratification (involving referenda in Denmark and Ireland) it came into force in July 1987.

Spinelli considered the Single European Act to be an inadequate response to Parliament's draft treaty initiative. He had, of course, half expected a disappointing outcome of the IGC and had warned Parliament at the time of its final vote on the draft treaty in 1984 that it might face the same situation as Hemingway's fisherman in *The Old Man and the Sea*, who, having caught the biggest fish of his life, found that by the time he had towed it back to port, only the skeleton remained, the rest having been nibbled away *en route* by the sharks. Spinelli, in what turned out to be one of his last speeches to Parliament before his death four months later, exhorted Parliament to persevere: 'We have arrived home, too, and all we have left are the bones of the fish. This is no reason for Parliament to give up the struggle. We have to get ready to venture out again, with better tackle to catch our fish and to save it from the sharks.'

In practice, the Single European Act proved to be important in relauching the process of European integration in the late 1980s, and stimulated a second version, the Treaty of Maastricht, in the early 1990s. These successive achievements certainly still fall short of Spinelli's aspirations. Nonetheless, significant progress has been achieved on a step-by-step basis that would not have occurred had Spinelli and the federalists not been part of the political equation, exhorting more radical and more decisive action.

Spinelli's great achievement was in putting an unambiguous federalist objective on the political agenda in the post-war development of Europe. His advocacy of such an objective created space for incremental developments in that direction. At times, the project may have appeared to fail in not immediately living up to Spinelli's aspirations. In a more historical perspective, however, the progress made in European integration seems more impressive, and no small part of the credit is due to those whose clarity of vision, courage and perseverance pointed the way. None rank higher than Spinelli in this respect.

Business means Europe –
Who built the market?

Maria Green Cowles

For many observers of the European Union, the term 'common market' is synonymous with 'business'. After all, creating a single market that today stretches from the northernmost shores of Finland to the southern islands of Greece would be the dream of many a business entrepreneur. Yet the giants of European industry were not among the early architects of the European integration movement. Indeed, it took three decades for industrialists such as Wisse Dekker of Philips, Pehr Gyllenhammar of Volvo, and Etienne Davignon, a former Commissioner who later took over the helm of Société Générale of Belgium, to emerge as leading proponents of the European project. While few business leaders were ardent promoters of European integration in the nascent years of the Community, a number of key industrialists later emerged as eminent Europeans to promote a new 'idea' of Europe and, in doing so, to set the agenda for the creation of the 1992 Single Market programme.

This essay begins by examining business leaders' limited participation in the early Community project. It then highlights the mobilisation of business leaders in EU policymaking in the late 1970s and early 1980s. The creation of the European Round Table of Industrialists and the political role of key industrialists behind the Single Market programme is highlighted in the third section. The essay concludes by examining the role of business leaders in the EU today.

Building a Europe without business

The Schuman Declaration in 1950 met with mixed responses from the European business community. Some members of the European League for Economic Cooperation (a group created at the time of the Marshall Plan to promote European industrial schemes) and the International Chamber of Commerce expressed their support. Other business leaders and organisations, however, largely distrusted the proposed project. German industry, for example, protested about potential interference from the European Coal and Steel Community (ECSC) in the economy. The *Conseil National du Patronat Français* (CNPF) expressed its dissatisfaction not only because of the ECSC's potential supranational intervention, but also due to the French organisation's uneasy relations with Jean Monnet during his tenure at the *Commissariat au Plan*.

The wary attitude of business towards the Community continued in 1955 when Jean Monnet, then President of the ECSC High Authority, resigned his position and created the Action Committee for the United States of Europe. This influential body was composed of leaders from Christian and Social Democrat parties as well as from trade unions. Noticeably missing from the ranks of the Action Committee were the leaders of business organisations. While Monnet's political persuasion favoured unions, the disagreements that arose between the CNPF and Monnet did not improve his perception of industry. As Max Kohnstamm, former secretary of the Action Committee pointed out, Monnet disliked business and 'hated' large firms which he viewed as too 'nationalistic' in orientation to support a European project. Indeed, the status of a number of the large companies suffered from their perceived or real activities during the Second World War. As a consequence, the foundations for the European Communities were laid and developed without the input or support of European big business.

For their part, the leaders of large companies paid little attention to the nascent Community, expressing greater interest in the creation of the General Agreement on Tariffs and Trade (GATT) during this period. Thus, while transnational business collaboration grew significantly in the Community between 1959 and 1968, the firms' political interest in the Community remained undeveloped.

In the early 1960s Fiat, the Italian carmaker, was the first non-Belgian firm to set up a special office for European Community affairs in Brussels. The company's presence in 1962 was largely due to the international outlook of Giovanni Agnelli, head of Fiat. The Italian industrialist, known for his trans-Atlantic and political connections, deemed it politically important to have a representative in the Community's headquarters. He assigned a former Italian diplomat, Manchese Cittadini Cesi, the task of creating the Fiat official liaison office and of 'building bridges' between the international civil servants and Fiat's structures. As a former Fiat official noted, because 'no one knew what the EC was,' the liaison officer's task was 'to explain to Agnelli what the Community was and to explain to the Community what Fiat was'.

Agnelli was not only the first major industrialist to see the potential importance of the Community, he was among the few business leaders to develop considerable political ties with Community institutions. Throughout the heyday of the boom of the 1960s, when intra-EEC trade increased some 80 percent between 1960 and 1964, only a handful of firms created 'European affairs' departments and met with Commission officials on EC legislative matters. During the 1960s Unilever and Royal Dutch Shell reportedly brought representatives to meet Commission officials once every two years. During these early years any meetings between business representatives and Community officials occurred more often than not at cocktail parties, rather than in Commission offices. As one former representative of a major British corporation noted, one of the qualifications for EC affairs representatives in the 1960s was to be 'a nice guy who could properly handle a glass of sherry'.

Indeed, few firms or business associations looked to the Community to provide a unified market. Many firms tended to develop their own national 'home' market and export to the rest of the Community states. This was particularly true of German firms which enjoyed the largest home market on the continent. Other firms, notably from smaller countries, set up 'nationally federated companies' in other EC member countries, complete with their own production and marketing departments. Anthony Rowley, author of *The Barons of European Industry*, stated the situation this way: 'There is no such thing as 'European' industry – there is French industry, German industry, British industry and so on. *Vive la différence*'.

One of the first signs of a change in big business's attitude toward the European Community occurred in 1967 with the creation of the *Groupe des Présidents des Grandes Entreprises Européennes* (the Group of Presidents of Large European Firms). The *Groupe des Présidents* was instigated by von Geldern, a senior director in Euratom – and a former top-level director at Philips, the Dutch electronics firm. Upon his arrival at Euratom, von Geldern was appalled at how little the Commission knew about European industrial concerns. The Commission was composed largely of individuals from the Social and Christian Democrat parties who had historical links with labour groups but little experience with business. As one former *Groupe des Présidents* official explained, von Geldern saw that:

> big business was not understood [by the Commission] and the importance of big business was not understood. ... Big business was seen as possibly a resistance to the federal idea because the national interests were so strong. There was the Italian motor industry, the German motor industry, the French motor industry, etc. The Commission did not view business as a natural supporter of the European idea.

Similarly, European industrialists were only vaguely familiar with the EC. Von Geldern contacted Baron Boël, Chairman of Solvay & Cie, and a committed European. The two men decided to form a group of top executives from large private firms (in general, three from each EC member state) to inform the executives of the impact of potential EC legislation and to discuss their concerns with Commission officials.

On 17 February 1967 the first meeting of the *Groupe des Présidents* took place with twelve senior executives present. The *Groupe* met twice a year without any publicity, hosted on a rotating basis by the company chairmen. The meetings of the *Groupe* were highly secretive for three key reasons. First, the members were concerned over any backlash that might occur from the unions if it became known that senior European industrialists were meeting together. Second, the *Présidents* were wary of the anti-capitalist movement of the 'New Left' in Europe. Third, the members were cognisant of the growing 'anti-multinational' sentiment of the time and did not want to jeopardise their relations with government officials. The two-day meetings included discussions with a Commissioner and later, when the UK companies joined the group in 1973, with a cabinet member of the member state where the meeting was taking place.

Table 1 – Members of 'Le Groupe des Présidents des Grandes Entreprises Européennes' at 17 February 1967.

G. Agnelli, *Fiat,* Italy

W. Baumgartner, *Rhône-Poulenc,* France

Baron Boël, *Solvay,* Belgium

L. Brouwer, *Royal Dutch Petroleum Company,* UK / Netherlands

M. Lambert, *Société Générale de Belgique,* Belgium

T. Neuman, *Arbed,* Luxembourg

F. Philips, *Philips,* Netherlands

L. Pirelli, *Pirelli,* Italy

A. Roux, *Compagnie Générale d'Electricité,* France

P. von Siemens, *Siemens,* Germany

A. de Voguë, *Saint-Gobain,* France

M. Winnacker, *Vorstand de Hoechst,* Germany

Source: Cowles, *The Politics of Big Business in the European Community,*
Ph.D. diss., The American University, 1994.

According to one member, the *Groupe des Présidents* was successful in these early years in that it 'showed the Commission that big business could be a key player, and was absolutely necessary for the internationalisation of the European economy'. At the same time, the Commissioners demonstrated to the industrialists that they were not 'merely a technocracy'. Moreover, heads of major European industries came to know one another – many for the first time – in the meetings. Certain members had met earlier, but not in Europe. Their introductions were first made in the United States at board meetings of American multinationals that began to form European subsidiaries in the 1950s.

The *Groupe des Présidents*, however, had a limited political role. Indeed, it did not aspire to have one at all. As one participant noted, it never viewed itself as a lobbying organisation, nor did it intend to promote European integration *per se*. Indeed, few participants espoused Boël's federalist aspirations. Some *Groupe des Présidents* members found Boël too 'utopian' in his views of Europe. Their participation in the group was based on the desire to 'defend their interests' *vis-à-vis* the Brussels establishment, to try to 'guide' the Commission in the proper direction – and not to promote a unified Europe. Over time, the meetings of the organisation became more of a social event for the chairmen until the group was merged with the European Round Table of Industrialists in the late 1980s.

The Commission and business:
a new partnership for Europe

The 1970s brought a renewed level of interest in Europe among business leaders. Large firms began to pay increasing attention to the activities of Industry Commissioner Altiero Spinelli who proposed an EC policy paper designed to 'address the economic and social problems raised by the activities of multinational companies'. Several pieces of legislation involving corporate disclosure and taxation, anti-trust, employment protection and development policy were proposed by Spinelli's office that would directly affect the bottom line of many large European companies.

In 1979 European Commissioner for Social Affairs, Henk Vredeling, followed Spinelli's lead and proposed a directive that would institutionalise employee participation in multinational firms. The 'Vredeling Proposal', as it became known, proved to be the catalyst behind the mobilisation of several large companies which sought to counter that proposal and other Commission initiatives *vis-à-vis* multinational firms. American companies, for example, reorganised themselves to create what is today the EU Committee of AmCham, the American Chamber of Commerce. Led by Imperial Chemical Industries (ICI), a handful of American and European representatives also created the European Enterprise Group, an organisation that proved instrumental in the revitalisation of the European association of employers' organisations, UNICE – the Union of Industrial and Employers' Confederations of Europe – in the 1980s.

Industry's views of the Commission and its programmes, however, were not entirely negative. In 1977, Etienne Davignon replaced Spinelli as the new Commissioner for Industrial Affairs and the Internal Market in the Commission headed by President Roy Jenkins. Davignon's arrival marked a turning point in the Commission's relations with European industry. In the first place, Davignon succeeded in moving away from the grand European-scale policies promoted by his predecessors to concrete actions on behalf of industries within particular sectors. The Commissioner pursued what he called a 'sectoral' as opposed to an 'ideological' approach to European industry and the economic crisis. Second, he was also instrumental in bringing leaders of major firms together to create specific measures designed to address these sectoral problems.

Davignon's open and deliberate contacts with leaders of European firms were unprecedented. Previous Commission officials had been reluctant to meet business leaders due to the Commission's own competition policies, the traditionally strong ties with labour unions, and the negative press coverage that such meetings might have carried during this period. Indeed, several commissioners protested against Davignon's business ties but Commission President Jenkins ultimately overruled their objections.

One of the Commissioner's best known proposals was the Davignon Plan for the European steel industry – a plan to restructure the industry by limiting national subsidies, closing outdated facilities, promoting mergers and funding the retraining of laid-off workers. To foster support for his programme, Davignon met with firms, labour groups and government leaders directly to discuss market shares and subsidisation practices. Davignon's meetings with steel companies, and later with firms from several other industries, began to change industry's views of the Commission. As one official from the Confederation of British Industry (CBI) pointed out, for the first time the business community viewed the Commission as a competent 'honest broker'. Moreover, during the economic malaise of the late 1970s Davignon demonstrated to many industrialists – including the heads of major European multinationals – that the European Community could forge solutions where national governments had failed.

In 1979 Davignon redirected his energies towards new technologies and the 'industries of the future', namely the European information technology (IT) sector. European IT producers were losing important market shares in digital integrated circuits, the foundation of the electronics industry. Furthermore, American and Japanese domination in the European telematics market signalled a growing technological gap between Europe and the rest of the industrialised world. Davignon invited the CEOs of the twelve largest European IT firms to discuss the means to promote growth in their industry. The companies were: Bull, Thomson and CGE from France; Siemens, Nixdorf and Allgemeine Elektrizitäts-Gesellschaft (AEG) from Germany; Olivetti and Societa Finanziaria Telefonica (STET) from Italy; Philips from the Netherlands; and General Electric Company (GEC), ICL and Plessey from the United Kingdom. Together they established a programme in which the firms would cooperate on 'pre-competitive research'. The group, later known as the Thorn-Davignon Roundtable, developed the European Strategic Programme for Research and Development in Information Technology (ESPRIT). Begun in 1984, the group's name also made reference to Gaston Thorn who was Commission President at the time.

The Thorn-Davignon Roundtable helped persuade a number of key industrialists – notably Wisse Dekker of Philips and Carlo de Benedetti of Olivetti – to become politically involved in promoting a 'new Europe' in the 1980s.

Business means Europe

In many respects, the oil crises and related economic stagnation of the 1970s took their toll on the European continent. During that decade Europe had been plagued by rising inflation, soaring unemployment and declining growth. During 1974-84, for example, European Community economic growth (Gross Domestic Product) averaged 1.8 percent compared to 2.7 percent in the US and 4.4 percent in Japan.

During the same period OECD figures show that official unemployment reached 10.8 percent in the EC compared to 9.5 percent in the US and 2.7 percent in Japan. Beginning in the 1980s, a number of industrialists began to look for a European response to address this 'Eurosclerosis'.

The industrialists' changing reasons were due to a number of factors. In the first place some CEOs were becoming disillusioned with national policies. During the 1970s the reinforcement of nationalistic trade programmes ensured greater barriers to trade and complicated corporate investment strategies. Moreover, while governments continued to subsidise ailing industries, government-sponsored research and development (R&D) programmes could not keep pace with the rising costs of R&D in critical technologies of the future.

National policies, however, were not completely to blame. While many of the largest companies emerged from the 1970s with a positive balance sheet, CEOs recognised that they could no longer afford to operate their companies along traditional lines. Internal reorganisation of companies *across* Europe was necessary to improve the interaction between R&D, production, financial and commercial functions. The 'federated national companies' were no longer viable if companies were to compete successfully for market share in the future. The globalisation of the world economy and the introduction of competition from the Far East brought this painful fact home to many companies.

Many CEOs recognised that getting a grip on their companies' cost structure was a *political* issue. Reorganising these firms required CEOs to pare budgets, to remove 'barons of subsidiaries', to consolidate R&D and other programmes and to lay off workers. The political difficulties facing business executives in carrying out company reorganisations, however, were many. The social welfare systems constructed by governments in the post-war era were designed to ensure employment for workers and, in times of economic downturns, to provide adequate social nets for the citizenry. Changes in government regulations were needed to modify these social welfare systems – changes that posed both political and ideological problems, changes that would require national and possibly Community involvement.

Whatever their motivations, leaders of major European companies began to voice their concerns. The viability of European industry had become intricately entwined with the notion of a competitive Europe.

Interestingly, the leading industrialist to articulate the business community's concerns came from outside the European Community. In 1982 Pehr Gyllenhammar, CEO of Volvo, the Swedish automobile manufacturer, began promoting what he later called a 'Marshall Plan for Europe'. Gyllenhammar maintained that an overall scheme was necessary 'to spur growth, and to build industry and infrastructure' in Europe. He found that European political leaders were either unable or unwilling to take the lead in relaunching Europe. Moreover, Gyllenhammar was well aware that existing European business groups such as UNICE were poorly-run organisations that could not promote a major European initiative. Through public addresses and articles in *International Management* and the *Financial Times*, Gyllenhammar called on European industry to 'play an active and important role in the formulation of the industrial strategies for future growth', noting that 'co-operation on a European level will be necessary'.

Gyllenhammar's actions were influenced by his meetings with Commissioner Davignon. The two men met on several occasions in 1982 to discuss the possibility of creating a cross-sectoral group of leading CEOs who could speak out on the European economic situation and EC industrial policy. While CEO groups such as the Business Roundtable existed in the United States, no such organisation could be found on the European Community level. The Groupe des Présidents, for example, refused to undertake political activity *vis-à-vis* EC policies. Moreover, the organisation was unwilling to accept non-EC members such as Swedish or Swiss entrepreneurs.

Davignon found in Gyllenhammar the individual needed to take on the task of organising such a group, despite the fact that he was an EC 'outsider'. Leading business journals recognised Gyllenhammar as one of Europe's 'bold new managers'. Both his admirers and detractors called him a 'political animal', known for his delight in seeking the spotlight, meeting with government officials and courting the press. He had a litany of ties with prestigious industrial and political leaders in the United States. Gyllenhammar was a board member of United Technologies, Vice President of the Aspen Institute, one of the five partners of Kissinger Associates and a member of the International Council of Chase Manhattan Bank. Fluent in English and French, he was well connected with the political establishment in most countries where Volvo had operations, especially in France.

Gyllenhammar decided to create a group of leading CEOs and enlisted the assistance of the Commission. The first list of potential industry members was drawn up in 1982 in the Commission's Berlaymont building by Volvo and Commission staff. The planning group included Fernand Braun, Director General for Industry and the Internal Market, Bo Ekman and Michael Hinks-Edwards, corporate planners with Volvo, and Pierre Defraigne, *chef de cabinet* to Commissioner Davignon. As one participant explained, in selecting the industrialists the group wanted progressive business leaders 'who had a reputation beyond management, who had weight in public opinion, who had *political influence*'.

Following the meeting Ekman, a close advisor to Gyllenhammar, travelled around Europe to meet with the business leaders and/or their top associates to discuss the strategy behind the group. As envisaged by Gyllenhammar, the goal was not merely to create a high-power lobby organisation. In addition, the purpose of the group would be to develop projects to promote the internal market, encourage European leadership in high technology, and provide an alternative form of job and wealth creation to that currently offered by member states. In short, the goal of the organisation was to relaunch Europe with an industrial initiative. Wisse Dekker of Philips, Umberto Agnelli of Fiat (with the support of his brother, Giovanni) and John Harvey-Jones of ICI, were among the early enthusiastic supporters of what became known as the 'Gyllenhammar Group'.

An inner circle of top associates of the CEOs was created including Ekman, Hinks-Edwards, Paolo Zannon (Fiat), Walter Grünsteidl (Philips), Paul Winby (ICI) and Bertrand Dechery representing the consulting firm, Telesis, which worked closely with Volvo. The associates picked the name, the 'Roundtable of European Industrialists', which was changed to the European Round Table of Industrialists (ERT) in the late 1980s, borrowing from the US Business Roundtable. Later that evening, in the deserted offices of the Berlaymont, the associates developed an agenda for the ERT that in time comprised six key areas: the internal market, infrastructure, technology, jobs, environment and finance.

On 6-7 April 1983 the CEOs of the ERT held their initial meeting in Paris to discuss plans for Europe's economic future. The participants included seventeen of Europe's leading businessmen, in what the *Financial Times* called a 'most unusual combination', of the 'Who's Who of European industrial heavyweights'. Commissioners Davignon and François-Xavier Ortoli participated in all but the final session of the Paris conference. As an influential figure in France and a former president of the European Commission, Ortoli was recruited to demonstrate to the French government the seriousness of the group's commitment to their programme.

Table 2 – Original Members of the European Roundtable of Industrialists at April 1983

Umberto Agnelli, Vice Chairman, *Fiat SpA*, Italy

Sir Peter Baxendell, Chairman, *Shell Transport and Trading plc*, UK

Carlo de Benedetti, Vice Chairman and Chief Executive Officer, *Olivetti & Co*, Italy

Wisse Dekker, President, *Philips Industries*, Netherlands

Kenneth Durham, Chairman, *Unilever plc*, UK

Roger Fauroux, Président-Directeur Général, *Compagnie de St. Gobain*, France

Pehr G. Gyllenhammar, Managing Director and Chief Executive Officer, *AB Volvo*, Sweden

Bernard Hanon, Président-Directeur Général, *Regie Nationale des Usines Renault*, France

John Harvey-Jones, Chairman, *ICI plc*, UK

Olivier Lecerf, Vice Chairman and Chief Operating Officer, *Lafarge Coppée SA*, France

Helmut Maucher, Managing Director and Chief Executive Officer, *Nestlé SA*, Switzerland

Hans Merkle, Chairman of the Board of Management, *Robert Bosch GmbH*, Germany

Curt Nicolin, Chairman, *ASEA AB*, Sweden

Louis von Planta, Chairman and Managing Director, *Ciba-Geigy*, Switzerland

Antoine Riboud, Président-Directeur Général, *BSN*, France

Wolfgang Seelig, Senior Vice President, *Siemens AG*, Germany

Dieter Spethmann, Chairman of the Board of Management, *Thyssen AG*, Germany

The ERT conference was the first occasion where European CEOs organised themselves to address European policy matters publicly. Indeed, the conference was a far cry from the secretive meetings of the *Groupe des Présidents* a decade earlier. At a press conference following the final session Gyllenhammar announced that '[N]ever before has such a group been assembled,' noting that a similar meeting would have been unheard of even two years earlier. The fact that this group of high-level industrialists had met signalled 'a new consensus that something has to be done' in Europe. Moreover, discussions among the industrialists were not limited to national issues, but demonstrated, as Paul Betts wrote in the *Financial Times* in April 1983, a 'level of concern above the nation state'.

A second ERT meeting took place on 1 June 1983 in Amsterdam to establish a charter for the organisation and to finalise a memorandum to Commissioner Davignon. Entitled *Foundations for the Future of European Industry*, this memorandum asserted the industrialists' 'will and ability to promote new wealth creation in Europe....But we cannot do this unaided ... we need supporting political action'. As the memorandum noted, this political action was necessary first and foremost in the creation of a unified European market:

> We cannot remove unaided the many obstacles in Europe which cause waste of valuable resources, and explain, in part, the weakening position of European firms in world markets. In reality, despite ambitions to liberalise trade, and the measures taken by the EEC, Europe remains a group of separated national markets with separated national policies and separated industrial structures. This prevents many firms from reaching the scale necessary to resist pressure from non-European competitors. The European market must serve as the unified 'home' base necessary to allow European firms to develop as powerful competitors in world markets.

According to the ERT document, the non-unified market resulted in three major obstacles to European industrial growth: 1) the highly unfavourable risk/return relationship for productive investments; 2) the European regulatory environment characterised by a proliferation of uncoordinated standards; and 3) fiscal, legal and political obstacles to the creation of transnational industrial structures. The ERT outlined specific measures and called on political leaders to revamp public policies for European private investment, end subsidies to obsolete industries, develop common standards and deregulate public markets in technology-intensive areas, and facilitate European merger and acquisition laws. The industrialists also appealed for the modification of regional and social funds and the Common Agricultural Policy in order to address the economic challenges of the 1980s. The core of the ERT plan, however, was to promote a unified European market. As the ERT charter stated, 'A halt to market fragmentation within Europe and the creation of unified European markets is essential'.

The ERT's strategy to attain a unified European market differed significantly from traditional approaches to the common market. The industrialists' approach was not limited merely to speeding up the removal of individual non-tariff barriers to trade. Nor did it resemble a European-wide deregulatory programme similar to that undertaken by Margaret Thatcher's government in the United Kingdom. Rather, ERT members believed that the creation of a unified market required additional measures that would promote the development of a competitive Europe. Initiatives were necessary to stimulate investment in technological development and industrial growth while firms undertook painful restructuring operations. Measures were needed to advance a *political-legal framework* under which these initiatives could be taken. The ERT strategy was, in effect, to offer a 'new Europe' – one that could effectively develop and market high technologies, create jobs through wealth creation and compete successfully in the world market.

In 1983 the ERT secretariat was set up in Paris. It issued press releases and attended to the day-to-day affairs of the organisation. The ERT secretariat was actually billed under the Volvo spare parts division. An annual membership fee of 200,000 French francs was collected from each ERT member for the budget which covered the secretariat, the meetings and background work on special projects. Fiat, Olivetti, Philips and Volvo seconded company officials to serve on the ERT staff and supervise project developments.

The ERT undertook several high-visibility projects that gave 'practical expression to the meaning of a unified market' – and further exposure to the ERT agenda. Over time the ERT agenda was heard by the Commission and by national governments as well. The ERT projects were largely led by firms based in the European Community, in consultation with national governments and EC institutions. Unfortunately, the projects proved to be a divisive issue to British members of the ERT who preferred a direct lobbying approach, and who detected that certain continental ERT companies would undoubtedly benefit disproportionally from participation in the European projects. Thus, in the autumn of 1983, John Harvey-Jones (ICI) and Sir Peter Baxendell (Shell) resigned from the ERT, followed shortly thereafter by Kenneth

Durham (Unilever). Harvey-Jones, however, continued to promote the idea of a unified European market, together with Dekker, de Benedetti and Jacques Solvay of Solvay & Cie. in a small committee attached to the *Groupe des Présidents*.

In January 1984, the CEOs of Olivetti and Wisse Dekker of Phillips announced the creation of the first ERT project. The European Venture Capital Association (EVCA) was designed to 'encourage transnational investments in Europe and … involve close relations between new technologically innovative firms and large industrial companies'. Venture capital for Europe-wide initiatives was still a relatively unknown and untried concept in 1984. ERT members believed that one of the reasons why Europe lagged in innovative technology compared to its global competitors was the lack of smaller, innovative companies. So ERT members opened their own venture capital firm, Euroventures, in January 1985 with initial capital of $30 million. As the first European-run venture capital group, Euroventures was developed around a pan-European 'network' of funds which encouraged cross-border developments.

In a news conference in London in December 1984 Gyllenhammar unveiled the second project undertaken by ERT members, *Missing Links: Upgrading Europe's Transborder Ground Transport Infrastructure*. The ERT's highly-promoted project comprised three major proposals that were designed to address the incomplete trans-European infrastructure network which precluded the development of a full common market. The first and most visible was an Anglo/French Channel road/rail link known as 'Euroroute'. Ian MacGregor, president of the British Steel Corporation, chaired the consortium, with the active support of a new intake of ERT members in 1984-5 – including Adolphe Demeure de Lespaul (Petrofina, Belgium), Sir John Clark (Plessey, UK), Jean-Luc Lagardère (Matra, France), Anthony Pilkington (Pilkington Brothers, UK), Stephan Scmidheiny (Eternit, Switzerland) and Poul Svanholm (United Breweries / Carlsberg, Denmark). While the Euroroute proposal was later abandoned in favour of the 'Chunnel,' the ERT project was recognised for demonstrating that such a project could be cost-effective if undertaken on a European scale, and that it could be financed by private funding. *The Economist* raised its hat to the ERT and its efforts to promote a European market in an article which noted, '[the ERT is] a growing force. The elusive group of do-gooding chief executives … is growing bolder…. The [*Missing Links*] transport proposals are one element in the group's campaign to rid Europe of its internal market barriers'.

The second proposal in the *Missing Links* project concerned the development of a Scandinavian road/rail link to northern Germany. The third, a European high-speed train system, later received considerable backing from national governments and rail systems. Both the Scanlink and high-speed train projects are under full development today. The *Missing Links* project provided the foundation for the future infrastructure work of the organisation – as well as the European Community.

In addition to promoting its projects to the press, the ERT's message was also heard because its members began to promote its agenda in private meetings with leading government officials. Nowhere were the links between ERT and government leaders closer than in France where the ERT played an important part in shaping French President François Mitterrand's European agenda.

Mitterrand was always a committed European, having been involved in larger European Socialist movements throughout his life. Two key decisions, however, cemented the French President's commitment towards Europe in the early 1980s. The first came in March 1983 when Mitterrand determined that the French franc should not be removed from the European Monetary System. The second came six months later when the French President proposed to relaunch Europe via an *industrial initiative*. In a memorandum circulated to fellow EC members, Mitterrand called for 'A New Step for Europe: A Common Space of Industry and Research' that would allow for 'the progressive construction of scientific and industrial cooperation capable of responding to the great challenge of the third technological revolution'. According to the document, the decline of European industry had no other origin than the fragmented European market: 'A customs union does not mean a homogeneous industrial space'. Mitterrand's support for a European industrial initiative can be attributed to lessons learned from the early nationalisation programmes as well as to the growing influence of the ERT on the thinking of the president and his key advisors.

The President began his term in office with an ambitious nationalisation programme. As early as January 1983, however, the CEOs of firms nationalised by the Socialists, led by Roger Fauroux of Saint-Gobain, put pressure on Mitterrand to depose Jean-Pierre Chevènement, the Minister of Industry who had sought considerable oversight of the companies' operations. The CEOs impressed upon Mitterrand that the success of his socialist experiment, notably the nationalisation policy, rested with the success or failure of the companies in the global marketplace. As the President came to acknowledge the rules of the global marketplace, the Socialist government was also forced to grapple with a series of setbacks in French high-technology industries, notably in telecommunications. Dual fears emerged of a 'technology gap' and French dependence on Japanese and American technological leadership.

With its domestic industry in trouble, the French government witnessed the increasingly successful cooperation of French and European firms in ESPRIT (the embryonic information technology programme), Airbus (the joint-European aircraft manufacturer) and Ariane (the European rocket programme designed to promote European autonomy in space). Mitterrand and his advisors became increasingly aware of the ERT's efforts to reinvigorate European industry through the promotion of a unified market, European high-technology cooperation, trans-European networks and improved education and training of the European workforce.

The ERT had privileged access to top French officials due to Gyllenhammar's personal relations with Mitterrand and with his closest advisor, Jacques Attali. Gyllenhammar's reception was facilitated by the French socialists' fascination with Swedish society's model of development. The ERT had also established strong ties with leading figures in French society, such as Michel Albert, co-author of the famous report to the European Parliament which first pointed out the costs of 'non-Europe'. The Paris location of the headquarters of the ERT also encouraged easy access between ERT staff and French government officials.

The French ERT members – who were the largest group within the ERT – also provided a critical link to the French government. Roger Fauroux of Saint Gobain, Olivier Lecerf of Lafarge Coppée and Antoine Riboud of BSN, were the 'young Turks' in the French Patronat who were instrumental in promoting change in early 1982 within the French employers' organisation, the CNPF. All three men were part of a new class of industrial managers in France, schooled in international competition and the ways of their foreign counterparts.

It was not only the ERT's access to the French government that mattered – it was the manner in which the group *presented itself* and was *perceived*. In the eyes of its French members, the ERT was a 'Christian Democratic/Social Democratic group' that did not share the ideology of Thatcherite capitalists. The ERT was not merely concerned with 'lobbying on issues' – an Anglo-Saxon preoccupation – but with creating *projects* or *des choses concrètes* to demonstrate their resolve to national governments.

It was no coincidence, therefore, that the proposals of the French government's industrial initiative in September 1983 largely reflected the ideas discussed in the original ERT memorandum and forwarded in private meetings by the ERT. The main elements of the government's initiative were to:

1. Give a new momentum to cooperation in research;
2. Define European norms/standards and open public procurement markets;
3. Ensure that European common commercial policy benefited European industrial development;
4. Favour alliances and cooperation among European firms;
5. Enlarge the Community's means of intervention;
6. Launch European infrastructure projects that support exchanges among companies and already existing interdependencies.

These proposals echoed the concerns of the ERT, especially the sixth one, which called for the creation of trans-European infrastructure projects. The ERT quickly took action to coordinate and reinforce its members' positions *vis-à-vis* the French government. For example, one month after the Mitterrand proposal, on 14 October 1983, a breakfast meeting was set up by the ERT with Michel Albert to review the Mitterrand government's plan and to develop strategies to promote the ERT platform further.

Mitterrand's industrial proposal was a prelude to his actions four months later. With the advent of the French presidency of the European Council in January 1984, Mitterrand launched a major diplomatic effort to address outstanding issues in the Community that had led to numerous stalemates in the past: reform of the common agricultural policy, change in the EC structural funds, agreement on enlargement negotiations with Spain and Portugal, and agreement on the budget. Mitterrand and his advisors began shuttling between Prime Minister Thatcher and Chancellor Kohl to discuss these issues. His advisors also held meetings with the ERT. In March 1984, for example, five members of the ERT – Agnelli, Dekker, Merkle, Riboud and Gyllenhammar – met with Jacques Attali, Mitterrand's confidant, at his home to discuss ERT projects and the goal of a unified market.

The French President's industrial initiative floundered, however, as national government and Commission officials failed to put its programme into effect. When Internal Market Commissioner Karl-Heinz Narjes produced a comprehensive package of proposals to complete a European common market in late 1984, there was no outpouring of support from government leaders. The Commission document listed hundreds of pre-existing pieces of legislation – ranging from standardisation to social actions and environmental issues – deemed necessary for the creation of an internal market. Business leaders, while pleased that a package was produced, found the Commission package 'unwieldy' and lacking 'a precise time-table'. Moreover, there was no strategy to ensure its implementation and no rationale for industrial growth. It became apparent to the heads of big business that industry needed to produce its own concrete programme.

The Single Market agenda was relaunched on 11 January 1985 in Brussels, when Wisse Dekker unveiled a plan, *Europe 1990*, before an audience of 500 people, including many of the newly appointed EC Commissioners. (The event had been scheduled for 13 November 1984 until Philips officials realised the new Commission would not be in Brussels until January 1985.) The plan laid out in precise terms the steps needed in four key areas – trade facilitation (elimination of border formalities), opening up of public procurement markets, harmonisation of technical standards, and fiscal harmonisation (eliminating the fiscal Value Added Tax frontiers) – to open up the European market within five years. The paper left little doubt about the importance of creating a united European market. As Dekker noted in his introduction: 'The survival of Europe is in fact at stake'.

Europe 1990 was not for Brussels consumption alone. Dekker sent the plan along with a letter to the heads of state and government of the European Community.

Wisse Dekker emerged as the new voice of European industry – and a recognised leader of the Single Market movement. In many respects Dekker also represented a new breed of European CEO. He had risen to the top echelon in Philips management, previously dominated by Philips family members, in part by overseeing company activities in Japan and the United Kingdom. He was well aware of the challenges facing the European electronics industry through growing global competition. It was Dekker who, in 1983, determined that his trusted aide, Koen Ramaer, should open up a Philips office in Brussels dedicated to ensuring the viability of European-level projects such as ESPRIT and to promoting a more competitive European market *vis-à-vis* the rest of the world. Ramaer, in fact, spearheaded the development of the *Europe 1990* plan along with four experts seconded from Philips.

The 'Dekker paper,' as it became known, was revolutionary, not only because it was proposed by the head of a major multinational, but because it produced what had escaped national and European policymakers – a simple plan for a unified market. In addition to providing a precise agenda, the paper introduced a number of new conceptualisations of what a unified European market might entail. In the trade facilitation area, for example, the 'ultimate goal' of the plan was to create *'frontiers without formalities* for goods traffic and the replacement of paper documents by data transmission via a telecommunications network used by traders, transporters, banks, and statistical and tax authorities..'. Of course, to implement this strategy, member states would also be required to develop a trans-European electronics-telecommunications network – one that Philips could undoubtedly provide.

While the Dekker paper was an initiative specific to Philips, it was soon embraced by the ERT. After all, many of the concepts developed in *Europe 1990* were first articulated in the ERT fora – most notably the creation of a trans-European communications infrastructure and the development of European-wide electronic databases. In June 1985 the Dekker paper and the *Missing Links* project were featured in an ERT document, *Changing Scales* – a 'scrapbook' of ERT activities prepared for ERT members but also sent to heads of government and numerous other high-level officials. Gyllenhammar personally delivered two copies to Attali, one designated for Mitterrand.

The Dekker speech and the *Missing Links* programme generated increased contacts between the European multinational firms and EC member state governments. The ERT also developed a 'Political Contact Programme' in order to target various government figures. Sometimes it was the member states that were first to contact the ERT for discussions.

ERT relations with the Commission grew and indeed strengthened with the new Delors Commission. On 14 January, three days after the Dekker speech, the newly installed President of the European Commission, Jacques Delors, appeared before the European Parliament and 'announced the new Commission's intention to ask the European Council to pledge itself to completion of a fully unified internal market by 1992, to be achieved with the help of a programme comprising a realistic and binding timetable'. Not surprisingly, many Brussels insiders regarded the Dekker paper as the primary influence behind Delors's Single Market proposal.

By March 1985 Delors had invited the ERT to an 'on the record' meeting with the Commission to discuss ERT goals. Members of the ERT secretariat met on several occasions with Delors's *cabinet* and other key Commission officials to prepare for the meeting. In addition, Gyllenhammar met privately with Delors on 28 May to discuss the 'official' ERT-Commission meeting on 14 June. Internal ERT correspondence reveals that during these background sessions, arrangements were made for 'things the Commission wants' and 'what the [ERT] can get out of the meeting'. As an ERT secretariat official put it:

> The EC is intrigued by the RT [Round Table] – are they [ERT members] really entrepreneurs or it is another UNICE? Do they mean what they say? The EC genuinely wants to meet the RT – and maybe use it as a *constituency* (beware!)

At the meeting of the European Council on 29-30 March 1985, the heads of state and government broadly endorsed the programme of the Commission and, echoing President Delors's statement, called for the creation of a single market by 1992. In the meantime, veiled threats by Wisse Dekker and other CEOs that European multinationals would move their companies' operations overseas if the European leaders did not follow through with their plans for a united Europe appeared on the front page of the *Financial Times*. As Dekker noted in one of many speeches on the European market, 'If Europe is neither able nor willing to develop its economic structure, then the consequences of that must be drawn'.

The European Council's endorsement sanctioned Internal Market Commissioner Lord Cockfield to move ahead with the Single Market project. For the next three months Cockfield and three other members of his team wrote the White Paper, incorporating the now-famous concept of mutual recognition and the new approach to harmonisation, and outlining the nearly 300 pieces of legislation necessary to create a single market. Unlike his predecessor, Cockfield and his associates managed to impose coherence on the single market concept.

The White Paper was far more comprehensive than the Dekker proposal. Initially, several industrialists feared that the White Paper was too encompassing and that member states would never follow through such a comprehensive document. Dekker also disliked the fact that Cockfield chose the 1992 deadline as opposed to the 1990 date proposed in the Dekker Paper. Lord Cockfield, however, adamantly refused to change either the contents of the White Paper or the date.

At the Milan Summit in June 1985 the heads of state and government followed up the declarations, 'welcomed' the White Paper and instructed the Community Institutions to draw up a precise programme of action. They also agreed to the creation of an Intergovernmental Conference (IGC) which later resulted in the Single European Act (SEA).

Several members of the ERT leadership took a keen interest in the governments' negotiations over the SEA between June and December 1985. It is not that they sought to influence the IGC negotiations; after all, the general foundation for the Single Market programme was already provided in the White Paper. The remaining governmental debates over the European Parliament's powers and procedures were of little importance to the industrialists. What *did* matter was the political will of the national leaders to take the decision to follow through their commitment to the Single Market. They had to be held to it.

Wisse Dekker contacted over thirty CEOs, including the EC members of the ERT, to send a strong, concerted message to the European Council that was to meet in Luxembourg in February 1986 for a final vote on the SEA. The message telexed to the Council members in the different EC languages was straight-forward: decide one way or another, but decide. Industry will then make its own decisions as to the future of its investment and growth strategies:

> As leading industrialists based in the European Communities ... we urge you to exercise your full influence so that the forthcoming topmeeting [sic] will produce concrete results. Not only is the credibility of European political leaders at stake but European industry badly needs a clear signal that the major objectives of the Treaty of Rome will be realised within the next 5 years. Even a clear statement that this would not be the case, would – although not hoped for – be helpful as this would end the prolonged period of uncertainty with which industry has to cope under the present situation and which forms a significant obstacle on the way to expanding our activities and intensifying our efforts to build a strong and competitive European position...

The SEA was formally signed by the member states of the Community at a ceremony in Luxembourg on 17 February 1986. While there is no evidence to suggest that the telex influenced the final vote of the European Council, the telex was the first time that the leaders of major European multinationals united to speak out forcefully on a treaty decision taken by the heads of state and government of the Community.

The story of the Single Market programme, of course, did not end with the signing of the SEA. Indeed, ERT members were not convinced that government leaders and their staffs would follow with the White Paper. Dekker, in particular, was increasingly concerned about the slow response of the member states to adhere to the internal market timetable. The ERT began to organise itself as a more visible lobby group by adding more members, including Davignon, the new head of Société Générale of Belgium. On 2 June 1986, at a symposium entitled 'Europe is Urgent,' Dekker announced the ERT's intention of creating a 'watchdog group' that would audit the member states' activities regarding the internal market programme. Over the next six months Dekker and his assistant, Walter Grünsteidl, developed the guidelines and recruited new members for the group. Using Cockfield's White Paper as a guide, the group was to monitor developments, identify and analyse significant delays and apply pressure to government leaders as well as domestic industry groups where progress was too slow.

On 1 December 1986 the first meeting of the Internal Market Support Committee (IMSC), as it was formally called, was held. One of its first actions was to send a telex to Prime Minister Thatcher, whose government held the EC Presidency at the time, offering the group's support to government leaders in promoting the internal market and pressing for further progress. Thatcher responded with letters to the IMSC members, expressing her appreciation of the IMSC's support.

The following month the IMSC members met the head of the new Presidency, Belgian Foreign Minister Leo Tindemans. The meeting marked the beginning of a new and continuing practice of the ERT – namely, meeting with senior government officials of the current presidency, usually including the head of state or government, to discuss the ERT's suggestions and concerns regarding developments and overall strategies of the European Community.

Meanwhile, IMSC members also met Delors and Cockfield to push their agenda. Members of the IMSC took to the two Commission officials a message first issued to government leaders at the Luxembourg summit: 'show political will, or European industry will invest elsewhere'. As the press release issued by the IMSC noted:

> If progress towards the implementation of the European market is as slow as at present, it is unavoidable that European industries might have to reconsider their long-term strategies in order to stay competitive, with the possibility of redirecting industrial investments to other parts of the world outside Europe. This could lead to a serious setback in Europe's industrial development with grave consequences for economic activity, employment and general welfare in Europe...

The industrialists made a strong plea to politicians at all levels to implement the provisions of the Single European Act according to the spirit of political good-will which existed at its conception, and the Commission's press release following the meeting noted that the ERT members would stay in close contact with the Commission regarding the progress of the Single Market programme.

In June 1987 the IMSC carried a similar message to Uffe Ellemann-Jensen, Foreign Minister of the newly-installed Danish Presidency. The presidency, however, was only mildly successful in achieving agreement on White Paper directives. As one IMSC member, Sir Patrick Sheehy of B.A.T Industries, noted in a letter to Cockfield in December 1987:

The IMSC ... remains in full support of your proposals as the only means of removing the barriers at the frontiers and we have taken every opportunity to say so to national governments. It will be no surprise to you to learn that we have had a very negative response. We have therefore decided to redouble our efforts to find ways of presenting our arguments in a persuasive way.

The uncertainty over the success of the Single Market programme ended with the German Presidency in 1988. A number of major decisions on the Single Market were taken, agreement was reached on the reform of the EC structural funds, Telecommunications Ministers met for the first time and approved action on the development of a common market in telecommunications services and equipment, and a green paper on copyright was presented to the Council. As the Commission noted in a rather celebratory issue of the official *Bulletin*, 'The question is no longer whether 1992 is plausible, but how to prepare for it and what it will mean'. Three years after the European Council welcomed the White Paper, the Single Market programme finally appeared irreversible.

Part of the success of the German Presidency can be attributed to growing familiarity with the White Paper requirements. Familiarity alone, however, is not a sufficient explanation. The underlying role of the European multinationals must not be overlooked. As Axel Kranse records, Delors himself noted that the success of the Single Market programme came 'thanks to many people and actors in what became a process ... the 1992 process. And I must admit the business actors mattered; they made a lot of it happen'.

Business leaders and Europe: then and now

The creation of the European Round Table of Industrialists and the promotion of the Single Market programme throughout the 1980s is the story of the rise of eminent business leaders who assumed a new role in the European Union. It is hard to imagine the development of the Single Market programme today without acknowledging the leadership and ideas of individuals such as Pehr Gyllenhammar and Wisse Dekker. Nor can one ignore the contribution of others: Giovanni Agnelli who began the first contacts with the Commission back in the early 1960s and who joined the ERT ranks in the 1990s; Carlo de Benedetti who first promoted the European Venture Capital Association and continues to play a leading role in the ERT today; and Etienne Davignon, the Commissioner who demonstrated to industrialists the positive role that the Community could play and who later joined their ranks.

The political role of business leaders, however, did not end with the Single Market programme. In 1988, Dekker took over as chair of the ERT, moved the organisation's permanent headquarters to Brussels and hired a full-time Secretary-General, Keith

Richardson. Members of the *Groupe des Présidents* were recruited to increase the size and stature of the organisation. New names appeared in the press as leading business people in support of European projects – names like Edward Reuter of Daimler-Benz, Jérôme Monod of Lyonnaise des Eaux-Dumez and Helmut Maucher of Nestlé. New initiatives were promoted and embraced by ERT members, notably in the area of Trans-European Networks (TENs). Today the ERT is recognised as one of the key promoters of TENs as codified in the Maastricht Treaty. In March 1994 the ERT created the European Centre for Infrastructure Studies in Rotterdam to promote EU infrastructure programmes further.

The ERT continues to follow an agenda-setting strategy, especially in promoting European industrial competitiveness. The ERT issued a series of 'mega-reports' to heads of state and government prior to European Council meetings in the early 1990s. The reports were in response to the perceived inability or unwillingness of member states to move forward with Community projects both during and after the Maastricht Treaty ratification crisis. The mega-reports outlined problems facing the Community as well as the industrialists' proposed strategies for addressing these issues. More recently, the ERT has provided notable input into the development of the 1996 IGC agenda.

More recently ERT members have extended their involvement to other key Community projects. Etienne Davignon and Giovanni Agnelli, for example, took office as chairman and vice-chairman respectively of the Association for the Monetary Union of Europe. Carlo de Benedetti served on the EU High Level Group on European information highways. David Simon of British Petroleum participated in the EU Competitiveness Group – an organisation proposed by the ERT in one of the mega-reports to the European Council.

The role of business leaders in the promotion of the European project has changed dramatically since the inception of the Community. Once viewed as 'too nationalistic' to support the European project, European CEOs proved themselves to be eminent Europeans in the promotion of the Single Market programme. Today, the ERT views itself as a 'strategic' organisation dedicated to generating ideas, setting agendas and moving forward 'practical policies' in key areas such as education, employment and infrastructure. Equally important, Community and member state officials alike also recognise European business leaders as critical participants in shaping and promoting the European Union's future.

Selected bibliography

This essay is largely drawn from Cowles (1994). Portions have been published in Cowles (1995a), and a separate treatment of the same ideas can be found in Cowles (1995b).

Bibliography

Drew, John (1979) *Doing Business in the European Community* London: Butterworths.

Cowles, Maria Green (1994) *The Politics of Big Business in the European Community*, Ph.D. dissertation, The American University.

(1995a) 'Setting the Agenda for a New Europe: The ERT and EC 1992' in *Journal of Common Market Studies*, Vol.33, No.4, December 1995, Oxford: Blackwell.

(1995b) 'The European Round Table of Industrialists: The Strategic Player in European Affairs' in Justin Greenwood, ed., *European Business Alliances*, Hertfordshire: Prentice-Hall.

Giesbert, Franz-Olivier (1990) *Le Président*, Paris: Editions de Seuil.

Gyllenhammar, Pehr (1982) 'Viewpoint' *International Management*, July.

(1983) 'What Europe needs is a new "Marshall Plan"' in *Financial Times*, 19 January 1983.

Krause, Axel (1992) *Inside the New Europe*, New York: HarperCollins.

Organisation for Economic Co-operation and Development (1985) *Economic Outlook*, Paris: OECD.

József Antall –
Prime Minister of Hungary

Péter Á. Bod

September 1948, Hungary. The Budapest Piarist College has been nationalised this summer. Despite that, a sixteen year old student is giving a speech in the debating society. There is still a debating society, still Piarist teachers, but not for long. Outside the school, a new tyranny is expanding. This month the State Security Authority, modelled after the Soviet NKVD, has been set up; the Hungaro-American Oil Corporation nationalised. The chief engineers will soon be taken to court; the Primate of the Catholic Church, Cardinal József Mindszenty, will soon be arrested and accused of treason, espionage and currency profiteering.

The communists and fellow-travellers already control most of society and the economy – with the Red Army standing behind them. Banks and companies are already all nationalised; small firms with over ten employees will have been expropriated within a year.

There is nothing especially Hungarian about this story. The script has been written in the Kremlin for the whole of its new Central European dominion: communists are to take control of the social democrats or socialists and drive the civic forces out of parliaments. This is the summer of the start of the Berlin blockade and of the Cold War.

Nevertheless, there are some brave souls in Budapest, Warsaw and Prague who still study the institutions and forms of democratic rule. One of them is József Antall. Speaking in the debating society about the geopolitical role of the United States, he starts:

> The significance of the United States of America in international politics, and concerning the consequences of its position as a superpower, is beyond dispute. Germany has twice plunged into war in recent decades to gain hegemony, first in Europe and then globally; her adversaries have twice owed the victory to the United States. The prophecy of Lajos Kossuth, made while in America in 1851, that the Union would intervene decisively in European affairs had twice come true. The sentences of this great Hungarian statesman proved once again true as the enormous military and economic power of the United States saved the Old Continent from the suffocating embrace of the German colossus. When freedom is endangered, the peoples of Europe turn to America.

The analysis is accurate, the style mature, yet the text could not be published until 45 years later (in *Magyar Szemle*), in the fourth year of the return to parliamentary democracy. That student became the Prime Minister of Hungary in 1990.

Back in 1948, the fate of the Central-Eastern European region seemed to have been sealed. *Cuius regio, eius religio* – a new system expanded as far as the Red Army had been able to march into Europe. 'Civilised Europe' was in ruins: Britain indebted, Germany defeated and still under punitive surveillance, France finally on the winning side but after a humiliating defeat. This Europe would hardly rise up in arms again even in self-defence, most certainly not for others. In Hungary, Czechoslovakia, Poland, in the eastern part of the defeated Germany, in the Balkans and in the Baltic states electors might still be allowed to vote, but not choose.

Yet, even under these conditions, there was a debating society where this student could discuss the similarities and differences of political systems: 'In the New World terms like "state", "government", "political party" carry meanings totally different from those in the European Continent and particularly in Hungary. The terms "state" and "government" evoke reflections over there different from those over here'.

Over there, over here

For centuries, this has been the framework of reference for intellectuals in the region east of the rivers Elbe and Leutha (the one time frontier of Charlemagne's empire) and west of the forests separating the Polish and Russian lands. This is Central-Eastern Europe, the land in-between. Intellectually, it has always been part of *Europa Occidens*, the *Christianitas*, the West. Economically, militarily and dynastically, however, it has only intermittently been part of the West.

Here, in this region, we like to say that we have belonged to Europe for one thousand years. But Europe has moved around us. As the Hungarian historian Jeno Szûcs has pointed out, when Stalin, Churchill and Roosevelt repartitioned Europe 1130 years after the death of Charlemagne, they merely reconstructed the eastern borders of the Carolingian empire – whose contours became the line where the iron curtain would drop. Churchill and Roosevelt must have taken into account more than just the probable advance of the Red Army; they only gave up at Yalta – or so could they comfort their consciences – what had always been a disputed area.

In 1948, the spirit of the older tradition still lives on: there are artists, teachers and academics who refuse, as long as it is physically possible, to accept that their country has been shifted back to the new Eastern empire. For long centuries, the continuity of the region's spiritual bonds has clashed with the volatility of its geopolitical affiliation. The clash of spirituality and reality has charged the Central-Eastern European intellectuals with a specific energy, hardly explicable to a Westerner. It is beyond easy comprehension how men of letters were able to preserve the feeling of belonging to Europe when their nation was in fact firmly subjugated to oriental rule. The intellectual was a keeper of hope, the conscience of the nation, creator and personifier of national or political programmes, at times a conspirator risking his/her freedom or life.

This Central-Eastern European type of intellectual is different from the West European intellectual who tends to spend his life – a life no longer endangered by despots – in the closed worlds of university, editorial office or artist's studio; but also different from the Chinese clerk who is but a bureaucrat of the empire. The intelligentsia on the periphery of Europe contains elements of both the former and the latter: while aspiring to retain artistic or academic independence, they most often live off the State since it is only the bureaucracy, and not the weak bourgeoisie, that can maintain a sufficient number of white collar workers in intellectual pursuits.

The intelligentsia, caught frequently between the bourgeoisie and the State, may assume a critical role when society reaches a cross-roads. Turning points in history call for those outside – or above – traditional political roles, those with a vision and will to redefine the national or political agenda. Intellectual as chief policy maker? Not unknown, but not common in mature Western democracies, in Central and Eastern Europe this has frequently been the pattern, and was certainly characteristic of the years 1989-90 when Havel the writer, Mazowiecky the journalist and Antall the historian all emerged as national leaders.

If this is a pattern, then there is logic behind it. The intellectuals' direct engagement with politics has always been prompted by the weakness of the body politic. Weak civic societies allow for, even call for, direct political activity by the intellectuals. Before the Second World War, Central-Eastern Europe was a region of belated social development with only a weak bourgeoisie. What happened to the region in the post-war years could only further weaken civic society. All Stalin needed from the small countries west of Russia was that they provide a buffer zone against an imagined Western attack and a military springboard for his war plans. Oriental rule, whether Byzantine or communist, rejects the concept of equal status and, built on a concept of hierarchy, aims to destroy markets including knowledge – since it is marketable and as such can become a means of distance from the state.

The Central-Eastern European intelligentsia has never been homogeneous, but sovietisation in the late-1940s and early-1950s definitively broke it up. There was some truth to the communists' claim that the Hungarian intelligentsia of the age could not be regarded as 'modern' or 'democratic'. It had inherited too much from a feudal past and had been too dependent on the powers that be.

In any case, the new regime, not trusting the old intelligentsia, recruited a new, malleable and more reliable one. This is the way the Jewish shoemaker, having survived humiliation and the extermination camp, would be made an officer of state security; the Communist tram conductor promoted to chief in the State Office for Religious Affairs and later Minister of Finance. The 1950s was the time for crash courses and quick promotions from factory shop level to the rank of chief executive. This was a singular period with sudden elevations and declines in social status. The accelerated recruitment of the cadres increased social mobility; many of those promoted to high positions very young did a good job. Others could not cope with the sudden increase of responsibility, and failed.

It was in this period that József Antall passed his final examination in the Piarist College and went on to the Budapest faculty of arts to study history, law, anthropology, economics and museology. After graduation he joined the Hungarian National Archives and also started to teach.

At that time, talking about politics was confined to reliable circles of friends and relatives: one talked behind closed windows with the radio playing loudly as a precaution against others listening. József's father, József Antall senior, was a man of note. In 1939, the anti-Nazi Prime Minister, Pál Teleki, promoted him to take charge of refugee affairs. He managed to perform his duties until 1944 when the Germans invaded Hungary and the Gestapo caught him. However, he survived the war and, once the front moved to the west, he was again in politics as State Secretary in the first provisional government, then Minister for Reconstruction during the coalition period. After the Communists took power, Antall retired from office and public duties. His home was certainly more than just a residence for the young Antall; it must have been an academy for politics as well.

The 1956 uprising

The young Antall was twenty-six when revolution broke out in 1956. As a teacher he threw himself into political organisation and was one of the founders of the Christian Democratic Youth Organisation, while his father was busily reorganising the Smallholders' and Civic Party. But the revolution was swiftly put down by the Russians. The younger Antall was detained for some time, then banned from teaching because he had 'expressed belief in multi-party democracy and called for independence and the withdrawal of the Soviet troops'. He subsequently made a living by working as a librarian. Jails and books and politics: close relations in this part of the world, as they had been for Alcide De Gasperi during the Second World War.

It is surprising how easily totalitarian rule seemed to collapse in Budapest in the autumn of 1956. The party bosses fled the country in a hurry, only to return on Soviet tanks thirsty for revenge. Their revenge was cruel and bloody. Over two hundred thousand Hungarians decided to escape before the border controls were reinstated; most of them were young, some of the brightest students, the driving forces of the uprising. But the spirit of the revolution was not broken immediately; the oppressors and their Hungarian clients were ostracised. The Russians felt that the regime had to be strengthened from inside. Their choice to undertake this task was János Kádár.

Kádár cruelly punished the working class: his machinery of 'justice' meted out hangings and life sentences mostly among working men and women. But Kádár was shrewd enough to know that memories fade and people gradually forget the past if not reminded. If they were not to be reminded, the intellectuals had to be properly handled. The Hungarian intelligentsia had by that time been decimated: some were in exile, some in jail, others banned from having their work published or from practising their profession. Perhaps for them the worst thing was the lack of hope of fundamental geopolitical change. The revolution may have overturned the totalitarian regime in one day, but the Soviet Union's control of the region was not seriously questioned by western governments. Yalta was alive; maintaining the status quo seemed the paramount western value. The uprising may temporarily have driven away the quislings of the eastern empire, but the empire itself was there to stay; the window of freedom and hope, opened wide in glorious October, had been firmly shut on that generation.

The new regime eventually managed the intellectuals so well that, barely two decades after the revolution was put down, the Yugoslav Djilas's vision of the intelligentsia as part of the new ruling class had come close to reality in Hungary. The revolution of 1956, like that of 1848, started as a demonstration by students. Intellectuals provided its leaders and strategists. It is symbolic that when Russian troops entered the empty halls of the Hungarian Parliament in the early hours of 4 November 1956, they found there one lone person busily hitting the keys of his typewriter: István Bibó, one of Hungary's most influential political thinkers and a Secretary of State in Imre Nagy's government, working at that moment on his famous proclamation to fellow Hungarians:

> ...I call upon the Hungarian people not to consider the occupying army – or the puppet-government which that army is likely to set up – as legal authority ... Now it is up to the world powers to demonstrate the force of the principles contained in the United Nations' Charter and the strength of the world's freedom-loving peoples.

The United Nations did not provide support for the revolution. The Kádár regime took root. The 'new-old' communist rulers managed to subjugate society, or what remained of the dynamic society of 1956. In the decades that followed the revolution, the peasantry ceased to exist: there remained only 'agricultural workers' in co-operatives. Similarly there was no longer a working class in Hungary but workers who spent eight hours a day in low pay, low intensity public sector jobs, doing after hours what untaxed jobs they could find.

And there was a new intelligentsia. While some eminent intellectuals were still in prison and only released as and when the government found it appropriate, certain prisoners proved to be weak under duress and were recruited as informers while in jail.

The real strength of the regime, however, lay not in threats and pressures but in promises. Kádár's promise, albeit a tacit one, to the blue collar workers was that as long as they did not bother about politics, the rulers would not interfere in their daily lives. This was the start of the 'liberal', 'enlightened' phase of Communist rule in Hungary which would later bring much praise for the regime from western journalists and politicians. A meagre deal like that could not have been made but for the historical weakness of civic society in the region. The Communists managed to convince the workers to leave politics to those with the requisite skills, that is, to the Party. Anyway, went the argument, just look at the intelligentsia: how comfortable they had found their role in 'building Socialism'.

From the early-1960s, certain key positions were reserved for the reliable only. These were jobs in the police, diplomacy, international finance and the media. Card-holding was required and 'reliability tests' had to be passed. One is tempted to say: an Orwellian world. But it was not; it was less organised and more Central European. There were many avenues into the inner circle, such as friendship or kinship with someone important. Up to a certain level, talent and skills would do. And then you reached a point which you would not be able to pass without surrendering to the Party.

Kádár's regime had softened a lot and, by the mid 1960s, became more tolerable than the rigid Stalinism of the pre-1956 period. Kádárism certainly differed from the communist regimes of neighbouring countries. The level of consumption in Hungary was higher, the constraints on intellectual life less strict. It was never clear where the exact limits lay since they were set by the Party leadership and not the law. Sometimes exciting articles appeared and sensational exhibitions were shown; this was one of the great periods of the Hungarian cinema. A part of the intelligentsia and the Party leadership started to interlock. Indeed it is appropriate to speak of the regime as that of Kádár and Aczél, since Aczél, responsible for cultural and media affairs within the top leadership, managed to link various sections of the Hungarian intelligentsia to himself and to the Party, and maintained the legitimacy of the regime among most of the intellectuals until the mid 1980s. He was simultaneously responsible for cultural affairs and the media on the one hand and the secret services on the other – he alone knew how much the two overlapped.

Influences

Yet there remained some who closely followed European trends of political thought throughout the period. It would be too much to say that they were preparing for the time after communism. The regime was strong, the Soviet Union showed no sign of weakness, western politicians and leading personalities developed warmer and warmer links with the representatives of the one-party states. No reasonable calculation could then have justified preparations for becoming at some time a non-communist politician. One could even have seemed ridiculous, like a stubborn monarchist in an established republic. But in this region there is a long tradition of maintaining one's moral stance against the odds; otherwise belief in the bonds with Europe could not have been maintained during one-and-a-half centuries of Ottoman domination, or patriotism under the rule of the Habsburgs.

József Antall was among those who managed to follow the intellectual and political events of the age. His later speeches and conversations reveal that he was much influenced by Ortega y Gasset, Röpke, Ludwig Erhard, László Németh and István Bibó, as well as the classic authors of Hungarian liberalism: József Eötvös, István Széchenyi, Kossuth and Ferenc Deák. In his political speeches he frequently referred to politicians whom he may have regarded as political role models: Schuman, De Gasperi, Adenauer, Monnet – the great generation of European unity. The remarkably successful restoration of democratic institutions in Germany after the Second World War and the economic miracle based on the *Sozialmarktwirtschaft* strongly shaped his political ideas and, once in office, his governmental principles.

Antall's enduring interest in politics must have had its roots in certain determining experiences of his youth. In the summer of 1993 he addressed a NATO workshop in what I regard as perhaps his most fascinating speech, in the Upper House of the Parliament building in Budapest. Seriously ill already, he recalled his early personal experiences and readings. He particularly mentioned to Averell Harriman's book, *Special Envoy to Churchill and Stalin*, in which Harriman refers to the first free municipal election in Budapest in October 1945: 'Budapest was jubilant. Jack McCloy and I wanted to go to the American mission, but we couldn't get in the door. There was an enormous crowd celebrating the victory under the American flag'. 'In fact I was there, a young lad,' added Antall, smiling.

Antall was without doubt a particularly disciplined politician and intellectual with a strong, supportive family background; but, although educated in and informed about the world's political affairs and European tendencies, he was not unique in Hungary or any other country of the region. The Poles also managed to keep windows of opportunity open to reflect on democracy and prepare for the future; the spiritual autonomy of the Church and the existence of some civic parties nominally independent from the establishment Party was largely maintained there throughout the decades. In Czechoslovakia the 1968 reform movement revealed how strongly democratic, western-type values were upheld among intellectuals, including some in top positions. During the years after the Prague Spring, the West learned the names of only a handful of Czech dissidents, yet many more longed for democracy.

The transition to parliamentary democracy and the market economy is still not complete, nor have any of the 'Visegrad' nations yet been allowed to join the core European institutions. Looking back from the present, one might even declare the period of the Antall government in Hungary – or, *mutatis mutandis*, that of Tadeus Mazowiecky and Hanna Suchocka in Poland – an historical accident. Yet that would be not only unfair, but largely incorrect, too. In spite of recent signs of restoration of an earlier style and the reappearance of former cadres, the civic governments that came to power after 1989-90 in Central-Eastern Europe were able to make their mark on the socio-economic structures and on the geo-political orientation of their countries.

Antall's rise to power

Just as Yalta in February 1945 once defined the geo-political place of the Central European region, the politically active perceived a redefinition at the time of the Malta summit between President Bush and General-Secretary Gorbachev in December 1989. It is not fully known what the American and Soviet leaders agreed upon there. Even the East European party bosses may not have been given a full account of the deal, but what briefing they did get made them change their behaviour. The signs were that Moscow had abandoned them. That impression also transformed the position of the latent political opposition. Cautious reorientation both within and outside the party-state had already started after Gorbachev launched his campaign of 'glasnost', but the message from Malta changed dimensions. No responsible politician would have risked another Hungary 1956, Czechoslovakia 1968, or Poland 1981 as long as his or her country was regarded – under the so-called Brezhnev doctrine – as a part of the 'Socialist camp' with no right to self-determination. But what if the Brezhnev doctrine were dead? Then the personal risks for politicians in opposition would be greatly reduced, and the call for a change of regime would not necessarily provoke Soviet intervention.

In 1989, the political landscape of Hungary totally changed. In response to the creation of opposition parties, the Party, that is the Hungarian Socialist Workers' Party, was transformed into two successor parties: one faithful to Marxism (Workers' Party), and another bigger one, the legal inheritor of the former establishment party with an undefined attitude to Marxism. As the leader of the 'true' party once remarked, 'We inherited Marx and they got the Capital'. Some of the opposition parties came into being by re-creating formerly banned, so-called historical parties like the Smallholder, Social Democratic and Christian Democratic parties; others were organisations without particular historical antecedents. The latter do not have the word 'party' in their name – which says a lot about the strong negative feelings concerning the Party and party politicking – the most important of them being the Hungarian Democratic Forum (MDF), the Alliance of Free Democrats (SZDSZ), and the Alliance of Young Democrats (FIDESZ).

Family traditions linked Antall to the Smallholders' Party. But, although the Small-holders invited him to join, he committed himself to the Democratic Forum, which he represented in the co-ordinating talks with opposition parties, then in the 'na-tional round table' talks from spring 1989. The many rounds of talks attempted to determine the constitutional form of the responsibilities of the prime minister and those of the president, and the legal and political guarantees between those in power and in opposition. At that time, the old Stalinist constitution still outlawed political opposition, and Soviet troops were still stationed on Hungarian soil. The opposition thus had every reason to demand guarantees. On the other hand, the Party bosses could not be sure about their victory in free elections, though most of them were confident on grounds of superiority in organisation and material strength; they, too, needed guarantees from the new forces.

No leader rose from the shopfloor in Hungary, unlike Walesa in Poland. No wonder: there is no working class in Hungary. In Poland, the misconceived crash industriali-sation programmes of the 1970s increased the size and social importance of the industrial workforce at a time when other countries were already entering the post-industrial age. In contrast, Hungary under the Kádár consolidation was not a land of the conscious worker but of the slick micro-entrepreneur who though officially em-ployed and paid by the state earned half of his income from businesses on the side, would not go on strike for better conditions or more pay, but rather minimised his time and effort in his official work-place. The chief personal strategy in 'reform-communist' Hungary was the private safeguard of one's interests. Representation to state-sponsored trade unions who were not much trusted or respected and certainly not regarded as eager to change the regime. The new parties were therefore confronted with a double task at their inception: to create a veritable programme for profound change, and at the same time mobilise the cautious and passive, if not suspicious, masses.At the first congress of the Forum in 1989, Antall recalled the words of his nineteenth century paragon József Eötvös: 'democracy should be organised not declared'.

In 1988-89, the MDF was an organisation of many valuable persons, though not a party. Most of its members were the intellectuals and professionals outside the nomenklatura: teachers, middle managers, veterinarians, preachers, lawyers. It was transformed into a party in the autumn of 1989, and József Antall was elected presi-dent. It was then the only party with a nation-wide network: the SZDSZ was pre-dominantly represented in the capital and larger cities, the FIDESZ in university centres. In 1989 Hungary needed a social force that was to create a constitutional democracy and market economy out of the bankrupt party-state, lead the economy out of the dying Comecon into the commonwealth of market economies, and eventu-ally, Antall hoped, link it to a unified Europe.

That was the challenge of the age. If there was any role Antall had prepared for, that was it. He had kept himself morally and politically intact throughout the decades.

Educated in the best traditions of Hungarian liberal-conservatism, he had not been lured by the promises of reform-communism or the vague concept of a 'third way'. He stood for changing the system rather than improving the declining regime. The historic occasion for change was somewhat unexpected, but Antall, the historian, grasped it. He volunteered to lead a movement which encompassed the politically active non-communist classes, a movement which organised itself around the concept of peaceful return to democracy and national sovereignty.

It did not take long for József Antall to rise to pre-eminence among the opposition leaders. His deep constitutional and historical knowledge and a sharp analytical mind were widely acknowledged, even by his foes. Politics seldom honours genuine contributions, but this is what exceptionally took place in 1990: the MDF won a plurality of votes at the spring election and Antall, by that time the president of the Forum, formed a government which he led until his death.

An important party cannot build its programme solely on the direct and short term interests of supporters and potential voters, yet nor can it survive without their continuing support either. To be adequate in the critical state of the Hungarian economy at the turn of 1989/90, the MDF's programme had to be tough, inviting at most understanding from its supporters, but not enthusiasm. Its programme aimed at an expeditious change of property rights, yet with an eye to the weaknesses, or lack, of market institutions and with the intention of broadening the middle classes.

As a major party, with a strong chance that it would come into government, the MDF had to deal with the issues of foreign debt, the state of the banking sector and the consequences of the dissolution of Comecon. The question was whether the party would stand for a genuine break with the socialist system – recognising the high social and economic costs of such a decision – or try to invent a 'third way' between socialism and market economy. The draft programme that was presented to its 1989 congress unambiguously called for a fully fledged market economy; although the inherited debt burden this would imply tremendous transitional costs. There were, and still are, many who hoped for a soft transition with perhaps strong support from the West, including write-offs or forgiveness on external debts. Antall nurtured no illusion about the external conditions, and recognised the shocks a determined change would imply, but he was also convinced that an irrevocable transformation could be achieved and that he had to achieve it. In a tough debate, the congress finally endorsed the economic chapter, but the debate on land and privatisation indicated that the general wish to have access to property would constantly clash with financial reality.

All new governing forces in the region were confronted with the fact that democratic political values had for the previous forty years been linked with opposition and lacked all governmental experience. The roots of opposition thinking went even deeper, as Antall stated in his acceptance speech to the congress:

In this part of Europe, our desire for freedom and our constitutional spirit were never weaker than in nations of more fortunate history; but they could realise them in institutions. Over here that spirit survived for decades in opposition.

As the president of a party preparing for government, he undertook the enormous tasks of turning his loosely organised movement into a genuine political party ('organising the democracy'); preparing the Forum for government; and placing his party movement on the political palette of Europe. It is extremely hard to turn an opposition movement into a party for government: the skills required to manage a country are not the same as those needed to fight for truth and social justice. Management skills can, no doubt, be acquired if history provides enough time. But it seldom does, and here it did not: the democracies of Central-Eastern Europe were reborn in deep economic crisis. The so-called reform-communist countries – Poland, Hungary and Yugoslavia – whose party leadership had experimented with certain market elements and opening to the West since the second half of the 1960s or early 1970s, had become heavily indebted by the 1980s.

For different reasons, income and output collapse was universal across all countries in Central-Eastern Europe, suffering a drop of about 20 per cent of GDP during the first three transition years. Economists had known for some time that a large part of the socialist economy was totally unproductive; that at least a third of jobs in factories and offices were just superfluous. Theoretical knowledge is one thing, personal experience another. Transition suddenly hit these societies in 1990-1. The voter would justifiably see it as a crisis, even if the governments had functioned perfectly – but they did not. The first governments did not generally last long. No wonder: to keep power or win elections is difficult in a recession, and what we had in the region after 1990 was much more than recession; it was a deep, protracted transformational crisis. True, the more advanced of the transition countries managed to resume growth after the tough first three years. Western observers cheered and advisers felt justified. If present growth trends continue, Poland's per capita national income in 1996 will reach the same level as in 1989, though that is not something to boast about.

Thus Solidarity in Poland and the Antall government in Hungary were confronted from the very start with the sinister foreign debt legacy of the previous regimes, while at the same time a new, democratic society had to be built. The chances of survival of these first governments were low: economic measures in the first few years counted against the politicians, who would not win on the economy; thus a non-economic issue would be needed to woo back the impoverished voters. In Croatia, Slovenia, and the Czech and Slovak republics, national independence issues provided extra legitimacy for incumbent governments, despite the economic hardships. In Lithuania, Poland and Hungary the voters let the forces of the nomenklatura back into power in the fourth year of transition.

The margins of victory may surprise observers, but the direction of events should not. Prime Minister Antall, an historian, was aware of the nature of Hungary's social changes in 1990; he called his team a 'kamikaze' government. Time was short, the economic and political institutions of democracy had to be created or re-created, the future of the country bound to Europe for good.

One of Antall's strategic goals well before the elections was to connect the MDF to the Western European party structure. As a result of his efforts, the Forum and two of its allies were accepted into the organisation of the European Democratic Union (EDU) which links Christian Democratic parties internationally. He himself was elected its vice president in 1990. He put much personal effort into organising the Hungarian branch of the European Movement of which he later became a vice-chairman, and also the Hungarian wing of the Pan-european Movement.

Antall was motivated in his efforts to construct strong cross-party links not just by his personal attachment to Christian Democracy. He was determined to create a modern party out of the non-socialist and non-nomenklatura Forum. In some ways a conservative by British standards, he defined the Forum's role in the centre of the Hungarian political scene, centre-right in parliamentary terms. Clear self-definition before the first free election was important since he sensed that the Socialists, the successor party to the Communists, would rely on significant sections of the old society and would build links to the SZDSZ with its leftist radical traditions: it was thus to the right of these parties that the political alternative had to be created. Some of his opponents both within and outside his party accused Antall of having 'stolen' the Forum, an organisation of allegedly plebeian origin, centre-left rather than cen-tre-right. And the term 'conservative' may really be misleading as applied to a move-ment which was the first to organise itself nation-wide at the end of the 1980s, firmly in opposition to the party-state, pursuing goals that critically touched the status quo. Parties to the left of the Forum, as well as most of the Hungarian media, have used the terms 'conservative' and 'patriotic' offensively. Antall knew very well how diffi-cult it was to restore values after decades of cynicism, yet he was convinced that a centre party could only be built on a clear moral stance and in cognisance of one's roots. He hoped that strong democratic institutions and a broad economic founda-tion would emerge after the turbulent first years of change to ensure Hungary's progress in true European fashion, rather than degeneration into unmitigated, peripheral capi-talism.

The 1990 spring elections offered Hungarian voters a plethora of political parties from which to choose, but the vast majority of the votes went to just six parties; and the same parties got into Parliament again four years later at the next elections. This stability may be read as a sign of maturity in Hungarian politics; what is disturbing is that the active membership of the parties is limited and mostly draws on people of an intellectual background.

Parties in the region have only a limited appeal and voting base and communicate with the public almost exclusively through the media. No party except the former establishment party has the necessary material base to enable it to be present in all major towns. The parties, with the exception of the former communists, have no communication channels, educational or youth or training centres of their own; all in a society which is deeply suspicious of the political 'party' as such, a society which – after decades of the ubiquity of politics – would like to stay away from public affairs, not fully understanding yet the connection between rights and duties.

Antall as Prime Minister had to expend much of his energy on cultural and media issues. Most of those who controlled and ran the Hungarian media held values different from his. One obvious reason for this might be the fact that the key personalities of the Press under communism had belonged to the closely controlled inner circle of the Party. The privatisation of the Press had mostly taken place before the changes and the new political forces inherited a given structure of communication. This structure predominantly preferred the liberal-left values and maintenance of the positions of the 'socialist establishment' to the values and programmes of the opposition, as it challenged the financial, cultural and power position of that nomenklatura. All in all, a determining part of the media and cultural elite defined the centre-right opposition forces as at best an unknown quantity, at worst a threat to their established position.

Many of his interlocutors on the international stage considered Antall not as an office holder from a small country, but as a statesman with global horizons and a strong sense of history. His advice was sought, although rarely heeded, about the possible directions and consequences of the disintegration of Yugoslavia and the Soviet Union. Western politicians still held to the concept of the unified South-Slav state, while he was already warning about the futility of maintaining the status quo and the tragic repercussions of its unavoidable breakdown. He was among the very first to react publicly to the putsch against Gorbachev in 1991 and, despite his good links to President Yeltsin, he never made a secret of his concern about the potential dangers of events in Russia for the world in general and for Central-Eastern Europe in particular. This is why he was eager to bind Hungary closely to the European political and security community. While influential leaders such as Kohl and Thatcher thought highly of him, the Western community was unable to forge a coherent strategy concerning Central-Eastern Europe. Antall saw it as an opportunity missed; the Western vacillation disappointed him.

Antall had good reason to think of time. Not long after he was appointed Prime Minister in 1990, he was diagnosed as seriously ill. He underwent the necessary operations and medical treatment with full self-control but it left him no respite. The tasks facing him as prime minister were huge, his time was short. Sensing that Hungarian citizens, unable to comprehend and digest all the twists and turns of the transformation, would demand explanation, not simply administration, he tried to interpret and explain in parliamentary debates and public speeches what was going on in his country and in this region. Antall took his audience seriously and did not try to court the media: there were no 'one liners', no 'sound bites'; the media found this style archaic.

Humourless, superior, hardhearted: this is the image some in the powerful media created of him. Those who knew him personally knew that the opposite was true. Never arrogant, he thought perhaps too much of ordinary people. Hardhearted he was not: he always instructed his Cabinet ministers to consider those on pensions or with large families when formulating budgets, since they would be least able to adjust to sudden economic changes. This was one of the reasons why he rejected the concept of 'shock therapy' for the economy, so heartily recommended by some foreign advisers. He was not humourless either; he knew how to diffuse the tensions of Cabinet meetings and political negotiations through a fine use of anecdote.

The last time Antall addressed the public was at the statue of St. Stephen on the occasion of Hungary's national holiday in August 1993. Stephen was the first Hungarian king, who bound his nation with force to the Europe of his age. St. Stephen's day provided the Prime Minister with an occasion to respond to critics:

> We are accused of retrospection. Only a fool can think that looking back to where we have come from means neglecting the present and forgetting about the future. Our history provides us with perspective, and this is what recharges us with strength and hope; knowing what hardship we have been through enables us to survive in the future.

Jószef Antall died in December 1993.

The Good Dissident Havel

Timothy W. Ryback

In April 1990, just three months after the 'velvet revolution' that swept Czechoslovakia's communist regime from power and elevated Vaclav Havel to his country's presidency, *Newsweek* magazine featured the former dissident on its cover. With a fetching Jack-Kennedy smile, his strawberry blond hair still dishevelled from his November tussle with destiny, the playwright-philosopher-dissident-turned-president seemed the very embodiment of democratic reform in the post-communist era. To emphasise Havel's unique role, a precious sobriquet accompanied the image: 'Philosopher King'.

In harking back to Plato's *Republic*, *Newsweek* was not just indulging in tabloid intellectualism. It was evoking a sense of the historic moment. After two post-platonic millennia strewn with the wreckage of false starts toward responsible political rule, with good kings gone foul or mad, with democrats turned despots or scoundrels, the world saw in Vaclav Havel a rare if not singular opportunity: an individual of uncompromising principle – 'living in truth', Havel called it – elevated to the highest political office not by personal ambition, but on the hopes of fourteen million countrymen. In November 1989 Vaclav Havel and a handful of fellow dissidents with headquarters in the basement rooms of the Laterna Magica Theatre helped orchestrate a protest movement that involved first students, then workers, then, it seemed, virtually every man, woman and child in the country. The dissidents brought the communist regime to the negotiating table, forced it to capitulate, then, in a gesture of breathtaking beneficence, called for national reconciliation. It was time, Havel insisted, for healing, not for vengeance. 'Our country, if that is what we want,' Havel proclaimed on his third day as president, 'can now permanently radiate love, understanding, the power of the spirit and ideas.' It is rare that the world has witnesssed such potential for enlightened political leadership. It is rarer still that so much potential has been lost – some have said squandered – so capriciously and so completely.

During the first two years of Havel's presidency, when he commanded the moral authority – and more importantly, the political mandate – to effect change, he not only promoted democratic values and economic reform, but also indulged himself in exuberant outbursts and childish antics followed by bouts of anxiety, self-doubt, and depression. Havel's equivocation on some issues paralysed the executive decision-making process; his intransigence on others – especially when principles were at stake – plunged the nation into rancorous feuding. Most significantly, Havel's initial insensitivity to the subtleties of Czech and Slovak relations, and his subsequent ineptness in brokering relations between the country's ethnic factions, allowed him to be outmanouevered by more adept politicians. In the end, Czechoslovakia was divided, without a referendum and against the will of the majority of its citizens. For all his high principles and commitment to civil society, Havel ultimately failed in his most fundamental duty as president: to preserve the nation he was elected to rule. Like the 'good soldier Svejk', the protagonist of Jaroslav Hasek's classic novel of the Great War, Havel has survived the upheavals of his age – the collapse of empires, the rise and fall of political destinies – with a wry, sometimes mischievous smile, a cigarette in one hand, and a bottle of Pilsner Urquell in the other.

'When you look at Havel, he is a kind of miracle,' says Jan Urban, a former dissident and one of Prague's leading political commentators. 'Whatever he touched in politics since 1989 he has lost; nevertheless, six years later he is more popular than ever.' By 'losing', Urban reasons, Havel has relinquished responsibility for the tough decisions which have devolved to the prime minister instead. Relieved of the nagging details of state – inflation rates, unemployment levels, trade deficits, a balanced budget – Havel has been elevated to the moral high ground. He can speak of lofty things like 'vision', 'moral principles', and, his favorite theme, 'responsibility', without worrying about their practical implementation. It is a role, Urban says, that Havel knows well. For years Havel sat in prison making moral pronouncements that were applauded internationally but had little impact on his own society; today, in Prague Castle, he remains an internationally acclaimed moral spokesman, who delivers an important moral message for those who care to listen, but who lacks the executive authority to realize his eloquently expressed ideals. 'After six years, Havel has come full circle,' Jan Urban says. 'He is once again a dissident.'

* * *

In May 1995, I visited the president at Prague Castle. Over the centuries, this many spired edifice, in whose shadow Franz Kafka penned some of the twentieth century's most haunting literary images, has been the residence of Bohemian kings, Habsburg emperors, Communist rulers, and, all too briefly, democratically elected rulers. Today, it is Havel's castle: the military guards wear uniforms – blue with red trim and a dashing red-white-blue sash – designed by Havel's artist friend, Theodor Pistek, who designed the costumes for the Milos Forman film *Amadeus*; the music that accompanies the changing of the guard was composed by Michal Kocab, a close Havel associate and former punk rocker; the walls of Havel's office – bearing bright psychedelic splashes, a female nude, a rainbow and a theatre ribald – were painted by another of Havel's artist-friends, Ales Lamr. A large portrait – from Havel's private collection – of a sensuous, dark-haired beauty dominates the wall behind a massive conference table where Havel receives foreign delegations. 'She is very seductive,' Havel once told the German actor Maxmilian Scheel. 'I enjoy watching her distract foreign dignitaries.' These playful flourishes are vestiges of Havel's first years in power.

In 1995 a quiet austerity prevails. Since January 1993, when Havel was elected president of the Czech Republic – he resigned as president of Czechoslovakia in July 1992, six months before the Czech and Slovak Federation was dissolved – the Castle budget has been slashed by forty percent, the staff reduced from four hundred to one hundred and fifty, and the presidential powers radically curtailed. The new constitution permits Havel to appoint judges and ambassadors, attend cabinet meetings and exercise a 'weak veto', which the parliament generally overrides with a simple majority. Havel passes most of his time receiving foreign dignitaries, attending gala dinners, travelling abroad, and, when time permits at the weekend, writing speeches for occasions of state and for the hundreds of honours he has received around the world. 'My speeches at universities or similar occasions such as those I have given when receiving the Philadelphia Liberty medal, or the degree at Stanford, or the Indira Gandhi Prize, or the Queen's Prize in New Zealand are different from those I deliver as a representative of my country,' Havel told me in his Castle Office. 'The formal speeches that I have written constitute in fact a series of thoughts or observations about the fate of this world and the present civilisation.'

The president has always taken words, language and ideas seriously. Just as Havel the student of road construction at Prague's Technical University in the late 1950s had attempted to draft a screenplay for Kafka's novel *The Castle*, so the stagehand turned playwright at Prague's Balustrade Theatre in the 1960s authored the absurdist satires *The Garden Party* and *The Memorandum*, and the dissident of the 1970s penned political essays – most notably the classic dissident tract 'The Power of the Powerless' – and the prison inmate wrote philosophical exigeses disguised as letters – one per week, four pages in length, to his wife Olga – so today, the president continues to express himself most eloquently through the written word. These days, however, his words come exclusively in the form of speeches, over two hundred and fifty to date, forming in aggregate a body of thought unparallelled in its thematic breadth, moral vigour and poetic elegance. When Havel addressed a joint session of the United States Congress in February 1990, invoking language from America's most sacred secular tract, *The Declaration of Independence*, one congressman remarked to a colleague, 'If I could string words together like that I could run for God.'

Havel is a modest man both in appearance and temperament. Although the days are long passed when Havel came to the Castle in a rag wool sweater and cords, his hand-tailored suits and flawlessly polished shoes have done little to straighten his stooped shoulders or improve his distinct slouching gait which resembles more of a shuffle than a walk.

Havel was just completing a briefing when I was escorted into the president's suite of offices by his spokesman, Ladislav Spacek. Havel glanced briefly at me, shook hands, murmured a welcome, then, accompanied by Spacek and a translator, led me into an adjoining room dominated by a sprawling seventeenth century map of Bohemia and Moravia. As we sat down at a table for four, Havel immediately lit a Camel cigarette, placed the pack on the table beside the ashtray, then bowed his head slightly and stared at the table, as if bracing himself for an interrogation. For the next forty minutes, I posed a series of questions regarding the state of affairs in the Czech Republic, the changes that have taken place since the revolution, the dissolution of Czechoslovakia, and, in particular, Havel's role as president of the Czech Republic. The president, who listened to the questions in English but responded in Czech, delivered extended verbal essays, speaking in a low murmur, focusing his attention on the floor, the table, the cigarette packet, never once looking me in the eye. When the allotted time was up, Spacek indicated to me that the interview was over. We rose from our seats, shook hands, and parted company. As I walked away, I came to the discomfiting realisation that I had played the part of the very worst kind of voyeur: the interview had proved to be an unpleasant intrusion for the observed, and an unfulfilling experience for the intruder.

The day after my interview with Havel, I called on Jan Urban. When he inquired about my meeting with Havel, I expressed my disappointment, telling him that the president's responses to questions had seemed rather formulaic and stylised, and, most curiously, that throughout the entire interview Havel had not once looked me in the eye. Urban was silent for a moment, then smiled knowingly. 'Eyes can betray,' he said curtly, then his voice fell into a deep resonant cadence. 'The dissident life meant surviving for years, years with the fear of betraying oneself or one's friends. This fear is still very deep inside.' Urban recalled how during the November revolution, the actor Petr Cepek came to the Laterna Magica Theatre to try and teach Havel to look straight into a camera. 'It was nearly impossible,' Urban told me. 'And at that moment, we realised that there is a subconscious instinct in many of us not to look into other people's eyes because in prison or in interrogation if you do it you can give yourself away.' Then I understood: my first encounter with Havel had not been an interview; it had been an interrogation.

* * *

A hundred kilometres northeast of Prague, not far from the German and Polish borders, is the town of Liberec, a centre of light industry set amid the rugged hills of northern Bohemia. Liberec's central square is dominated by a McDonald's, a Photo-Quick, and a neo-gothic town hall on whose facade the city has erected a memorial to the nine young people killed during the Warsaw Pact invasion of 1968. It is a modest monument: a plaque with nine tank track links cast in brass, each bearing the name of one victim inscribed in verso, a simple but eloquent statement to the sheer brutality of their deaths. It is also a milestone of sorts, marking Havel's emergence as one of the twentieth century's most prominent dissidents.

It is hard to say exactly when Vaclav Havel became a dissident. Havel himself claims that his first step towards dissidence was taken in 1965 when he joined the editorial board of *Tvar*, a progressive literary magazine. Havel's official biographer, the former dissident Eda Kriseova, says that Havel was a dissident of sorts, possibly at the age of fifteen, when, warmed by the literary tinder of Kafka, Beckett and Ionescu, he joined a reading circle named the 'Thirty-Sixers', and that he was certainly a dissident by age twenty, when, as an aspiring writer – with a pocketful of unpublished poems and one 'letter to the editor' to his credit – he threw a writers' conference into turmoil by denouncing the assembly for its 'hypocrisy', 'blunders' and 'misguided notions of truth'. According to Ivan Klima, a leading figure of the dissident movement and currently one of East Europe's most distinguished writers, Havel's early plays – *The Garden Party, The Memorandum, The Increased Difficulty of Concentration* – suggest a playwright who was as political as he was theatrical.

In August 1968, as the Soviets were preparing to crush the liberal reforms of the Prague Spring, Havel was on holiday with his wife, Olga, and the actor Jan Triska in Liberec. Havel was thus able to witness the Soviet invasion as tanks and troops entered Liberec. 'I saw Soviet tanks smash down barricades on the main square and bury several people in the rubble,' Havel later recalled. 'I saw a tank commander start shooting wildly into a crowd.'

In the desperate hours and days that followed the Warsaw Pact invasion, Havel joined activists across the country in denouncing the invasion. He penned daily commentaries for broadcast from the Liberec radio station, watching how townspeople brought food, medicine and flowers, and then how, in the months following the invasion, as 'normalisation' set in, the solidarity dissipated. Thousands fled abroad; millions more retreated from public life to protect an apartment, a job, a child's future. Havel, for his part, banished from the Balustrade Theatre, where he worked as the house playwright and dramaturge, withdrew to Hradecek, his rustic country home in northern Bohemia, to 'live in truth', which was another way of saying that he refused to abandon, as most of his countrymen already had, the ideals of the Prague Spring. Twenty-year old Jan Palach tried to make essentially the same point when, on a bitter January afternoon, six months after the invasion, he walked to Wenceslas Square, doused himself with several litres of kerosene and struck a match.

At Hradecek Havel gathered around him much of the outcast genius of the Prague Spring: painters, playwrights, actors, poets, novelists, philosophers, journalists, translators, professors and, eventually, a six-man underground rock band called the Plastic People of the Universe. During the Prague Spring, the Plastics, who at the time called themselves The Primitives, had emerged as one of Prague's leading interpreters of Frank Zappa, Lou Reed and Captain Beefheart. Following August 1968, when the government deemed their music 'counterrevolutionary', the band withdrew into the underground where they developed their own brand of Bohemian rock that attracted a small but devoted following. In a massive police raid on 27 March 1977, the Plastic People and a hundred other members of Bohemia's underground rock scene were taken into custody. While most were eventually released, four musicians were placed on trial, charged with 'corrupting the youth'. They were sentenced to prison terms lasting from twelve to eighteen months. For Havel, the Plastics' trial was a watershed moment: 'The objects of this attack were not veterans of old political battles,' Havel later wrote in his essay *The Trial*. 'They had no political past, or even any well-defined political positions. They were simply young people who wanted to live in their own way, to make music they liked, to sing what they want to sing, to live in harmony with themselves, and to express themselves in a truthful way.' In December of that year Havel, along with Jan Patocka and a handful of other dissidents, drafted Charter 77, a landmark human rights declaration that urged the Czechoslovak government to respect the basic individual rights of its citizens – freedom of speech, freedom of expression, the right to a fair trial.

'The inception of Charter 77 was that it was not an organisation,' says Wendy Luers, president of the New York-based Foundation for a Civil Society. It was to be a 'loose collection of people' who 'signed the original document which called upon the Czechoslovak government to respect the agreements that they had signed in Helsinki.' The Helsinki Accords, one of the major achievements of the detente era, formally committed the Prague government to respect international norms for human rights. Invoking the Helsinki mandates, Charter 77 signatories – eighty in all – and members of a subsequent human rights organisation known by the acronym VONS (Committee for Unjustly Persecuted Persons) tracked and reported on human rights abuses in Czechoslovakia, issuing hundreds of reports to the international community.

Until the appearance of Charter 77, Czechoslovakia's dissident community had by and large been left in peace. In April 1975, after writing an 'open letter' denouncing the 'painful and degrading buffoonery' of public life under communist rule, Havel had packed a bag and waited to be arrested; the government's only response was to return his letter with a note admonishing him for having made the letter available to 'hostile press agencies'. However, within two months of the publication of Charter 77, Havel was in prison, charged under Article 112 of the Czechoslovak Criminal Code, with 'actions injurious to the interests of the republic abroad'. He was, in his own words, 'terrified'. In March 1978 Havel agreed to resign as a Charter spokesman in exchange for a reduced prison term. The communist daily newspaper, *Rude Pravo* announced Havel's early parole in a front page article that included excerpts from his 'compromise' with the government. Upon his release, Havel was devastated to learn that three other signatories remained in prison. 'I became entangled in a web of my own inappropriate politeness, inexperience, credulity, incomprehensible stupidity and even less comprehensible underestimation of my opponents perfidy,' Havel later wrote of the incident.

Milos Forman, the filmmaker and Havel's close friend from boarding school days, in looking back over Havel's career as a dissident – which included four separate prison terms – recalls his friend's unshakeable resolve, his quiet dignity, his incorrigible wit and, above all, his courteousness. 'I think the thing that was mightily surprising and shocking to his jailers when he was a dissident, was his politeness,' Forman told me. 'When they would ask him, "Alright, who else was at that meeting?" Havel would say, "I understand it is important for you to know who was there, and that you would like me to cooperate, but I am very sorry, and I apologise, but my conscience will not allow me to answer".'

The spirit would not bend, but the body eventually broke. In January 1982, two-thirds of the way through a four and a half year prison sentence in Valdice, Havel contracted pneumonia. When his right lung collapsed, prison authorities fearing Havel was on the verge of death, transferred him – with a hundred-and-four degree fever, still in pyjamas, and handcuffed in the back of a police van – to the medical ward of the Pankrak Prison forty miles away. When Havel recovered sufficiently, he was moved to a public hospital, and eventually, in March 1983, was released. He was arrested for the last time on the afternoon of 23 January 1989, following an unofficial ceremony to mark the twentieth anniversary of Jan Palach's self-immolation on Wenceslas Square. His trial and subsequent imprisonment sparked a public protest that generated thousands of signatures and compelled the government to halve his nine-month prison sentence. By May he was free; by the end of the year, he was president of Czechoslovakia.

The persecution was over, but the trauma lingered. 'I am the kind of person who would not be in the least surprised if, in the very middle of my presidency, I were to be summoned and left to stand trial before some shadowy tribunal, or taken to a quarry to break rocks,' Havel confessed in the summer of 1990. 'Nor would I be surprised if I were suddenly to hear reveille and wake up in my prison cell, and then with great bemusement proceed to tell my fellow prisoners everything that had happened to me in the past six months.'

While Havel's closest friends, including Milos Forman and Zdenek Urbanek, the country's leading translator of Shakespeare, who have known Havel since the 1950s, readily admit that Havel takes pleasure in his celebrity contacts – his circle of associates extends from former German president Richard von Weizsäcker to the British rock star Mick Jagger – Havel's 'integrity', 'humanity' and, above all, his 'modesty' remain unaffected. Havel, they insist, still prefers the pub to the palace. But many former dissidents disagree, and the post-revolutionary disillusionment with Vaclav Havel has been surprisingly fierce. In Prague, former associates of Havel, once privy to the president's confidences and now held at arm's length by Castle bureaucrats, talk about abandoned revolutionary ideals, about the seduction of power. Some whisper their criticisms in confidence, others shout them across the room, still others air them on the radio and in the press. In 1990 when Havel rebuked a former dissident, Jiri Cibulka, for publishing lists of suspected state security police (Stb) collaborators in his newspaper, *Respekt*, Cibulka lashed back in print with 'Vasku, ty isi prase!' – 'Vaclav, you are a pig!' Although on that occasion the president sued his former associate for libel, Havel generally endures the criticisms with quiet stoicism, trying to understand the anger, the disillusionment, the jealousy. 'Havel takes criticism very seriously,' says Wendy Luers. 'It hurts him when people criticise him. He is a very insecure person. He has a tremendous need for affirmation, to hear he is doing the right thing.'

Havel can find abundant solace in public opinion polls that consistently identify the president as the most trusted public figure in the country, with approval ratings in excess of seventy percent, a full twenty points higher than any other political leader. The Czechs not only trust Havel; they like him. Having tired of Vaclav Klaus's arrogance and pragmatism, they have developed a new appreciation for Havel's modesty and principles. They also understand that Havel's talk of 'politics of morals' and 'responsibility' has, in the eyes of the international community, transformed this modest Central European nation, with its ten million citizens and eight thousand square miles of territory – a geographic and demographic entity roughly the size of Ohio – into a model of 'civil society' in the post-totalitarian world.

* * *

Despite international recognition, the Czech Republic is only half the country it was before 1 January 1993 when the Czechoslovak Federal Republic broke into two autonomous states. Today, most Czechs and Slovaks still express bewilderment at the speed and course of the dissolution. The parliaments had been deadlocked, Slovak nationalists clamoured for autonomy, there was repeated talk of a public referendum on the fate of the country, and finally, on a hot day in the summer of 1992, the federation's two leading political figures, Vaclav Klaus from Prague and Vladimir Meciar from Bratislava, emerged from six hours of negotiation in the Villa Tugendhat near Brno to declare that the Czechoslovak Federal Republic was 'beyond salvation'. Most people also remember that the majority of the population, including the federal president, Vaclav Havel, was against the idea.

Opinions vary greatly on whether or not the Czechoslovak federation could have been saved. Looking at the political and economic chaos in neighbouring Slovakia, where the GNP has fallen by fifty per cent and Meciar appears to have established himself as a virtual dictator, many Czechs express astonishment that they ever shared a common state with their unruly neighbours. Pointing to multi-national states that have survived nationalistic tensions – Belgium and, most recently, Canada – many observers insist that the federation could have survived, and cite a trail of missed opportunities: greater sensitivity for the Slovaks on Havel's part, an amendment to the electoral laws permitting the creation of national parties that could include Czechs and Slovaks, a moderated privatisation process, a Czech willingness to accommodate the Slovak desire for a loosely confederated state, and, perhaps most significantly, a public referendum on the future of the federation. 'If a referendum could have taken place at that time,' claims Rupnik, 'it would have got overwhelming support for Czechoslovakia, and would have cut the ground from under the feet of the nationalist politicians in Slovakia, who were making political mileage exclusively out of anti-Prague rhetoric.'

Havel insists that by the summer of 1992 he had exhausted every constitutional option for preserving the federation; that the Slovak drive for autonomy was inexorable. 'With more presidential powers, I might have been able to make the division process more complicated perhaps, but I don't think I would have been able to halt it while remaining a democrat,' Havel told me. 'Only a dictator could have had the capability to stop it altogether, and of course it has never been my ambition to become that.' Havel told me he did not wish to become 'another Tito'. Havel may have only needed to be another Tomas Masaryk, the philosopher-president – also hailed in his day as a 'philosopher-king' – who in 1918 carved the Czecho-Slovak Republic from the ruins of the Habsburg Empire, and over the next two decades, through a deft balance of cultural sensitivity and political cunning, nurtured a Czechoslovak nationalism. But Vaclav Havel was no Tomas Masaryk. 'I have the feeling that even today Havel does not understand the problem of the Czechs and Slovaks,' Milan Sladnik, Havel's advisor on Slovak relations, remarked in the summer of 1992. 'I do not want to suggest that he consciously ignored the problem, he simply had no idea what it was all about. Foreign relations were more important for him than resolving the situation between Czechs and Slovaks. He simply marginalised the issue. But by doing this the problems continued to mount and in the end he did not know what to do.'

While Havel cannot be held responsible for destroying Czechoslovakia – that dubious honour belongs to Klaus and Meciar – he was certainly the one person in the country – I have been told repeatedly – who could have saved the federation. There is a final sad irony to the dissolution of Czechoslovakia. Although Havel told me that he refused to resort to 'undemocratic' means to preserve the federation, by not exercising a stronger executive hand, he ultimately allowed the single most important decision of this newly-resurrected democracy to be decided by two men – Meciar and Klaus – making what the Czech emigré writer Jan Novak has called a 'back-room deal'.

* * *

Vaclav Havel's last official act as federal president was to host a 'garden party' for friends and journalists at Lany. On Friday 17 July, following a declaration of sovereignty by the Slovak Republic, Havel submitted a brief written statement to the federal parliament, saying it was clear to him the federation could no longer be preserved, that by presiding over the dissolution of the state, he would betray his presidential oath to preserve the country, and that he would therefore step down from office the following Monday. The journalist Marcela Pecháčková recalls that shortly before six o'clock on Monday evening, as Havel's executive duties officially ended, the president conducted a final press conference. At six o'clock, he looked at his watch and said, 'I am no longer president.' An hour or so later, Pecháčková encountered Havel walking through the woods of the estate with several advisers. He said he was going back to the palace to watch the evening news. In that instant, Pecháčková said she understood that 'President Havel' had once again become 'Citizen Havel'.

With Havel's resignation not only had the last hope for preserving the federation vanished, the two and a half year 'reign of the dissidents' had come to an end. Since the revolution the dissident ranks had been progressively reduced. Vaclav Maly, an original signatory to Charter 77 and a key figure in the November 1989 revolution, withdrew immediately from political life to resume his pastoral work as a Catholic priest in a small Prague parish. Michael Kocab, the punk rocker who was given responsibility for overseeing the withdrawal of Soviet forces from the country, resigned his post when the last Soviet transport departed, declaring his public service complete. 'I used to be into one kind of heavy metal,' Kocab told Mick Jagger at the time, 'now I'm handling another kind.' A handful of parliamentarians, exposed as former secret police informants, stepped down in disgrace. The rest were voted out of office in the June elections. 'By the spring of 1992, there was a general sobering in the country,' says Ladislav Venys, Director of Prague's Centre for Democracy and Free Enterprise. 'People were worried about their jobs, about the economy. They wanted the era of dissidents behind them, and to see professional politicians running the country.' Reflecting on the mood at the time, even Havel's authorised biographer, Eda Kriesova, admitted the president looked and sounded like a political relic. 'Vaclav Havel started to appear to citizens as too moral, too intellectual, too soft, and not strict enough,' Kriesova has written. 'In fact, too democratic.'

Although Havel had spent 935 days in office playing the 'reluctant' president, telling the *Financial Times* in March 1990, 'One day in this job is one hundred times worse than one day in prison,' it was clear almost immediately that he intended to run for president of the Czech Republic. In autumn 1992 Havel opened an office on the ground floor of his apartment building – built by his father – installed four assistants, what he called his 'VH Team', or publicity team, and set to work campaigning for the presidency of the Czech-speaking remnants of the federation. Havel conducted interviews with journalists, received foreign dignitaries and, through contacts facilitated in large part by Michal Kocab, aggressively courted the country's political leaders, especially Vaclav Klaus whose party had swept the June elections. Havel's message was clear: he had learned his lesson. Havel would function as a mature and responsible political partner, something which had not always been the case in his first period in office. 'In the end, he has shown himself to be very much like other politicians,' one unnamed diplomatic source in Prague said of Havel at the time. 'He has come down off his pedestal and entered the grubby world of wheeling, dealing and making compromises. In a way it is a shame.'

It is hard to say exactly why Havel decided to run again. Eda Kriesova insists that Havel considered the revolution 'his baby' and felt a 'deep responsibity' to nurture a civil society. Michal Kocab claims that Havel was the only viable candidate. Others have said that Havel, never one to admit defeat, wanted the presidency as a matter of pride. In an unrelated context, Milos Forman shared with me a revealing anecdote from Havel's boarding school days. 'I remember playing soccer,' Forman told me over breakfast the day of Harvard commencement. 'For some reason, he thought that he must be everywhere where the ball is, so in ten minutes, he was exhausted. He'd be dead, because he was always running after the ball.' Forty-five years later, having expended his energies on the political playing field, having been outplayed and outmanoeuvred by more capable players, Havel was still unable to give up the ball.

The key issue that autumn was the relationship between Klaus and Havel. Although Klaus and Havel had clashed repeatedly on issues of principle and policy, Klaus publicly endorsed Havel's possible candidacy for the presidency of the Czech Republic. Havel, for his part, knew that his political fate lay in Klaus's hands. 'Klaus is the leader of the winning party and the leading coalition party,' Havel conceded in an interview on 20 October 1992 in *Lidovy Noviny*. 'I am, of course, dependent on them to an extent because the candidacy for the office of president depends on them.' But, Havel insisted, he saw no problem in 'cooperation' with Klaus. 'We are both mature and respect each other's opinions.' Two weeks later, in a Sunday evening television appearance, Havel outlined his vision for the new presidency. He proposed that the president be elected by direct, popular vote, rather than by the parliament, and enumerated the advantages: the president could provide a stabilising force in turbulent political times; he would have a popular mandate to break parliamentary deadlocks; his increased strength could enhance the country's international stature. Most post-communist countries, Havel observed, had decided on direct elections for the president; Havel wanted the same for the Czech Republic. Three days after Havel's television appearance, the ruling council of Klaus's ODS delivered Havel a public rebuff: there would be no direct election of the president. 'I cannot say anything about this at the moment,' Havel responded when asked for a response. 'This is an opinion which I must think over, analyse.' But there was nothing to analyse. With the ODS commanding thirty-four per cent of the popular vote – twice the number of any other party – Klaus, as head of the ODS, would determine the shape of the new republic's constitutional order.

Until 17 November 1992, the third anniversary of the November Revolution, when Vaclav Havel officially announced his candidacy, it had generally been assumed that Havel was indeed the only man for the Czech presidency. It therefore came as a rude surprise when a number of ODS delegates expressed a desire to consider alternative candidates. Numerous concerns were raised: Havel was still too closely associated with the Civic Movement that had taken a severe beating in the June elections; Havel had fostered considerable animus with his lenient treatment of the former communists; Havel had alienated virtually the entire population with his public apology to the Germans for the post-war expulsion of three million Sudeten Germans from Czechoslovakia. More importantly, there seemed to be a viable alternative to Havel in Jan Strasky, a brilliant young technocrat who served as the federation's last prime minister, and who, for a time, was ranked as the most popular politician in the country. 'Havel had just assumed that he would be the only serious candidate for the presidency,' one source close to the president told me. 'He was terrified by the prospect that he actually might not get the job.'

By mid-January 1993 Klaus, who remained committed to Havel, had rallied his coalition partners, but by then two additional candidates had emerged: Marie Stiborova, representing the reformed communists, and Miroslav Sladek, the standard bearer for the country's ultra-nationalists.

With the election to be decided by simple majority in the two-hundred seat house, Klaus's coalition, if no delegates broke ranks, would deliver one hundred and four votes, just enough to push Havel into the presidential office. But on the morning of 26 January 1993, when the parliament convened to vote, delegates insisted on a secret ballot. Party discipline could not be enforced; nor, as it turned out, could basic democratic civility. In a televised session of parliament, during which delegates were permitted to take the floor and comment on the three presidential candidates, the Republican Party staged a filibuster. One after the other, the eleven Republican representatives and three other opposition delegates rose to condemn the former Czechoslovak president in the most scandalous terms, denouncing him as a liar, an alcoholic, a drug addict, a state security agent, a communist, and a lackey to the Germans. When Jan Vik, one of the Republican delegates, accused Havel of inflicting 'large scale damage' on the country, pointing in particular to Havel's 1990 'amnesty law' that emptied prisons and allegedly flooded the country with criminals – and when it became clear that Milan Uhde, the chairman of the parliament, himself a former dissident, was not going to intervene – scores of deputies, embarrassed and outraged, left the hall in protest. It required a bomb threat that temporarily forced an evacuation of the hall to silence the Republican tirade. (A television viewer later confessed to having made the bomb threat; he said he that he simply 'couldn't watch that filth any more.') Havel, seated in a separate room, followed the proceedings on a television monitor, grim-faced and silent. 'He didn't say anything, but you could see by the expression on his face that these things hurt him a great deal,' a close Havel associate recalls. 'It took him a very long time to get over this incident.'

Late that evening, when the delegates reassembled in the hall to cast their ballots, Sladek received fourteen votes, Stiborova forty-nine, and Havel one-hundred and eight. Although Vaclav Havel had been elected the first president of the Czech Republic, it was a pyrrhic victory, a political success won at a high personal and political price. Three weeks later, when Havel held his inaugural address before the parliament, delegates listened dismissively – some derisively – to Havel's plea for a 'politics of morality' and 'courage'. Klaus was said to have sat reading a newspaper. The message was clear to everyone: Havel was president, but Klaus ran the country.

When Jan Urban spoke of Vaclav Havel as a 'miracle', he was, of course, alluding to the fact that despite Havel's political defeats and compromises over the last six years, the Czech President is as respected today – both at home and abroad – as at any time in his career, that despite his repeated failures in office, opinion polls continue to identify him as the most popular figure in the country. In a country dominated by the rigorous economic policies – and towering arrogance – of Vaclav Klaus, Czechs have developed a renewed appreciation for Havel's modesty, idealism and moral convictions, a comfort in the fact that while the presidency has changed dramatically over the last six years, their president Havel does not seem to have changed at all. For his part, Havel has generally viewed the incongruities of his life in philosophical rather than in political or sociological terms, say in terms of Immanuel Kant, or Martin Heidegger, or Jan Patocka, or, on more than one occasion, in terms of Franz Kafka. 'I have always harboured a feeling that I somehow understand Kafka better than others,' Havel wrote to his wife from prison in 1982, 'not because I can claim a deeper intellectual insight into his work, but because of an intensely personal and existential understanding of experience that borders on spiritual kinship.' Like a hapless character from a Kafka story – *The Penal Colony, Before the Law, The Trial* – the dissident Havel lived in a state of 'existential guilt' subjected to random arrests, gruelling interrogations, bizarre trials and even more bizarre verdicts. Havel understands Kafka. 'I am even secretly persuaded that if Kafka did not exist, and if I were a better writer than I am,' Havel recently claimed, 'I would have written his works myself.' In the end, through a rare combination of moral strength and political ineptness – call it *surrealpolitik* – Havel may have provided a fitting conclusion to Kafka's most celebrated work, his unfinished novel, *The Castle*. By ascending to the presidency Vaclav Havel completed Joseph K.'s interrupted journey: he reached the 'castle', the locus of power, only to discover upon his arrival – a Havelian twist to a Kafkaesque plot – the powerlessness of the powerful. In the end, the 'miracle' Jan Urban thought he perceived reveals itself to be just one more turn in a life filled with subtle ironies, gentle absurdities, and monumental incongruities.

The Marlene Dietrich Fan Club – Poland's Intellectuals in Opposition

Konstanty Gebert

'If forced to choose between Stalin and Hitler,' Adam Michnik used to say, 'I choose Marlene Dietrich'. For most of his life the veteran Polish dissident was faced with choices of this kind – and survived by consistently refusing to accept them. In a country whose fate for more than half a century was shaped by the fact that, having rejected Hitler, it was then given over to Stalin, he is not the only one. His friends, Jacek Kuron and Zbyszek Bujak, to name but two, could easily say the same thing. They could even form the Marlene Dietrich Fan Club.

On 23 June 1989 154 *Solidarnosc* MPs entered the building of the *Sejm*, the Polish Parliament, for the first time. The hastily assembled group, dubbed 'Walesa's team', had won all the seats it could have won: 35 percent of a total of 440, under a political contract negotiated with the Communists barely two months earlier.

Some of the new parliamentarians were all but unknown to the wider public, their sole claim to the people's vote being campaign posters showing them with Lech Walesa, wearing the characteristic *Solidarnosc* badges in their lapels. Others had long been household names, symbols of principled opposition to oppression for some, enemies of the State for others.

Now they stood all together in front of the entrance gate: old-time Communist revisionist and opposition organiser Jacek Kuron, who had spent eight and a half years in prison; leading dissident intellectual Adam Michnik, who had spent five and a half years in prison; and underground *Solidarnosc* leader Zbyszek Bujak, who had spent four and a half years underground. Facing them at the door of the Sejm stood the Communist Minister of the Interior, general Czeslaw Kiszczak, their hitherto nemesis and general Jaruzelski's second-in-command. He was the one responsible for Kuron and Michnik's prison sentences, for Bujak's years underground, for the sufferings years of martial law had brought the entire nation. With a smile and a handshake, he greeted the new parliamentarians. His smile said, 'It's business as usual'.

'No, Mr. Minister,' said Adam Michnik with his trademark stutter when his turn came. 'In the Polish Sejm, I do the greetings'. 'Welcome, general,' he added, extending his hand to his astonished enemy. Power was slipping from the general's grasp. He was soon to become history. Michnik, Kuron, Bujak and the others were there to make it.

The fates of the three became inseparably joined together in the 1970s, when the intellectual opposition reached out to worker protesters and set up the Committee to Defend the Workers (KOR). Bujak, then a young worker at the Ursus tractor works near Warsaw, had read Vaclav Havel's essay *The Power of the Powerless* in a *samizdat* publication. Profoundly transfixed by the future Czech president's analysis of 'living the lie', he sought out the publication's editors to ask them what he could do to fight it. He met Adam Michnik and in no time was running an underground publication himself. *Samizdat* had come to Ursus.

By passing on the virus of independent thought to Zbyszek Bujak, Michnik was in fact repaying an old debt. Born in a family of pre-war Polish-Jewish communists (the difference is important: pre-war communists had an idealistic streak that their post-war apparatchik successors clearly lacked), he quickly came under the sway of veteran revisionist Jacek Kuron. Twice expelled from the party for his unorthodox views, co-author of the 1964 *Open Letter to the Party*, an early opposition programme, Jacek Kuron had become an educator. Young people flocked to him, and he inculcated in them the ideas and values of his left-wing and fiercely patriotic home: Kuron's father, a democratic socialist, had fought against the invading Bolsheviks in 1920.

Bujak's family was the antithesis of left-wing, let alone communist or socialist. Poor Catholic peasants from near Warsaw, they had moved closer to the city in search of jobs. Young Zbyszek's high school education and factory job meant for them social advancement. The system was designed to fulfil the aspirations of millions of Zbyszek Bujaks, and to derive its legitimacy from them. But just as the regime found out it could not count on the loyalty of critical communists and their children, it was soon to discover that the new proletariat made up of peasant sons it had created was just as undependable.

For Kuron, the turning point was Poland's abortive democratic socialism movement of 1956. A workers' uprising in the city of Poznan had been drowned in blood, but had forced the Communist party to renounce Stalinism and change its leadership. After a few giddy months of experimenting with a free press, workers' councils and Polish patriotic feeling, the new Gomulka regime gradually regained control of the situation. The horrors of Stalinism were gone for good, true, but so was the hope of combining Socialism with democracy. By the late 1950s, when Kuron was drawing his political conclusions, Bujak was in kindergarten, Michnik in elementary school.

In 1968 Michnik, by then a university student, became one of the leaders of a students' movement for democracy, soon to be brutally crushed by the police, while the media staged an anti-Semitic campaign to vilify its real and putative activists. But history put an ironic twist to the story: the students' revolt was triggered by the government's decision to ban the theatre performances of *Dziady*, a nineteenth-century patriotic Polish masterpiece about the struggle against the Russians. And so Michnik first went to jail both as an accused Jewish traitor and as a Polish patriot, a counter-revolutionary inspired by Western intelligence and a campaigner continuing the democratic socialist tradition. He still relishes the paradox.

Bujak's turn came in 1976, when a series of strikes against price hikes started in the Ursus factory near Warsaw where he was a worker. The repression was brutal, but engendered a wave of solidarity from the opposition intellectuals. *Samizdat* spread and found its way to Ursus too, and Bujak eventually found his way to the opposition.

The intellectual opposition became simply the opposition, then a movement. But the magnitude of change became apparent only in the summer, when strikes paralysed the Baltic seacoast. 'Do not burn down committees, set up your own,' Jacek Kuron called out, in reference to the violent workers' riots of 1970, in which a local party committee building was burnt down. The workers did, giving birth to *Solidarnosc*. Within months, the new union grew to become nine and a half million strong – in a country of 38 million inhabitants.

Bujak, Kuron and Michnik were at the centre of the action. Bujak was swiftly elected chairman of *Solidarnosc*'s Warsaw chapter, the union's largest. He also served on the union's national executive, to which both Kuron and Michnik were attached as advisers. They knew the entire movement was living on borrowed time. A Polish military or Soviet crackdown was an only too real possibility, as was the danger of the movement spinning out of control. Adam Michnik, accused together with Jacek Kuron by the official media of being wild-eyed radicals, acted to defuse tensions. When in March 1981 an angry mob surrounded a police station in a town near Warsaw, Michnik arrived on the scene: 'My name is Adam Michnik and I'm an anti-Socialist element' he announced himself, using a standard propaganda epithet to gain credibility with the crowd. Thanks to his powers of persuasion, the siege of the police station was lifted.

Bujak, younger than these two men and more action-oriented, was sometimes accused of excessive radicalism. He supported, for instance, a mass rally against violence, set for 17 December, which the authorities had labelled a 'dangerous provocation'. The rally never took place: martial law was imposed four days earlier. And further proof of Bujak's radicalism lay in his repeated calls for free elections, a move that would have been suicidal for the authorities.

The three activists were confronted not only with the impressive power machine of the Communist state. There were also dissensions within the union itself. Nine and a half million people were more than just a trade union. They were the nation organised; indeed, there are many European countries that have fewer citizens than *Solidarnosc* had members in 1981. It is hardly surprising, therefore, that all shades of opinion were expressed within the union, including authoritarian nationalism tinged with anti-Semitism. KOR was seen by these particular activists as an enemy, both for its liberal politics, and for the fact that the membership included persons with a Jewish background, like Michnik, or reformed ex-Communists, like Kuron.

Opponents of KOR, dubbing themselves 'true Poles', led a vicious but unsuccessful campaign against Zbyszek Bujak, accusing him of being 'manipulated by dark anti-national forces'. They also violently attacked Kuron and Michnik, despite the fact that they were *Solidarnosc* advisers. This campaign did not end even with the onset of martial law in December 1981, and it was a harbinger of future political splits in the movement.

The military, having staged their coup, placed Michnik and Kuron under administrative detention. Bujak escaped and went underground, becoming a living legend until his capture in 1986. But though the union was badly hurt, it was not defeated. Key structures survived or were recreated underground, strategic debate continued, and the three became key participants. In a manifesto smuggled out of jail and published in the underground press in March 1982, Jacek Kuron abandoned his habitual cautious stance. Claiming that a mass explosion of social unrest against the military regime was all but unavoidable, the veteran organiser called upon the underground leadership to lead the protest, in fact to organise an uprising. Responses from fellow prisoner Adam Michnik and underground leader Zbyszek Bujak were swift and scathing. In separate texts also published in *samizdat*, the two activists argued against any violence and in favour of a non-violent 'long march' to the final victory. This debate determined the strategy of the entire movement. The crucial principles of non-violence, social self-organisation and setting up an alternative ('independent' or 'underground') society were adopted as guidelines and impressively adhered to. Kuron was quick to recognise he had been wrong and his opponents right, and took it in his stride. 'Looks like I've taught them well,' he quipped.

The debate of 1982 was a crucial turning point for the politics of the three. During the 1970s, their opposition activity was more an outgrowth of moral outrage than a long-term project with clearly defined goals, and in the heady days of 1981 decision-making could barely keep abreast of day-to-day developments. But in 1982 they had to design a strategy and tactics for a mass underground movement of indeterminate duration and uncertain hopes. The choices they would be making would affect the political future of the underground; that is of the lives thousands of men and women. And the odds were high: especially in the first months of martial law, the military courts did not hesitate to pass down prison sentences of up to ten years for 'activity hostile to the State'. Not only individual freedom was at stake: people could, and did, get killed during street demonstrations, strikes, and in police custody. Perhaps it would have been more sensible to advocate discontinuing the struggle, especially as it seemed hopeless.

The international community, for all its moral posturing, regarded martial law in Poland as an event occurring within the Soviet sphere of influence, and therefore 'legitimately' beyond the scope of international intervention, even if it were only political. Western governments might put pressure on Poland's rulers and their Soviet patrons, to prevent and condemn excessive violations of human rights, but the coup itself would be allowed to stand. No hopes there.

None looking eastward either. The Soviet Union, which would cease to exist barely ten years later, seemed then as solid as ever, and as uninterested as ever in giving the Poles even minimal leeway. Not that the three activists were terribly radical in their demands: they argued for a Finlandisation of their country, hoping Moscow would grant it the status it had granted its northern neighbour: internal freedom in exchange for subordination in matters of foreign policy and defence. To people like Kuron it was obvious that this would have been in the Soviet Union's interests as well: would it not be better for Moscow to have, on its western border, a compliant partner rather than a crushed nation, hoping for revenge? But the Soviets did not see it that way. They were happy with the current arrangement, which had served them well for four decades.

Nor would the Polish Communists allow themselves to be upstaged. At a Warsaw party General Kiszczak once met Stefan Kisielewski, an unorthodox Catholic columnist with close ties to the opposition, and a very strong partisan of establishing parallel ties with the Soviets. 'I've heard you are trying to ring the Kremlin behind our backs,' the general remarked. 'But do you have the phone number?' 'Well, no' replied Kisielewski. 'Ah gentlemen, you see, we do,' said Kiszczak grinning. So much for that hope – until Gorbachev came along.

Not only was there not much hope to be seen East or West, but Polish society itself was badly split. While the military coup came as a shock to almost all Poles – including Communist party members, tens of thousands of whom had given up their party membership in the following months – at the same time it had a feeling of unavoidability about it which gave it a legitimacy of sorts. 'At least,' many people thought, 'there will be goods to be bought in the stores once again'. And it did seem hopeless to fight it. On the other hand, the determination of the militant minority seemed boundless. It derived less from political planning than from a sense of recovered dignity: the subjects of the Communist regime had suddenly experienced the thrill of being citizens. And the teaching of the Polish Pope still resounded in their minds: 'You are a child of God. It is not permitted for you to be a slave'. These people would not give up – so their leaders should follow suit.

And follow suit they did. They stuck to the union's conditions for compromise: repeal of martial law, liberation of all prisoners, re-legalisation of *Solidarnosc*. When the authorities suggested in 1983 that political prisoners could be liberated if they promised to refrain from political activity for some time, Kuron thought the offer should not be rejected out of hand: after all, it affected the lives of hundreds of imprisoned activists. He received permission from prison authorities to talk to his fellow-prisoner Michnik about it. Michnik, hearing Kuron's opinion, promptly threw him out of his prison cell. At the same time Bujak, in the underground, rejected Kiszczak's offers of safe conducts for informal negotiations.

This loyalty to the cause seemed heroic at first, then, with the passage of time, foolish. But by the late 1980s the regime was so badly in trouble that it had no option but to negotiate with the undefeated underground. Mikhail Gorbachev, the new man in the Kremlin, told Jaruzelski that the Russians would not bail him out this time: they had too many problems of their own. Martial law was lifted, political prisoners released. *Solidarnosc* leader, Lech Walesa, after much soul-searching, agreed late in 1988 to sit down and negotiate. Kuron, Michnik and Bujak were to be part of his team.

But the very same factors which had forced the regime to negotiate had radicalised much of the opposition. 'No negotiations with the Communists!' the radicals clamoured. 'We will win anyhow'. 'Possibly – but at what cost?' was the negotiating team's reply. 'Let us choose the Spanish way,' advocated Adam Michnik, referring to the negotiated transition to democracy after the death of General Franco. He warned that the alternative was to go the way Iran or Lebanon went: a triumphant revolution imposing a new totalitarianism, or an unending civil war. Bujak and Kuron agreed.

'The people usually enter the palaces of power after a successful revolution,' mused Jacek Kuron watching the *Solidarnosc* delegates enter the Warsaw palace of government for the round table talks in January 1989. 'This time, however, they are entering the palace to prevent one from happening'.

They were successful. A year after the talks started, parliamentary elections took place, and then the Communists were swept from power in a bloodless takeover, which led the opponents of the negotiations to mutter darkly about secret deals supposedly made *under* the round table. When the ex-Communists won the parliamentary elections in 1993, and in 1995 the Presidency, the conspiracy theorists were sure that this was ultimate confirmation of their suspicions and accusations.

Nobody has ever produced proof of such deals, but the fact is that both sides drew close during the negotiating period and in the months of power-sharing following the elections of 1989. A particularly strong mutual attraction developed between Adam Michnik and generals Jaruzelski and Kiszczak. They each discovered the human being in their former enemy and came to understand, if not share, his values and motivations. Michnik publicly defended general Jaruzelski from accusations of having betrayed Poland by declaring martial law, and went to court as a character witness for the defence during the trial of general Kiszczak for the deaths of striking miners shot by police in the first days of the coup. To his detractors, this was ultimate proof of an ever-present collusion between 'pink' Michnik and the communists; many of his former comrades from the opposition now hate him bitterly for it. To others, it was Michnik's way of achieving ultimate triumph – extending a helping hand to his former tormentors, now abandoned by fortune. He had promised to do as much in one of his letters from prison.

The other two activists also made similar, if less spectacular gestures. Bujak apologised in public for *Solidarnosc*, when the union moved right – and got immediately expelled by the Ursus chapter of the union. This particular chapter remains today a hot-bed of right-wing anti-Semitic activism. Kuron did not seem drawn to former Communist leaders, but attempted repeatedly to build bridges between the two Polands – the one that had triumphed in 1989, and the one which, for whatever reason, did not participate in that triumph. This shared political sensitivity brought the three together.

And it enlarged the rift between their segment of the movement and that centred around Lech Walesa. Originally, Michnik had hoped that the unity of the movement, which had been its force during the underground years, could be maintained for some time still. This was wrong: the movement, once free of the primary necessity of defeating the Communists, splintered, as it rightly should, along its different political fault-lines. Its elites articulated that division. Less than a year after its victory at the polls, *Solidarnosc* waged its 'war at the top'.

Ostensibly, it was about Lech Walesa. The charismatic leader, who had led the movement to victory and then became the architect of the new political constellation that enabled *Solidarnosc* to create a government, felt left out. His original vision was, like Michnik's, one of unity – with him pulling the strings. But by spring 1990 new political formations had sprung up. Kuron and Bujak were instrumental in setting up a movement called ROAD (Civic Movement for Democratic Action), with Michnik eventually lending a sympathetic hand. It expressed the traditional democratic and left wing sympathies of much of the dissident intelligentsia, which it assumed were shared by much of society at large.

'Not so,' claimed their opponents from the Centre Alliance, which became the standard bearer of more conservative, national and Christian values. Much of *Solidarnosc* expressed its support for the Alliance, and Walesa became its natural leader. The chairman of *Solidarnosc* then went on to call for early elections for the presidency, still occupied by general Jaruzelski, and declared himself a candidate. When Michnik's paper, *Gazeta Wyborcza*, refused to endorse him, Walesa promptly denied it the right to use the *Solidarnosc* logo on its masthead. This came to Michnik and his friends as a major shock. Few people, excepting Walesa himself, could claim to have done more than them for the values the logo stood for. Nor did it earlier occur to anyone that the logo could be anybody's exclusive property. The break was sharp and bitter.

ROAD and *Gazeta* endorsed Tadeusz Mazowiecki, Poland's first non-Communist prime minister, for the presidency. The conservative Catholic thinker turned politician seemed surprised at the company he found himself in – but despite political differences there was a natural affinity between him and the non-Walesa group. 'We are neither left nor right of centre,' quipped one prominent ROAD activist, irritated by Centre Alliance's constant attacks on their supposedly left-wing inclinations, 'but West of it'. 'True,' replied Centre, 'and you stay there too damn much'. The Mazowiecki camp became branded as alien: intellectual, liberal, Western – unavoidably: Jewish. And lost the election, as it should have expected, but did not.

The political scene fragmented further, as Michnik, studying the impact of his direct political involvement on the credibility of his paper withdrew from active politics. On the other hand Bujak, in a move reflecting perhaps his working-class background, moved toward Labour Solidarity (later renamed Union of Labour), a small new left-wing party that rejected the division between former Communists and oppositionists, while stressing the need of a social agenda to address the interests of those made redundant by Poland's galloping economic reforms. Only Jacek Kuron, the veteran organiser, soldiered on within a mainstream party – Democratic Union, later renamed Freedom Union, which developed from Mazowiecki's electoral committees.

But Polish politics did not end with Walesa's presidency, or with the victory of the former opposition's right wing in parliamentary elections one year later. The new government decided to settle accounts with the past by promoting a law which would 'lustrate' all prominent public figures in order to root out former secret police agents and collaborators. A first list containing many suspect parliamentarians was leaked and proved to be full of baseless accusations against hitherto respected personalities. The three opposed what Bujak called 'a witch-hunt'. They believed this kind of global and necessarily imprecise settling of accounts smacked of ulterior motives. 'I haven't been such a coward then to need to be so brave now,' commented Adam Michnik. And Jacek Kuron, also a determined opponent of 'lustration', publicly asked forgiveness from a very highly respected former *Solidarnosc* activist whose name was one of many unjustly placed on the leaked list. 'This is exactly what we had fought against,' he said.

Though the three also later found themselves more than once on the same side of political struggles: against the anti-abortion law, for example, or against excessive Church presence in political life, their roads have now truly parted. When in 1995 Jacek Kuron ran as Freedom Union candidate for the presidency, Bujak was supporting the Union of Labour candidate, while Michnik published a common manifesto with a leading member of the eventually victorious ex-Communist Democratic Left Alliance, stressing the necessity of 'historical reconciliation'.

Of the three, Bujak seems to have fared best. He has youth on his side, a well-defined constituency and well-honed political instincts. He is clearly a possible future prime minister, and knows he can afford to wait. In the meantime, he has taken up philosophy at Warsaw University to complete his secondary education. Adam Michnik still writes a fiery editorial from time to time, but in the stable democracy which Poland aspires to be, there is less and less to be fiery about. And Jacek Kuron's political career is now all but over, his experience – gathered in fighting a system that most Poles now consider history – considered useless by many. He rejoins other legendary figures of the Polish opposition including Mazowiecki and Walesa, in the shadow of the immensity of their victory. But, as opposed to them, he retains public approval ratings of 75 percent and higher. Nobody comes remotely close to him in this.

But at least now they can choose Marlene Dietrich for the fun of it, instead of rebelling against unacceptable choices.

Russia at the Gates – Gorbachev's European House

Elizabeth Teague and Julia Wishnevsky

Is Russia an integral part of Europe, or does its unique mix of European and Asiatic influences mark it out as a country separate and apart? This age-old question was given fresh urgency by the liberalising reforms of President Mikhail Gorbachev, who came to power as leader of the Soviet Communist Party in March 1985. Gorbachev sought to relax the Soviet Union's repressive political and economic systems and to move his country away from confrontation and toward cooperation with the community of western nations. Gorbachev's policies helped to end the Cold War and free Russia from the isolation into which it had been cast by the Bolshevik Revolution of October 1917. But his policies also had effects that Gorbachev had not foreseen, since they led to the collapse of the Communist Party, the disintegration of the Soviet state and the break-up of the Soviet Union into fifteen independent countries.

Gorbachev says he launched his reforms because 'Soviet society had rejected the communist system. It was impossible to control everything by force in such a huge country'. He goes on, 'We were late starting our reforms. Developments such as the Khrushchev reforms [in the late 1950s and early 1960s], the Kosygin reforms [in the mid-1960s] and the dissident movement all showed that the country had lost its way and was searching for a new path'. Gorbachev believes that his foreign policies were a success but his domestic policies were a failure. The criterion he uses is a moral one. His aim, he says, both at home and abroad, was 'to combine politics and morality so that the two would become inseparable. Politics was so immoral, it was so false, nothing was as it appeared to be.... That was the hardest part of our policies and I must admit that we were only partially successful. We failed at home but we succeeded abroad'.

Slavophiles and westernisers

Gorbachev's reforms placed him squarely in the 'Westernising' camp in a debate that has preoccupied Russians for centuries. This debate focuses on Russia's relationship to the rest of the world, but at its heart is the enigma of Russian identity.

Russia's attitude to the outside world has always been complex. Russia's most densely populated regions lie in Europe and it was there that the first Russian state took shape in the ninth century. By the eleventh century, Kievan Rus – as that first state was called – was one of the main centres of Christian civilisation and a hub of European trade and manufacturing. But Russia sees itself as a *Eurasian* country and has vital trade and security interests in both Europe and Asia. The Mongol Conquest of 1240 cut Russia off from the western world for nearly two hundred and fifty years. In the sixteenth century, when the princes of Muscovy had defeated the Golden Horde, Russia began its rapid eastward expansion across Siberia. A century later, Russia had pushed its borders to the shores of the Pacific Ocean. Today, two-thirds of Russia's territory and most of its natural wealth lie east of the Urals. Russians have traditionally been a Christian nation and their closest ethnic ties are to their fellow Eastern Slavs in Ukraine and Belarus, yet Russia is also home to millions of Moslems, and Tatars make up the country's second largest ethnic group. 'Scratch a Russian,' runs the saying, 'and you'll find a Tatar'. In the seventeenth and eighteenth centuries, Russians commonly used the word 'Europe' as shorthand for 'the civilised world,' yet Russians have traditionally regarded Europe with mixed emotions of envy, longing, suspicion and superiority. 'In Europe,' wrote Dostoevsky, 'we Russians are seen as Tatars; in Asia, we are seen as Europeans'.

Until the time of Peter the Great, Russia was isolated from the rest of Europe. And for all Peter's efforts to modernise his country and transform it into a great European power, its political system remained closer to what liberal Russian intellectuals consider 'Asiatic despotism' than to the western democratic tradition. 'In one form or another,' says Kenneth Minogue, 'non-European civilisations have almost invariably been ruled despotically'. With its deeply rooted tradition of authoritarian rule, Russia has, until the most recent past, stood apart from the European model of pluralistic democracy, rule of law, market economy and human rights.

In the 1840s, a debate broke out within the Russian intelligentsia that continues to this day. The 'Slavophiles' argued that destiny had fated Russia to follow its own path. Though the Slavophiles did not reject western values in themselves, they insisted that Russia's unique combination of semi-Asiatic roots and Orthodox religious heritage could not be reconciled with the individualistic and materialistic values of the western world. The 'Westernisers,' for their part, did not deny the intrinsic value of Russia's cultural heritage. But they argued that, if Russia was to overcome its backwardness and realise its potential as a great power, it must adopt some western customs and find ways of integrating with the rest of Europe. Otherwise, Russia would be condemned forever to exclusion and impotence.

'Everything is rotten..'.

'We can't go on living like this!' was the cry in the months leading up to Gorbachev's accession to power. The system created by Lenin and Stalin was grinding to a halt.

The problem was not that the Soviet system did not work, but that it worked worse than the western model. An economy founded on state ownership and central planning could not compete successfully with economies based on private property and free enterprise. As the populations of the Soviet Union and eastern Europe grew increasingly urbanised and educated, they became more and more resentful of the restrictions imposed on them by their aging and corrupt leaders. Eduard Shevardnadze, who was to serve as Gorbachev's foreign minister, recalled in a television interview in 1991 how, as he and Gorbachev strolled along a Black Sea beach one winter day in 1984, the future Soviet president had exclaimed: 'Everything is rotten, from top to bottom. It's all got to be changed!' At that time, Shevardnadze said, neither man had any clear vision of the future. 'We simply came to the conclusion that we couldn't go on living like this any more, that everything had to be destroyed. But how it was to be done, and what problems would face those who began the work, of these things we did not speak at that time ..'.

Indeed, Gorbachev identified himself with the Westernising camp well before he became leader of the Soviet Union. He first spoke of his vision of a 'common European home' in December 1984. When, in March 1985, he was appointed general secretary of the Communist Party of the Soviet Union (CPSU), he began the mammoth task of setting the Soviet empire on a new track.

Bolshevism as radical westernisation

Lenin, the leader of the October Revolution, was a Westerniser of the most extreme kind. He and his fellow Bolsheviks rejected Russian traditions and did not identify with the Slavophiles in any way. The philosophy they adopted was a western one, developed in and for the West by Karl Marx and Friedrich Engels, both of whom distrusted Russia and openly doubted whether communism could take root there.

The Bolsheviks rejected nationalism and patriotism: one of their favourite slogans was 'The proletariat has no fatherland!' They overthrew the autocracy not in order to build a socialist paradise in Russia or to improve the lives of Russian workers and peasants, but to 'break capitalism at its weakest link' and launch a process of permanent revolution that would spread throughout Europe and beyond. But the form of Marxism that they implanted in Russia was so extreme that it alientated the outside world and turned the infant Soviet state into an pariah. Soon the Bolsheviks found that, to hold on to their new-won power, they had to close down opposition newspapers, arrest and imprison all those who thought differently, and abolish the embryonic forms of representative democracy and private property that had begun to take shape in Russia at the end of the nineteenth century.

The Bolsheviks tried to destroy everything that could make Russians normal people and Russia a normal country. They replaced religion by militant atheism, severed family bonds and rewrote the laws of economics and morality. Soviet men and women were declared to be a new type of human being. All this the Bolsheviks did, not because they wanted to cut Russia off from the rest of humanity, but because they hoped to develop a new civilisation that would transform the world.

Stalin discarded the idea of permanent revolution because he saw how difficult it was to achieve, and replaced it with the doctrine of 'socialism in a single country'. His leadership marked the abandonment of Lenin's effort to reform Russia and a reversion to authoritarian rule. In order to buttress his own power, Stalin cut the Soviet Union off from the outside world, instituted terror against his own people, banned books and deported entire nations. Only in the last months of the Second World War, as the Soviet army advanced towards Berlin, did Stalin resurrect the goal of 'export of revolution' and seek to install communist regimes in neighbouring countries. Post-war Europe was split into two. The idea that Europe could be physically divided into 'eastern' and 'western' halves was, Milan Kundera has argued, an artificial creation of the Cold War, invented by Stalin and his henchmen to justify Soviet domination over large swathes of central, southeastern and eastern Europe.

Growing up in Stalin's shadow

Stalin was tightening his grip over Soviet society when Mikhail Gorbachev was born into a peasant family in Russia's breadbasket, the northern Caucasus, in 1931. Gorbachev, who was ten years old when Germany invaded the USSR, was too young to see military action. Eduard Shevardnadze, who subsequently became the chief executor of Gorbachev's 'new thinking' in foreign policy, was born into the family of a schoolteacher in the west of Georgia in 1928; he, too, was too young to serve in the war. But Aleksandr Yakovlev, who later became Gorbachev's closest political associate, was eighteen when war broke out and was immediately dispatched to the front. The son of peasants living to the north of Moscow, Yakovlev was to become the main theoretician of *glasnost*, or openness in public life.

In 1950, Gorbachev won a rare and coveted place to study law at Moscow State University, the most prestigious institute of higher education in the Soviet Union. While his training was inevitably influenced by the prevailing Stalinist orthodoxy, Gorbachev has often expressed pride that he trained as a lawyer. At university, he met and married a fellow-student, Raisa Maksimovna. Gorbachev is a private man and his wife has, throughout the years, been his closest confidante.

Work in some form of state or Communist Party administration was virtually the only career open to ambitious Soviet youngsters and, on graduating from university in 1955, Gorbachev returned to his native Stavropol Region as a full-time official in the Communist Youth League (Komsomol). There he began his ascent up the provincial Communist Party hierarchy. Through the Komsomol he met Shevardnadze, who was making a similar career in his native Georgia. Yakovlev, meanwhile, studied what he calls 'a kind of history' at a provincial college, and worked briefly on a local newspaper before landing a job in the Propaganda Department of the Communist Party apparatus in Moscow. A turning point in his life occurred in 1959 when Yakovlev was sent abroad as one of the Soviet Union's first exchange students. He spent a year studying American history at Columbia University in New York, but he was not happy in the US and returned to Moscow with strong anti-American views.

As these brief sketches show, the three men who were to be primarily reponsible for transforming Soviet foreign policy in the second half of the 1980s came from obscure but by no means untypical backgrounds. All three grew up in the Stalin period and joined the Communist Party at an early age. None had any association with dissident or opposition movements. They were not, however, untouched by Stalin's Terror: Gorbachev's paternal grandfather was sentenced to seven years in a labour camp for hiding grain from the state during collectivisation, while Shevardnadze's parents-in-law were both sent to the camps. But such experiences were shared by thousands and even millions of Soviet citizens. What prompted three men from such relatively unremarkable backgrounds to turn Soviet foreign policy on its head?

Outside influences

One obvious reason is that, while still young men, all three felt the impact of Nikita Khrushchev's de-Stalinisation campaign. In this, they were typical of their peers. The late 1950s and early 1960s produced a generation of liberal Soviet intellectuals who became known as the *shestidesyatniki* ('sixtiers'). When Gorbachev embarked on his reforms, it was from this generation that his closest aides and supporters came.

Also crucial was the bitter disappointment felt by many of the *shestidesyatniki* when, in August 1968, Khrushchev's successor Leonid Brezhnev crushed the attempt by communist leaders in Czechoslovakia to build 'socialism with a human face'. The promulgation of the Brezhnev Doctrine, which amounted to an assertion that the countries of central and eastern Europe were not free to choose their own political and economic systems, dashed hopes that similar reforms might be launched in the Soviet Union. Yakovlev, who was sent to Prague soon after the invasion to get the propaganda machine back on track, has spoken of the 'shame' he felt when he saw how Czechs and Slovaks resisted Soviet tanks. Gorbachev himself visited Prague in 1969 as a member of a Communist Party delegation. It is not known what impression the visit made on him at the time but, during his university days, he had formed a close friendship with a Czech student, Zdenek Mlynar, who was to play a key role in the Prague Spring. In her biography of Gorbachev, Gail Sheehy records that Mlynar visited Gorbachev and his wife in Stavropol in 1967, so Gorbachev must have been informed about events in Czechoslovakia. After he launched his own reforms, Gorbachev explicitly said that he saw the Prague Spring as a model, as did several of his aides. Two of his closest foreign policy advisers, Anatolii Chernyaev and Georgii Shakhnazarov, worked in Prague in the early 1960s, on the editorial staff of the journal *World Marxist Review,* and forged links with reform-minded communists there.

Gorbachev and Shevardnadze, who built their careers outside Moscow, flourished in the 1970s. Gorbachev was appointed Communist Party boss in Stavropol Region, while Shevardnadze became Party leader in Georgia. Yakovlev's career took a downturn, however. In 1973, he published an article criticising Russian nationalism that provoked such an uproar that he was banished to Canada as Soviet ambassador. Yakovlev remained in virtual exile for ten years, until Gorbachev arranged his return to Moscow.

As Brezhnev and his fellow oligarchs clung to power, ambitious officials of Gorbachev's generation grew increasingly impatient. Brezhnev's later years were especially frustrating for enterprising local leaders who tried to run their regions efficiently. Gorbachev says that it was while he was Party boss in Stavropol that he first appreciated the necessity for systemic reform. Shevardnadze's experience was the same. Like Gorbachev, he took an interest in agriculture and had some success with experiments that encouraged farmers to take initiatives. But, Shevardnadze later told a television interviewer, he understood the need for radical reform when it dawned on him that, however successful the small-scale innovations in which he and Gorbachev took such pride, they could make only a small dent in the system as a whole. 'I realised,' he says, 'that you couldn't make an economic reform in a single district'.

Of course, patronage played an important role in Soviet politics. In 1979, after his predecessor as Stavropol Party boss had moved to a higher post in Moscow, Gorbachev found himself summoned to the capital and put in charge of Soviet agriculture. He also won the trust of Yurii Andropov, head of the KGB. In 1980, Gorbachev entered the Politburo. At 48, he was by far the youngest member of the leadership. Once in the Kremlin, however, Gorbachev grew increasingly frustrated by his inability to improve Soviet agricultural performance. He says it was then that he realised for the first time how serious the Soviet economic crisis was. 'The situation was especially intolerable,' he recalls, 'in view of the success of other states, including those that had suffered defeat in the Second World War. The population became very dissatisfied with the state of affairs: they began to call strikes and to send petitions to the centre'.

Gorbachev and his associates were the first generation of Soviet citizens to see the outside world from anything other than a tank and to be able to make first-hand comparisons between the communist and western systems. Even for the Soviet elite, however, travel was not a right but merely a reward for good behaviour. This was a further source of frustration. Words were coined to distinguish those who had permission to travel (*vyezdnye*) from those who did not (*nevyezdnye*). 'Our generation was different,' Gorbachev says:

We felt the urge to see the world, to travel, to meet people... We felt isolated because we weren't allowed to go abroad and meet anyone we wanted. Everything was parcelled out in tiny portions. The Central Committee apparatus gave permission for officials to travel abroad, while for ordinary citizens the decision rested with a commission headed by the secretary of the Party committee at the factory. You had to provide character references and names of people who would sign guarantees for you and, of course, an evaluation of your reliability from the KGB.

Gorbachev and his wife seized every opportunity to travel. Following a group visit to France in 1966, they took the unusual step of renting a car and spent several weeks driving around the country on their own. In 1972 Gorbachev went to the Netherlands on an official delegation; three years later, he visited West Germany; in 1977 he and his wife holidayed in Italy at the invitation of the Italian Communist Party. In the spring of 1983 Gorbachev made an official visit to Canada where he met Yakovlev; legend has it that the two men sat up an entire night talking. In December 1984, shortly before he was elected General Secretary, Gorbachev made a fateful visit to London where he established an immediate rapport with Margaret Thatcher. When he left, the prime minister made her famous pronouncement: 'I *like* Mr Gorbachev. We can do business together'.

These visits made a profound impression on Gorbachev. They might even be likened to the tour of western Europe made by Peter the Great at the end of the seventeenth century, which opened the eyes of Russia's first Westerniser to the advantages of other countries and made him eager to apply western practices and inventions within his own borders. Peter's experience was repeated by many Soviet citizens when they first travelled abroad. Taught from childhood that western propaganda was lies and that the populations of capitalist countries were impoverished and downtrodden, many became profoundly angry when they realised they had been lied to. Gorbachev's trips to Canada in 1983 and Britain in 1984 had another effect, too: they reminded western leaders that a generational shift was in the offing in the Kremlin and alerted them that the next Soviet leader might be very different from the aging oligarchs of the Brezhnev era.

Anatolii Chernyaev realised early on that Gorbachev was unlike other apparatchiks. In his memoirs, Chenyaev recalls accompanying Gorbachev to Amsterdam in 1972.

> Gorbachev showed no interest in the city's legendary red-light district, but we dragged him to see a blue movie. He blushed at what he saw. Perhaps he was angry. But he was silent. When I got back to Moscow, I told Boris Ponomarev [the official in charge of Soviet relations with western communist parties] that we had a find in Gorbachev: someone who could keep up the image of the CPSU among the fraternal parties. There were few such people – at any rate, I'd never met any.

Chernyaev's anecdote reveals much about the hypocrisy that pervaded the Soviet leadership in the late Brezhnev years, against which Gorbachev and his associates were to revolt. Their revolt came about not as the result of a sudden revelation but through a slow evolution of their thinking, yet it is probably safe to say that by 1985, however, neither Gorbachev nor Yakovlev believed in Marxism-Leninism in the orthodox sense of that term. By the time Gorbachev became Soviet leader, his ideas could perhaps be best described as broadly resembling those of a social democrat of the west European type. That, at any rate, is what can be deduced from the policies he began to enact. His emphasis was less on orthodox socialist priorities such as the redistribution of wealth and the provision of social welfare and more on the need for democratisation and social justice. Yakovlev, for his part, appears to have undergone a profound transformation during his decade in Canada, where he became a close friend of prime minister Pierre Trudeau. By 1985 his ideas could perhaps be described as closest to those of a west European liberal democrat. Indeed, cadres secretary Yegor Ligachev has been called the only true Marxist in Gorbachev's Politburo. Gorbachev and Yakovlev did not always live up to their principles, as the dispatch of Soviet troops to crush mass demonstrations in Tbilisi in 1989, Baku in 1990 and Vilnius in 1991 tragically testified, but they did, on the intellectual level, reject the use of violence by the state and consciously eschewed it against the Soviet Union's eastern European neighbours.

Gorbachev in power

It was during his visit to London in December 1984 that Gorbachev first described Europe as 'our common home'. At the time, few western leaders paid any attention. This was partly because the phrase had already been used by Brezhnev during an official visit to Bonn in November 1981. 'We would have a good idea,' Chernyaev later told the BBC's Angus Roxburgh, 'but nobody in the world would believe us, because Brezhnev also used to use these pretty words'. It was, however, one of Gorbachev's hallmarks that he took concepts that his predecessors had employed as propaganda tools and tried to give them real meaning. Chernyaev told the BBC's Stephen Dalziel in 1995 that, in his opinion, the lack of trust between East and West had been the most dangerous feature of the Cold War and that Gorbachev's most important achievement was to persuade western leaders to trust him. Gorbachev finally got their attention, Chernyaev argued, not because he came forward with fresh initiatives, but 'because he was a *normal* person'.

Gorbachev's early foreign policy moves were accordingly aimed at breaking down the wall of distrust between East and West. During his first two years in power, his foreign policy agenda was dominated by arms control issues and Soviet relations with the United States formed the main focus of his attention. However, Gorbachev explains that his vision of a 'common European home' differed from earlier blueprints, such as General de Gaulle's concept of Europe stretching 'from the Atlantic to the Urals,' precisely because it included the United States of America. 'We were realists,' Gorbachev asserts, 'so we did not try to exclude America from the continent of Europe. Europe could not ignore the United States: that would only create new splits and new dangers'. In other words, Europe for Gorbachev represented less a geographical or even a political entity and rather a cultural community founded on democratic norms and embracing both Europe and North America. Gorbachev explains: 'We envisaged a big European house: it would have different apartments but normal communications would be possible between them, and it would be a single home whose inhabitants would observe common rules. There would be a room for America. I thought it would take fifty years to build such a house ..'.

Early on, Gorbachev made a fateful decision. Soon after he became Party leader, he signalled to the leaders of the East European Communist Parties that he intended to give them leeway to decide matters in their countries without Soviet interference. Gorbachev claims this message was first intimated to the East European leaders when they came to Moscow to attend the funeral of his predecessor, Konstantin Chernenko, but the first public indication that Moscow might abandon the Brezhnev Doctrine came in February 1986. Addressing his first CPSU Congress as Party leader, Gorbachev declared that 'no party has a monopoly of the truth'. Later that same year, a Politburo memorandum was prepared on the basis of expertise provided by Moscow's main think-tank devoted to the study of eastern Europe. The institute's leading specialist on East Germany, Vyacheslav Dashichev, argued that the eastern European states were a dangerous financial and political liability to the Soviet Union, and that Moscow would not be able to mend its fences with the West until it relaxed its grip on eastern Europe.

There were indeed strong reasons for the USSR to disengage from its 'outer empire'. Gorbachev was aware that some form of East-West rapprochement was essential to give Moscow a breathing space from the arms race and to allow the reinvigoration of the flagging Soviet economy. And, with the rise of the Solidarity trade union movement on their doorstep, Gorbachev and his colleagues were acutely aware that they must placate the disgruntled Soviet population if they wanted to prevent a repetition of Poland's workers' revolt inside the USSR.

In the autumn of 1986, Timothy Garton Ash has recorded, Moscow sent word through private channels to all the East European Communist Party leaders that from now on they should conduct their internal affairs as they saw fit. By the same token, the East European leaders were put on notice that those whose policies failed to command popular support could no longer expect to be bailed out economically or militarily by Moscow. Gorbachev recalls:

I told my East European colleagues that from now on they were responsible for what happened and we would not interfere. They went away saying, 'We've heard all this before, from Brezhnev and even from Chernenko'. So they paid no attention. [Gustav] Husak [leader of the Communist Party of Czechoslovakia] came and asked for advice on personnel appointments. [Erich] Honecker [the East German leader] was not on our wavelength at all, so we let him go his own way. Those closest to us were [Poland's General Wojciech] Jaruzelski and [Hungary's Janos] Kadar.

There is a parallel here with the way in which Yakovlev was encouraging *glasnost* in the Soviet media. Soon after his appointment as propaganda chief, Yakovlev informed Soviet newspaper editors that, from now on, they should stop asking for instructions from above and make their own decisions about what to publish. After decades of interference and control, the decision simply to stop meddling – to do nothing – was for the Soviet leadership a revolutionary departure.

Revolutionary though Soviet foreign policy was in the hands of Gorbachev and Shevardnadze, Gorbachev turned out to be extraordinarily blinkered when it came to the 'inner empire,' that is, the USSR's non-Russian republics. When his policies of *glasnost* and democratisation encouraged strong independence movements in Estonia, Latvia, Lithuania, Moldova, Georgia and Armenia, Gorbachev stubbornly refused to allow these republics the same rights to independence and self-determination that he was prepared to countenance in eastern Europe. He consistently opposed the idea of the break-up of the Soviet Union and resorted to threats and violence in a self-defeating effort to keep the Soviet Union together. The use of Soviet troops against civilians in Tbilisi, Baku and Vilnius left an ugly stain on the record of his leadership.

'New thinking'

In 1986, Gorbachev first spoke of the need for 'new thinking' in Soviet foreign policy. As the concept evolved, it turned out to include several elements. One was renunciation of the use of force in international relations, memorably summarised by Shevardnadze as recognising that 'you don't enhance your own security by making your neighbours feel insecure'. A key element, according to Gorbachev, was the desire 'to free the Soviet Union from ideological confrontation'. In this respect, he says, his policy was fundamentally different from the doctrine of peaceful coexistence promulgated by Khrushchev. Recognising the realities of the nuclear age, Khrushchev abandoned Lenin's insistence that war between capitalism and socialism was inevitable. However, Khrushchev did not renounce the Marxist aim of world revolution or abandon the weapons of ideological struggle ('We will bury you!' he told western leaders). 'But our idea,' Gorbachev says, 'was to to replace ideological confrontation with the principle of freedom of choice.... No-one has the right to force a foreign model on others, not the communist model, nor the American way of life, nor western values'.

If the nations of central, southeastern and eastern Europe were to be free to choose the political and economic systems they wanted, the Soviet Union had to recognise that it had no right to force them to change their minds. Gorbachev spelled this out in a landmark speech to the UN General Assembly in December 1988. 'Force or the threat of force can no longer be, and should not be, instruments of foreign policy,' he declared. It was immaterial whether the states in question were capitalist or socialist: 'Freedom of choice is a universal principle. It knows no exception'.

This meant rejecting not only Khrushchev's legacy but also Lenin's notorious assertion of 1920 that the Bolsheviks recognised no moral or ethical values save those that served to advance the interests of proletarian class struggle. Casting aside seventy years of Soviet support for the ideology of class warfare, Gorbachev spoke on Soviet television in October 1986 of 'the primacy of common human values'. In a nuclear age, he declared, the preservation of the human race must take precedence over all other interests. Nothing that Gorbachev said or did demonstrated more clearly than that one statement the seriousness of his desire to bring about a rapprochement between his country and the western world.

On a visit to Prague in April 1987, Gorbachev said his vision of the common European home 'assumes a degree of integrity, even if its states belong to different social systems and opposing military-political blocs'. This statement has been cited by some commentators to argue that Gorbachev's idea of a common European house was one in which the socialist states, with their centrally-planned economies and single-party dictatorships, would be as much as at home as the pluralistic democracies and market economies of western Europe and North America. If so, this would suggest that all Gorbachev had in mind was a revival of the détente policies of the Brezhnev era. It is true that Gorbachev was, as has already been stressed, tragically blinkered as far as the aspirations for independence of the peoples of the Soviet Union's 'inner empire' were concerned. As for the 'outer empire,' however, Gorbachev was true to his word: his leadership did allow the eastern European countries to choose their own paths. Therefore, his statement in Prague may also be interpreted as expressing the principle of free choice. Support for this interpretation came in an address in Strasbourg in July 1989, in which Gorbachev set out his view of Europe more clearly than ever before. 'The social and political order changed in some countries in the past,' he stated on that occasion, 'and they may change in the future too, but this is entirely a matter for each people to decide. Any interference in internal affairs, or any attempt to limit the sovereignty of another state – friend, ally or any other – is inadmissible'.

This is not the place for a blow-by-blow account of the unravelling of the Soviet bloc, of which excellent accounts already exist. Suffice it to say that 1989 saw the initiative pass irrevocably to the grassroots. In February of that year, the Hungarian leadership consented to the formation of rival political parties. In June, Poland's fiercely anti-communist Solidarity movement won a landslide victory in the first more or less democratic elections held in eastern Europe since the imposition of Soviet rule. In August Jaruzelski agreed, after a telephone call from Gorbachev, that the Polish communists would enter a coalition government in which Solidarity would be the senior partner. Anti-regime demonstrations became more and more frequent in East Germany and Czechoslovakia. In early October, Gorbachev met Honecker in Berlin and tried, unsuccessfully, to persuade him to launch East Germany on the reform path. Gorbachev's parting words were prophetic. 'History,' he said, 'punishes those who come late'. Honecker was deposed within two weeks.

In Helsinki at the end of October Gorbachev declared that the USSR had no right, 'moral or political,' to interfere in eastern Europe. Meanwhile the spokesman of the Soviet Foreign Ministry, Gennadii Gerasimov, was telling reporters that the Brezhnev Doctrine had been replaced by the 'Sinatra Doctrine,' a reference to Frank Sinatra's song 'I Did It My Way'. On 1 November Gorbachev called on East Germany's new leaders to 'avoid an explosion' by opening the country's borders to the West. On 9 November they did so. 'When the people started to come through the Wall,' Gorbachev chuckles, 'it proved that Marx was right to speak of the defining role of the working masses. We did nothing in November 1989, and that was the right decision'.

Gorbachev did nothing, either, in December 1989 when Romania's Nicolae Ceausescu was overthrown, nor when Vaclav Havel was elected president of the Czechoslovak parliament. But the decision for which Gorbachev will be known in history, and in which Shevardnadze also played a key role, came when he consented to the unification of East and West Germany.

In fact, the question of German unification is believed to have been less of a stumbling block for the Soviet leadership than whether or not a united Germany should remain in NATO. At first, Gorbachev insisted that the new Germany must be neutral. But when he came to Washington for a summit with the American president in early June 1990, Gorbachev responded positively to a suggestion from George Bush that it should be left to the German people to decide whether or not a united Germany should be in NATO. Gorbachev's interlocutors were astounded; so too were his aides. The most likely explanation for Gorbachev's unexpected decision was that, by the middle of 1990, he was coming under intense pressure from hardliners in the Soviet leadership and felt he had to make concessions in order to win western support to shore up his position at home. Independence campaigns in the non-Russian Soviet republics were tearing the USSR apart, while Gorbachev's nemesis, Boris Yeltsin, had just become the first popularly elected leader in Russian history. Yeltsin's decision to assert Russia's independence from the central Soviet authorities rendered the collapse of the Soviet Union inevitable. 'Never before,' write Michael Beschloss and Strobe Talbott, 'had Gorbachev's domestic difficulties made him so desperate for the benefits of good relations with the United States'.

Gorbachev's decision to allow a united Germany to join NATO provoked fury within much of the Soviet elite, especially the military, and he lost control of the situation. In an attempt to appease his opponents, Gorbachev lurched toward the hardliners, prompting Shevardnadze at the end of 1990 to resign his post as foreign minister. In the spring of 1991, Gorbachev sought to contain centrifugal forces within the Soviet state by negotiating a new Union Treaty with the Soviet republics. The prospect of the loss of central control only increased the virulence of the hardliners, culminating in the attempted coup of August 1991. Four months later, the Soviet Union disintegrated and Gorbachev resigned from his post as the country's first and only president.

Eurasian colossus

Over the past three centuries, numerous efforts have been made to modernise Russia's economy and reform its political system. These have invariably involved Russia's opening to the West. Mikhail Gorbachev clearly believed that the openness and flexibility of western countries gave them a competitive advantage and that the Soviet Union stood to gain by joining such a community. In stressing the links between his country and Europe, he made a serious and sustained attempt to move away from despotism and towards government by consent. In some respects his policies were successful. Most notably they made it possible for Russia to emerge from the isolation in which it had languished since 1917. But Gorbachev also made tactical errors and pursued policies that were inherently contradictory. This was especially true of his attitude toward the constituent republics of the Soviet Union. As a result, his reforms had effects that were often very different from those he intended. There is certainly no sign that Gorbachev had any inkling that, as a result of his policies, his country would disintegrate, its Communist Party would collapse, and he himself would be forced into retirement.

On the evidence, what Gorbachev seems to have wanted in 1985 was to make the USSR into a superpower he could be proud of. He wanted the Soviet economy to work more efficiently and the Soviet Union to become a pleasanter place for its citizens to live in. Above all, Gorbachev wanted to lead a 'normal' country. He had studied the western world at first hand and knew that the model he had in mind for his own country was represented by such nations as France, West Germany or Canada. He understood that, for that to happen, the Soviet Union had to set its 'outer empire' free. At the same time, however, Gorbachev wanted to keep the USSR's 'inner empire' intact. The contradictions in this agenda led to what can only be described, in the light of Gorbachev's apparent objectives, as a debâcle.

The impact of Gorbachev's policies on the countries of central, eastern and southeastern Europe was immense. His decision to stop interfering in their affairs represented an extraordinary renunciation of the Soviet imperial imperative even if it was prompted by a mistaken belief that, left to their own devices, eastern Europe's communist leaders would see the error of their ways and start to behave like democrats. Gorbachev's efforts led to the end of the Cold War, the unification of Germany and the return of the eastern European nations to the European family. The politically-inspired division of Europe into 'East' and 'West' was expunged. The end of the Cold War made it possible for the Baltic States, the Czech and Slovak Republics, Hungary, Poland, Ukraine and other states to forge or renew links with western Europe that have already brought these countries into the Council of Europe and that some of them hope will soon bring them into the European Union and NATO as full-fledged members.

It is not yet clear what the long-term effect on Russia will be. Russia has made enormous strides on the path to democracy and the market, and in 1996 joined the Council of Europe, yet Russian citizens would be the first to say that it is still not an entirely 'normal' country. Perhaps Russia, in many ways the least western of European countries, occupies so unusual a geopolitical position that it cannot and should not aspire to normalcy. Instead, perhaps, Russia is destined to remain, like a colossus, with one foot on European soil and the other planted in Asia, attracted by the West and its values and appreciative of them and yet, at the same time, shaped by its own unique history, traditions and experience into an entity unmistakably different from the rest of Europe.

Selected bibliography

The authors followed the rise and fall of the Gorbachev leadership as analysts at Radio Free Europe/Radio Liberty Inc., and this essay draws on their monitoring of the Soviet print and broadcast media throughout the 1980s. In connection with this essay, interviews were conducted in Moscow in July 1995 with President Mikhail S. Gorbachev and Aleksandr N. Yakovlev. Unless otherwise indicated, the quotations in the text are taken from these interviews.

Bibliography

Beschloss, Michael R. and Strobe Talbott (1994) *At the Highest Levels: The Inside Story of the End of the Cold War*, London: Warner Books.

Chernyaev, A.S. (1993) *Shest' let s Gorbachevym* (*Six Years With Gorbachev*), Moscow: Kul'tura.

Garton Ash, Timothy (1993) *In Europe's Name: Germany and the Divided Continent*, London: Jonathan Cape.

Gati, Charles (1990) *The Bloc that Failed*, Bloomington: Indiana University Press.

Gorbachev, Mikhail (1987) *Perestroika: New Thinking for Our Country and the World*, London: Collins.

Malcolm, Neil, ed. (1994) *Russia and Europe: An End to Confrontation?* London: Pinter.

Minogue, Kenneth (1993) *Politics: A Very Short Introduction*, Oxford: Oxford University Press.

Pryce-Jones, David (1995) *The War that Never Was: The Fall of the Soviet Empire*, London: Weidenfeld and Nicolson.

Roxburgh, Angus (1991) *The Second Russian Revolution*, London: BBC Books.

Sheehy, Gail (1991) *Gorbachev: The Making of the Man Who Shook the World*, London: Mandarin Books.

Steele, Jonathan (1994) *Eternal Russia*, London: Faber and Faber.

Tchoubarian, Alexander (1994) *The European Idea in History in the Nineteenth and Twentieth Centuries: A View from Moscow*, London: Frank Cass.

Walker, Martin (1994) *The Cold War*, London: Vintage.

White, Stephen (1990) *Gorbachev in Power*, Cambridge: Cambridge University Press.

Thatcher and Kohl –
Old Rivalries Revisited

Alan Watson

On 11 December 1898 Prince Bernhard von Bülow addressed the Reichstag in Berlin. His purpose was to look towards the new century. With uncharacteristic foresight he warned the Chamber that 'in the new century Germany must be either the hammer or the anvil.' The caution and the calculation of Bismarck had been replaced by the restless and often reckless ambition of his successors. Germany headed into the twentieth century doomed to be both hammer and anvil and to involve her European neighbours in the same experience. Britain might still have felt itself to be impervious to continental entanglements but within two decades was to be drawn into the continental maelstrom. 'We do not desire to put anyone else in the shade, but we want our place in the sun,' von Bülow assured the German Reichstag; but as the century closed Britain occupied the best place in the sun. Rivalry between Imperial Britain and Imperial Germany became inevitable and conflict all too probable. For the Imperialists around Kaiser Wilhelm II all that was needed was care in passing through 'the danger zone', those years when Germany's new fleet would not be able to survive a surprise attack by the Royal Navy. Once through that period the future looked rosy. The German Ambassador in London at the turn of the century expressed it well: 'If people in Germany would only sit still, the time would soon come when we could have oysters and champagne for dinner.' In the event, miscalculation was the order of the day and oysters and champagne gave way to the shells and mud of the First World War.

As we approach the end of our century it is worth recollecting these unhappy developments at the close of the nineteenth. Then as now assumptions were made about the inevitability of Anglo-German rivalry and the possibility of confrontation. In his important speech at Leuven University in February 1996 Chancellor Kohl restated his faith in European Union and his fear that, unless the pace of integration is maintained, Europe could repeat the conflict of the first half of the twentieth century. Of course the Chancellor does not fear a repetition of the world wars of the twentieth century but he has consistently warned that Europe must go either forwards or backwards and, if the latter, then conflict becomes inevitable and its outcome unpredictable.

On the British side, the late Nicholas Ridley in his interview with the *Spectator* magazine fumed against the whole process of European integration as 'a German racket, designed to take over the whole of Europe'. For Nicholas Ridley conflict was preferable to defeat. 'I am not sure I'd rather not have the shelters and the chance to fight back than simply being taken over by economics.' Even as robust an optimist about Anglo-German relations as Sir Oliver Wright, Britain's former Ambassador in Bonn, has sounded the tocsin of impending confrontation. In his Robert Birley Memorial Lecture in March 1995 he said of the 1996 inter-governmental conference 'it seems to me that, judging by ministerial speeches, Britain and Germany are far apart, indeed on collision courses.' So do old rivalries have new resonance? Is Anglo-German competition, confrontation and conflict endemic to our age, as to an earlier one? Above all, did the relationship between Helmut Kohl as Chancellor and Margaret Thatcher as Prime Minister lead to the revisiting of Anglo-German rivalry and its revival? Did they set both countries on a collision course into the twenty-first century?

That the relationship between Margaret Thatcher and Helmut Kohl was neither warm nor close is beyond dispute. The reasons for this are important, especially where the differences of character and style between them reflected and shaped policy differences. Old rivalries found fresh form. Yet, equally important is the question whether these differences of both personality and policy in reality expressed differences of national interest. If they did, then these differences are indeed likely to shape relations into the next century. If they did not, then the ill humour and disagreement which so often characterised the relationship between the two may lack potency and the potential for future conflict.

The evidence abounds that Margaret Thatcher carried with her the intellectual and emotional baggage of hostility to Germany. There is far less evidence of Kohl's wariness towards Britain, although within the German Foreign Office scepticism about Britain's commitment to Europe remained acute throughout the period of Margaret Thatcher's premiership. On particular occasions Kohl personally became exasperated and angered by the evidence, as he saw it, of British insensitivity to German interests, disdain for her position and hostility to her hopes.

It is appropriate to start with Margaret Thatcher for, on balance, she set the tone and Kohl reacted.

Despite the difficulties of the Kohl/Thatcher relationship they were both assisted and the cause of Anglo-German cooperation furthered by another relationship, namely that between Charles, now Sir Charles, Powell and Horst Teltschik. Charles Powell, seconded by the Foreign Office to work with Margaret Thatcher, became in many ways its leading critic and her stoutest defender. His ability to read her mind and express her thoughts was rivalled only by Bernard Ingham, her incorrigible press secretary. Charles Powell's opposite number in Bonn was Horst Teltschik whose understanding of his chief matched Powell's own. In his memoirs Horst Teltschik describes how on 9 February 1990 Charles Powell, as his main 'counterpart in 10 Downing Street', spent some three hours explaining to him Margaret Thatcher's position on Germany and German reunification. He explained that she belonged to another generation, that there was between both countries a cultural gap and that the bottom line would always be that Margaret Thatcher would feel herself 'uneasy' with the prospect of a large and strong Germany. In conversation Sir Charles Powell speaks of Mrs Thatcher's 'wellspring of instinctive anti-Germanism'.

This instinctive anti-Germanism may well have led to the decision to hold the famous – or infamous – Chequers seminar in March 1990, the minutes of which were subsequently leaked. Margaret Thatcher was so alarmed by the prospects of enhanced German power in Europe that she called together experts on that country's history, economics and politics to discuss what might be in store. On balance the academics who attended were positive. The historian, George Urban, stated later that 'Our unanimous clear advice was that Germany ought to be embraced as a partner and helped as a friend.' The German-born Professor of History at Columbia University, Fritz Stern, said that the discussion acknowledged that 'The Germans had changed profoundly since 1945.' Charles Powell, whose summary of German characteristics caused most of the brouhaha, himself recalls the seminar as being 'frank, but very positive in its conclusions'. He insists that there never was a specific list of German attributes. Instead he had pulled together all the various characteristics that had been attributed to the Germans into a single list at the end of a six-hour discussion. This list, however, was hardly flattering. In alphabetical order it was 'angst, aggressiveness, assertiveness, bullying, egotism, inferiority complex, sentimentality'. Little is known of Margaret Thatcher's own contribution to the discussion, but according to Charles Powell, 'She revelled in it and was affected by the positive conclusions although nothing could change her instinctive jumpiness about Germany.'

That jumpiness undoubtedly stemmed from wartime memories and emotions. In the view of another former British Ambassador in Bonn she had absorbed the 1945 view of Europe in which, from a British perspective, Germany was the foe and France the unreliable ally. Lord Howe remembers her antipathy towards and fear of Germany, and Karl-Günther von Hase, one of Bonn's former Ambassadors in London and a doyen of the annual Anglo-German Königswinter Conferences, recalls with continuing astonishment the depth of her feelings. In 1990 Margaret Thatcher was invited to one of these conferences, held that year in Cambridge. Its purpose was to celebrate forty years of cooperation at Königswinter Conferences. It was her first visit and her clear view was that the audience would not be friendly. In particular the sort of 'Brits' who attended Königswinter Conferences were her natural enemies – 'Euro-federalists and the like' remembers Charles Powell. Chancellor Kohl attended the same conference and it fell to Sir Oliver Wright to determine the seating arrangements for dinner. He decided it was far too risky to put them next to each other. Instead he sat between them, putting Christopher Mallaby, the British Ambassador, on the Chancellor's right and the then German Ambassador in London, Hermann von Richthofen, on her left. On this somewhat strained and unhappy occasion, the Prime Minister gave Karl-Günther von Hase the full benefit of her instinctive anti-Germanism. It would be, she warned, 'at least another forty years before the British could trust the Germans again!'

What then of the German side of this strained relationship? Were the old rivalries and prejudices endemic with them as well? Thomas Kielinger, one of Germany's most expert writers about Britain and an eminent journalist, believes strongly that after Margaret Thatcher's speech at Bruges in 1988 the feeling in Bonn was that 'Britain could not be trusted on Europe'. This unease, indeed scepticism about Britain's commitment and intent, had been formalised at the time of British entry into the European Community. It was and remained the thinking of the German Foreign Office. All the developments during Margaret Thatcher's premiership confirmed the view.

Karl-Günther von Hase remembers well the papers being discussed in the German Foreign Office in 1972 and 1973 when British membership of the EEC was confirmed. It was thought that there might be four ways in which British membership would affect Europe. The first was that the United Kingdom might take a lead in Europe. After all, the United Kingdom uniquely had a world position. Its special relationship with the United States was vague but had substance. It had emerged from the Second World War as the sole European victor. Its position in the United Nations, the reputation of its armed forces and the skills of its diplomatic service, all buttressed such a premier position. The second option was that the United Kingdom would become 'a normal member' of the European Community. It would not lead nor would it follow. It would behave as France, proud of its history and careful of its sovereignty. The third option was that Britain would respond to membership in a consistently minimalist manner. It would do what was necessary to stay in the Club, it would obey the rules but it would do so with reluctance and even resentment. It would complain and it would strive to put a brake on the process of forward integration. The fourth and most pessimistic option examined by the German Foreign Office was that the United Kingdom would in fact use its membership to 'torpedo' the enterprise from the inside. Perfidious Albion would enter the Community only to seek to destroy it. Her real preference would be for a loose trading area, devoid of political ambition and stripped of all supranational power.

In practice, the German Foreign Office view at the end of the Thatcher years was that the United Kingdom had acted somewhere between the third and fourth options. She had done what was required to remain a member, but with reluctance and resentment. On occasion she had acted to torpedo the enterprise.

The judgement is partially unfair and in some respects acknowledged to be so. Britain under Margaret Thatcher's leadership was an enthusiastic exponent of the Single Market, but perhaps in part for the very reason that the Single Market would make its own rules and escape the hand of Brussels. Again, it is acknowledged in

Bonn that Britain has always implemented European Union regulations, indeed she has done so to an extent and with a thoroughness quite different from many of her partner nations. Yet the implementation of European directives pales as a test of Euro-fidelity when one looks at the more critical current and future issues of 'widening and deepening' the Community. The suspicion in Bonn has always been that when Britain urges the widening of the Community it does so because it believes that wider will be looser. More member states will mean less cohesion. Depth will be sacrificed for breadth.

These German Foreign Office fears and suspicions of Britain were undoubtedly shared by Chancellor Kohl in his dealings with Margaret Thatcher. Again and again his experience seemed to confirm the gloomiest of Bonn's official forecasts.

This tale of instinctive anti-Germanism on Mrs Thatcher's side and intuitive suspicion of Perfidious Albion on Kohl's side should not be taken to imply personal discourtesy on either side. Margaret Thatcher as Prime Minister and Helmut Kohl as Chancellor were both acutely conscious of the dignity of their office and the representational role conferred by such office. In contrast to Mitterrand who was head of state as well as head of government, Kohl and Thatcher personified only the executive arm of power, not the symbolic expression of the state. However, both are intensely patriotic and acutely aware of their country's status. Helmut Kohl is a post-war politician. While deeply regretting the crimes of the Third Reich, he can feel no personal remorse as he was in no way involved. His pride in a Germany which existed before Nazism, survived that appalling period and has succeeded since, is well-known. It has led him sometimes to insensitivity, as when he persuaded President Reagan to visit a cemetery containing the graves of members of the Waffen SS. However, it has also informed and driven his instinctive leadership of Germany at the unique moment of its reunification. He grasped a possibility of ending his country's division because he felt the need so deeply. Patriotism is not a dirty word in Helmut Kohl's dictionary; Margaret Thatcher's national pride is the very essence of her political consciousness. Helmut Kohl was led to do the right thing over reunification by his sense of nationhood; Margaret Thatcher was guided to success in the Falklands War by the same emotion and instinct.

Their roles as the embodiment of the executive arm of their two nations ensured personal courtesy and dignity. Charles Powell remembers that on every single occasion on which Helmut Kohl visited the Prime Minister in Britain he brought a personal gift. This was unusual for heads of government and reflected his willingness to work hard at a personal relationship. Mrs Thatcher herself acknowledged this courtesy – the human dimension of Kohl's approach. During her nightmare visit to Paris in November 1992 for the CSCE Summit, her leadership under threat, she sensed even before the news of the first ballot that her position as Prime Minister was gravely at risk. In Paris she noted:

It was characteristic of Helmut Kohl that unlike the other leaders I had met he came straight to the point, namely the leadership election. He said it was good to talk about these difficult issues rather than bottle them up. He had been determined to devote this evening to me as a way of demonstrating his complete support. It was unimaginable that I should be deprived of office. Given that the Chancellor and I had strong differences on the future course of the European Community and that my departure would remove an obstacle to his plans – as indeed proved to be the case – this was big-hearted of him. With a more serpentine politician I would have assumed this to be merely insurance against my victory. For Chancellor Kohl, whether as ally or opponent, was never devious. So I was very moved by his words and by the real warmth of his feeling. I tried to overcome my confusion.

The one, often cited, example of personal discourtesy by Helmut Kohl towards Margaret Thatcher turns out to be apocryphal. The story has it that, at a time when both Margaret Thatcher and Helmut Kohl found themselves on holiday in Austria, they agreed to meet at Salzburg. Helmut Kohl came on his own, Margaret Thatcher was accompanied by a number of staff, including Charles Powell. After a not altogether happy exchange of views in which Margaret Thatcher had characteristically started to lecture Helmut Kohl on his duties and responsibilities to the Western Alliance, the story goes that he made his apologies, explaining that after all he would have to leave shortly to attend a meeting with the President of the Federal Republic, Richard von Weizsäcker, back in Bonn. He then left, rather to the Prime Minister's surprise. At a loss as to what to do with the unexpected bonus of a few empty hours in Salzburg, she sought Charles Powell's advice. His suggestion was that they should walk through the city, find a suitable restaurant and take afternoon coffee. This they proceeded to do, only to find to their horror, embarrassment and astonishment the German Chancellor sitting in the corner consuming a large cream cake. They left in some disarray.

That at least is the story, but it is emphatically denied by Charles Powell. He insists it simply did not happen, and certainly it would have been a discourtesy entirely out of character for Helmut Kohl in his relationship with the British Prime Minister.

The truth is that the German Chancellor worked hard at the relationship, not simply in terms of personal gifts and politeness, but also in seeking to understand the character of the Prime Minister. He undoubtedly failed. Was he genuinely disorientated and puzzled by the sharp contrast between Margaret Thatcher's hospitality and warmth as a hostess at Chequers and at 10 Downing Street and her 'no-holds-barred' approach to argument and disagreement? Perhaps he had a somewhat old-fashioned view of women in politics. Certainly he believed that she should do more to woo him and he was willing to do a great deal to woo her. At the Williamsburg Economic Summit in May 1983 Kohl took Geoffrey Howe by surprise. Supposedly having

President Mitterrand in mind Kohl said to Geoffrey Howe: 'Can you not encourage Margaret to be more ready to woo her colleagues?' However, he may also have been thinking of himself.

The trouble was that he simply could not read her right. Hermann von Richthofen remembers one of her visits to Frankfurt at which she expressed a strong interest in meeting the then Head of the Bundesbank, Karl Otto Pöhl. Chancellor Kohl had briefed the Bundesbank chief to show the Prime Minister the Bank's collection of coins, believing that these would interest her. Pöhl knew better. 'The Chancellor has asked me to show you our assembly of coins,' he said to her, 'but I expect you would prefer not to see them'. He was right.

Again, on her visit to Helmut Kohl's home town of Oggersheim, the Chancellor went to great trouble to serve a gargantuan lunch from his own kitchen. According to Mrs Thatcher it consisted of potato soup, pig's stomach, sausage, liver dumplings and sauerkraut. He consumed several helpings. Unenthusiastically she pushed the German equivalent of haggis around her plate with her knife and fork. Afterwards they drove to the nearby cathedral of Speyer. She described her lunch as *gemütlich* ('that is, I think, the German word') and she had difficulty with the crowd outside the cathedral but 'understood' that they were critical of the British and US military presence in Germany. Once inside, Kohl urged Charles Powell to emphasise to the Prime Minister that in such a cathedral, which was both German and French, the Prime Minister should understand that he was as much European as German. The cathedral was of no great interest to the Prime Minister and once she was back in her plane to London she poured a drink, kicked off her shoes and complained to Charles Powell: 'My God, that man is *so* German!'

All these stories – verified or denied – can be dismissed as little more than the tittle-tattle of the power circuit. However, more was involved than an incompatibility of personal chemistry. The inability of either to speak the other's language certainly played an important role, but far more significant were the differences that stemmed from political culture and political attitude. It is worth identifying these political elements because they were to have a considerable impact on policy differences between the two leaders. Margaret Thatcher was not a consensus politician. Her whole political experience was of the confrontation of a House of Commons in which Government and Opposition implacably face each other across the floor. In the view of one German diplomat, she was 'a typical barrister, only giving away a point well after midnight!' It was a style of debate she was to deploy to great effect during the prolonged battle to win a readjustment of the Community budget. Her determination was that Britain should 'get its money back' and the barrister's skills were deployed remorselessly to that end. By contrast, Kohl came from a background in which coalition and consensus were the essential preconditions of power. His own Government depended on the support not just of the Bavarian CSU, but also of the

Liberal FDP. In every decision that he took he always had to think 'of the next battle', namely persuading his partners in government to agree. Kohl seems to have been genuinely surprised by the confrontational nature of British politics, just as Margaret Thatcher and indeed Geoffrey Howe, were somewhat startled by the German system. Neither side envied the other's way of doing things.

There was, too, a very different sense of history. Margaret Thatcher's history was that of the island race. It was peopled by heroes and villains. It was specific. By contrast, Helmut Kohl, a historian by academic training, loved the broad sweep of history. He believed the British Prime Minister lacked any sense of history. He confided to his own Foreign Office that Margaret Thatcher was 'pre-Churchillian' while he was 'post-Churchillian'. What he meant by this was that, while Margaret Thatcher may have been an instinctive practitioner of the balance of power, she simply had not understood its actual operation in the nineteenth century, nor its enormous potential for damage and conflict.

Then there was the sharp contrast in their interpretation of free enterprise and capitalism. Helmut Kohl came from the Christian Democratic tradition which was in sentiment and strategy far closer to that of the 'one nation' Toryism that Margaret Thatcher so deplored and which she strove to destroy. The Manchester Liberalism of Margaret Thatcher's analysis and advocacy he found distasteful. It produced what he once described to Hermann von Richthofen vividly as 'an elbow society', in others words, a society in which people elbowed each other out of the way. His was the path of *Mitbestimmung*, in which workers and managers co-operated together in the direction of companies, in which a generous and comprehensive welfare state protected management and workers alike from the worst ravages of 'capitalist competition'. All this was anathema to Margaret Thatcher, particularly when it manifested itself in European legislation. She saw the Social Chapter of the European Commission legislative programme as a classic example of German dominance in Europe. Works Councils and co-determination, government spending and social benefits were part and parcel of the advancing frontier of the state which she had rolled back in Britain and had no intention of succumbing to via Brussels.

That was the burden of her speech in Bruges, and the same determination ensured that, far from being united by their commitment to capitalism, she and Helmut Kohl were divided by it.

Finally there was the issue of rhetorical style, shaped by the very different theatres of the British House of Commons and the Bundestag. She felt Kohl's style to be light, overblown and often vacuous. She was known to dismiss him from time to time as a 'gasbag'. He saw her debating style as aggressive, mean, narrow and insensitive. If his was a sunny temperament, hers was overcast. These differences of style and background were to play an important role in the substantial rivalry between the two leaders over the key policy issues of the period, issues which help to illuminate the real nature of the competition between Kohl and Thatcher at a crucial period of European development.

There were three principal issues which divided the German and British Governments during the period of Margaret Thatcher's premiership. Chronologically, these were: first, the prolonged and often bitter battle by the Prime Minister to win a recurring refund on Britain's budget contribution to the European Community; second, the Prime Minister's determined resistance to the idea of postponing or cancelling the introduction of new, short-range nuclear missiles in Europe; and third, the fundamental difference between the Prime Minister and the German Chancellor on German reunification and European integration. It was this last issue that eventually led to her own downfall.

The chronological order of these divisive issues also expresses their increasing importance. While Britain's budget contribution mattered a great deal to the British Government, it was a somewhat peripheral issue to the rest of Europe. It seemed to confirm Britain's role as the reluctant and complaining European, an all too obvious reminder to the German Foreign Office of the accuracy of its predictions when Britain originally joined the Community. Yet the issue did not strike at the heart of German/British relations, it exacerbated rather than jeopardised them. The nuclear missile issue was more damaging. The two governments took diametrically opposed positions because fundamental national interests seemed to be involved. Moreover, Margaret Thatcher's stance exemplified to the Germans a disregard, even a contempt for their own national sensitivities and self-interest. The third issue, that of German reunification and European integration, did go to the very heart of the British/German problem. Here were two quite opposed views of the future of Europe and, on the reunification of East and West Germany, a perceived incompatibility of national interests.

Each of these crises involved a heightened sense of tension and a more direct and singular confrontation between the two leaders. On the issue of Britain's contribution to the Community budget, Kohl was just one of Margaret Thatcher's European colleagues who had to be cajoled and persuaded. As Lord Howe remembers: 'The structure of the European Council was kaleidoscopic. There were many variations in alliances and in argument.' Indeed, Helmut Kohl was to prove himself not unsympathetic to the Prime Minister's insistence that Britain must 'get its money back'. After all, the Federal Republic was the biggest contributor to the Community budget and, while sometimes relishing the influence of being Europe's paymaster, the German Chancellor was always acutely aware of the German taxpayers' disenchantment and the need to balance what Germany paid with real gains to Germany's farmers. This was the basis of their mutual understanding on the issue. Margaret Thatcher always acknowledged that Chancellor Kohl had to get something for his own people, just as she had to get her money back. She wrote of Kohl in her memoirs that he had 'the sure touch of a German provincial politician'. This in no small measure meant a willingness to trade.

The 'trade' came at the 1984 European Council held at Fontainebleau. Margaret Thatcher had leverage – Spain and Portugal were joining the European Community and the extra resources that would be needed as a consequence could only material-ise if the United Kingdom agreed to future budget-sharing arrangements. The Prime Minister pushed for a two-thirds refund. President Mitterrand agreed to go to 60 percent. Kohl moved to 65 percent. The Prime Minister insisted on 66 percent and with Gallic charm the French President responded that 'Of course, Madam Prime Minister, you must have it!' Margaret Thatcher remembers that the moment the deal was done the German Chancellor returned to the special subsidy for his farmers. It was the sort of horse-trading the Prime Minister accepted as inevitable and, indeed, inherent in a Common Market.

Of course, the agreement did not disguise the different interests involved. Helmut Kohl's Agriculture Minister once explained to Sir Oliver Wright, British Ambassa-dor in Bonn, that the Common Agricultural Policy (CAP) was indisputably 'a good thing for Germany'. It kept the countryside, and in particular the Bavarian country-side, neat and beautiful, and above all it prevented the peasantry moving to the towns where they were likely to be suborned by the opposition Social Democrats (SPD). Economically and politically the CAP made sense for Germany.

It did not do so for the United Kingdom. Margaret Thatcher always saw the CAP as 'a stitch-up' between France and Germany. However, her price for at least tolerating the CAP was her budget refund and she got it. The difficulty lay not in the difference of interests, nor in the way that they were reconciled, but in the misunderstanding born of the process. According to Thomas Kielinger, Helmut Kohl agreed that Mrs Thatcher 'had a point in getting her money back'. Germany needed to look after its money, too. The difficulty arose from his expectation that he and the other Commu-nity states would receive a *quid pro quo* for the budget settlement. Helmut Kohl believed that he and Germany had scored 'Brownie points' by supporting Margaret Thatcher and that she would be as sympathetic to German interests as he had been to those of Britain. But far from dispelling Margaret Thatcher's alleged anti-Europeanism, the budget settlement seemed only to encourage it. She was ready for further battles ahead and intended to engage in them.

There was clearly scope for misunderstanding. The British Prime Minister felt that Britain was getting nothing less than it deserved. She would owe no favours as a consequence of the agreement. She was also persuaded that the budget settlement had cleared the decks. The United Kingdom was now able and willing to concen-trate on making a reality of first the common market and then the single market. She was as frustrated as Chancellor Kohl to discover that old rivalries immediately reas-serted themselves. Helmut Kohl, in close partnership with France, moved on to a further and, as she saw it, federalist agenda. No sooner was the budget question dealt with than talk began of the intergovernmental conference and moves to 'ever closer union'. Somehow the continental powers, led by Germany, seemed remorselessly determined to erode British sovereignty. From Helmut Kohl's perspective, Margaret Thatcher's opposition to Europe seemed not to diminish but to grow.

The question of the deployment of modernised short range nuclear weapons in central Europe bought a sharper clash, engaging a stronger emotional commitment on the part of both leaders. Chancellor Kohl had always been a consistent supporter of NATO. He had accepted the need during the years of Brezhnev confrontation to modernise NATO nuclear forces. He was under no illusion, however, about German public opinion. The Germans, East and West, were only too aware of the misfortune of their front-line status. In any tactical nuclear exchange in Europe they would be the first victims. Allied nuclear weapons such as the advanced Pershing and Cruise missiles, like their Warsaw Pact equivalent, were targeted as well as located on German soil. In any tactical nuclear exchange in central Europe, German casualties would inevitably be catastrophic. Chancellor Kohl was willing to stand up to German public opinion on the issue of tactical nuclear weapons modernisation while the Cold War seemed to justify it. He was persuaded that NATO had to mean business if it was to be able to do business with the Soviets. However, the advent of Gorbachev changed the entire situation.

While 'Gorby-mania' gripped German crowds and television commentators, the Chancellor saw quite suddenly a vista of new and startling possibilities. In Jacques Delors's famous phrase, history was about to accelerate. Bismarck, the earlier unifier of Germany, had sensed 'the mantle of fate' and reached to grasp it before it passed by. Helmut Kohl's instinct was to do the same. The first step was not German reunification. It was, as Sir Charles Powell believes, his realisation of a unique opportunity to get rid of nuclear weapons on German soil. He took it, as later he was to grasp the opportunity of reunification.

At a meeting in Frankfurt in 1989 Margaret Thatcher and the German Chancellor discussed the situation. As always for the Prime Minister the issues of NATO and the contest with communism were essentially simple. In her memoirs she recalls urging the Chancellor to put the case for short-range nuclear forces to German public opinion by asking one fundamental question: did they value their freedom? Their freedom had begun on the day the Second World War had ended; NATO had preserved it for four decades. She professed to understand his difficulties in dealing with German public opinion and left their meeting convinced that he and she were in basic agreement. She was wrong.

It became clear over the ensuing months that the German government wanted to delay modernisation and deployment and to include short range nuclear weapons in an overall discussion of arms control in central Europe. This was anathema to the British Prime Minister and her reaction, and that of the Americans, led to recriminations in the German media. German opinion was sensitive to the charge that Germany was soft on the Soviets. The Foreign Minister, Hans Dietrich Genscher, felt that Britain was simply insensitive to Germany's national interest: after all Germany was the target. In March 1989 the Federal President, Richard von Weizsäcker, took the unusual step of giving an interview in which he made it clear that Germany could not and should not be bullied on the issue of short-range nuclear weapons.

German unease with the modernisation of short-range nuclear weapons contributed to one of the unhappiest conversations recorded between the British Prime Minister and the German Chancellor. At the meeting already described, which took place at Helmut Kohl's home town of Oggersheim in Rhineland-Palatinate, Margaret Thatcher's fear that he was manoeuvring to accept what the terminology of the time described as 'the third zero' became paramount. The third zero meant negotiating away the third arm of NATO's nuclear defence, namely short-range weapons. The *Gemütlichkeit* of the meeting at Oggersheim rapidly evaporated as she reminded him that he had originally proposed an early NATO summit on modernisation and that she had supported him. There had been their joint statement at Frankfurt. In her words:

> He began to get agitated. He said he did not need any lectures about NATO. But the fact was that Germany was more affected than anyone else by short-range nuclear weapons and that therefore German interest should be given priority. I retorted that, contrary to what he said, short-range nuclear forces did not affect only Germany. Our troops were on German soil ... At this, Chancellor Kohl became still more worked up. He said that for years he had been attacked as the vassal of the Americans. Now he was suddenly being branded a traitor!

In the event the impasse was resolved by the new American President, George Bush. It was done in a way which confirmed Margaret Thatcher's worst fears and fuelled her determination to resist Germany's increasing power and influence in Europe. At Oggersheim she believed she had been able to bring Kohl into line, but clearly she had failed. Instead, he had appealed to the Americans and, on 19 May 1989, the American line on short-range nuclear weapons modernisation changed. They were willing to concede the principle of negotiating on such weapons. President Bush and his Secretary of State, Jim Baker, were not loyal Thatcherites as Reagan had been. In her own words, 'The new American approach was to subordinate clear statements of intention about the Alliance's defence to the political sensibilities of the Germans. I did not think this boded well'.

Worse was to come. On 31 May of that year, President Bush spoke in Mainz, lauding the Germans as 'partners in leadership'. Later, in London, he was to explain that the British were also partners in leadership, but the writing was on the wall. In the event, nuclear weapons modernisation was postponed and subsequent events were to render the process irrelevant. But to the Germans Margaret Thatcher had seemed impervious to their interests. In Thomas Kielinger's words, she had taken 'not a blind bit of notice' of German sensitivity. From her perspective, the Germans had shown themselves to be untrustworthy on the most crucial issue, and more ominously they had won the ear of Washington under the new administration. The next great clash on reunification would only confirm Germany's pre-eminence in Europe and America's acceptance of it.

Most evidently on the future course for Europe and for Germany, but in reality on all the issues that separated them, it was Margaret Thatcher's nationalism that played the key role. This was true on Britain's EC budgetary settlement, on short-range nuclear weapons, on the dangers of German pre-eminence and on the perils of European federalism. She was motivated and driven by nationalist sentiments and perceptions. Had Helmut Kohl ever expressed to her directly his view that she was pre-Churchillian while he was post-Churchillian, she would simply not have understood him. She felt herself to be Churchillian. Winston Churchill was her hero, his defiance of continental dictatorship her ideal, his victory her inspiration. Certainly she did not have, as Helmut Kohl would express it, 'Churchill's sweep of history', but she had his tenacity and it was this which she would apply remorselessly in defence of national sovereignty.

Never was her nationalism more clearly nor more eloquently expressed than in the speech she made at Cheltenham following the Falklands War. There on Saturday 3 July 1983 she proclaimed:

> We have ceased to be a nation in retreat. We have instead a new found confidence, born in the economic battles at home, tested and found true 8,000 miles away. We rejoice that Britain has rekindled that spirit which has fired her for generations past and which today has begun to burn as brightly as before. Britain has found herself, again, in the South Atlantic and will not look back from the victory she has won.

To Helmut Kohl such glorification of war, such intense association with victories past, such a synthesis of martial and economic achievement were literally incomprehensible. He, like all Germans, was embarrassed by Germany's past military prowess. He, like most Germans, saw the future as an escape from nationalism, a rejection of precisely the attitudes that Margaret Thatcher exemplified. Their positions were incompatible.

So, while Helmut Kohl admired Margaret Thatcher's strength of leadership, he wondered openly how it was that she could pour a fortune into the Falklands conflict without counting the cost and at the same time fight for every last penny of her money on Europe's budget. To her the contrast was self-explanatory. She believed in recapturing the Falklands; she opposed much of the process of European integration and thus the purpose of the Community budget. Again, Helmut Kohl was anxious in the cathedral of Speyer to persuade Margaret Thatcher that he was as much European as German. Her reaction afterwards was that in this he had been so very German. Her visceral instinct was that a federal Europe would inevitably be a vehicle for German power and that the extension of German power must be contrary to British interests. If Germany was up, Britain would be down.

This then was the core of Margaret Thatcher and Helmut Kohl's profound disagreement over European union and German unification. On the latter, she was to admit defeat – in her assessment, her only real defeat in foreign affairs. However, the reasons for this only strengthened her determination to oppose further European integration. It had been French weakness which had frustrated her attempts to slow or halt German reunification. If only President Mitterrand had done what he had said, or said what he had thought, all would have been different. The other factors which combined to frustrate her were the attitudes of the USSR and the United States. To her dismay President Bush favoured German and European integration and failed to grasp the centrality of the transatlantic bond between Britain and the United States which for her was the ark of the covenant – a community of 'blood, language, culture and values'. Had her ally and soulmate, Ronald Reagan, still been in the White House, things might have been different. Then there was Russia and Gorbachev, who incomprehensibly had 'sold the pass' for German gold. As she commented bitterly in her memoirs, 'The Soviets were prepared to sell reunification for a modest financial boost from Germany to their crumbling economy.'

All this left Margaret Thatcher in a minority of one – not a position that worried her. Indeed, she was willing to rejoice in isolation. As Britain's later and somewhat Eurosceptic Foreign Minister, Malcolm Rifkind, was to express it: if in Europe Britain had to choose between her interest and her influence, she should always opt for the former and not the latter.

In her memoirs, which are unrivalled for sheer candour, Margaret Thatcher was to be totally clear in her explanation of how in her mind the perils of German reunification and European integration coalesced. She began with Germany's national character, the subject of the Chequers seminar. She did not believe in collective guilt but argued that, since Bismarck, Germany had 'veered unpredictably between aggression and self-doubt... the true origin of German angst is the agony of self-knowledge'. Here is the now familiar leitmotif summarised in Charles Powell's list of German characteristics. The Germans allegedly had disturbing and unattractive character faults and, as this was a question of character, nothing could, of course, change it.

In her memoirs she then moved on from this analysis to explain why European Union would fail to contain the Germans, who had, so to speak, within their genes, character traits which would always make them threatening to the rest of Europe. In fact, Germany was more, rather than less, likely to dominate within the framework of a federal Europe: for a reunited Germany would be simply too big and powerful to be just another player; 'Germany is by its very nature a destabilising rather than a stabilising force in Europe'.

It is at this point that Margaret Thatcher arrived at the nub of her argument. In a single sentence she revealed Germany's role in her Eurosceptic view of Europe. She wrote, 'Only the military and political engagement of the United States in Europe and the close relations between the other two strongest Sovereign States in Europe – Britain and France – are sufficient to balance German power and *nothing of the sort would be possible within a European super-state.'*

She thus laid out her argument with brutal candour, or what Geoffrey Howe vividly describes as 'gut candour'. The Germans, because of innate character defects and because of their very size and geographic position, would always destabilise and pose a threat to their neighbours. That threat was no longer military, but was now economic and political. The German drive to dominance, however, was consistent and inherent. The only way to contain it was through bilateral and trilateral alliances. Mrs Thatcher did not refer to the precursors of such alliances, namely those used to restrain and deter Wilhelmian Germany before the First World War. However, her instinct was clearly pre-Churchillian rather than post-Churchillian, pre-First World War rather than post-Second World War. Such alliances exemplify the traditional power diplomacy of the nineteenth century and, as she so accurately foresaw, are inconceivable in a European Union.

Thus there were for her only two ways to prevent the nightmare materialising. One was to prevent German reunification, the other to frustrate European integration. As it proved impossible to stop German reunification, the solution to the problem imposed by the Second World War, namely the division of Germany, no longer applied. The only course for the future was to prevent Europe becoming a coherent and cohesive union, so that the balance of power could once more have free play.

All of this did not detract from Margaret Thatcher's opposition to communist rule in Eastern Germany. She deplored communism wherever she found it and she had no wish to perpetuate the dictatorship of the Communist Party in the so-called German Democratic Republic. However, the fact was that her fear of German power was greater than her repugnance to Soviet influence. She was concerned to protect Gorbachev's position and she was irritated that he was less stout in his own defence than she was willing to be. In one of the most extraordinary turns in the saga of Margaret Thatcher's relationship with Germany she went so far as to propose to President Bush during a telephone conversation on 24 February 1990 that it would be best if at least some of the Soviet forces in Eastern Germany were allowed to stay for a transitional period *'without any specific terminal date..'*. She emphasised to a somewhat bewildered US President that:

One had to remember that Germany was surrounded by countries, most of which it had attacked or occupied on mainland Europe in the course of this century. Looking well into the future *only the Soviet Union – or its successor – could provide such a balance ... to German dominance in Europe.*

As she comments in her memoirs:

President Bush, as I afterwards learnt, failed to understand that I was discussing a long term balance of power in Europe rather than proposing an alternative alliance to NATO. It was the last time that I relied on a telephone conversation to explain such matters.

Nevertheless, this telephone exchange was the clearest indication that when push came to shove Margaret Thatcher was willing to do all in her power to slow German reunification. Her preferred solution was for a democratic but independent Eastern Germany in harmony with its Western neighbours.

Surprisingly this most fundamental confrontation of German and British positions does not seem to have involved direct personal acrimony between Helmut Kohl and Margaret Thatcher. Only at one point did she become furious. This concerned Helmut Kohl's famous ten point speech to the Bundestag at the close of 1989. In it, the Chancellor spelt out the road to reunification, stating for the first time to the parliament that the goal was nothing less than the unity of the German state. For Margaret Thatcher, this was a development 'without any previous consultation with his allies and in clear breach of, at least, the spirit of the Paris Summit'. The fifth of Kohl's ten points was the proposal to develop confederate structures between the two German states with the goal of creating a federation. His tenth point was a commitment by his government to work towards unity and reunification. Mrs Thatcher felt that this speech was at best devious and manipulative, at worst a betrayal of the Chancellor's friends and allies. Advisers on both sides, who were close to the events, are in retrospect less apocalyptic. Charles Powell remembers that his colleague in Bonn, Horst Teltschik, did not feel the German government to be steering events, but rather pursuing them. Reunification was being made by popular opinion on the ground in Eastern Germany rather than being manoeuvred from Bonn. He also feels that in general terms the thrust of Kohl's speech was known in advance, a recollection confirmed by other Germans close to the event. Whatever the truth of the matter, however, Margaret Thatcher felt betrayed.

Kohl's imperturbability is less easy to explain. Certainly he was fully aware of Margaret Thatcher's position. After all, Charles Powell had explained it with great clarity to Horst Teltschik. Probably he was more offended and shocked by François Mitterrand's attitude than by Margaret Thatcher's. Mitterrand was his friend and ally. Germany's special relationship was with France and yet Mitterrand, both in conversations with Margaret Thatcher and in his somewhat frantic consultations with political leaders in Poland, Russia and East Germany, evidenced a deep disquiet at German reunification. In Charles Powell's view, François Mitterrand's opposition to the creation of the single German state made Margaret Thatcher's contribution 'pale by comparison'. It may be that the French President's reaction, together with that of Mrs Thatcher, confirmed Kohl in his determination to press ahead with the next stage of European integration. The Maastricht Treaty was Kohl's answer to the fears of Germany's neighbours. He was willing to be bound in, even to the extent of sacrificing the Deutschmark itself. Yet while his neighbours' concerns fuelled his Europeanism, they do not seem to have disturbed his sleep. The probable explanation is that Kohl had indeed sensed the 'mantle of fate' and had the confidence of a man who has grasped it with both hands.

In essence, no western country could deny the Germans their right of self-determination and the one power that could do so, the Soviet Union, no longer wished to. This was decisive.

Chancellor Kohl may indeed have had a more perceptive understanding of Margaret Thatcher's agony than was realised at the time. Hermann von Richthofen claims that the Chancellor understood very well that Britain had sacrificed her Empire, her economy and her world position to stop Nazism. Given this, the re-emergence of a united, powerful and successful Germany must have seemed a bitter outcome. What the Chancellor could not understand was the way in which the Prime Minister allowed this sentiment to overwhelm her own commitment to democracy and self-determination. She seemed to be denying to the Germans what she proclaimed as the right of every other nation. Significantly Charles Powell emphasises Margaret Thatcher's sense of the 'injustice' of this reunification. Britain had given all to stop Germany coming out on top and yet this was the result.

It is at this point that one must step back from the events and emotions of the time and ask whether, in the confrontation of policies and personalities, real as opposed to imagined interests were at stake. Were these real rivalries or simply old memories revisited?

The answers vary. The three issues of divergence and disagreement – short-range nuclear weapons in Europe, the European Community budget and the linked questions of reunification and European integration – were each very different.

In retrospect, Margaret Thatcher's insistence on the modernisation and deployment of short-range nuclear weapons on German soil did not represent a critical British interest. She saw the issue above all else as a test of German fidelity to NATO. Any weakness implied the Germans being soft on the Soviet Union and possibly – the ultimate nightmare – trading neutrality for unification. In the event, Kohl's greatest diplomatic achievement was undoubtedly to negotiate the unification of his country without compromising its membership of NATO. Indeed, unification was to mark the territorial advance of NATO. In her memoirs, Margaret Thatcher simply notes the outcome of Kohl's talks with Gorbachev at the crucial meeting in Stavropol in the Caucasus in July of 1990; she does not congratulate him on it. Yet this outcome was surely an astonishing achievement. For decades both sides in the Cold War had been mesmerised by the possibility of removing the Iron Curtain at the price of German neutrality. Now the border had gone, yet Germany remained firmly anchored in the NATO alliance. Thus her concern over Kohl's 'wobbliness' on nuclear armaments proved unnecessary.

On the question of Britain's money and the European Community budget, clear national interests were involved. It was important to the United Kingdom that an unfair contribution should be rectified – not just on an occasional basis but as part of a permanent readjustment. This was a real victory for Margaret Thatcher and one which the Germans recognised as irritating but fair. Was there, however, a clash of national interests involved? In essence not, for Germany also gained from an acceptance that net contributors could not forever provide Europe with a blank cheque. As the Community's paymaster, Germany had a greater interest in this recognition of reality, particularly by southern member states, than any other. National interest was involved for both Britain and Germany but not in substantive opposition to each other.

It is on reunification and European integration that the clash between Margaret Thatcher and Helmut Kohl expressed a profound difference of perceived national interest. Yet here again the issue is far from clear cut. For example, one aspect of Margaret Thatcher's concern was Germany's position in eastern Europe. According to Margaret Thatcher's memoirs, in her conversations with President Mitterrand at the Elysée Palace on 20 January 1990 the President had shared her worries about the Germans' so-called 'mission' in eastern Europe. She recalls 'I said that we must not just accept that the Germans had a particular hold over these countries but rather do everything possible to expand our own links there'. In the event, however, Germany's 'mission' in eastern European countries has translated principally into an advocacy of their membership of the European Union, a cause equally supported by Britain. It may well be that Britain and Germany favour the enlargement of the European Union to embrace Poland, the Czech and Slovak Republics and Hungary for different reasons. The Germans fear chaos at their eastern borders and will feel safer with eastern Europe snugly incorporated into the Union. The British Government favours eastward expansion in order to stabilise those countries and at the same time somewhat dilute the European Union. The fact is, however, that eastern Europe is not a cockpit of conflicting German and British interests.

There are, however, two specific and crucially important areas of perceived disagreement and difference of national interest. The first turns on Britain's relative position in the world after German reunification. The second involves the transfer of British national and parliamentary sovereignty to Brussels.

The impact of German reunification on Britain's role in the world has centred around two bilateral relationships. The first is the Franco-German 'axis' as Margaret Thatcher chose to describe it. The other is Britain's 'special relationship' with the United States.

The Franco-German alliance, with its historic roots in the agreement struck between Konrad Adenauer and Charles de Gaulle, has long irritated Britain's political establishment. The British have striven to accept the relationship with good grace, arguing that it is in everyone's interest, including Britain's, that the age-old enmity between France and Germany has ended. However, in so far as the Franco-German axis has excluded Britain from influence, and indeed from a presence, at the heart of Europe, it is privately deplored by the country's political leaders. That it has done so for so long may well represent a spectacular 'own goal' by successive British Governments. By being the reluctant Europeans, the British again and again have confirmed the very Franco-German axis they so dislike. However, the events of German reunification in 1989-90 confirmed in a brutal manner the primacy of the relationship between Paris and Bonn. In conversation President Mitterrand repeatedly shared, endorsed and echoed Margaret Thatcher's own dislike of German unity. At their meeting at the Elysée Palace on 20 January 1990 he was open about his frustration, 'That unless you were wholeheartedly for reunification you were described as an enemy of Germany'. The difference between his position and that of the Prime Minister was that he simply did not believe that anything could be done to stop German reunification. Margaret Thatcher's anger at this commonality of position rendered ineffective by pusillanimity of public expression was acute. She had waved in front of a startled President a map that she kept in her handbag showing Germany's prewar borders, warning him that this could be the Germany of tomorrow. However, as she herself recalls it:

> Mitterrand had a choice between moving ahead faster towards a Federal Union in order to tie down the German giant or to abandon this approach and return to that associated with General de Gaulle – the defence of French sovereignty and the striking up of alliances to secure French interests. He made the wrong decisions for France... but it must be said that his judgement that there was nothing we could do to halt German reunification turned out to be right.

In her view, one reason why things did turn out this way was simply France's unwillingness to compromise its special relationship with Germany. Thus reunification confirmed the Franco-German axis and enhanced it because Germany's augmented power strengthened the imperative of binding her into Europe.

German reunification also seemed to confirm the weakening of the special relationship across the Atlantic. For Margaret Thatcher this special relationship was an article of faith. As she said frequently, and as Ronald Reagan also believed, 'The ties of blood, language, culture and values which bound Britain and America were the only firm basis for US policy in the West'. In her memoirs, she adds ironically, 'Only a very clever person could fail to appreciate something so obvious!' President Bush turned out to be just such a clever person, as did his Secretary of State, James Baker. The argument that only a united Europe could check German power was in her judgement 'propagated by the French but swallowed by the United States State Department too'. It had the additional benefit as an argument for the Americans that 'a German-led United Europe would allow the Americans to cut back on the amount they spent on Europe's defence.'

In his account of the Thatcher government, Lord Howe looks at this switch in American priorities with a cool, professional eye:

> The United Kingdom was only one of five medium-sized European nations and by no means the most successful or influential in Continental politics, so neither Bush nor Baker was likely to accept the thesis which Margaret Thatcher had enunciated.

That thesis was, of course, that the special relationship with Britain alone was the only sure foundation for the Atlantic alliance and US policy in Europe.

German reunification threatened that power relationship in international affairs which the British Prime Minister most treasured. At the same time it confirmed Britain's exclusion from the key relationship between the Germans and the French. The combination of these two developments certainly led to a diminution of British influence and prestige. There was, thus, a tangible clash of national interest.

Margaret Thatcher's opposition to political integration in Europe is too well known to need recounting. It may well be that, as was later claimed, she had not read the small print of the Single European Act and had thus failed to understand that its economic provisions were designed to further political integration as well. What is undeniable is that Margaret Thatcher saw the Single European Act and the creation of the Single Market in 1992 as the end point of the process of integration. She did not wish to go further. Certainly she was implacably opposed to all the objectives so often expounded by Helmut Kohl – the strengthening of the European Parliament, the move to a European currency, the expansion of the European dimension of policy-making in social affairs, security questions and foreign policy. All this would erode the sovereignty of Westminster and nullify the proud defiance of Britain in 1940. Far from believing, as Helmut Kohl did, that any halt in Europe's integration could lead to disintegration and retreat, Margaret Thatcher's conviction was that any further integration would lead to eventual break-up and disharmony. Their analyses were incompatible.

Yet, again, the question has to be asked whether these analyses reflected a true difference of national interest. The jury is out. There are those who would argue that even though Maastricht may have been 'a treaty too far', Britain's national interest is best pursued from within an integrating Europe rather than outside its borders. The argument continues to divide British politics and British parties as well as British public opinion. Margaret Thatcher's concluding position as Prime Minister was resoundingly hammered home in her last speech to the House of Commons. What should Britain's reaction be to further steps down the European road? She had no doubt: 'No, no, no'.

The relationship between Margaret Thatcher and Helmut Kohl was unique. Both leaders embodied political skills and instincts which each admired in the other. Both leaders were careful to give to the other the dignity of office which both felt they deserved. However, both leaders sensed an incompatibility of policy, position and interest. Towards the close of Margaret Thatcher's premiership these differences became increasingly acute and public. The arguments live on today with growing resonance. 'Good friends and bad relations' has become something of a cliché in defining the position of the two countries. As has been argued, it is open to dispute whether this is indeed accurate and certainly whether it is inevitable. Anglo-German rivalry is a fact of the past. Whether or not it need be a characteristic of the future lies with the governments of both nations. It is evident that, whatever the differences may be, the greater interest of both countries is to continue the partnership and friendship which has achieved so much in the post-war period. Should rivalry persist and grow, the interests of both will suffer. History places a mighty responsibility on political leadership in both Germany and Britain. It teaches the cost of confrontation. Konrad Adenauer always argued that wisdom in politics consists in avoiding the avoidable mistakes of the past. He was surely right.

The Theory and Practice of Delorism

Charles Grant

Jacques Delors did more than any individual since Jean Monnet to advance the cause of a united Europe. He made such an impact because he combined qualities that are rare in a single politician. Most modern politicians are fixers who get things done: George Bush and Bill Clinton, François Mitterrand and Jacques Chirac, Felipe González and John Major have been essentially managers of parties and governments. Of course, they have had their principles and ideals, some a little bit to the left, and some a little bit to the right. But their emphasis on pragmatism has often meant that the business of solving short-term problems buries the principles and ideals.

Then there are ideologues and thinkers, strategists who generate ideas and have a vision of how society, or the political system, needs changing. Not many of these intellectuals flourish in the real world of politics. They generally reside in think tanks or academia, perhaps with hopes of becoming a ministerial adviser. Some of them become mainstream politicians – Tony Crosland and Keith Joseph in Britain, Pierre Mendès-France and Alain Madelin in France, Newt Gingrich in the United States, Oskar Lafontaine in Germany – but few are great successes.

Jacques Delors is one of the few politicians who possesses both sorts of quality. No other recent European leader – except perhaps for Margaret Thatcher – has paid such attention to ideas and to implementation, to ideology and to detail, to principle and to power.

This essay explores Delors's political and social ideas; his methods of putting them into practice; and, finally, some of the adverse results of those methods. But first, it is worth recalling Delors's achievements (defined as such if they promoted his goal of European integration), for the problems which beset his last years at the Commission have tended to obscure them. Arriving in Brussels in 1985, Delors decided that the creation of a single market by the end of 1992 would be the Commission's chief priority. He had a big hand in the Single European Act (SEA), the constitutional reform which allowed the '1992 programme' to be implemented. The success of that project gave the EC the confidence and momentum to aim for more ambitious targets, and attracted the interest of countries in the European Free Trade Association (EFTA). He thought up the European Economic Area, which extended the single market to five members of EFTA (three of which, Austria, Finland and Sweden, joined the European Union – as the EC became in November 1993 – in January 1995, the month that Delors retired).

There would not have been a treaty on economic and monetary union (EMU) if Delors had not cajoled Helmut Kohl and the other leaders into appointing the Delors Committee in 1988. If and when Europe has a monetary union, the central bank will be based on the design – Delorist in parts – of the Maastricht Treaty of 1991. Some of that treaty's provisions for political union disappointed Delors, yet it was he, in the autumn of 1989, who propelled the EC towards that goal. In 1989 and 1990, Delors welcomed German reunification warmly and ensured East Germany's smooth entry into the EC. He helped to conclude 'Europe agreements' with six East European states, thereby tightening their political and economic ties to the EC.

Delors played a central role in the negotiation of the budgetary packages of 1988 and 1992, which would, among other things, quadruple the regional aid budget. He oversaw two reforms of the Common Agricultural Policy (CAP), which cut its share of the EC budget from 65 percent to 45 percent. He invented the Social Charter, the 'social action plan' of employment laws and – at the Maastricht summit – the 'social chapter'. In 1993 Delors provoked a wide-ranging debate on the causes of European unemployment.

That is not a bad record for a man who, having been born into a poor Parisian family in 1925, had little formal education; whose father stopped him going to university so that he could, at the age of 19, become a clerk in the Banque de France; who always felt ill at ease in political parties and so disliked elections that he never stood for France's National Assembly; and who did not become a minister until the age of 55, or Commission President until the age of 59.

The foundations of Delorism

When I began to research a biography of Jacques Delors, Pascal Lamy, his *chef de cabinet* for most of the time that he was president, told me that if I wanted to understand Delors I should read Emmanuel Mounier. This Roman Catholic philosopher, who died in 1950, is now largely forgotten. But in the 1940s and 1950s Mounier's doctrine of 'personalism' had a huge impact on a generation of young, left-wing French Catholics that included Delors. Personalism aimed for a middle way between communism, which denied the individual, and liberalism, which denied the community. But personalism is not just another word for social democracy, for it has an ethical dimension. Mounier wrote: 'Man masters himself through his relationship with other people and things, in work and in camaraderie, in friendship, in love, in action, in meeting, and not through standoffishness'.

When I had read Mounier and then heard Delors say that 'the individual is a person who cannot be reduced to other people, and who cannot live without participating in communities which bind him to other people,' I realised that Delors remains, to this day, an ardent personalist. But I doubted that personalism had much to do with the politics he practised in Brussels. Since finishing the biography, however, I have become convinced that many of Delors's most important principles – federalism, subsidiarity, opposition to Anglo-Saxon capitalism, belief in a 'European model of society' and support for a communitarian version of socialism – derive, at least indirectly, from personalism.

Delors says that personalism remains his principal analytical tool for understanding life and people. Like Mounier, he mistrusts the world of politics and has, throughout his career, been torn between the desire to remain pure and analytical on the out-side, and the wish to join the *mêlée* in an effort to implement his ideas. The last time that Delors confronted this dilemma was at the end of 1994, when he had to decide whether to be a candidate for the French presidency. Delors's decision not to run confounded the cynics who had presumed that his apparent lack of ambition was an act and that, in reality, he was just as power-crazed as the next politician.

Much of Mounier's writing is an angry polemic against totalitarianism and liberal capitalism. 'The classical notion of man has been broken up: people affirm the absolute of the individual, the race, the class, the nation'. The modern world had divided man into little pieces. 'Each broken fragment withers on its own: we search to rebuild him, to bring together his body and his mind, meditation and works, thought and action.' Like Marx, Mounier stressed the unity of theory and practice. 'Man is only man when committed.'

Throughout his career, Delors has been a strong critic of the atomism of modern western society, and especially of American *laissez-faire* capitalism. That reflects, in part, France's traditional penchant for Colbert rather than Adam Smith. But some of Delors's vehemence – such as when he tried to stop a GATT deal in 1992, rather than cede to what he saw as American 'bullying' over cuts in farm subsidies – stems from his personalism. Liberalism, wrote Mounier, was 'linked to individualism, its dominant trait is strongly egocentric, it saps the essence of our humanity, which is not only about worrying about how to co-exist within the mutual limitation of our fantasies, but also about collaboration, devotion, a common destiny and sacrifice for the common future'.

Delors's Mounierist view of socialism is close to the 'communitarianism' now in vogue in Britain and the United States. For Delors, socialism is not primarily about equality, efficiency, power or an ideological analysis of economic forces. It is about morality: the way individuals, groups and institutions treat people. He has defined socialism as 'a rejection of the idea that each individual stays in his niche. The individual should become a social being, participate in collective life and see his civic spirit raised'. Delors stresses that each individual is morally responsible for his actions. 'I never believed the state could make people happy. You have to allow everyone to fulfil themselves and that means giving them a margin of manoeuvre; each person should have his chances and take his responsibilities. Thus liberty, responsibility and solidarity go together.'

One of Delors's obsessions in Brussels was the need to preserve a 'European model of society'. He has defined this as:

> Different from the Japanese model in that it doesn't exert so much psychological or sociological pressure on the individual, and allows a bit more space for self-fulfilment. But society is more present than it is in the United States. The Europeans have always found a kind of balance between the individual and society. That goes back to the basis of their civilisation, to Christianity, to Roman Law, to the Greek *civitas*, and in the recent period, to the influence of social democracy.

In other words, European society comes closer to Delors's personalist ideal than does American or Japanese society. Delors attributes three essential characteristics to the model:

> First, a social and economic system founded on the role of the market. Second, we have a state which intervenes, regulates and fills lacunae left by the market. The third element is the role of professional bodies and trade unions, the 'social partners', which help to make people more responsible. There are no longer enough of such intermediary groups, between the state and the individual, with the result that political leaders are often unduly guided by opinion polls. These three elements have to, on the one hand, produce enough competitiveness to maintain the standard of living and to prevent unemployment from rising, and, on the other, provide citizens with cover against the risks of sickness, old age and so on. Leave on one side the less essential question of redistribution of wealth: you can favour a European model which is strongly redistributive, or one that is less so.

When European unemployment began to rise, in the early 1990s, Delors worried that the EC's faltering competitiveness would undermine the European model. So he persuaded the governments to ask the Commission to produce a white paper, 'Growth, competitiveness, employment', for the Brussels summit of December 1993. The central message of the white paper, much of which he wrote himself, was that governments had to liberalise labour markets if the European model was to survive. The white paper argued that some EU countries should allow employers to sack workers more easily, and that others should cut unemployment benefits, taxes on low incomes and minimum wages. They should all reduce the non-wage costs of employment.

Many of the governments have, subsequently, followed some of these prescriptions, but they have not done enough to reduce European rates of unemployment to American levels. Since leaving the Commission Delors has spent a lot of his time worrying about how to save the European model. He has become critical of welfare states in which 'this desire for equity has led to an excess of welfare, where nobody is responsible for anything'. He would favour a pensions system that, in addition to the state pension, gave people incentives to take out personal plans. 'The problem with a purely collective system is not only that it requires economic growth, and the right sort of demographic trends, but also that it doesn't make people think about their futures in a responsible way. If social democrats are not capable of founding a welfare system which is fairer, and gives a sense of responsibility to everyone, they'll be defeated by the disciples of Hayek, whose system – although harsh and unpitying – at least allows one responsibility.' Delors's insistence on moral responsibility is rooted in his Christianity and personalism.

When Delors was Commission President, of course, he had no sway over welfare states. But he managed to nurture the European model in other ways. In 1988 Delors and the European Parliament became frustrated that a dialogue between ETUC, the European confederation of trade unions, and UNICE, the European employers' lobby, had borne little fruit. So he launched an EC 'social dimension' which included the Social Charter, a set of non-binding statements on workers' rights, and the 'social action programme', with twenty-seven proposals for binding directives. Many of these directives were passed, despite opposition from the British government. One gave mothers the right to 13 weeks of maternity leave, with pay of no less than health benefits in their country; a second set a maximum working week of 48 hours (with exceptions) and a minimum of four weeks annual paid holiday; a third regulated the hours that children could work.

Delors had several reasons for steering the EC into social policy. He worried that the 1992 programme was making the EC seem like a cornucopia for capitalists, and that the trade unions might therefore oppose it. He listened to the unions' complaints about social dumping – the idea that investment would flow to countries with the lightest labour regulations – and to their pleas for directives to prevent it. But when asked to justify EC involvement in social legislation, he said that some directives – such as that limiting child labour – aimed not so much to limit social dumping, but rather to 'express common European values'.

Delors wanted the EC's social dimension to strengthen the role of trade unions. That had been an *idée fixe* of Delors, ever since he became active in the *Confédération Française des Travailleurs Chrétiens* in the 1950s. He believes that, beyond the unions' practical benefits to their members, they are a crucial part of civil society, and that the richness of that civil society is a strength of the European model.

When Delors worked in the *cabinet* of Jacques Chaban-Delmas, France's Gaullist prime minister from 1969 to 1972, he promoted '*la politique contractuelle*'. That is untranslatable but has some of the meaning of 'social contract' and 'corporatism'. The idea was that the two sides of industry should negotiate regularly. That was an innovation in France, where the government and employers had, to a large extent, ignored the trade unions. Nationalised industry by nationalised industry, Delors persuaded the managers and the unions to agree on contracts which set out procedures for negotiating on pay and conditions; some contracts set formulae for future pay increases. Delors had another success with 'formation permanent', adult training. He asked the trade unions and the employers to negotiate a national convention on training, which the government then turned into a law. The Loi Delors, as it was known, gave all employees the right to training throughout their careers, and obliged the government and the employers to find the money.

At the Commission Delors tried to create a kind of EC-wide politique contractuelle. During the intergovernmental conference (IGC) on political union in 1991, he suggested that, if the social partners could agree on pan-European conventions, the results could be turned into EU law. That became one of the most contentious provisions of the Maastricht treaty's social chapter – the others being that laws on working conditions and worker consultation would be subject to qualified majority voting. John Major would not accept the social chapter at the Maastricht summit, and it needed Delors's negotiating skill to break the deadlock. He thought up the scheme whereby 11 countries would 'opt in' to the social chapter, leaving Britain outside.

It is too early to tell if the pan-European conventions will come to much. UNICE and ETUC tried to negotiate an agreement on worker consultation, but UNICE pulled out because of opposition from British employers. The Commission then resorted to a directive which, passed in 1994, requires about 1,200 multi-national companies to set up workers' councils. Because Britain did not sign the social chapter, these companies do not have to invite British workers onto the councils; in practice most of them have thought it good for labour relations to do so. Then, in 1995, the social partners agreed to a convention giving all new parents the right to three months unpaid leave; this may soon be EU law.

Another Delorist influence on the Maastricht treaty was the clause on 'subsidiarity'. In areas which did not fall within the EC's exclusive competence, the treaty said, it 'shall take action only if and in so far as the objectives of the proposed action cannot be sufficiently achieved by the member-states and can therefore, by reason of the scale or of the effects of the proposed action, be better achieved by the Community'. Delors would not have got that clause without support from the British, who thought subsidiarity would curb overweening Brussels institutions, and the Germans, who thought it would transfer their own federal principles to the EC.

Delors began to champion subsidiarity in 1988, when he found it a useful tactic for deflecting the criticism that the EC had become too intrusive. But the principle also lay close to his deepest-held beliefs. Popes Leo XIII and Pius IX had made subsidiarity a foundation of the social teaching of the Roman Catholic Church. They thought it should guide relations between society and the individual, and between social groups of different levels. It meant that society should respect the autonomy of the person, but also that it should create the conditions which allowed the individual to flourish. Delors liked the idea of the higher levels of government taking a paternal interest in those below them. He told the European Parliament in 1991 that subsidiarity is not only about limiting the intervention of a superior authority, but also 'an obligation on this authority, *vis-à-vis* the persons or groups at a lower level, to provide the means for their self-fulfilment'.

When Delors defines federalism as 'a clear distinction between the levels of power,' he makes it sound like subsidiarity. The virtue of federalism is to 'allow people to live together, while retaining their diversity, because the division of powers is clear. I'm for a federal Europe not to increase the powers of the Community but because one knows who does what'.

Jacques Delors's federalism, of course, is based on many more influences, experiences and ideologies than personalism. Delors has never described in detail the kind of European federation that he would like to see. That is probably wise. Like Marx, who refused to describe a communist society, Delors knows that history is a process that does not stop at any given state. But from what Delors has said and written, one can infer something of his vision.

The 'institutional triad' that Monnet first invented for the European Coal and Steel Community (ECSC) – the Commission (which began as the High Authority), Parliament and Council of Ministers – must, at all costs, be maintained. In particular, the Commission should retain its monopoly of the right to initiate legislation, which allows it to set the EU's agenda and is its principal source of strength. In the long run Delors would like the influence of the Council of Ministers, which represents the national governments, to diminish, and that of the Parliament and the Commission to grow. The Commission would evolve into an EU executive, responsible to the Parliament. The Council of Ministers would become a senate-style revising chamber, leaving the Parliament the major say on legislation. Delors has said very little about the European Court of Justice, whose rulings have done much to advance European integration; he appears to be suspicious of judges becoming involved in politics.

Delors believes that the member states should transfer interest-rate policy, the co-ordination of macro-economic policy and some of their foreign and defence policy to EU institutions. Decisions in these and other areas of EU competence should normally be taken by majority vote. Delors believes that, if Europe fails to build a tighter and stronger federation, it risks becoming dependent on America or Japan. In that sense Delors is a European nationalist.

Delors spent ten years at the head of an institution whose *raison d'être* is European unity. Since the Commission would benefit from a more unified EU, almost all its commissioners and presidents become federalists in the job. But Delors was a believer before he arrived. Little of Delors's federalism stems directly from Mounier, who was unsympathetic to the idea of a united Europe. Mounier apart, however, France's left-wing Catholic milieu was fervently federalist in the post-war years.

Many of the founding fathers of the ECSC, such as Robert Schuman, Alcide De Gaspari and Konrad Adenauer, had been strong Catholics. *Citoyen 60*, the review which Delors edited from 1959 to 1965, carried editorials in favour of a federal Europe and monetary union.

Two years in the European Parliament, from 1979 to 1981, stimulated Delors's curiosity in the Community, but it took the experience of being French finance minister, from 1981 to 1984, to convince him that France could not solve its economic problems alone. During the franc crisis of March 1983, when Mitterrand had to decide whether to continue with 'reflation in one country' and let the franc float, or to impose austerity and stay in the Exchange Rate Mechanism (ERM), Delors persuaded him to choose the path of Europe. Since then French governments of left and right have followed Delors's strategy of conquering inflation through a *franc fort*. 'I've always believed in the European ideal, but today it's no longer a simple question of idealism, it's a matter of necessity,' he said in 1983.

Jean Monnet, whose portrait hung in Delors's Brussels office, was a huge source of inspiration. Delors consciously sought to emulate Monnet's methods and to build on his work. He never met Monnet, who died in 1979, but read his *Memoirs* when they appeared in 1976. Delors absorbed, from Monnet, a great distrust of 'inter-governmental' bodies in which decision-making required unanimity. Delors would not have struggled so hard against the inter-governmental 'pillars' of the Maastricht treaty, which covered foreign policy and judicial affairs, if he had not shared Monnet's conviction that inter-governmental meant inefficient.

Monnet believed in the potential beneficence of supranational bodies, saying that 'human nature cannot be changed, but common rules and institutions, which bind and protect at the same time, can change behaviour for the better'. He said that in the Community's worst moments, the European spirit survived in the institutions, which 'once created have their own force, that supersedes the will of man'. Delors shares that faith and has described the Commission as 'a militant memory of European construction'. Delors also owed to Monnet his method for promoting European integration, of which more later.

Indirectly, Delors's federalism does mesh with his personalism. At the most obvious level, he believes that individuals cannot fulfil themselves except in a community; and he thinks that European nations can achieve more in a community than on their own. Beyond that, both are tied to his idea of subsidiarity. He said in August 1995:

In my mind personalism and federalism have always been strongly linked. They both believe in devolving authority to the lowest possible level. And also that the lower levels should have the means to fulfil their roles. At all levels of society, responsibilities need to be clearly defined, and clearly assured. In that there is a complete coherence between federalism and communitarian personalism.

Delorism in practice

All these ideas drove and inspired Delors. His historical significance, however, rests on the practice rather than the theory of Delorism. When Delors arrived in Brussels he found a Commission that had drifted, rudderless, for many years. It had few successes to its credit and scant respect from the rest of the world. Individual commissioners and officials ran parts of the organisation as semi-independent fiefs. Discipline was slack, working hours were short and morale was low.

Ten years later, Delors had changed the course of European history, despite the fact that a politician can more easily make a mark on a national government than on European institutions. The constitutions of nation-states are hierarchical: a prime minister or president with a parliamentary majority has huge opportunities for bringing about change. The European Union, by contrast, is a complex network of supranational bodies (the Commission, the European Parliament and the Court of Justice), inter-governmental bodies (the Council of Ministers) and national governments. The three sorts of institution contribute to the legislative and to the executive process. For instance, both the Council of Ministers and the Commission take decisions on aspects of the CAP, while national governments administer those decisions.

The links between the various bodies are horizontal. The EU has no leader with a strong executive authority. Ultimately, the Council of Ministers takes the most important legislative and executive decisions. Beforehand, however, officials from several parts of the Commission, the Council of Ministers' secretariat, the European Parliament and national ministries may be consulted. Euro-MPs, commissioners, junior ministers, EU ambassadors and hundreds of lobbyists may also be involved. Committees, 'working groups' and all-night meetings, rather than powerful individuals, are the cogs which drive this machinery forward. The Union never has been and never will be a right-wing or a left-wing entity; too many people of too many persuasions have to agree to the compromises. Decision making is so slow and consensual that decisive leadership from the centre is almost impossible – as Delors's predecessors discovered.

That Delors provided such leadership is remarkable, for the Commission President has few formal powers. He (there has yet to be a she) is *primus inter pares* among the college of 20 commissioners (17 in Delors's day). The President has one vote, like all the others. He gains some authority from having a seat at Group-of-Seven summits, and at EU meetings of heads of government and foreign ministers. And he does decide, after consulting the national capitals, which commissioner does which job. But should the President find a commissioner awkward, rebellious or just plain incompetent, he cannot sack him or her. Unlike ministers in a government, commissioners are not bound by a common affiliation to a party or coalition. They have little incentive to bury their differences for the common good or to respect the president.

Given this inheritance, how did Delors make such an indelible mark? Luck played its part. The Community had begun to regain momentum just before his arrival. The Fontainebleu summit of June 1984 settled five years of argument over Britain's budget contribution. Big business was worried about 'Eurosclerosis' and economic liberalism was coming into vogue. France, Germany and Britain, the most influential member-states, had strong leaders who believed that economic deregulation and some kind of institutional reform were necessary. Anyone becoming president of the Commission in January 1985 would have faced exciting opportunities. But it is doubtful that many people would have seized the opportunities with such skill as Delors.

Delors began by turning the Commission upside down. He gave it a sense of purpose and taught it to respond to his will. Power and ideas started to flow top-down instead of bottom-up.

He brought about this revolution by concentrating power in the presidency. He could not have done so without Pascal Lamy, the *chef de cabinet* who planned and implemented the presidential regime. Lamy's intellect, energy, efficiency and forcefulness are impressive. He chose and trained Delors's *cabinet* (private office) as an elite squad of commandos, dedicated to enforcing the President's will. As George Ross has noted, their task was 'to make the Commission function more like a real government and less like a college, while simultaneously preserving the collegiate forms and ethos'.

Lamy designed a system to suit the President's strengths and weaknesses.

> From my experience of working with Delors [when he was finance minister], I knew what he liked and didn't like doing, and what he could and could not do. It was like designing a custom-built car for a driver who has particular skills. If you want to make good use of Delors's resources, you should leave strategy, communication and negotiation to him, and take care of the rest.

So Lamy's role was to run the administration, which never interested Delors, and to be ruthless when necessary, for Delors disliked personal confrontations. Lamy also had to push Delors to take decisions, for he is inclined to procrastinate.

The Delors *cabinet* was more hierarchical than those of most other commissioners. Its members seldom met as a group and did not see the President unless he happened to be working on their subject. The *chef de cabinet* alone had an overview of their work. The point of the hierarchy was to save Delors time. Unlike a typical managerial politician, whose work revolves around briefings from staff and meetings, Delors liked to spend time by himself, reading, thinking and writing.

Delors and Lamy worked symbiotically. Lamy's cool and sober temperament balanced Delors's changeable emotions. Lamy's down-to-earth realism restrained Delors's flights of fancy. As Jérôme Vignon, head of the Cellule de Prospective, the Commission's in-house think tank, once remarked, 'Lamy's role is to listen to Delors's twenty ideas and tell him which are the nineteen which will not work'.

Lamy helped Delors to guard his moral image. When something nasty happened in the Commission, people assumed Lamy and not Delors was responsible. Lamy set the style – aggressive, dedicated and frugal – for the Delors *cabinet*, which, in turn, transmitted these values to many other parts of the Commission. When members of the Delors team leaned on, shouted at or bullied other officials, the justification was simple: there was no other way to get things done.

Delors's system of command and control depended on more than his *cabinet*. He and Lamy installed their own men in key posts, creating a network of supporters. The point of the network, like the *cabinet*, was to gather information and to carry out the President's wishes. In 1987 Jean-Louis Dewost, a Frenchman, replaced a German as head of the legal service. Vignon took over the Cellule de Prospective in 1989. In 1990 Bruno Dethomas, Delors's spokesman, became chief spokesman of the Commission. The boundaries between the *cabinet* and the secretariat-general – whose job was to co-ordinate the work of the various directorates-general, and which reported directly to the President – became blurred. David Williamson, the Briton who became secretary-general in 1987, became one of Delors's most trusted aides. Ironically, Williamson became more enmeshed in the Delors network than his predecessor, the Frenchman Emile Noël, had been.

The *cabinet* of Sir Leon Brittan, who was competition commissioner and later trade commissioner under Delors, criticised Williamson for allowing Lamy to tamper with the minutes of Commission meetings. An official of the secretariat-general took the minutes and passed them to the President's *cabinet*. The minutes were then returned to the secretariat-general, sometimes amended to make it appear that there was more support for the President's viewpoint than there had been. The college of commissioners had to approve the final version of the minutes, but, given the President's clout, few commissioners dared to oppose the 'corrections' which Lamy had insisted on.

The 'Delors mafia' – as its enemies called the network – strengthened during Delors's second term (1989 to 1992) and third term (1993 to January 1995). Riccardo Perissich, an able Italian and a Delors loyalist, became director-general for the single market in 1990. Jean-Louis Cadieux, a friend of Lamy, took charge of eastern Europe in the same year. In 1993 Gunter Burghardt, a German who had been Delors's deputy *chef de cabinet* in his first term, became director-general for foreign policy.

Delors and his cabinet became increasingly dependent on the network, especially when important tasks had to be carried out rapidly. In July 1989, when the Paris G7 summit asked the Commission to co-ordinate the West's aid to eastern Europe, Delors mobilised the network rather than the directors-general. The secretariat-general and the President's *cabinet* wrote the greater part of the budgetary packages which Delors launched in 1987 and 1992. The network drafted the Commission's contributions to the IGCs of 1986 and 1991; the commissioners did not even see the draft treaty on EMU – published in their name in December 1991 – before they read about it in the newspapers.

Any commissioner who wished to make a formal proposal was required by the rules to notify the president's *cabinet* ten days in advance. That allowed Lamy considerable control over the Commission's agenda: if he disliked a proposal he would badger the commissioner's *cabinet* to withdraw it, usually with success. The Delors *cabinet* justified all this centralisation in the name of efficiency. If every commissioner could propose amendments to presidential initiatives, noted one member, the results would be watered down and meaningless. 'You can't delegate much when there is no constitutional means of exerting authority.'

France's administrative tradition considers strategic thinking and centralisation to be virtues. *Hauts fonctionnaires* may have fewer qualms about the ends justifying the means than do civil servants in some countries. But Delors and Lamy did much more than import the French tradition to Brussels. They transformed a horizontal power structure into a vertical one, resembling a steep pyramid. The secretariat-general, the President's *cabinet* and Delors formed the apex. The formidable Sir Leon was one of the few commissioners to establish a foothold on the upper slopes of the pyramid. The weaker commissioners languished at the bottom, excluded from the decisions which mattered. Many of Delors's fellow commissioners were inconsequential politicians who made no mark on their portfolios and have already been forgotten. By appointing such people, the governments gave Delors a justification for augmenting his own power.

Delors the man

Delors's achievements depended as much on his personal qualities as on his method of managing the Commission. Few politicians can equal his energy, imagination, determination and cunning. Delors was no less dedicated to his work than Margaret Thatcher was to hers. On a typical day he entered the Commission's headquarters at 8 a.m. He would leave at 9 or 10 p.m., taking work home. And he spent most of the weekend working, either in the office or at home. His appetite for reading reminded Lamy of 'a whale who sucks in enormous quantities of water and keeps the plankton'. While reading, Delors fills small, grey notebooks with summaries and comments.

Having risen to prominence through hard work rather than birth or education – Delors attended evening classes for six years, instead of university – he understood that application was a source of power. He was influential at EC summits because he knew the nitty-gritty better than anyone else. His ability to explain complex issues succinctly – whether the principle of subsidiarity or Europe's failing competitiveness – gave him extra sway at such events. When Ruud Lubbers, the Dutch prime minister, chaired the Maastricht summit, he often interrupted the debate and asked Delors to summarise the issues and the position of each country. Delors would respond with an off-the-cuff speech of a few minutes, impressing even John Major with his objectivity.

The EC's prime ministers and foreign ministers often relied on Delors to unearth compromises where others could find none. Niels Ersbøll, the Danish secretary-general of the Council of Ministers in the Delors years, observed: 'No task is too humble for Delors to perform: he's the mechanic who works out the lowly details which make an agreement possible. He is brilliant at satisfying a country by finding tiny changes in a text, or a sum of money, which others would not have thought of because they would not have known the details.' Both the Brussels summit of 1988 and the Edinburgh summit of 1992 depended on Delors to put together the final agreements on the huge budgetry packages – for five years and seven years, respectively – which they settled.

A typical example of Delors's deal-making derring-do occurred at a foreign ministers' meeting in July 1993. There was deadlock on how to divide up 96 billion ecus of EC aid for backward regions. The Belgian presidency called Delors from his sickbed, where sciatica had laid him low. He arrived at 9.30 p.m., hobbling with a walking stick and under the influence of painkillers.

Delors invited each country's foreign minister and ambassador, country by country, to a 'confessional' in a small room. He held out slightly larger amounts of money than the Commission had previously offered. One ambassador recalls Delors being 'like a Turkish carpet salesman, applying rudeness, finesse, insight and diplomatic skill, all at the same time, while promising more than there really was'. When the ambassador demanded a larger portion of the regional budget for his country, Delors told him that he was crazy and had gone too far. Delors directed his curses at the ambassador, avoiding eye contact with the minister. 'If you think I'm not honest, say so!' he yelled. The most extraordinary aspect of Delors's performance, notes the ambassador, was that he guessed the minister's bottom line. If the Commission president had offered one ecu less, the minister would have vetoed the agreement. 'It was as if he had bugged our delegation room,' says the ambassador. The other ambassadors reported similar powers of divination on Delors's part.

By 6 a.m. everyone had accepted Delors's offers, but no one knew what they added up to, for nothing had been written down, except on a small scrap of paper that Delors himself carried. He had offered some countries an upper and a lower limit, rather than a precise amount, which made it hard to calculate the total. Some officials estimated that Delors had promised 1-2 billion ecus more than the 96 billion ecus available. The complexity of the EC's structural funds allowed him scope for creative accounting, yet he had taken risks. In October 1993, when the Commission published the exact amounts of each country's allotment, the Irish accused Delors of reneging on a promise and almost rebelled. But the deal stuck.

Delors's fertile imagination proved a constant source of strength. Some of his ideas – the EC 'social dimension', for instance – were inspired by fundamental principles; more often – as with the many compromises he forged – his ideas were solutions to particular problems. All through his career, Delors has relied on the force of his ideas to gain recognition. That is why, unlike his friend and rival, Michel Rocard, Delors has never been at ease in political parties. Delors has always preferred to work in political clubs, where the atmosphere is more congenial to intellectual debate.

In the early 1960s, when Delors edited *Citoyen 60*, and ran the club of the same name, he promoted schemes for *politique contractuelle* and decentralisation; subsequent French governments of left and right put several of these into practice. In the 1970s his new club, *Échange et Projets*, published a set of proposals for giving workers more statutory rights; many of these ended up in the *Lois Auroux*, passed when Delors was French minister of finance.

Since the principal task of the European Commission is to make proposals, the institution suited Delors perfectly. In 1985 he drafted several parts of the Single European Act, such as the 'co-operation procedure', which gave the European Parliament the power to amend some laws. In 1987 the governments approved Delors's suggestion that they should agree on a budgetry package of five years, to avoid the time-consuming annual haggle. In the Delors Report on EMU, in 1989, he was responsible for the emphasis on monetary union and economic convergence proceeding in parallel; that bridged the gap between those who thought one or the other should come first. In 1992 he sent the governments reams of paper on how the EC could, in practice, apply subsidiarity, while the following year he inspired the white paper on Europe's failing competitiveness.

Other than the right of proposal, a Commission President has few formal means of influencing European politics. His real clout depends on the informal links that he cultivates with national politicians, especially the prime ministers and foreign ministers. Men such as Felipe González, Ruud Lubbers, Giulio Andreotti, Geoffrey Howe, Wilfried Martens and Jean-Luc Dehaene appreciated Delors's personable, engaging character, and, more important, his usefulness. They agreed, some of the time, with his philosophy of European integration, and thought him so crucial to that process that he deserved favours.

At the Milan summit of June 1985, Andreotti, then Italy's foreign minister and in league with Delors, persuaded Bettino Craxi, Italy's prime minister, to call a vote on the holding of an intergovernmental conference (IGC). Mrs Thatcher, caught off guard, lost the vote. When the Luxembourg summit of December 1985 considered the fruit of that conference, Howe helped to convince Mrs Thatcher that she should sign the Single European Act. At the G7 summit in Paris, in July 1989, President Bush, having just lunched with Delors in the White House, ensured that the Commission won the job of co-ordinating the West's aid to eastern Europe. There were sometimes unstated trade-offs. In the autumn of 1992, for instance, González knew that Delors was committed to increases in the regional aid budget, while the Beneluxers feared that attempts by the large countries to weaken the Commission would lead to them dominating the EC. So when, at the Birmingham summit, the British floated new procedures for limiting the Commission's powers, González, Lubbers and Dehaene battled, successfully, against change.

Delors's most important friend, by far, was Helmut Kohl. In February 1988 Kohl broke the deadlock over Delors's first budgetary package by committing extra German cash. Soon afterwards Delors persuaded Kohl to support the idea of a single currency, and it was Kohl who suggested, at the Hanover summit of June 1988, that Delors should chair a committee on EMU. The following year, at the Strasbourg summit, Kohl overrode Theo Waigel, his finance minister, and Karl Otto Pöhl, his central bank governor, by agreeing on a starting date for the IGC on monetary union. And in 1990 and 1991, when the Commission came under attack in the negotiations on political union, Kohl – some of the time – was prepared to defend it.

Delors and Kohl hit it off personally. Both are inclined to strong emotions and a certain rustic earthiness. They share a caustic sense of humour and a strong Catholic faith. They believe in the necessity of Franco-German friendship and in the federal destiny of Europe. They trusted each other not to be tricky. According to Horst Teltschik, Kohl's former diplomatic adviser:

> The triangular relationship of Kohl-Delors-Mitterrand was pivotal. Delors mediated between Kohl and Mitterrand and – never afraid of stating his own views forcefully – tried to infuence them while doing so. He understood our domestic problems and helped Mitterrand to do so, such as when we wanted the IGC on EMU postponed until after the November 1990 German election.

Kohl found it handy having a friend at the head of the Commission. 'On many big issues we've worked to defend German interests, rather than French ones – and more often than we have defended British interests,' said one of Delors's (French) aides. Thus when Leon Brittan, the competition commissioner, tried to cut Germany's subsidies to its coal industry, Delors blunted his attack. The aide said that Delors helped Germany more than other members because 'it served the cause of European construction'.

Delors's handling of the German question turned friendship with Kohl into *Blutbruderschaft*. From the fall of the Berlin Wall until the day of reunification, Delors greeted the prospect of German unity with more warmth than any other European politician. While Thatcher and Mitterrand did their best to slow down the process, Delors made sure that the EC did not create difficulties for the Germans. There were no disputes over the procedures by which the five East German *Länder* joined the Community, or over cash questions such as their entitlement to regional funds. In the summer of 1990 the Commission dealt with all the complications in a package of sixty directives which, when rubber-stamped by the Council of Ministers, enabled the five *Länder* to join both West Germany and the EC on 3 October 1990. Delors was, alongside Enrique Baron, the President of the European Parliament, the only foreigner invited to Germany's unity celebrations.

Delors was a strategist who plotted a course and stuck to it with tenacity, but he also had a general's tactical instinct for spotting an opening, timing an offensive and concentrating resources on a target. In both these respects, Delors followed the example of Monnet and showed that he had some of the same skills. Delors was more effective than most politicians because, like Monnet, he knew what he wanted. In his first presidential speech to the European Parliament, in January 1985, Delors set out his plans for the next four years: a single market, a revision of the Treaty of Rome, a 'European social space' and moves towards monetary union. No one can say they were not warned.

The experience of running the Commission reinforced Delors's enthusiasm for Monnet's approach to European integration. Monnet believed that deadlines concentrated the minds of governments. The dates which appeared in the Treaty of Paris (which set up the ECSC) and the Treaty of Rome gave Delors the idea of creating a single market by the end of 1992. A more fundamental part of the Monnet method, according to Max Kohnstamm, for many years a Monnet aide, involved 'looking for the point which, when touched, would set off a series of consequences. What counts is having the ability to find that strategic point'. That would appear to be self-evident for any political leader, yet few of them have a broad enough vision to be able to apply such tactics.

Monnet had written: 'There are no premature ideas, only opportunities for which one must learn to wait.' Delors shared that obsession with the importance of timing. Before taking any initiative, he agonised over whether the moment was right. In the autumn of 1984, before arriving in Brussels, Delors considered four different themes around which Europe could be relaunched: institutional reform, closer defence co-operation, monetary union and a single market. His tour of the (then) ten governments convinced him that only the market had a chance of success. He judged, correctly, that when governments saw the 1992 programme, they would agree to reforming the institutions so that it could be implemented. Hence the Single European Act which, with its crucial innovation of majority voting on single market laws, gave the EC a new momentum.

In 1988, seeking to apply the 'Monnet method' again, Delors pushed the governments to consider EMU. The prospect of another treaty revision triggered a new debate on the institutions. In 1989 Delors decided, perhaps prematurely, that the 12 were ready for some kind of 'political union', and he campaigned for a more supranational constitution. But the political union enshrined in the Maastricht Treaty – agreed in December 1991 – turned out too inter-governmental for his liking. Delors's sense of timing deteriorated towards the end of his presidency. In the spring of 1992 he tried to drag the EC closer to federalism, just when public opinion and some governments were starting to pull the other way.

Delors's Presidency – the balance sheet

Delors's presidency had its flops as well as its fillips. Delors himself complains of his failure to achieve a European industrial policy. He would have liked the Commission to sponsor high-tech industries such as high-definition television and semiconductors. But the Commission's inability to create specifically European ventures, in industries that were increasingly global, was probably no bad thing. Many free-traders would point to Delors's behaviour in the Uruguay Round of GATT talks as the nadir of his presidency. It is true that, in November 1992, Delors tried (and failed) to sabotage a GATT agreement, but his actions appeared to have little effect on the final result.

The two biggest weaknesses of the Delors presidency stemmed from the methods and manner by which he sought to implement his ideas. The first is that, despite Delors's huge impact on the Commission, he failed to carry out the fundamental reforms it needed. Indeed, his personalised system of command and control caused some harm. The second is that, from 1990 to 1992, he tried to push the EC too far, too fast. Delors's slipping sense of timing and his sometimes over-bearing style contributed – along with much else – to an anti-federalist backlash.

As Delors began his third and final term as President, in January 1993, Commission officials began to speculate that the Delors regime was doing more harm than good. 'By relying excessively on informal channels, the formal channels have become atrophied and the morale of the senior officials has suffered,' said one member of the Delors *cabinet*. He thought the Commission's poor morale in 1992 and 1993 could be blamed only partly on the external shocks – economic recession, the Yugoslav war and Denmark's vote against Maastricht – which had damaged the EC. He believed the institution would have better weathered the crises if the Delors network had not undermined its structures and stability.

A member of the Brittan *cabinet* observed that any good President would need a network: 'He cannot rely solely on his fellow commissioners or on directors-general, for some of them will be incompetent, or display national prejudice or simply not be on the same wavelength'. But many other commission officials thought the power of the cabinets and the networks had increased, was increasing and ought to be diminished. When Delors arrived in Brussels he had promised the directors-general that he would restore their authority. Yet he did nothing to restrain the cabinets' power, and in 1989 even increased the size of commissioners' cabinets from five to six. Many directors-general had become preparers of files for their commissioners, rather than true advisers. When Delors planned a new initiative, he seldom consulted even the more able of his directors-general, unless he or she happened to belong to the network.

Many of the Commission's weaknesses in 1985 were still weaknesses when Delors left ten years later. Ability was only one factor that influenced promotion. Directors-general decided junior appointments and the full Commission ruled on senior ones. But decisions on jobs were seldom made without months of struggle between rival networks of influence. Governments insisted that the appointment of directors-general should, informally, reflect national quotas. The directors-general ran their departments as independent baronies which pursued their own priorities and seldom communicated – DG5 proposed a law to ban cigarette advertising while DG6 raised subsidies to tobacco farmers. Directors-general with more than enough staff resisted the secretary-general's efforts to make them deliver posts to over-stretched directorates.

Many commissioners had no idea how unhelpful and inefficient some of their departments appeared to the outsiders – consultants, lobbyists, researchers, lawyers, business people and recipients of regional aid – who had to deal with them. Letters to the institution often went unanswered. Outside consultants working for the Commission were often paid more than a year late. The Commission also mistreated some of its own people. The example of an official who was expected to start work before he had received a contract, and then, when the three-year contract was coming to an end, was not told whether it would be renewed until the day it expired, is not an isolated one.

Delors occasionally dabbled with reform. In 1991 Carlo Trojan, the Dutch deputy secretary-general, drew up a report on the Commission's inadequacies. Its hint that the cabinets had too many staff annoyed enough commissioners to ensure that the report gathered dust. In 1993, after a series of meetings between Delors and the directors-general, they won the right to discuss policy initiatives as a group, and some powers to reorganise their departments.

But neither Delors, nor Lamy, nor Williamson tried to tackle the Commission's fundamental weaknesses. For instance the number of directorates could have been reduced, to prevent duplication of resources. Some departments which administered existing policies, rather than planned new ones, could have become autonomous agencies. Had the influence of the cabinets on appointments been curbed, ability would have counted for more; an independent appointments body could have ensured a fair balance among the nationalities.

If Delors and his team had managed to push through some major reforms, they might not have had to depend so much on unconventional management methods. In June 1993 Lamy conceded that the Delors system concentrated too much on taking short cuts to get things done: 'Probably we should have changed the structure of the system, but we thought it wasn't a priority'. Delors himself acknowledged in the same month, 'The pyramidal structure became too strong. It's true that Lamy held the system in an iron grip, to change it. But this authoritarianism was necessary for a while, since nothing worked'. In his third term Delors sought to moderate his regime, noting: 'After the pyramidal phase there is a phase of relaxing the constraints, to try and get more collegial behaviour. That implies that my collaborators don't reign by terror, that they're a bit more open and that they refer to me before hitting hard'. The style did soften a little, and Lamy himself left in May 1994. But the essence of the Delors system remained in place until Jacques Santer arrived. However much Delors's mind focused on loftier matters, he knew about the methods used by Lamy and his band and must take responsibility.

Delors was a difficult man to work with. Living on his nerves, he was liable to explode if something went wrong. Perhaps because of the puritan streak which made him frugal, he would not tolerate imperfection, either in his own or in his colleagues' work or behavour. His barbed comments on those who had benefited from an elite education revealed, from time to time, a sense of insecurity. 'I've got an inferiority complex because I didn't attend the *grands écoles* or do proper studies,' he admitted. Delors's successes in Brussels made him more self-assured. In his second and third presidential terms, talk of resignation and explosions of choler became less frequent. But there were still, on some reckonings, about a dozen resignation threats – both direct and indirect, to the college of commissioners and to the Council of Ministers – every year.

Few politicians are capable of such humility and such pride as Delors. He was humble about his person but proud of his office. However, during the long years in Brussels, Delors began to identify his person with his office, the Commission and even the EU. The pride – sometimes verging towards arrogance and occasionally towards authoritarianism – became increasingly prominent. Niels Ersbøll noted that 'the private Delors is modest, but the public figure is surrounded by EC ambassadors, Commission officials and journalists who hold him in awe. It would take a very strong personality to resist all that'.

Delors made more mistakes in his last years as President, Ersbøll believes, because he had less objective advice and because the EC's agenda grew so large. For instance in 1991, the year of the Maastricht treaty, Delors also had to cope with a major reform of the CAP, the Uruguay Round of GATT talks, the forging of the European Economic Area between the EC and EFTA, and the negotiation of 'Europe agreements' linking the EU to Poland, Hungary and Czechoslovakia – not to mention the effects of wars in the Gulf and Yugoslavia.

Delors's behaviour during the IGC on political union, which ran through 1991, shows that he was getting out of touch with what governments – and sometimes voters – were prepared to accept. He pushed a federal agenda, apparently oblivious of the growing tide of anti-Commission sentiment in national capitals. His support for institutional reforms that had no chance of being adopted undermined his authority. The strength of his own convictions may have weakened his judgement: he believed, passionately, that unless Europe followed his constitutional prescriptions it was doomed to decline. This was an issue on which, against his normal nature, he would not compromise.

The Commission's draft treaty, much influenced by Delors, appeared in sections between February and June 1991. It proposed a new legislative system, whereby the Council of Ministers and the European Parliament would agree on laws that laid down general principles; the Commission would write regulations to fill in the details. Although the Council and the Parliament would be able to veto regulations they disliked, most governments treated the proposed system as an outrageous attempt by the Commission to grab more power. The section on foreign policy was even more provocative: the Commission, or the country holding the EC presidency, or a group of at least six member-states would have the right of initiative, but not individual governments.

Few governments took this document seriously and it was ignored by Luxembourg, which was chairing the IGC, in its own draft treaty. Instead of a single Community, this proposed three 'pillars': the existing EC for economic policy, plus new intergovernmental bodies, one for foreign policy and another for judicial co-operation. The role of the Commission, the Parliament and the European Court of Justice would be minimal in the new pillars – which meant that governments such as Britain and France liked the scheme, and Delors hated it.

Advocates of a single Community, such as Delors, acknowledged that diplomacy and co-operation among interior ministries could not be subject to the usual EC procedures; for instance it would not be practicable to give the Commission the sole right of initiative. But they thought that, so long as a single Community embraced all that the member states did together, there was, in the long term, the prospect of the EC's usual procedures applying to everything. Delors was convinced that the pillars would undermine Monnet's proven institutional model.

When the federalist Dutch took over the chairmanship of the IGC in July 1991, they tore up Luxembourg's draft treaty. With Delors's support, the Netherlands came up with a new treaty that proposed a single Community. Delors denies that he helped to write the Dutch draft. However, he discussed it on the phone with Ruud Lubbers, the Dutch prime minister, and saw the draft ten days before it was published. In September the EC foreign ministers savaged the draft: even Germany and Italy, which were sympathetic to the idea of a single Community, argued that, because Britain and France would never accept it, the pillars would have to be brought back.

The Dutch did restore the pillars, in yet another draft treaty. In the last weeks before the Maastricht summit, Delors did everything he could to change its foreign policy provisions – which he described in the European Parliament as 'inapplicable and crippling'. The plan for the EC to manage external economic relations and for the member states to run diplomacy was 'organised schizophrenia'. Delors demanded some element of majority voting and a greater role for the Commission, which would, according to the draft, be merely 'associated' with foreign policy. Yet the governments would not budge. With hindsight it may be argued that Delors had a point: the institutional mechanisms of the Maastricht treaty have failed to produce strong or effective EU foreign policies. But the kind of procedures that Delors envisaged were simply not practical politics in 1991.

Delors was so dissatisfied with the Maastricht treaty that, straight after its signature, he launched a campaign for a further round of institutional reform. On French television he called for a European nuclear deterrent and suggested that the Commission should become a European executive, responsible to both the European Council and the European Parliament. Delors told his officials to start mulling over new constitutional schemes. In June 1992 the Commission was due to report to the Lisbon summit on the consequences of the EC's imminent enlargement. In April Delors told the European Parliament that the Commission's Lisbon report would 'certainly be a political, institutional and intellectual shock for the 12 member-states, which have not yet reflected enough on what, for example, a Community of 35 would look like'.

Delors stirred up this constitutional debate in the middle of Denmark's referendum campaign on the Maastricht treaty. Some of his officials' ideas leaked into the Danish press and, after some embellishment, helped the anti-Maastricht campaigners to argue that centralisers in Brussels would deprive small states of their rights. Thus Delors contributed, however unwittingly, to a '*Nej*' vote of 50.7% in June 1992. The Danes threw the EC into a series of crises: intense debate leading to the narrow vote in favour of the treaty in France's referendum, Britain's reluctance to ratify it and the near-destruction of the ERM. Delors had to forget about his hopes for a further dose of political union.

On 1 January 1993 Delors was asked by *France Deux* if the EC should not have concentrated on the single market, rather than take on so many ambitious projects all at once. He demurred, saying that the EC had had to advance quickly because of German unity, the rapid changes in eastern Europe and the unstable nature of the ERM. Otherwise, the 'forces of national introversion and disintegration are so strong that we would have risked losing everything we have gained over the past 40 years'. Sir Leon Brittan disagrees: 'Delors tried to push the Community too fast. He could not take the citizens with him because they did not understand what was happening'.

Many EC governments felt antipathy towards Delors and his institution, and so were reluctant to defend them against the attacks – many of them unjust – which multi-

305

plied in 1992. That governmental hostility, which had been growing since 1990, influenced as well as reflected public opinion. Some of the resentment was inevitable: Delors's plans for a federal Europe would, by definition, curb the role of national politicians. But some of it was a reaction to Delors's personal style of running the Commission.

Governments complained of the Commission waging petty territorial warfare against the Council of Ministers. Its main interest in foreign policy seemed to be to enlarge its own role. National capitals liked neither the Commission's tendency to preach, nor the over-detailed character of some of its proposals, particularly on environmental and labour law. Delors's sidelining of several commissioners, and his concentration of authority in the presidency, did not endear him to governments.

However, much of the EC's unpopularity had nothing to do with Jacques Delors. The EC's failure to bring peace to Yugoslavia damaged its image. Unemployment began to rise in 1991, feeding protectionist sentiment and hostility to the EC's single market. Some members of the ERM could not maintain their exchange rates against the D-mark because, when German interest rates were high, their recession-hit economies needed cheap credit. The Bundesbank insisted on a tight monetary policy to balance the German government's financing of reunification through inflationary borrowing. The consequent ERM crises – from September 1992 to July 1993 – cast doubts over the EC's plans for monetary union.

Nevertheless, much of the hostility to Brussels was a reaction against the EC's increasing sway over people's lives. Many Danes, for instance, were upset that the EC had banned their favourite Ingrid Maria apples, on the ground that they were too small. German public opinion feared that it would have to exchange the D-mark for a weaker Euro-currency. In Britain many Conservative activists became obsessed with the erosion of parliamentary sovereignty. In September 1992, during the French referendum campaign on the Maastricht treaty, farmers who feared that CAP reform would cut their incomes led the '*Non*' camp.

It was not a coincidence that the EC began to become more powerful in 1985, the year that Delors became president. He played a necessary, though not sufficient role in relaunching the European idea, and in its becoming sufficiently influential to incite fear. Indirectly, therefore, he helped to make the tidal wave of anti-federalist sentiment which almost engulfed the final years of his presidency. The Eurosceptics in Britain, France, Germany and the Nordic countries would have been lost without Delors. The political careers of Bill Cash, Philippe de Villiers, Sir James Goldsmith and Manfred Brunner – all opponents of further integration – would never have flourished if the EC had remained in the *status quo ante* Delors.

Of Delors's many ideas and principles, he will be remembered, above all, for his federalism – a doctrine which had, by the mid-1990s, fallen thoroughly out of fashion. Yet federalism, as an approach to tackling Europe's problems, will not disappear. As Delors wrote in 1992, 'The construction of Europe corresponds both to an ideal and to a necessity'. The ideal – noble though it is to some – may be forgotten; but the necessity cannot be ignored. However much some national elites and some elements of public opinion argue for the repatriation of powers to governments, the reality is that, as European economies become more closely intertwined, the EU's role in economic policy-making is bound to grow. The pressure for EMU – to create a stable, non-inflationary currency zone, run by something other than the Bundesbank – may wax or wane from year to year, but will remain.

There is much less inevitability about the European nations strengthening their political bonds. But the progressive enlargement of the EU will require constitutional changes, in order to maintain its efficiency and accountability. The European states will co-operate more on defence policy, within a NATO framework, because it is cheaper and potentially more effective, and because the Americans will press them to do so. And governments will, however fitfully, struggle to reach more coherent common foreign policies, if only because experiences such as the Yugoslav war highlight the cost of their absence.

Selected bibliography

Some of the material in this essay has already appeared in '*Delors: Inside the House that Jacques Built*', published by Nicholas Brearley in 1994.

Delors, Jacques (1992) *Le nouveau concert Européen*, Odile Jacob.

  (1994) *L'Unité d'un homme*, Odile Jacob.

Grant, Charles (1995) *Delors: architecte de l'Europe*, Georg Editeur.

Maris, Bernard (1993) *Jacques Delors, artiste et martyr*, Albin Michel.

Milesi, Gabriel (1995) *Jacques Delors: L'homme qui dit non*, Edition no.1.

Mounier, Emmanuel (1947) *Qu'est-ce que c'est le personnalisme?*, Senil.

Rollot, Alain (1993) *Delors*, Flammarion.

Ross, George (1995) *Jacques Delors and European integration*, Polity Press.

Interviews

Sir Leon Brittan – 2 April 1993

Jacques Delors – 19 May 1993, 5 June 1993 and 5 August 1995

Niels Ersbøll – 1 March 1993

Max Kohnstamm – 4 May 1993

Pascal Lamy – 7 June 1993

Horst Teltschik – 11 May 1992

Brief Biographical Notes

This section gives brief biographical notes on close to one hundred personalitites who contributed in various ways to shaping contemporary Europe, and who are mentioned in this collection but are not themselves the central focus of these essays.

Dean Acheson

Born April 1893. Died October 1971. US Democrat politician. Assistant US Secretary of State 1941-5. Under-Secretary of State 1945-7. Secretary of State 1949-53.

Michel Albert

Born February 1930. French civil servant and financial expert. Director of Economic Structure and Development, EEC Commission 1966-9.

Giulio Andreotti

Born January 1919. Italian Christian Democrat politician. Prime Minister 1972-3, 1976-9, 1989-92.

Jacques Attali

Born November 1943. Special adviser to the French President 1981-91. President European Bank of Reconstruction and Development 1991-3.

Clement Attlee (1st Earl Attlee)

Born January 1883. Died October 1967. British Labour politician. Deputy Prime Minister 1942-5. Prime Minister 1945-51. Leader of the Opposition 1951-5.

Egon Bahr

Born March 1922. German Christian Democrat politician. State Secretary and Minister in Federal Chancellor's Office 1969-74.

Edouard Balladur

Born May 1929. French Gaullist politician. Member of staff in Pompidou's administration. Prime Minister 1993-5.

William Henry Beveridge (1st Baron)

Born March 1879. Died March 1963. British Liberal academic whose writings influenced post-war social policy, as well as federalist thought.

Ernest Bevin

Born March 1881. Died April 1951. British Labour politician. Minister of Labour and National Service 1940-5. Secretary of State for Foreign Affairs 1945-51.

Johan Willem Beyen

Born May 1897. Died April 1976. Dutch banker and diplomat. Minister of Foreign Affairs 1952-6. Ambassador to Paris 1958-63.

Georges Bidault

Born October 1899. Died January 1983. Prime Minister of France 1946 & 1958. Foreign Minister 1946-8, 1954. Delegate to Council of Europe 1949.

Charles Bohlen

Born August 1904. Died January 1974. US diplomat. Counsellor, Department of State 1951-3. Ambassador to the USSR 1953-7.

Robert Boothby (Baron of Buchan and Rattray Head)

Born 1900. Died July 1986. British Conservative politician. Delegate to the Consultative Assembly of the Council of Europe 1949-57.

Heinrich von Brentano

Born June 1904. Died November 1964. German Christian Democrat politician. President of the parliamentary section of the CDU 1949-55. Foreign Minister 1955-6.

Aristide Briand

Born 1862. Died March 1932. French politician and lawyer. Foreign Minister on several occasions. Early advocate of a federal Europe.

Leon Brittan (Sir)

Born September 1939. British Conservative politician. Offices include Home Secretary 1983-5, Secretary of State for Trade and Industry 1985-6. European Commissioner for competition policy 1989-92, for economic relations 1993-94, for external trade since 1995.

David K.E.Bruce

Born February 1898. Died December 1977. US diplomat. Ambassador to France 1949-52. Special American representative to the High Authority of the ECSC 1953-4. Ambassador to the Federal Republic of Germany 1957-9.

R.A.Butler (Baron Butler of Saffron Walden)

Born December 1902. Died March 1982. British Conservative politician. Offices include Chancellor of the Exchequer 1951-5, Foreign Secretary 1963-4.

Jacques Chaban-Delmas

Born March 1915. French Gaullist politician. President of the National Assembly 1958-69, 1978-81, 1986-8. Prime Minister 1969-72.

Jacques Chirac

Born November 1932. French Gaullist politician. Prime Minister 1974-6. Mayor of Paris 1977-95. President of the French Republic 1995-.

Winston Churchill

Born November 1874. Died January 1965. British Conservative politician, first held office in 1906. Prime Minister and Minister of Defence 1940-5 and 1951-5. Leader of the Opposition 1945-51.

William L. Clayton

Born 1880. Died 1966. US government official from 1940. Acted *inter alia* as Assistant Secretary of Commerce, Administrator of Surplus War Property Administration and Assistant Secretary of State in Charge of Economic Affairs.

Francis Cockfield (Baron)

Born September 1916. British civil servant, businessman and Conservative politician. Secretary of State for Trade 1982-3. European Commissioner for the internal market 1985-8.

Alfred Duff Cooper (1st Viscount Norwich)

Born February 1890. Died January 1954. British Conservative politician. Served in Second World War government. Ambassador to France 1944-7.

Richard N. Coudenhove-Kalergi (Count)

Born November 1894. Died July 1972. Half-Hungarian/half-Japanese advocate of an integrated Europe. Founded Paneuropean Movement 1923. Founded European Parliamentary Union 1947.

Bettino Craxi

Born February 1934. Italian Socialist politician. Prime Minister 1983-7.

Stafford Cripps (Sir)

Born April 1889. Died April 1952. British Labour politician. Ambassador to the USSR 1940-2. Government minister 1942-7. Chancellor of the Exchequer 1947-50.

Hugh Dalton (Baron)

Born 1887. Died February 1962. British Labour politician. Taught economics at London University 1919-36. Chancellor of the Exchequer 1945-7.

Etienne Davignon (Vicomte)

Born October 1932. Belgian civil servant. European Commissioner for industry 1977-84. Chairman of the Société Générale de Belgique since 1989. Chairman of the Association for the Monetary Union of Europe.

Allen Dulles

Born April 1893. Died January 1969. US diplomat and intelligence officer. Director of Council on Foreign Relations 1942-5. CIA Director 1953-61.

John Foster Dulles

Born February 1888. Died May 1959. US Secretary of State 1952-9.

David Eccles (1st Viscount)

Born 1904. British Conservative politician. President of the Board of Trade 1957-9.

Anthony Eden (1st Earl of Avon)

Born June 1897. Died January 1977. British Conservative politician. Foreign Secretary 1935-8, 1940-5 and 1951-5. Prime Minister 1955-7.

Dwight D. Eisenhower

Born 1890. Died 1969. Chief of Staff of US Army 1945-8. Supreme Commander NATO forces in Europe 1950-2. US Republican President 1953-61.

Ludwig Erhard

Born February 1897. Died May 1977. German Christian Democrat politician. Minister for Economic Affairs 1949-63. Vice-chancellor of the Federal Republic 1957-63. Chancellor of the Federal Republic 1963-6.

Niels Ersbøll

Born April 1926. Danish diplomat. Served in embassy to NATO 1958-60, mission to EFTA 1963-4, EFTA secretariat 1960-3. Ambassador to EC 1973-7. Secretary-general EU Council 1980-94.

Amintore Fanfani

Born February 1908. Italian Christian Democrat politician. Prime Minister 1954, 1958-9, 1960-3, 1982-3. Foreign Minister 1965, 1966-8.

Edgar Faure

Born August 1908. Died March 1988. French Radical-Socialist politician. Prime Minister 1952, 1955-6. MEP 1979-88.

J. William Fulbright

Born April 1905. US Democrat senator 1945-74. Chairman Senate Committee on Foreign Relations 1959-74.

Hans-Dietrich Genscher

Born March 1927. German FDP politician. Foreign Minister 1974-92.

Valéry Giscard d'Estaing

Born February 1926. French politician. President of French Republic 1974-81. MEP 1989-93.

Pehr Gyllenhammar

Born April 1935. Swedish businessman. Managing Director of Volvo from 1971. Member of Round Table of European Industrialists since 1979.

(William) Averell Harriman

Born November 1891. Died July 1986. US diplomat. Ambassador to the USSR 1943-6. Ambassador to UK 1948. US Secretary of Commerce 1946-8. US Special Representative in Europe for the Economic Cooperation Administration (Marshall Plan) 1948.

Edward Heath (Sir)

Born July 1916. British Conservative politician. Offices include President of Board of Trade 1963-4. Prime Minister 1970-4. Negotiated British entry to EC 1972.

Hinchingbrooke (Lord) (Victor Montagu)

Born May 1906. British Conservative politician. Disclaimed peerages 1964.

Etienne Hirsch

Born January 1901. Civil servant. Colleague of Jean Monnet in the *Commissariat au Plan*. President of the Commission of Euratom 1959-61.

Paul Hoffman

Born 1891. Died 1974. US businessman and administrator. Administrator of the Economic Cooperation Administration (Marshall Plan) 1948-50.

Geoffrey Howe (Baron Howe of Aberavon)

Born December 1926. British Conservative politician. Offices include Chancellor of the Exchequer 1979-83, Foreign Secretary 1983-9.

Cordell Hull

Born October 1871. Died July 1955. US Democrat politician. Secretary of State 1933-44. Nobel Peace Prize 1945.

George F. Kennan

Born February 1904. US diplomat. Ambassador to USSR 1952-3. Author of many books on the Cold War period.

Kurt Georg Kiesinger

Born April 1904. Died March 1988. German Christian Democrat politician. Chancellor 1966-9. Member of the Consultative Assembly of Council of Europe 1950-8.

Henry Kissinger

Born May 1923. US Republican politician. US immigrant 1938, naturalised 1943. Secretary of State 1973-7. Nobel Peace Prize 1973.

Karl Lamers

Born November 1935. German Christian Democrat politician. Member of the Bundestag 1980-. Spokesman on foreign policy for CDU/CSU.

Pascal Lamy

Born April 1947. French civil servant. *Directeur de cabinet* of President of European Commission 1985-95.

Harold Laski

Born June 1893. Died March 1950. Professor of Political Science at the University of London. Member of Labour Party Executive Committee 1936-49.

Walter Layton

Born December 1929. British economist and journalist. *Chef de cabinet* of Commissioner Spinelli 1971-3.

Joseph Luns

Born August 1911. Dutch diplomat and politician. Permanent delegate to the United Nations 1949-52. Foreign Minister 1952-71. President of NATO Council 1958-9. Secretary-general NATO 1971-84.

John J. McCloy

Born 1895. Died 1989. US administrator. Assistant Secretary of State for War 1941-5. President International Bank for Reconstruction and Development, 1947-9. US military governor and US High Commissioner for Germany 1949-52.

R. W.G.('Kim') Mackay

Born Australia 1902. Died 1960. Labour politician in Great Britain. Strong proponent of European integration, present at the Congress of the Hague.

George C. Marshall

Born December 1880. Died October 1959. US General. Chief of Staff of US Army 1939-45. Secretary of State 1947-9. Attended major international peace conferences during and after the Second World War.

Angus Maude (Baron Maude of Stratford-upon-Avon)

Born 1912. Died April 1992. British Conservative politician and journalist.

David Maxwell Fyfe (1st Earl of Kilmuir)

Born May 1900. Died January 1967. British Conservative politician. Offices include Lord Chancellor 1954-62. Member of the Council of Europe 1949.

René Mayer

Born May 1895. Died December 1972. French politician. Prime Minister 1953. President of ECSC 1955-7.

Pierre Mendès-France

Born January 1907. Died October 1982. French politician. Head of French Financial Missions 1944. Minister of National Economy 1944-5. Prime Minister and Foreign Minister 1954-5. Governor for France of International Bank of Reconstruction and Development and Monetary Fund 1946-58.

Guy Mollet

Born December 1905. Died 1975. French Socialist politician. Minister of State dealing with the Council of Europe 1950-1. President of the Consultative Assembly of the Council of Europe 1954-6.

Herbert Morrison (Baron Morrison of Lambeth)

Born 1888. Died March 1965. British Labour politician. Member of War Cabinet 1940-5. Deputy Prime Minister 1945-51. Foreign Secretary 1951.

Karl-Heinz Narjes

Born 1924. German FDP politician. European Commissioner for the internal market 1985-8.

Emile Noël

Born 1922. French. Secretary of Council of Europe 1950-2. Director of Secretariat of Ad Hoc Assembly 1952-4. *Chef de cabinet* of the President of the Consultative Assembly of Council of Europe 1954-6. Secretary-general to the European Commission from the early 1970s to 1987.

François-Xavier Ortoli

Born February 1925. Secretary-general of Interministerial Committee for European Economic Co-operation 1961-. President of European Commission 1973-6. Commissioner for economics and finance 1977-84.

Antoine Pinay

Born 1891. French politician. Prime Minister 1952. Foreign Minister 1955-6.

René Pleven

Born April 1901. Held various ministerial posts in the Fourth Republic, including ministry of National Defence 1949-50 and 1952.

Karl-Otto Pöhl

Born December 1929. German banker and civil servant. Chairman of the European Commission's Monetary Committee 1976-77. President of the Bundesbank 1980-91.

Georges Pompidou

Born July 1911. Died April 1974. French Gaullist politician. Prime Minister 1962-8. President of the French Republic 1969-74.

Paul Ramadier

Born 1888. Died 1961. French Socialist politician. Held ministerial office before and after the Second World War.

Paul Reynaud

Born October 1878. Died September 1966. French lawyer and politician. Held various posts in French governments, including Prime Minister 1940. Delegate to Council of Europe 1949.

Franklin D. Roosevelt

Born January 1882. Died April 1945. US Democrat President 1933-45.

Duncan E. Sandys (Baron Duncan-Sandys)

Born January 1908. Died November 1987. Diplomat and later Conservative politician. Son-in-law of Winston Churchill. Founder in 1947 of the European Movement. Member of Parliamentary Assemblies of Western European Union and Council of Europe 1950-1 and 1965-87.

Jacques Santer

Born May 1937. Luxembourg Christian Socialist politician. Prime Minister 1984-94. MEP 1975-9. President of European Commission since 1995.

Walter Scheel

Born July 1919. German FDP politician. Foreign Minister 1969-74. President of the Federal Republic 1974-9. MEP 1958-61.

Eduard Shevardnadze

Born January 1928. Soviet and Georgian politician. USSR Foreign Minister 1985-91. Founder of the Movement for Democratic Reform 1991. Chairman of the Georgian State Council since 1992.

Arthur Christopher Soames (Baron Soames)

Born 1920. Died 1987. British Conservative politician. *Inter alia* Parliamentary Private Secretary to the Prime Minister 1952-5. Ambassador to France 1968-72. Vice-President of the European Commission 1973-7.

Horst Teltschik

Born 1940. German civil servant. Federal Republic Under-secretary of State 1982-90. Foreign policy consultant to the Christian Social Union.

Gaston Thorn

Born September 1928. Luxembourg Democrat politician. Prime Minister 1974-9. MEP 1959-69. President of the European Commission 1981-4.

Leo Tindemans

Born April 1922. Belgian Christian Democrat politician. Prime Minister 1974-8. Foreign Minister 1981-9. Secretary-general of the European Union of Christian Democrats 1965-73. MEP 1979-81 and 1989-.

Arnold J. Toynbee

Born 1889. Died 1975. British historian. Director, Royal Institute of International Affairs, 1925-55. Director of Research Department of the Foreign Office 1943-6.

Harry S. Truman

Born May 1884. Died December 1972. US Democrat politician. Vice-President January-April 1945, then assumed Presidency. Elected President 1949-52.

Pierre Uri

Born November 1911. French banker. Economic and financial councillor to the economic *Commissariat au Plan* 1947-52. Rapporteur for the French delegation at the Schuman Plan (1951) and the Messina Conference (1956).

Paul van Zeeland (Viscount)

Born November 1893. Died September 1973. Belgian politician. *Inter alia*: President of the League of Nations Assembly, President of the OEEC and the Committee of Ministers of Council of Europe.

Simone Veil

Born July 1927. French politician. Held ministerial posts 1974-9 and 1993-5. Member of the European Parliament since 1979. President of the European Parliament 1979-82. Chair of the Liberal and Democratic Group 1984-9.

Karl-Günther von Hase

Born December 1917. German politician. Federal Republic Secretary of State for Information 1962-7, Defence 1967-9. Ambassador to UK 1970-7.

Friedrich von Hayek

Born May 1899. Died March 1992. Austrian economist. Naturalised British 1938. Professor London 1931-50, Chicago 1950-62, Freiburg 1962-9.

Richard von Weizsäcker

Born April 1920. German Christian Democrat politician. Governing Mayor of West Berlin, subsequently President of the Federal Republic of Germany 1984-94.

Henk Vredeling

Born November 1924. Dutch politician. Offices include Minister of Defence 1973-6. MEP 1958-73. European Commissioner for employment and social affairs 1977-81.

Barbara F. Wootton (Baroness Wootton of Abinger)

Born 1897. Died July 1988. British academic and Labour politician. Professor of Social Studies, University of London, 1952-7. Later Labour leader in the House of Lords.

David Williamson

Born May 1934. British civil servant. Secretary-general to the European Commission since 1987.

Harold Wilson (Baron Wilson of Rievaulx)

Born March 1916. Died 1995. British Labour politician. Prime Minister 1964-70, 1974-6.

Aleksandr N. Yakovlev

Born December 1923. Soviet and Russian politician. Soviet Ambassador to Canada 1973-83. Member of the Politburo 1987-90. President of the Democracy Foundation since 1993.

Boris Yeltsin

Born February 1931. Soviet and Russian politician. Candidate member of Politburo 1986-8. Chairman of the Supreme Soviet 1990-1. President of the Russian Federation since 1991.

List of contributors

Péter Á. Bod

    Director for Eastern Europe at the European Bank for Reconstruction and Development.

Jean-Louis Bourlanges

    Member of the European Parliament, European Peoples Party.

Richard Corbett

    Political Adviser to the Party of European Socialists

Maria Green Cowles

    Assistant Professor at the University of North Carolina at Charlotte.

Sir Julian Critchley

    Conservative Member of Parliament for Aldershot.

François Duchêne

    Writer and biographer of Jean Monnet, former director of the International Institute for Stratgeic Studies

Konstanty Gebert

    Writer and journalist with the *Gazeta Wyborcza*, Warsaw.

Charles Grant

    Journalist, biographer of Jacques Delors, defence editor of *The Economist*.

John Harper

    Professor of American Foreign Policy and European Studies at the Paul H. Nitze School of Advanced International Relations at the Bologna Center of the Johns Hopkins University.

Thomas Jansen

    Member of the Forward Studies Unit at the European Commission, former secretary-general of the European Peoples Party.

Dick Leonard

Former Brussels correspondent of *The Economist*, consultant for the Centre for European Policy Studies.

Richard Mayne

Former speech-writer to Monnet, writer and broadcaster.

Roger Morgan

Professor of Political Science at the European University Institute, Florence.

John Pinder

Former director of the Policy Studies Institute.

Timothy W. Ryback

Writer on Eastern Europe, Director of the Salzburg Seminar.

Elizabeth Teague

Former Researcher with Radio Free Europe, and at the Organisation for Cooperation and Security in Europe.

Alan Watson CBE

Visiting Professor at the Catholic University of Leuven, chairman of Burston-Marsteller, formerly with the European Commission.

Julia Wishnevsky

Former Researcher with Radio Free Europe, author of numerous articles on Russia and the Soviet Union.

List of editors

Martyn Bond

Martyn Bond began his career with the BBC in 1966. He lectured in West European Studies at the New University of Ulster, Coleraine from 1970-73. He then became Press Officer at the Council of Ministers in Brussels in 1974. From 1981-3 he was the BBC Correspondent in Berlin. After further service in Brussels he was appointed Head of the European Parliament Information Office in London in 1989. During the 1980s he was Chairman of the International Advisory Council of the Salzburg Seminar and from 1994 a Governor of the English College in Prague.

Julie Smith

Julie Smith is a Hanseatic Scholar at the University of Hamburg. She was previously a researcher at the Royal Institute of International Affairs. She has recently completed her doctoral thesis, *Direct Elections to the European Parliament: A Re-evaluation.* Her most recent publication is *Voice of the People: The European Parliament in the 1990s.*

William Wallace

William Wallace is Reader in International Relations at the London School of Economics and Professor of International Studies at the Central European University. He was director of studies at the Royal Institute of International Affairs from 1978-90, and was Walter F. Hallstein fellow at St. Athony's College, Oxford, 1990-95. His most recent publications include *Regional Integration: The West European Experience* (Brookings, 1994) and *Policy-Making in the European Union* (with Helen Wallace, OUP, 1996).